TIER

Published by The Institute for Evidence-based Reform, LLC
Brandon, MS 39047

Printed in the United States of America. Cover art copyright 2014 by Jay Miller.

All Internet links in this book are correct as of March 2014 but may have become inactive or otherwise been modified since that time. If you identify an inactive or modified Internet link, please e-mail info@evidencebasedreform.com with the words "Link Update" in the subject line. Please specify the Internet Link, the book title, and the page number on which the link appears.

Academic Behavioral INTERVENTIONS

EVIDENCE-BASED INTERVENTIONS FOR ALL STUDENTS

Contents

Some of the most common feedback we hear from educators and parents is, "Why isn't there a book on helping children with behavior problems?" or "How can I help my student or child struggling with school work?" We also hear many educators when faced with a student with problem behaviors or academic difficulties say, "I was not trained or educated on how to deal with…." Have you ever asked a friend or a colleague for an intervention or strategy to help your child or student? Have you been told to implement an intervention but found no support (i.e., materials, procedures, etc.) to help you implement it? Did you find that some of the steps of the intervention were vague or missing? Did you try the strategy/intervention and then find that it didn't work exactly as described? Did you know how to modify or change the procedures when a situation arose that was unusual? If you have met with any of these scenarios or faced any of these questions, then this book was written for you!

Before You Intervene…Things You Need To Know

This book is for educators, parents, and others who need interventions for children who are at risk in reading and/or mathematics or children with social, emotional, and/or behavior issues. Legislation that has been introduced in the past decade such as *No Child Left Behind* and *Individuals with Disabilities Education Improvement Act* mandate that evidence-based practices be used in school settings (Smith, Daunic, & Taylor, 2007). In addition, mental health agencies, school counselor organizations, and departments of health and human services are also advocating for the same type of evidence-based practices. However, educators, mental health professionals, and parents are left to wonder which interventions are supported by such evidence. This book offers the very guidance you may be seeking by providing the research behind each intervention included in this book. Many books and articles may describe an intervention but often leave out important details or not list materials needed or not explain how to make a necessary modification—any of these omissions hindering you from implementing an intervention with integrity. This book gives you detailed steps, lists materials (or provides the actual materials), and addresses modifications needed to ensure treatment integrity! .This treatment integrity means that each person and/or agency can be held accountable in that the intervention that was decided upon by the person or team is supported by research and implemented in the way it was intended.

The majority of the material in this book is procedures for implementing interventions and conducting integrity checks for those interventions. Because, you, the reader will be using many of these pages as reference for implementing an intervention or checking someone else's procedural integrity, you will notice that we have written the procedures in the imperative form—addressing "you" (the reader)—so that each step is direct, clear, and quickly recognized. We expect that you will read the procedures before you take any action, but we also expect that you may need to have the procedures handy for reference.

How to Use This Book

We recommend that you read the entire introduction before you begin any intervention implementation. The introduction is provided to lay the groundwork for your understanding not only of the interventions but also how and why the book is organized as it is. This book is arranged in an order that specifically supports your full comprehension of the purpose and the process for interventions; each part, especially the introduction, is critical for full understanding and the greatest opportunity for success when implementing an intervention. The introduction provides a first look at the order of the sections of the book and provides a brief overview of the matrix of intervention strategies, Interventions, interventions including the instructional hierarchy, how to use interventions, selecting children for intervention, and phasing out interventions, data collection, glossary.

Matrix of Intervention Strategies

The matrix provides a quick way to identify an intervention for a particular behavior and for which grades, settings, group, and skill the intervention is appropriate. You will see in the Matrix of Intervention Strategies the mention of learning stages such as acquisition, proficiency/fluency, maintenance, generalization, and/or adaptation. These stages in the Instructional Hierarchy of Learning are explained in the introduction.

Interventions

The interventions in this book are organized into four primary categories: 1) engagement, participation, and work completion interventions; 2) math interventions; 3) reading or reading related interventions; and 4) behavior interventions. To guide you in selecting an intervention, the following basic information about the appropriate group and goal of the intervention is provided at the beginning of each intervention.

Age/Grade
Setting
Individual or Group
Tier
Desired/ Appropriate Behavior
Skill Level

The age or grade level of the interventions ranges from preschool to high school. Most of these interventions are appropriate for a wide age range of children. The settings identified for implementing these interventions include school, home, group home, clinic, and in-patient settings. Some interventions are specifically designed for individual use; others are specifically designed for group use; but many can be used for either an individual or a group. Interventions are not just for children who are struggling. Rather, many interventions can benefit all children, both academically and behaviorally. The tiers identified are the three tiers commonly used by educators. Tier 1 includes the school-wide instructional and behavioral practices available to all children. Tier 2 includes strategic interventions for students who are struggling either academically and/or behaviorally and not responding to Tier 1 efforts. Tier 3 includes intensive, individualized interventions for those students who need more support either academically and/or behaviorally and are not responding to Tier 2 efforts (Johnson, Kaase, Medley, Cates, & Doggett, 2011). In the case of academic interventions at Tier 3, the intervention is generally provided in addition to and outside of the general instruction provided for the specific child who is the focus of the intervention. The desired or appropriate behavior addressed by the intervention is also described, for example, "student engagement in learning" or "work completion, compliance, keeping hands and feet to self, appropriate language, prepared for class/school, homework completion." Finally, the skill level is described. The skill levels are descriptors of the functioning or instructing sequence for children. The skill levels are based on the Instructional Hierarchy of Learning described in more detail below.

The Instructional Hierarchy of Learning

The Instructional Hierarchy of Learning should be used when selecting an intervention. The five stages conceptualized as an instructional hierarchy of learning by Haring and Eaton (1978) are acquisition, fluency/proficiency, maintenance, generalization, and adaptation. In order for a child to begin a new behavior, the child must first acquire the behavior and perform the required behavior fluently. Then the child must be able to maintain the behavior and generalize the behavior. Finally, the child must be able to adapt the skill to new circumstances. When learning a new material, all children should progress through these stages. Certain interventions may be more effective than others depending where in the instructional hierarchy of learning a student is at the time of the intervention. Children may perform in different ways as they progress through each stage (Haring & Eaton, 1978). It is important to first conceptualize what each stage entails.

Acquisition involves first demonstrating the steps that lead to a new skill. Until a child responds to a task accurately, the task cannot become an acquired skill. Demonstration and modeling have been used to help children acquire unknown skills (Haring & Eaton, 1978). Once a child has acquired the skill, the child can then move on to increasing the ***fluency*** or ***proficiency*** of the skill.

Fluency/Proficiency involves a child demonstrating the skill with little errors and increasing speed. Producing the skill fluently is important if the student wants to ***maintain*** the skill over time and apply the skill to different areas. Drills, active repeated responding, and reinforcement of accurate responding can increase fluency.

Maintenance is described as the child performing a behavior or skill after the "formal" instruction has been taught. Maintenance is equivalent to the state reached when you never forget how to swim or ride a bicycle. It is only after maintenance has been reached that children can progress to ***generalizing*** and applying their newly acquired skills. One method to establish and continue maintenance of skills is to periodically and systematically question the student while rewarding appropriate answers.

Generalization has been achieved when children who have acquired a new skill and can fluently respond using that skill can also apply the skill in novel situations. Generalization involves responding accurately even when the setting, events, cues, and/or triggers change. Practice involves applying the learned response with other learned responses to solve problems. However, on the flip side, discrimination training involves teaching children to display one type of response when certain cues, signals, or triggers are present but not when other cues are present. For example, the interventionist teaches a child using discrimination training to multiply (response) when presented with the x sign (i.e., cue or signal).

Adaptation is the final stage in the instructional hierarchy of learning. Once a student has generalized the skill to new situations, he/she must then learn to adapt or modify the response to apply it to other problems.

Preparing to Use the Interventions

Almost all of the interventions in this book are presented in two parts. The first part has the title of the intervention, such as "Response Cards." In this part you will find the following information presented in this order: Research and Rationale, Materials, Procedures, Adjustments/Modifications, and References. The Research and Rationale section provides a very brief summary of the research that supports the intervention, settings in which the intervention has been used, and/or the behaviors to which the intervention has been applied. The Materials section provides a detailed list of the materials necessary for implementing the intervention. The Procedures section provides a step-by-step guide to implementing the intervention or conducting the procedural integrity check. The Adjustments/Modifications section provides guidance about how the intervention may be modified for different tiers of intervention or in different settings.

The second part provides information about the Procedural Integrity Checklist and then the Procedural Integrity Checklist itself. *Interventions* are implemented by an interventionist, who is anyone designated as implementing an intervention or the person primarily responsible for implementing an intervention. Depending on the setting and circumstances, an interventionist may be a general teacher, special education teacher, teacher assistant, school psychologist, behavior specialist, clinician, parent, or another appropriate adult. *Integrity checks* are conducted by someone *other than the interventionist.* We refer to the person conducting an integrity check as an observer. Depending on the setting and circumstances, an observer may be a principal, assistant principal, school psychologist, treatment specialist, behavior specialist, counselor, lead teacher, or another appropriate adult other than the interventionist.

If you are an interventionist: You should read through the procedures for an intervention at least once prior to attempting an implementation. Also, read the integrity checklist so that you are aware of the specific behaviors the observer will be assessing. Reading the integrity checklist procedures and integrity checklist will help you understand what to expect when you are being observed and also emphasize to you what the key parts of the intervention are. If you have been assigned one of these interventions to implement, then you should also know who will possibly observe you as you implement the intervention. If you are implementing one of these interventions on your own without it being assigned to you, then it is a good idea to find someone who can be an observer and check your implementation of the intervention. As you are implementing an intervention, you generally have too many other tasks to manage to be able to adequately assess your own implementation. If you are asking someone to observe and check your implementation, then make sure you ask someone who can be a critical friend, that is, someone who can provide you honest and constructive feedback in the interest of helping you improve and better serve the child or children who are the focus of the intervention. You know the difference between someone who cares about helping you and children versus someone who is going along because they do not want to "rock the boat." Pick the right person for the job of observer. You will be glad you did!

If you are an integrity observer: You should read through the procedures for an intervention at least once prior to reading the integrity checklist procedures and the integrity checklist. As an observer who will be assessing implementation, you want to have a good knowledge of the specific behaviors that the interventionist is ideally attempting to implement. Your job as an observer is to provide honest and constructive feedback in the interest of helping the interventionist to improve and to better serve the child or children who are the focus of the intervention. As an observer you should always try to *provide* *feedback on the same day that an observation is conducted.* For a first-time observation of an interventionist who is implementing an intervention for the first time, you should also try to provide the feedback orally before providing the written feedback. When feedback is provided only in writing, the interventionist may find it difficult to capture the care or underlying spirit of the written remarks. By providing feedback orally first, you can better communicate your intention, meaning, and care. Also, providing feedback orally provides an opportunity for you and the interventionist to discuss any feedback that is not clear. Always try to start feedback with comments about what aspects of the intervention the interventionist did accurately or well. Providing this positive feedback first is important because individuals often have a hard to time "hearing" positive feedback after receiving constructive feedback. Make sure that that you state the feedback constructively if there is something that the interventionist did not implement or implemented only partially or if there was some other deficiency in the implementation. For example, if you are observing an interventionist implementing the Response Card intervention and you observed the interventionist immediately ask for a response from children instead of providing the child an appropriate amount of think time in response to the prompt, then you would want to provide constructive feedback based on the following example:

I observed that as soon as you presented a question, you asked children to give their response. It is good that you are trying to keep a quick, energetic pace but remember that you need to provide the children with an appropriate amount of think time prior to asking for their response. Next time you implement Response Cards, try silently counting to three or looking at the clock in the back of your room and waiting for five seconds to go by before asking for responses.

Finally, as the procedural integrity checklist observer, you should make a copy of each completed procedural integrity checklist to include in individual student files for documentation of the intervention integrity. If you, as the procedural integrity checklist observer, are observing multiple children in an intervention, you can complete all parts of the checklist *except* the children's names, the date, and your signature. After the observation, you can make as many copies of the completed checklist as you need, complete each with a child's name and the date and then sign each and place them in the files of the children who were in the observed classroom or intervention session. *You should never affix your signature to the checklist before you make copies.*

Selecting Children for Interventions

Schools, agencies, or parents/caregivers should not use one source of data to determine who should be selected for an intervention. Data that are collected—whether it is from the school's statewide assessment data, progress monitoring, other sources, office discipline referrals, teacher interviews or parent interviews—have inherent bias, meaning that there is some error in using one data source. For example, the school's statewide assessment data are collected only once a year and represent only a sample of what a student can do. Therefore, to base a decision solely on these data is problematic. The same can be said for any other measure. The data should converge to demonstrate that a student needs help. For example, the student may demonstrate inadequate performance on a statewide assessment, formative or summative assessment, and other sources of data. Two potential ways to determine if the child needs an intervention are a) discrepancy from peers or b) lack of improvement in comparison to peers (rate of improvement).

First, when examining the data from data sources, the school, agency, or parent/caregiver can identify children who are discrepant from peers at data collection point 1 (e.g., fall universal screening or parent interview one) and at each data collection period following. Thus, the agency at the time that the data were conducted would want to consider examining this child more closely to determine if he or she demonstrates a need based upon whether there is a convergence of data (i.e., multiple sources of data like previous universal screening scores, previous social skills measures) instead of waiting for failure.

Second, when the school, agency, or parent/caregiver reviews the data sources and determines that the child is not necessarily discrepant from peers but is not making the same amount of progress as his or her peers, an intervention may be warranted. If the school or agency or adult does not consider the child's rate of improvement, the child will eventually become discrepant from peers and may fail. We as caregivers, educators, and mental health professionals never want to wait until a child is failing socially, academically, or emotionally. We want to be preventive!

Phasing Out Interventions

So when do you stop an intervention? The interventionist should graph the child's current performance level and the goal which tells the interventionist how quickly the child needs to progress to achieve the goal. By plotting the child's progress, the interventionist can even determine the actual rate/slope at which the child is progressing with an intervention. The average rate of improvement is defined as can be described algebraically as the slope of a **line.** Slope is defined as: the vertical change over the horizontal change on a Cartesian plane (x-axis and y-axis graph). Graphical display allows the interventionist to use a set of standards to create more ambitious goals.

After the intervention has been deemed to have been implemented with high integrity based upon the checklist, the decision rules can be applied. Both academic and behavioral processes use the same decision rules:

Decision Rule #1: There has been no change; thus, the interventionist needs to try another intervention or seek help from a professional with experience dealing with the child's concern.

Decision Rule #2: There is a change, but the child has not met the goal:
2a: Continue with the same intervention and continue monitoring.
2b: Alter the intervention and assess response.
2c: Refer to a qualified professional.

Decision Rule #3: There is change, and the child has met the standard:
If the child just met the goal, then consider keeping the intervention in place to ensure success. If the child met and exceeded the goal, the interventionist can consider terminating the intervention or phasing out the intervention.

If the interventionist is phasing out the intervention, there are several things to consider. If the intervention does not entail some kind of consequence (e.g., reward), then the interventionist can phase out by reducing the amount of time spent on the intervention. For example, the child spends 5 days a week for 20 minutes a day doing an intervention; then the interventionist can reduce it to 3 days a week for 20 minutes. The interventionist needs to assess progress to ensure the child is maintaining or growing appropriately. If the child continues to have success, then the interventionist can continue to decrease the frequency as the data indicate. If the intervention has a consequence component (e.g., daily reward, hourly feedback, every 5 minutes earns a break), then the interventionist will want to phase out the amount or schedule of delivery of the consequence. For example, the child is earning a break every 5 minutes for appropriate behaviors in the classroom and has met the goal; then the interventionist will increase the interval to 6 minutes (as an example). If the child continues to be successful according to the data, then the interventionist can increase the interval again. If the child is unsuccessful, then the interventionist will want to go back to the 5-minute interval until the child's performance is stable before trying again to increase the interval.

Data Collection

Effective implementation of interventions requires data. To know whether an intervention is effective or not, you must understand the starting point for the intervention. In the Data Collection section, you will find detailed steps that address how to collect baseline data through progress monitoring. The Data Collection section also provides procedures for specific types of observations required and are collected solely for the purpose of a specific intervention.

Glossary

A Glossary is included to define key terms and phrases used in the book. Even if you feel you are familiar with many of the terms, we recommend that you review the Glossary before reading the interventions so that you will understand how we intend these terms to be used with and interpreted for the interventions.

References

Haring, N. G., & Eaton, M. D. (1978). Systematic instructional technology: An instructional hierarchy. In N. G. Haring, T. C. Lovitt, M. D. Eaton, & C. L. Hansen (Eds.), *The fourth R: Research in the classroom* (pp. 23-40). Columbus, OH: Merrill.

Johnson, K.N., Kaase, K.J., Medley, M.B., Cates, G.L., & Doggett, R.A. (2011). The Essential Elements Matrices: Is RtI a Set of Interrelated or Independent Components? *Journal of Evidence-Based Practices for Schools, 12(1)*, 15-39.

Smith, S. W., Daunic, A., Taylor, G. (2007). Treatment fidelity in applied educational research: Expanding the adoption and application of measures to ensure evidence-based practice. *Education and Treatment of Children, 30(4),* 121-134.

Intervention Strategies Matrix (Skill Area)

	Grade Level					Setting				Individual (I) or Group (G)	Tier	Behavior	Skill Level				
Intervention	Pre-K	K-2	3-5	6-8	9-12	School	Home	Clinic	In-Patient				Acquisition	Fluency	Mainten-ance	Generaliz-ation	Adaptation
Engagement, Participation, Work Completion Interventions																	
Active Student Engagement	X	X	X	X	X	X		X	X	I or G	1	On-task, participation, work engagement, work completion		X	X		
Response Cards	X	X	X	X	X	X	X	X	X	I or G	1, 2, 3	Engagement in learning	X	X	X		
Good Behavior Game		X	X	X	X	X	X	X	X	I or G	1, 2	Appropriate classroom behavior including on-task, speaking with permission, remaining in seat, respectful		X	X		
Mystery Motivator	X	X	X	X	X	X	X	X		I or G	1, 2, 3	Any desired behavior such as work completion, compliance, keeping hands and feet to self, appropriate language, prepared for class/school, homework completion		X	X	X	
Additive Interspersal Technique	X	X	X	X	X	X	X	X	X	I	1, 2, 3	Independent seatwork, task completion, on-task, homework completion, etc.		X	X		
Math Interventions																	
Folding-In Math	X	X	X	X	X	X	X	X	X	I	1, 2, 3	Fluency with a variety of math facts	X	X	X		
Cover, Copy, Compare – Math		1st	X	X	X	X	X	X	X	I	1, 2, 3	Accuracy and fluency in math skills with two or more steps to complete	X	X	X		
Accelerated Math		2nd	X	X		X				I or G	2, 3	Fluency in math skills	X	X	X		

	Grade Level					Setting				Individual (I) or Group (G)	Tier	Behavior	Skill Level				
Intervention	Pre-K	K-2	3-5	6-8	9-12	School	Home	Clinic	In-Patient				Acquisition	Fluency	Mainten-ance	Generaliz-ation	Adaptation
Look Ask Pick			4th	X	X	X	X	X	X	I	2, 3	Adding and subtracting like and unlike fractions	X	X	X		
Reading or Reading Related Interventions																	
Folding In – Sight Words	X	X	X	X	X	X	X	X	X	I	1, 2, 3	Fluency with a variety of sight words or sight vocabulary	X	X	X		
Cover Copy Compare – Spelling		X	X	X	X	X	X	X	X	I	1, 2, 3	Accuracy in spelling words	X	X	X	X	
Word and Sentence Repeat		1st	X			X	X	X	X	I	1, 2, 3	Reading with accuracy and fluency, reading comprehension		X	X		
Partner Reading		1st	X	X	X	X	X	X	X	G	1, 2, 3	Reading fluency; secondary benefits may include increased accuracy, increased reading level, increased vocabulary, and increased comprehension		X			
Semantic Mapping			X	X	X	X	X	X	X	I or G	1, 2, 3	Concept and vocabulary development, support for reading fluency and comprehension	X	X	X		
Behavior Interventions																	
Active Supervision	X	X	X	X	X	X			X	G	1	Increase in pro-social behaviors, appropriate behaviors in unstructured settings		X	X		
Behavior Contracts	X	X	X	X	X	X	X	X	X	I or G	1, 2, 3	Homework completion, academic performance, reduction in office referrals, home responsibilities (e.g., chores)		X	X		

	Grade Level					Setting				Individual (I) or Group (G)	Tier	Behavior	Skill Level				
Intervention	Pre-K	K-2	3-5	6-8	9-12	School	Home	Clinic	In-Patient				Acquisition	Fluency	Mainten-ance	Generaliz-ation	Adaptation
Behavior Interventions																	
Daily Behavior Report Card	X	X	X	X	X	X	X	X		I	2, 3	work completion, compliance, keeping hands and feet to self, appropriate language, prepared for class/school, homework completion		X	X	X	
Check In-Check Out			X	X	X	X				I	2, 3	Homework completion, academic performance, reduction in office referrals		X	X	X	
PreCorrection	X	X	X	X	X	X	X	X	X	I or G	1, 2	Homework completion, academic performance, reduction in office referrals, general appropriate behavior, home responsibilities (e.g., chores)		X	X		
Time-In	X	X	X	X	X	X	X	X	X	I or G	1, 2, 3	Compliance, on-task, generally appropriate classroom behavior		X	X		
Compliance Training	X	X	X			X	X	X		I	1, 2, 3	Compliance		X	X	X	
Positive Peer Reporting	X	X	X	X	X	X	X	X	X	I	1, 2, 3	Increase appropriate prosocial behavior		X	X	X	

	Grade Level					Setting				Individual (I) or Group (G)	Tier	Behavior	Skill Level				
Intervention	Pre-K	K-2	3-5	6-8	9-12	School	Home	Clinic	In-Patient				Acquisition	Fluency	Mainten-ance	Generaliz-ation	Adaptation
Behavior Interventions																	
VR VI Reinforcement	X	X	X	X	X	X	X		X	I or G	2, 3	On-task, attentive behavior as well as specific targeted appropriate behaviors such as compliance, talking with permission, or remaining in seat or area		X	X		
Break from Work	X	X	X	X	X	X	X	X	X	I or G	1, 2, 3	Task completion, on-task, task accuracy		X	X		
Structured Breaks		X	X	X	X	X	X		X	I	2, 3	Appropriate self-removal from difficult situations that have typically resulted in negative, sometimes verbally aggressive behaviors		X	X		
Self-Monitoring		2nd	X	X	X	X	X	X	X	I	2, 3	On-task, task accuracy, task completion, anger management, relaxation, hand raising to ask a question, making appropriate comments, exercising		X	X	X	
Self-Management		2nd	X	X	X	X	X		X	I	2, 3	Homework completion, academic performance, on-task behaviors, anger management, exercising, work productivity		X	X	X	
Pleasant Events Diary				X	X	X		X	X	I	2, 3	Positive mood, healthy behaviors, social behaviors, relax/calm (reduction in nervous behaviors)		X	X		

	Grade Level					**Setting**				**Individual (I) or Group (G)**	**Tier**	**Behavior**	**Skill Level**				
Intervention	Pre-K	K-2	3-5	6-8	9-12	School	Home	Clinic	In-Patient				Acquisition	Fluency	Mainten-ance	Generaliz-ation	Adaptation
Behavior Interventions																	
Habit Reversal	X	X	X	X	X	X	X	X	X	I	2, 3	Reduction in repetitive (habit) behaviors, thumb sucking, hair twirling, hair pulling, stuttering, tics, etc.	X	X	X	X	

Intervention Strategies Matrix (Alphabetical Order)

	Grade Level					Setting				Individual (I) or Group (G)	Tier	Behavior	Skill Level				
Intervention	Pre-K	K-2	3-5	6-8	9-12	School	Home	Clinic	In-Patient				Acquisition	Fluency	Mainten-ance	Generaliz-ation	Adaptation
Accelerated Math		2nd	X	X		X				I or G	2, 3	Fluency in math skills	X	X	X		
Active Student Engagement	X	X	X	X	X	X		X	X	I or G	1	On-task, participation, work engagement, work completion		X	X		
Active Supervision	X	X	X	X	X	X			X	G	1	Pro-social behavior, appropriate behavior in unstructured settings		X	X		
Additive Interspersal Technique	X	X	X	X	X	X	X	X	X	I	1, 2, 3	Independent seatwork, task completion, on-task, homework completion, etc.		X	X		
Behavior Contracts	X	X	X	X	X	X	X	X	X	I or G	1, 2, 3	Homework completion, academic performance, reduction in office referrals, home responsibilities (e.g., chores)		X	X		
Break from Work	X	X	X	X	X	X	X	X	X	I or G	1, 2, 3	Task completion, on-task, task accuracy		X	X		
Check In-Check Out			X	X	X	X				I	2, 3	Homework completion, academic performance, reduction in office referrals		X	X	X	
Compliance Training	X	X	X			X	X	X		I	1, 2, 3	Compliance		X	X	X	
Cover Copy Compare Math		1st	X	X		X	X	X	X	I	1, 2, 3	Accuracy and fluency in math skills with two or more steps to complete	X	X	X		
Cover Copy Compare Spelling		X	X	X	X	X	X	X	X	I	1, 2, 3	Accuracy in spelling words	X	X	X	X	

	Grade Level					Setting				Individual (I) or Group (G)	Tier	Behavior	Skill Level				
Intervention	Pre-K	K-2	3-5	6-8	9-12	School	Home	Clinic	In-Patient				Acquisition	Fluency	Mainten-ance	Generaliz-ation	Adaptation
Daily Behavior Report Card	X	X	X	X	X	X	X	X		I	2, 3	work completion, compliance, keeping hands and feet to self, appropriate language, prepared for class/school, homework completion		X	X	X	
Folding-In Math	X	X	X	X	X	X	X	X	X	I	1, 2, 3	Fluency with a variety of math facts	X	X	X		
Folding-In Sight Words	X	X	X	X	X	X	X	X	X	I	1, 2, 3	Fluency with a variety of sight words or sight vocabulary	X	X	X		
Good Behavior Game		X	X	X	X	X	X	X	X	I or G	1, 2	Appropriate classroom behavior including on-task, speaking with permission, remaining in seat, respectful		X	X		
Habit Reversal	X	X	X	X	X	X	X	X	X	I	2, 3	Reduction in repetitive (habit) behaviors, thumb sucking, hair twirling, hair pulling, stuttering, tics, etc.	X	X	X	X	
Look Ask Pick			4th	X	X	X	X	X	X	I	2, 3	Adding and subtracting like and unlike fractions	X	X	X		
Mystery Motivator	X	X	X	X	X	X	X	X		I or G	1, 2, 3	Any desired behavior such as work completion, compliance, keeping hands and feet to self, appropriate language, prepared for class/school, homework completion		X	X	X	

	Grade Level					Setting				Individual (I) or Group (G)	Tier	Behavior	Skill Level				
Intervention	Pre-K	K-2	3-5	6-8	9-12	School	Home	Clinic	In-Patient				Acquisition	Fluency	Mainten-ance	Generaliz-ation	Adaptation
Partner Reading		1st	X	X	X	X	X	X	X	G	1, 2, 3	Reading fluency; secondary benefits may include increased accuracy, increased reading level, increased vocabulary, and increased comprehension		X			
Pleasant Events Diary				X	X	X		X	X	I	2, 3	Positive mood, healthy behaviors, social behaviors, relax/calm (reduction in nervous behaviors)		X	X		
Positive Peer Reporting	X	X	X	X	X	X	X	X	X	I	1, 2, 3	Increase appropriate prosocial behavior		X	X	X	
PreCorrection	X	X	X	X	X	X	X	X	X	I or G	1, 2	Homework completion, academic performance, reduction in office referrals, general appropriate behavior, home responsibilities (e.g., chores)		X	X		
Response Cards	X	X	X	X	X	X	X	X	X	I or G	1, 2, 3	Engagement in learning	X	X	X		
Self-Management		2nd	X	X	X	X	X		X	I	2, 3	Homework completion, academic performance, on-task behaviors, anger management, exercising, work productivity		X	X	X	

	Grade Level					Setting				Individual (I) or Group (G)	Tier	Behavior	Skill Level				
Intervention	Pre-K	K-2	3-5	6-8	9-12	School	Home	Clinic	In-Patient				Acquisition	Fluency	Mainten-ance	Generaliz-ation	Adaptation
Self-Monitoring		2nd	X	X	X	X	X	X	X	I	2, 3	On-task, task accuracy, task completion, anger management, relaxation, hand raising to ask a question, making appropriate comments, exercising, etc.		X	X	X	
Semantic Mapping			X	X	X	X	X	X	X	I or G	1, 2, 3	Concept and vocabulary development , support for reading fluency and comprehension	X	X	X		
Structured Breaks		X	X	X	X	X	X		X	I	2, 3	Appropriate self-removal from difficult situations that have typically resulted in negative, sometimes verbally aggressive behaviors		X	X		
Time-In	X	X	X	X	X	X	X	X	X	I or G	1, 2, 3	Compliance, on-task, generally appropriate classroom behavior		X	X		
VR VI Reinforcement	X	X	X	X	X	X	X		X	I or G	2, 3	On-task, attentive behavior as well as specific targeted appropriate behaviors such as compliance, talking with permission, or remaining in seat or area		X	X		
Word and Sentence Repeat		1st	X			X	X	X	X	I	1, 2, 3	Reading with accuracy and fluency, reading comprehension		X	X		

Engagement, Participation, & Work Completion Interventions

Active Student Engagement: Procedural Integrity Checklist

Age/Grade:	Preschool – High School
Setting:	School, Clinic, In-patient
Individual or Group:	One or more
Tier:	1
Desired/ Appropriate Behavior:	On-task, participation, work engagement, work completion
Skill Level:	Fluency to maintenance

Rationale & Research Support

Research indicates children who are actively engaged during instruction learn more than passive learners (Brophy & Good, 1986; Fisher & Berliner, 1985; Heward, 1994; Rosenshine & Berliner, 1978; Ryan & Deci, 2000;). Therefore, monitoring the level of active student engagement across classrooms is an important task for a school leader. This checklist provides a procedure for an observer (e.g., assistant principal, lead teacher) to conduct brief classroom observations to monitor active student engagement.

Active engagement is defined as **80% of the children engaging in exercises or activities** that include, but are not limited to, writing, answering questions, discussions. It is NOT passive listening, silent reading, copying notes, or test taking.

Materials

Stopwatch or other timing device

Procedure for Integrity Checklist Observer

1) The observer conducts *unannounced, random* observations of groups (e.g., classrooms) to observe for student active engagement. The observer should create a table of individuals being observed and times in advance to ensure that all individuals and groups are observed and that the times are randomly spread across the entire school day. Ideally, all individuals/groups will be observed at least once a week initially.
2) The observer completes the Procedural Integrity Checklist (see page 24) information about the interventionist, group (class, period), location, date, time, observer name, and observer signature.
3) The observer determines the number of children required to be actively engaged to meet the definition of 80% or more of children engaged. This number can be determined by multiplying the total number of children in the group by 0.8 and rounding any partial value (e.g., 15.2) to the next whole number (e.g., 16). A table of common group sizes with this calculation completed is provided on the observation form.
4) The observer observes the group for ten 30-second intervals, or a total of five minutes. The observer puts a slash (/) in each 30 second interval in which the behavior (active student engagement) is present at **any time** during the interval. For example, 80% of the children may not be actively engaged in the first 5 seconds but are actively engaged the rest of the interval (25

seconds). The observer would put a single slash in the interval since Active Engagement occurred during the interval. Active student engagement is counted as present during a 30-second interval if 80% or more of the children are engaged *at any point* during that 30-second interval in exercises or activities that include, but are not limited to, writing, answering questions, discussions. It is NOT passive listening, silent reading, or test taking. Leave the 30-second interval box empty if the behavior was not observed at any point during the interval.

5) Write the number of slashes across the row in the Observed Total cell at the end of the five-minute observation.

6) Divide the Observed Total by the Possible Total (10) to obtain a Percent Observed.

7) *The minimum observation is one five-minute observation*. Additional five-minute observations may be completed at the discretion of the observer. Indicate in the Observation Completed column if the five-minute observation was completed by writing Y(es) or N(o). A Y or N should be written in each of the cells in this column.

8) Write any constructive feedback comments in the "Feedback" section.

9) At an appropriate time following each observation, the observer provides the observed individual with oral feedback regarding active student engagement, starting with positive behaviors observed, and a copy of the Active Student Engagement Procedural Integrity Checklist. *The feedback should be provided the same day of the observation.*

10) After the initial observation, the observer should observe an interventionist weekly until active student engagement is demonstrated 90% or more of the time on three consecutive observations (across more 3 or more days), meaning that the children need to display 80% active engagement in 9 out of the 10 interval (90%). Once an interventionist demonstrates active student engagement 90% or more of the time on three consecutive observations, the frequency of observation for the interventionist may be reduced to once every four weeks.

11) The observer records the Percent Observed student engagement for each interventionist and an average for all interventionists weekly. The observer monitors the trend in the Percent Observed by interventionist and for all interventionists to ensure that the Percent Observed is increasing or is maintained at a level of 90% or higher.

References

Brophy, J. and Good, T. (1986). Teacher behavior and student achievement. In M.C. Wittro (Ed.), *Handbook of research on teaching* (3rd Ed., pp. 328-375). New York: Macmillan.

Fisher, C. W. & Berliner, D. C. (Eds.). (1985). *Perspectives on instructional time*. New York: Longman.

Heward, W.L. (1994). Three 'low-tech' strategies for increasing the frequency of active student response during group instruction. In R.Gardner III, D.M.Sainato, J.O.Cooper, T.E.Heron, W.L.Heward, J.Eshleman, & T.A.Grossi (Eds.), *Behavior analysis in education: Focus on measurably superior instruction* (pp. 283-320). Monterey, CA: Brooks/Cole.

Rosenshine, B. & Berliner, D. (1978). Academic engaged time. *British Journal of Teacher Education, 4,* 3-16.

Ryan, R. & Deci, E. (2000). Self-Determination theory and the facilitation of intrinsic motivation, social development, and well-being. *American Psychologist.* Vol. 55, No. 1, 68-78.

Active Student Engagement: Procedural Integrity Checklist

Interventionist: ______________________ Date: __________ Time: __________

Group: ______________________ Observer: ______________________

Location: ______________________ Signature: ______________________

Directions

- Determine the number of students required to be actively engaged to meet the definition of 80% or more of students engaged.
- Put a single slash (/) in each 30-second interval in which the behavior (active student engagement) is present at any time during the interval. Active student engagement is counted as present during a 30-second interval if 80% or more of the students are engaged in exercises or activities that include, but are not limited to, writing, answering questions, discussions. It is NOT passive listening, silent reading, copying notes, or test taking.
- Leave the box empty if the behavior was not seen at any point during the ENTIRE interval.
- At the end of the five-minute observation, write the number of slashes across the row in the Observed Total cell.
- Divide the Observed Total by the Possible Total (10) to obtain a Percent Observed.
- The minimum observation is one five-minute observation. Additional five-minute observations may be completed at the discretion of the observer.

Determine the number of students in the group required to be actively engaged

Number of students present in group = ______

Number of students required to be actively engaged (80% or more of group) = _____

Minimum Number of Student Actively Engaged based on Group Total			
Group Total	Number Equal to 80% or more	Group Total	Number Equal to 80% or more
11	9	21	17
12	10	22	18
13	11	23	19
14	12	24	20
15	12	25	20
16	13	26	21
17	14	27	22
18	15	28	23
19	16	29	24
20	16	30	24

Observation (Each box represents a 30-second interval.)

	Observation Completed (Y or N)	0:00		1:00		2:00		3:00		4:00	5:00	**Observed Total (# of /'s)**	**Possible Total**	**Pct Observed (Observed/ Possible)**
1st Observation													10	
2nd Observation													10	
3rd Observation													10	
Totals (Only count rows for which an observation was completed.)														

Across all observation, the number of intervals active student engagement was observed = _____ out of _____ = ______ %

Feedback:

Response Cards

Age/Grade:	Preschool – High School
Setting:	School, Home, Clinic, In-patient
Individual or Group:	One or more
Tier:	1, 2, & 3
Desired/ Appropriate Behavior:	Engagement in learning
Skill Level:	Acquisition to maintenance

Rationale & Research Support

The response cards procedure is an intervention that increases children's active engagement and provides a means for a teacher or interventionist to immediately assess and to provide feedback to the whole class, a group of children within the class, or individual children. The basic procedure for response cards is for all children to respond simultaneously to a prompt by using a card with pre-printed answers, a white board, interactive white board, or other technology. The interventionist then assesses the responses and provides feedback to children.

The response cards procedure has been shown to increase student performance on both short-term and delayed assessments (Cavanaugh, Heward, & Donelson, 1996; Christle & Schuster, 2003; Maheady, Michielli-Pendl, Mallette, & Harper, 2002; Randolph, 2007). This procedure has also been shown to decrease off-task and disruptive student behavior (Armendariz & Umbreit, 1999; Gardner, Bullara, Heward, Cooper, & Sweeney, 1993; Randolph, 2007). The response cards procedure has been demonstrated to be more effective than hand raising (Narayan, Heward, Gardner, Courson, & Omness, 1990). Research has shown that the response cards procedure is effective at all educational levels from primary through college with a variety of subjects (Cavanaugh, Heward, & Donelson, 1996; Kellum, Carr, & Dozier, 2001; Randolph, 2007; Marmolejo, Wilder, & Bradley, 2004).

Materials

Any one of the following:

- Response cards (see pages 30-35)
- White boards with dry erase markers and erasers
- Electronic responders with an interactive white board
- Other technology or materials which may be made for this purpose

Procedure for Interventionist

Introducing the procedure to children

1) Inform children that they will be responding to questions and prompts in a new way.
2) Show children a response card or white board. (See page 28 for examples of response cards.)
3) Model how to use the response card correctly by demonstrating examples of the different responses a child will provide using the response card. For example, if using a Yes/No response

card, provide examples of using the response card when the response would be Yes and examples when the response would be No. Be sure the demonstration includes the use of selected prompts for children to show their responses (e.g., "Cards up" or "Answer please"), the proper placement of cards or white boards (e.g., below chin), and the instruction for children to put down their cards or white boards (e.g., "Cards down" or "Boards down and clean").

4) Distribute the response cards or white boards to children. If using white boards, distribute an appropriate marker and something for erasing the board (e.g., tissue, paper towel, eraser) to each child.

5) Provide the children with an opportunity to practice responding to several prompts using the response cards or white boards. A suggestion is to use material from a previous lesson or class session for this practice. Provide children with praise and corrective feedback. When using response cards or white boards, children should be facing the interventionist.

6) Once all children consistently respond on cue with cards/boards in the proper position, then conclude the introduction of response cards. At this point, it is also a good idea to instruction children on the procedure for putting the materials away or for collecting materials, whichever is appropriate for the setting.

Daily procedure

1) Prior to the class period, determine what material will be used with the response cards. Initially, it may be helpful to plan the questions or prompts that will be used with children when they use the response cards.

2) Prior to the class period, prepare a student list or seating chart that will be used to keep a tally of student incorrect responses. This information will be used later to make decisions about differentiating instruction for groups or individual children.

3) Distribute the response cards or white boards if children do not have them at their seats. If using white boards, you may also need to distribute an appropriate marker and something for erasing the board (e.g., tissue, paper towel, eraser) to each child.

4) Ask a question or provide a prompt to which children will respond by using the response cards or white board.

5) Give the children a few seconds to choose an answer or to write a response. Generally, 3-5 seconds should be sufficient for recall types of demands. Generally, more time will be required for a response requiring higher cognitive demand.

6) Prompt children to show their responses with a cue such as "Cards up" or "Answers please." Be sure that children hold or display the cards/boards in the manner they were trained.

7) Scan the class as a whole to assess the response. The goal is for 80% or more of the children to respond correctly.

8) Put a tally mark on the student list or seating chart (prepared in step 2 above) beside the name of each student who responds incorrectly. If more than one skill or concept is assessed during the session, noting the skill or concept is necessary. The notation can be made by using a single letter abbreviation for the skill or concept as the tally mark. For example, a mathematics teacher might be

addressing communicative and distributive properties. The teacher might simply indicate an incorrect response addressing communicative property with a "c" as the tally mark.

9) Provide feedback to children.
   a) If 80% or more of the children respond correctly, the following steps are appropriate:
      i) Affirm the correct response by clearly stating it for the whole class (e.g., "36 is the correct response." or "Pronoun is the correct response.") and providing a brief supporting explanation or rationale.
      ii) Prompt children to put down their response cards or white boards with a cue such as "Cards down" or "Boards down and clean."
      iii) Move on to the next question or prompt to which the children will respond.
   b) If less than 80% of children respond correctly, the following steps are appropriate:
      i) Prompt children to put down their response cards or white boards with a cue such as "Cards down" or "Board down." If using white boards, do not instruct children to clean their white board at this point so that they can see their response.
      ii) Ask children who responded correctly to explain how they solved the problem.
      iii) Ask children who did not respond correctly to explain how they solved the problem; provide feedback to the children on where their thinking was incorrect.
      iv) Affirm the correct response by clearly stating it for the whole class (e.g., "36 is the correct response." or "Pronoun is the correct response.") and providing a brief supporting explanation or rationale if not already provided by the children who responded correctly.
      v) If using white boards, prompt children to clean their white boards with a cue "Clean boards."
      vi) Re-teach or model the knowledge or skill if appropriate.
      vii) Following steps 5-9 above, ask a new question or provide a new prompt on the knowledge or skill until 80% or more of the children respond correctly.
10) Continue asking questions or providing prompts until the knowledge or skill has been adequately assessed.
11) At the end of the session, using the response cards or white boards, prompt children for the procedure for putting the materials away or for collecting materials, whichever is appropriate for the setting.
12) While children are putting away or collecting materials, review the student list or seating chart and take note of any children who responded incorrectly during the session. Based on the patterns presented in the data, determine if children should receive individual or small group instruction at another time (e.g., when the rest of the class is engaged in independent practice). If these data cannot be reviewed immediately, the data should be reviewed prior to the next time these children will be receiving instruction in this content area.

2

Important Things to Note

1. When using response cards or white boards, try to maintain a quick, energetic pace.
2. Periodically (at least once per session) praise children for appropriate and correct use of the response cards procedure.
3. The responses on the response card or white board should be legible from the front of the room so that the interventionist can quickly and accurately assess all responses.
4. When using white boards, keep the responses to one to two words if possible. Be sure to train children to write the responses large enough to be seen by the interventionist at the front of the room.
5. If more than one method for arriving at the correct response is possible or more than one correct response is possible, the interventionist should validate these other methods or correct responses. Affirming these alternatives will help children to generalize the knowledge or skill that is the focus of the learning.

Examples of Response Cards

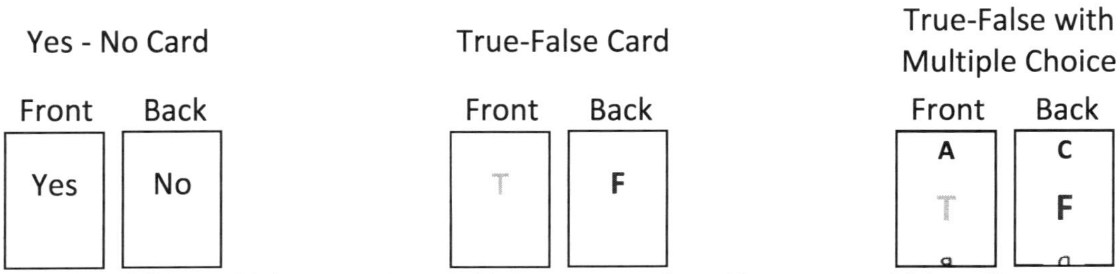

Note: For children with less experience with response cards and for younger children, the response card design should be simple. More complex designs such as the True-False with Multiple Choice example should be reserved for children with more response card experience and/or older children.

References

Armendariz, F., & Umbreit, J. (1999). Using active responding to reduce disruptive behavior in a general education classroom. *Journal of Positive Behavior Interventions, 1,* 152-158.

Cavanaugh, R. A., Heward, W. L., & Donelson, F. (1996). Effects of response cards during lesson closure on the academic performance of secondary students in an earth science course. *Journal of Applied Behavior Analysis, 29,* 403-406.

Christle, C. A., & Schuster, J. W. (2003). The effects of using response cards on student participation, academic achievement, and on-task behavior during whole-class math instruction. *Journal of Behavioral Education, 12,* 147-165.

Gardner, R. III., Bullara, D. T., Heward, W. L., Cooper, J. O., & Sweeney, W. J. (1993, October). *Effects of response cards on elementary students' participation and disruptive behavior during whole-class instruction.* Paper presented at The Ohio State University Conference on Measurably Superior Instruction, Columbus, OH.

Kellum, K. K., Carr, J. E., & Dozier, C. L. (2001). Response-card instruction and student learning in a college classroom. *Teaching of Psychology, 28,* 101-104.

Maheady, L., Michielli-Pendl, J., Mallette, B., & Harper, G. F. (2002). A collaborative research project to improve the performance of a diverse sixth grade science class. *Teacher Education and Special Education, 25,* 55-70.

Marmolejo, E. K., Wilder, D. A., & Bradley, L. (2004). A preliminary analysis of the effects of response cards on student performance and participation in an upper division university course. *Journal of Applied Behavior Analysis, 37,* 405-410.

Narayan, J. S., Heward, W. L., Gardner, R., Courson, F. H., & Omness, C. K. (1990). Using response cards to increase student participation in an elementary classroom. *Journal of Applied Behavior Analysis, 23,* 483-490.

Randolph, J. J. (2007). Meta-analysis of the research on response cards: Effects on test achievement, quiz achievement, participation, and off-task behavior. *Journal of Positive Behavior Interventions, 9,* 113-128.

Instructions for Making Response Cards

These instructions are for creating response cards with options for True/False responses, multiple choice responses (A, B, C, or D), or any other response that requires only two choices (e.g., Fact/Opinion, Yes/No). Two responses cards in two different colors are created for each participant. The interventionist should use the Response Cards procedures for training participants and proper implementation of response cards.

Materials

- 8.5 X 11 inch card stock or other heavy weight paper in two colors (Two pieces of card stock — one color of each — will provide a set of response cards for three participants.)
- Printer or copier that can accept card stock paper
- Laminating equipment or material (optional)

Instructions

Note: It may be helpful to test out these instructions on plain or scrap paper before using card stock paper since the proper way to feed paper through a printer or copier multiple times depends on the specific printer or copier used.

1) Choose the color card stock for the two response cards per participant. One color (e.g., green, blue) is for the A, B, and T(rue) response card. A second color (e.g., pink, red, orange, yellow) is for the C, D, and F(alse) response card.
2) Starting with the card stock selected for the A, B, and T(rue) response card, print or copy page 1 of the Response Card – A B and True provided on pages 32-35
3) Take the printed or copied card stock which now has the letters A and B printed three times across the page and turn the paper over and print or copy page 2 of the Response Card – A B and True document. The paper will now have three Ts (for True) across the page and the three As and three Bs across the page similar to the following graphic.

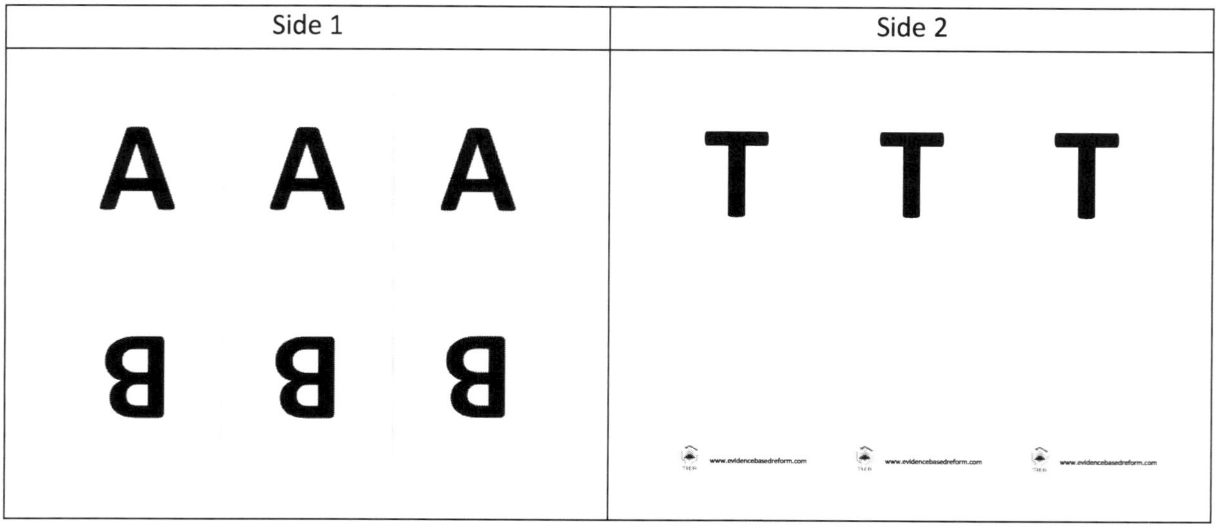

4) The A and B side of the card has very faint lines that serve as guides for cutting the paper into three response cards.
5) Now take the card stock (second color) selected for the C, D, and F(alse) response card and print or copy page 1 of the Response Card – C D and False document.
6) Take the printed or copied card stock which now has the letters C and D printed three times across the page and turn the paper over and print or copy page 2 of the Response Card – C D and False document. The paper will now have three Fs (for False) across the page on one side and the three Cs and three Ds across the other side of the paper.
7) The C and D side of the card has very faint lines that serve as guides for cutting the paper into three response cards.
8) (Optional) Laminate each response card to make the response cards last longer.
9) Prior to using the response cards for the first time in the classroom, develop a procedure for quickly distributing the response cards to children. For example, the procedure may be that the number of response cards needed for each row of participants is counted out prior to use and the cards are simply given to the first participant in the row who takes one of each response card and passes the rest back.
10) Remember to refer to the Response Cards procedures for training participants and proper implementation of response cards.

A

B

A

B

A

B

T T T

TIER www.evidencebasedreform.com
TIER www.evidencebasedreform.com

C D

C D

C D

F F F

Response Cards: Procedural Integrity Checklist

Age/Grade:	Preschool – High School
Setting:	School, Home, Clinic, In-patient
Individual or Group:	One or more
Tier:	1, 2, & 3
Desired/ Appropriate Behavior:	Engagement in learning
Skill Level:	Acquisition to maintenance

Procedure for Integrity Checklist Observer

1) The observer (e.g., principal, assistant principal, lead teacher) completes the Procedural Integrity Checklist (see page 37) information about the interventionist, group (class, period), location, date, time, observer name, and signature.
2) The observer assesses an interventionist's implementation of the response card procedure in the classroom. An initial observation should occur within the first couple of weeks of an interventionist's implementing the response cards procedure so that feedback can be provided to the interventionist early in the implementation.
3) The observer should observe the interventionist for the presence of behaviors 1-11 on the Checklist and mark Yes if present or No if not present.
4) If less than 80% of children respond correctly to a presented question or prompt, then the observer should mark Yes that this situation was observed and indicate Yes or No if behaviors 12-14 were present.
5) At the completion of the observation, the observer should count the number of behaviors marked Yes and write the number on the line for "Number of behaviors marked Yes."
6) The observer will write the total number of behaviors observed (either 11 or 14) and calculate the percent marked Yes. A chart is provided for determining the percent marked Yes. If less than 80% of behaviors are marked Yes, then provide feedback immediately to the interventionist and conduct another observation the next day or as soon as possible.
7) The observer should write any constructive feedback comments in addition to any notations made beside any individual behavior in the "Feedback" section.
8) At an appropriate time following each observation, the observer should provide the interventionist with oral feedback regarding implementation of the intervention, starting with positive behaviors observed, and a copy of the Response Cards: Procedural Integrity Checklist. *The feedback should be provided the same day of the observation.*
9) After the initial observation, the observer should assess the interventionist implementing the response cards procedure 3-4 times per school year. If the intervention is used for Tier 2 or Tier 3, then observe approximately every other week or twice a month after the initial observation

Response Cards: Procedural Integrity Checklist

Interventionist: ______________________ Date: __________ Time: __________

Group: ______________________ Observer: ______________________

Location: ______________________ Signature: ______________________

Behaviors to Observe	Yes	No	Comments
1. The interventionist has a quick and efficient procedure for distributing response cards or white boards and materials (i.e., makers, erasers, paper towel, etc.)			
2. The interventionist asks a question or provides a prompt appropriate for response cards/white boards.			
3. The interventionist gives children a few seconds to choose an answer or to write a response.			
4. The interventionist prompt children to show their responses with a cue such as "Cards up" or "Answers please."			
5. The interventionist scans the class as a whole to assess the response.			
6. The interventionist records or marks each child who responded incorrectly.			
7. The interventionist affirms the correct response by clearly stating it for the whole class (e.g., "36 is the correct response." or "Pronoun is the correct response.") and provides a brief supporting explanation or rationale.			
8. The interventionist prompts children to put down their response cards or white boards with a cue such as "Cards down" or "Boards down and clean."			
9. The interventionist moves to the next question or prompt only if 80% or more of the children respond correctly.			
10. The interventionist maintains a quick, energetic pace during the use of the response card intervention.			
11. The interventionist praises children at least once for appropriate and correct use of the response cards procedure.			
If less than 80% of children respond correctly: Was this observed? __Yes __No			
12. The interventionist asks children who responded correctly to explain how they solved the problem.			
13. The interventionist asks children who did not respond correctly to explain how they solved the problem and provides feedback to the children on where their thinking was incorrect.			
14. The interventionist re-teaches or models the knowledge or skill if			

Number of behaviors marked Yes = _____ out of _____ = ______ %

Feedback:

Percent

1 out of 11 = 9%	1 out of 14 = 7%
2 out of 11 = 18%	2 out of 14 = 14%
3 out of 11 = 27%	3 out of 14 = 21%
4 out of 11 = 36%	4 out of 14 = 29%
5 out of 11 = 45%	5 out of 14 = 36%
6 out of 11 = 55%	6 out of 14 = 43%
7 out of 11 = 64%	7 out of 14 = 50%
8 out of 11 = 73%	8 out of 14 = 57%
9 out of 11 = 82%	9 out of 14 = 64%
10 out of 11 = 91%	10 out of 14 = 71%
11 out of 11 = 100%	11 out of 14 = 79%
	12 out of 14 = 86%
	13 out of 14 = 93%
	14 out of 14 = 100%

TIER

Good Behavior Game

Age/Grade:	Kindergarten – High School
Setting:	School, Home, Clinic, In-patient
Individual or Group:	One or more
Tier:	1 & 2
Desired/ Appropriate Behavior:	Appropriate classroom behavior including on-task, speaking with permission, remaining in seat, respectful
Skill Level:	Fluency to maintenance

Rationale & Research Support

The Good Behavior Game (GBG) is an approach to the management of behaviors that rewards children for displaying appropriate on-task behaviors during instruction, small group, or large group times. The GBG is an interdependent group contingency procedure in which the consequence is delivered to all members of the group contingent upon the collective group's performance. The group of children is divided into two teams and a point is given to a team for any inappropriate behavior displayed by one of its members. The team with the fewest number of points at the game's conclusion each day wins a group reward. If both teams keep their points below a preset level, then both teams share in the reward. An alternative implementation of the GBG is to earn points for exhibition of appropriate behavior. Specifically, following a specified number of minutes, teams may earn a point for on-task, appropriate behavior. The team with the most points shares in the reward.

Referrals for problem behaviors often include more than one child; these referrals may reflect classwide or group-wide concerns rather than individual concerns. In such cases, efficiency may be increased when using group oriented contingencies (Tingstrom, Sterling-Turner, & Wilczynski, 2006). The program was first tested in 1969; several research articles have confirmed that the GBG is an effective means of increasing the rate of on-task behaviors while reducing disruptions in the classroom (Barrish, Saunders, & Wolf, 1969; Harris & Sherman, 1973; Medland & Stachnik, 1972). Since that time, research continues to indicate that the GBG can be used to increase on-task behaviors and decrease disruptive behaviors as well as increase peer acceptance and increase observed proximity to peers for children who had exhibited disruptive behaviors and experienced peer rejection (Christ & Christ, 2006; Ruiz-Olivares, Pino, & Herruzo, 2010; Witvliet, Lier, Cuijpers, & Koot, 2009).

Materials

1) Large paper or other method for visibly posting teams' points
2) MotivAider® (optional for use with the 15-second intervals with the observations)
3) Cool Timer (optional if needing a countdown timer and is a free download from harmonyhollow.net)
4) List of Rewards

Procedure for Interventionist

1) Decide when to schedule the game. The interventionist first decides during what activity or period(s) of the day the game will be played. As a rule of thumb, interventionists should pick those times when the entire group is expected to show appropriate behaviors. Blocks of time devoted to

reading, math, content instruction, independent seatwork, or small group work are the most appropriate for putting the game into effect.

2) Determine target behaviors. Teams earn points for engagement in target behaviors. The target behaviors must be stated in a positive manner (e.g., on-task, speaks with permission).
3) Based on the procedure determined in step 2, clearly define the target behaviors that will be scored during the game.
   a) All target behaviors should be operationally defined so that they are clear, observable, and measureable. Examples are as follows:
      i) *Speaks only with permission* is defined as any period of time that the child raises a hand to speak or speaks during a time that is designated by the interventionist (e.g., choral responding) and all individuals have permission to speak. Any incident of talking out loud without the permission of the interventionist or unauthorized vocalization (e.g., shouts, whistles, grunts, noises) is not considered speaking with permission, and the team would not earn a point for that time period.
      ii) *Remains on-task is defined as* speaking with permission, remaining in designated area, physically oriented toward instructional stimuli or the interventionist, and working on classroom assignment. Engaging in tasks that have been indicated as allowed by the interventionist is not considered off-task. For example, if children are allowed to get up and sharpen their pencil without permission, that behavior is not off-task.
4) Collect baseline data.
   a) Using the target behaviors, an observer (can be the interventionist or other adult such as the school psychologist, behavior specialist, counselor, etc.) should conduct observations prior to beginning the intervention during the time that has been set for the game to take place.
   b) The observer should conduct at least three different observations using a momentary time sampling procedure.
      i) Momentary time sampling observations are conducted by observing children at the beginning of each interval and recording the behaviors they are exhibiting at each specified (e.g., each 15 seconds) moment in time. See Conducting Direct Observations for a detailed description of the observation procedure and sample forms.
      ii) The observer randomly selects five children for observation. The observation lasts for 20 minutes with 15-second intervals. At the beginning of each interval, the observer looks at a targeted child for 3 seconds and records the observed behaviors. At each interval, a different child is observed until all 5 children have been observed and then the observer starts over with the first target child and continues throughout the observation.
      iii) Calculate the percentage of occurrence of each behavior to determine the average exhibition of the target behavior during the observation. These totals should be used for baseline and additional observations should be conducted weekly for progress monitoring. Percentages are calculated by totaling the number of occurrences for each behavior and dividing by the total possible occurrences for each behavior. See Conducting Direct Observations for an example.

5) Decide upon suitable daily and (perhaps) weekly rewards for teams winning the game.
    a) The Interventionist should choose rewards that are more likely to effectively motivate children to take part in the game. Interventionists find that children are motivated by the promise of free time and therefore often use free time as a daily reward. For example, one interventionist's reward system included giving her daily 4th-grade game winners the privilege of wearing a "victory tag," putting a star next to their name on a "Winner's Chart," lining up first for lunch, and getting 30 minutes of time at the end of the day to work on preferred, educationally related topics.
        i) If using a daily reward, the reward should be based on the points earned that day.
        ii) If using a weekly reward, the reward can be provided based either on the weekly total of points or on the daily points for a specific number of days that week. For example, if the teams earn their set points for 4 out of 5 days that week, they earn their weekly reward.
    b) When choosing rewards, interventionist should consider using reinforcers that fit naturally into the context and mission of the setting/classroom. For example, allowing winners to play quietly together at the end of the school day may help to promote social skills, but dispensing material rewards (e.g., comic books) to winners is less likely to contribute directly to educational and social goals.
6) Introduce the game to the class once behaviors are clearly defined. Ideally, the interventionist should set aside time for an initial group discussion. The interventionist states that the group will be playing a game and presents a schedule that clearly sets forth the times during which the game will be in effect.
    a) The interventionist next divides the group into two teams. For ease of recording, the interventionist should divide the class down the center of the room into roughly equal halves for two teams or thirds for three teams. To build a sense of team spirit, the interventionist may encourage groups to name their teams.
    b) The interventionist informs the children that engaging in the target behavior(s) will earn points for the team to which they belong.
    c) The interventionist explains that both teams can win and earn the reward if they meet specific criteria. For example, if the interventionist has a set criterion of 10 points, then both teams earn the reward if they earn 10 points.
    d) When introducing the game to children, the interventionist should clearly review examples of acceptable and unacceptable behaviors so that all children know and understand the rules before the game begins. To more effectively illustrate those rules, the interventionist may recruit children to demonstrate acceptable and unacceptable behaviors, or the interventionist may describe a number of behaviors and ask the class to decide with a show of hands whether such behaviors are acceptable.
7) Put the game into effect.
    a) The interventionist is now ready to start the Game. During those times that the game is in effect, the interventionist continues to carry out usual procedures/instructional practices. The only alterations in the routine are as follows:
        i) At the beginning of the time period, the interventionist introduces the game and reminds the group of the target behaviors

ii) The interventionist reminds teams of how they earn points and how those points lead to rewards.
iii) The interventionist notes and publicly records any points earned by either team and posts scores where they are visible to everyone in the room (e.g., on a whiteboard, a large piece of paper).
iv) If working with children in a small group, the interventionist can record points on a small note pad and later transfer them to a more visible location.
v) The interventionist can also choose to publicly announce when another point has been earned as a reminder to the group about acceptable behavior. The interventionist should encourage the group by giving positive feedback.
vi) The interventionist must keep a weekly tally of points for each team, if teams are competing for weekly as well as daily rewards.

b) The interventionist should be as consistent as possible in scoring behaviors. The interventionist should praise winning teams as well as reward them for their efforts, with that praise tied to specifically observed behaviors. The interventionist may want to alter the game somewhat as necessary (e.g., changing rewards or clarifying definitions of acceptable and unacceptable behaviors with children). When any alteration is made to the game, no matter how small, the interventionist must share the change with the teams before the change is put into effect.

8) Progress Monitoring
   a) Momentary time sampling observations should be continued at least once per week as the intervention is being conducted.
   b) Compare percentages calculated on the observations each week to determine if the GBG is increasing or decreasing target behaviors.

Tier 1

For Tier 1, introduce the GBG as a whole group procedure with no specific target children. The target behaviors should be basic group rules that are expected to be followed by all children. Points can be earned and whole class or group rewards can be used on a weekly basis.

Tier 2

For Tier 2, identify a small group of target children due to the occurrence of specific disruptive behaviors. Target behaviors are determined based on the goals for those children whose behaviors need to be decreased or increased. Gather baseline data on the targeted children who are identified for the intervention. If only one child is identified, the collection of baseline data as it has been described should continue for five children being observed; however, the one target child must always be one of the five children selected and must be observed during each game. The same procedure is followed if 2 or 3 children are identified for intervention.

Adjustments/Modifications

1) If only a few children are preventing their team from earning points during the game, the interventionist should consider forming them into a separate team. While not the norm, occasionally a single child or small group of children may be tempted to undermine the game by deliberately preventing their team from earning points. (Such children may find the resulting negative social attention of other members of their team to be its own reward!) A simple remedy

for this problem is to modify the Game by making those disruptive children into a separate team. The game will continue unchanged, except that there will be one additional team competing for rewards.

2) If the interventionist determines that children are losing motivation with the rewards, the interventionist should consider using an "unknown" reward at the end of the day. Each winning team can draw a reward from a bag and will earn the reward that is pulled from the bag that day.
3) If the interventionist is using positively stated behaviors and the group must earn points for appropriate behavior following a given period of time, the interventionist should consider using a countdown timer with a smart board in the room. If an inappropriate behavior occurs, the timer should be re-started. Once the time reaches zero, the team(s) should earn a point for the exhibition of appropriate behavior.
4) The interventionist may also choose to use target behaviors worded in a negative fashion. More specifically, the target behaviors can be stated in a way that describes the inappropriate behavior (e.g., off-task, talking out). If inappropriate behaviors are the targets, the teams will be "earn" points when they engage in the inappropriate behavior. In this version of the game, the team that "earns" the fewest points will be given a reward at the end of the day. Another option is that a criterion of points (e.g., 5 points) is set, and each team with fewer than 5 points earns a reward.

References

Barrish, H.H., Saunders, M, & Wolf, M.M. (1969). Good behavior game: Effects of individual contingencies for group consequences on disruptive behavior in a classroom. *Journal of Applied Behavior Analysis, 2,* 119-124.

Christ, T. J. & Christ, J. A. (2006). Application of an interdependent group contingency mediated by an automated feedback device: An intervention across three high school classrooms. *School Psychology Review, 75,* 78-90.

Harris, V.W. & Sherman, J.A. (1973). Use and analysis of the "Good Behavior Game" to reduce disruptive classroom behavior. *Journal of Applied Behavior Analysis, 6*, 405-417.

Medland, M. B. & Stachnik, T.J. (1972). Good-behavior game: A replication and systematic analysis. *Journal of Applied Behavior Analysis, 5,* 45-51.

Ruiz-Olivares, R., Pino, M. J., & Herruzo, J. (2010). Reduction of disruptive behaviors using an intervention based on the good behavior game and the say-do-report correspondence. *Psychology in the Schools, 47,* 1046-1058.

Tingstrom, D. H., Sterling-Turner, H. E., & Wilczynski, S. M. (2006). The good behavior game: 1969-2002. *Behavior Modification, 30,* 225-253.

Witvliet, M., Lier, P.A., Cuijpers, P., & Koot, H. M. (2009). Testing links between childhood positive peer relations and externalizing outcomes through a randomized controlled intervention study. *Journal of Consulting and Clinical Psychology, 77,* 905-915.

3

Good Behavior Game (GBG): Procedural Integrity Checklist

Age/Grade:	Kindergarten – High School
Setting:	School, Home, Clinic, In-patient
Individual or Group:	One or more people
Tier:	1 & 2
Desired/ Appropriate Behavior:	Appropriate classroom behavior including on-task, speaking with permission, remaining in seat, respectful
Skill Level:	Fluency to maintenance

This document provides the procedure for checking the implementation integrity of the GBG procedure and a procedural checklist. The GBG procedure is described in a separate document. The GBG program was developed as an efficient Tier 1/2 intervention for reducing problem behavior. GBG was designed as an approach to the management of classrooms behaviors that rewards children for displaying appropriate on-task behaviors

Procedure for Integrity Checklist Observer

1) The principal or other appropriate staff (e.g., counselor, behavior specialist, therapist, school psychologist) completes the Procedural Integrity Checklists (see pages 45-46) information about the teacher, group (class, period), location, date, time, and observer name. The first checklist is for the initial training day for the group and the second checklist is for the daily implementation.
2) The observer observes the designated adult's implementation of the GBG procedure. An initial observation should occur within the first two weeks of implementing the GBG procedure so that feedback can be provided to the designated adult early in the implementation.
3) The observer observes the designated adult or child for the presence of behaviors 1-8 on the Checklist and marks Yes if present or No if not present. If there was not an opportunity to observe some of the behaviors, then mark N/O for not observed.
4) At the completion of the observation, the observer counts the number of behaviors marked Yes and writes the number on the line for "Number of behaviors marked Yes."
5) The observer writes the total number of behaviors observed (i.e., the total behaviors marked Yes or No) and the percent marked Yes.
6) The observer writes any constructive feedback comments in addition to any notations made beside any individual behavior in the "Feedback" section.
7) At an appropriate time following each observation, the observer provides the designated adult with oral feedback regarding the implementation of the intervention, starting with positive behaviors observed, and a copy of the GBG Procedural Integrity Checklist. *The feedback should be provided the same day of the observation.*
8) After the initial observation, the observer should observe the designated adult implementing the GBG procedure 2-8 times depending on the length of the implementation (e.g., approximately every other week or twice a month).

Good Behavior Game (GBG): Procedural Integrity Checklist

Initial Training Procedures

Interventionist: ______________________ Date: ________ Time: ________

Child: ______________________ Observer: ______________________

Location: ______________________ Signature: ______________________

N/O = Not Observed

Behaviors to Observe	Yes	No	N/O	Comments
1) Time of day for GBG to be conducted is determined.				
2) Target behaviors are defined in clear, observable, measureable terms.				
3) Baseline data are collected for at least 3 days prior to implementation.				
4) Suitable daily or weekly rewards are determined.				
5) Game is introduced in a whole group discussion				
6) Examples of acceptable and unacceptable behaviors are reviewed and practiced with the group.				
7) Clear schedule is created for times the Game will be in effect.				
8) Group is divided into equal teams (unless reasons are presented for the need of an additional team or no team at all for Tier 1 implementation).				

Number of behaviors marked Yes = _____ out of _____ = ______ %

Percent
1 out of 8 = 13%
2 out of 8 = 25%
3 out of 8 = 38%
4 out of 8 = 50%
5 out of 8 = 63%
6 out of 8 = 75%
7 out of 8 = 88%
8 out of 8 = 100%

Feedback:

Good Behavior Game (GBG): Procedural Integrity Checklist
Daily Intervention Procedures

Interventionist: ______________________ Date: __________ Time: __________

Child: ______________________ Observer: ______________________

Location: ______________________ Signature: ______________________

N/O = Not Observed

Behaviors to Observe	Yes	No	N/O	Comments
1) The interventionist introduced/reminds the group of the target behaviors at the beginning of the time period.				
2) The interventionist reminds teams of rewards and how the points are earned and noted.				
3) The interventionist acknowledges addition of points at appropriate times during instructional period.				
4) Points are clearly visible in the room.				
5) If points are earned in a small group, the interventionist appropriately documents those points at the conclusion of the group.				
6) The interventionist gives feedback to encourage success.				
7) The interventionist reviews and tallies points with the groups.				
8) The interventionist gives rewards or announces when they will be given (e.g., extra recess or free time at end of day).				

Number of behaviors marked Yes = _____ out of _____ = ______ %

Percent
1 out of 8 = 13%
2 out of 8 = 25%
3 out of 8 = 38%
4 out of 8 = 50%
5 out of 8 = 63%
6 out of 8 = 75%
7 out of 8 = 88%
8 out of 8 = 100%

Feedback:

Mystery Motivator

Age/Grade:	Preschool – High School
Setting:	School, Home, Clinic
Individual or Group:	One or more
Tier:	1, 2, & 3
Desired/ Appropriate Behavior:	Any desired behavior such as work completion, compliance, keeping hands and feet to self, appropriate language, prepared for class/school, homework completion
Skill Level:	Fluency to generalization

Rationale & Research Support

The Mystery Motivator intervention has been successfully used to decrease off-task behavior and disruptive behavior in preschool to high school classrooms (Hoag, 2006; Kraemer, Davies, Arndt, & Sawyer, 2012; Murphy, Theodore, Aloiso, Alric-Edwards, & Hughes, 2007; Rhode, Jensen, & Reaves, 1993; Schanding & Sterling-Turner, 2010). It can be used as a classroom behavior management tool as well as a Tier 2 or 3 intervention to target individual children. Mystery Motivators are unknown rewards that use anticipation to maintain children's interest. A critical component is the "hype" associated with the unknown reward. Children involved in the intervention are required to meet a specific criterion in order to gain access to the motivator.

Materials

1) Mystery Motivator Chart
2) Set of markers that include an invisible marker
3) List of rewards

Procedure for Interventionist

1) Define the target behaviors.
    a) Choose no more than 3 - 5 target behaviors.
    b) Operationally define the target behaviors so that they are clear, observable, and measureable. Examples are as follows:
        i) *On-task*: Child's eyes are oriented towards interventionist, working on assignments, moving around the room in order to put up work or gather materials that are to be used for current assignment, speaking to adult or other children as given permission and for the purpose of completing current assignment, using materials in an appropriate fashion.
        ii) *Speaks only with permission*: Child raises hand to speak or speaks during a time designated by the interventionist (e.g., choral responding to questions) when all individuals have permission to speak. Any incident of talking out loud without the permission of the interventionist or unauthorized vocalization (e.g., shouts, whistles, grunts, noises) is not

considered speaking with permission, and the child would not earn a point for that time period.

2) Determine the time of day that the Mystery Motivator intervention will be played. As a general rule, interventionists should pick those times when the entire group is expected to show appropriate behaviors. The most appropriate blocks of time for putting the intervention into effect are times devoted to reading, math, content instruction, independent seatwork, or small group work.

3) Collect baseline data. Using the target behaviors, an observer should conduct observations prior to beginning the intervention during the time that has been set for the intervention to take place. These observations can be completed by the interventionist or an observer who is someone other than the interventionist working with the child on the intervention (e.g., school psychologist, behavior specialist, or other adult). Conduct at least three different observations using the Momentary Time Sampling procedure (see Conducting Direct Observations on page 377).

4) Review target behaviors and procedures with group.

   a) Set aside time for an initial group discussion and introduce the intervention to the group once the behaviors have been selected and clearly defined. State that the group will be playing a game and present a schedule clearly setting the times during which the intervention will be in effect.

   b) Inform the children that engaging in the target behavior(s) will earn the group the right to use the Mystery Motivator Chart.

   c) Provide examples of acceptable and unacceptable behaviors when introducing the intervention to children. It is important that all children know the rules before the intervention begins. To more effectively illustrate those rules, children may be recruited to demonstrate acceptable and unacceptable behaviors, or the interventionist may describe a number of behaviors and ask the group to decide with a show of hands whether such behaviors are to be scored.

   d) Show the children the Mystery Motivator Chart for the week. Explain the following procedures:

      i) Invisible M's are placed on the chart for some of the days of the week but not for every day.

      ii) During the targeted time period for the day (e.g., math group or reading class), the children's behaviors will be observed. If they engage in the expected target behaviors during the allotted time, they will earn the right to color in the Motivator chart for that day.

      iii) If the children are separated into small groups, the interventionist will observe and document if the children have engaged in the expected target behaviors while in their respective groups.

      iv) If the invisible M is revealed, then the children will earn the selected reward at that time or at the end of the day.

      v) If there is no M in the chart for that day, the children will be praised for their behavior and earning the right to color in the chart. They will be encouraged to engage in expected target behaviors again the next day.

e) It is important to note that at the beginning of the intervention, the interventionist should have a richer schedule of reinforcement. Specifically, the invisible M should be placed on 4 of 5 days that week. As the intervention progresses, the scheduled can be thinned out to 3 or fewer days each week.

5) Determine appropriate daily rewards for the children.

   a) Choose rewards that will effectively motivate children. For example, one interventionist's reward system included giving her 4th-grade children the daily privilege of wearing a "victory tag," putting a star next to their name on a "Winner's Chart," lining up first for lunch, and having 30 minutes of time at the end of the day to work on fun, educationally related topics.

   b) Choose rewards that reinforce and fit naturally into the context and mission of the setting/classroom. For example, allowing winners to play quietly together at the end of the school day may help to promote social skills, but dispensing material rewards (e.g., comic books) to winners is less likely to contribute directly to educational and social goals.

   c) Ask children to suggest possible rewards they would like to earn.

6) Monitor the plan. Determine if specific target behaviors defined in step 1 have increased expected behaviors or decreased unwanted behaviors. Continue to use the Momentary Time Sampling observation described in Conducting Direct Observations to compare behavior and determine effectiveness.

Adjustments/Modification

1) For individual children at Tier 2 or 3, the Mystery Motivator can be used as described above. However, individual children can be targeted for improvement in specific behaviors. The specific behaviors for the group should be chosen based on the behaviors for the target children. The observations that are conducted for baseline and progress monitoring should be done for the target children to determine if the intervention is increasing or decreasing the specific behaviors.

2) For increased intensity for individual children, the Mystery Motivator can be used in conjunction with the Daily Behavior Report Card (See intervention for Daily Behavior Report Card on page 205). Specifically, children who are monitored more frequently throughout the day (e.g., each class period or every 30 minutes) can use the Mystery Motivator chart if they reach their individual daily goal.

References

Hoag, J. (2006). Effects of mystery motivators vs. expected reinforcers on disruptive behavior in preschoolers (Doctoral dissertation, Hofstra University, 2007). *Dissertation Abstracts International, 67,* 6041B.

Kraemer, E. E., Davies, S. C., Arndt, K. J., & Sawyer, H. (2012). A comparison of the mystery motivator and the Get 'Em On Task interventions for off-task behaviors. *Psychology in the Schools, 49,* 163–175.

Murphy, K., Theodore, L., Aloiso, D., Alric-Edwards, J., & Hughes, T. (2007). Interdependent group contingency and mystery motivators to reduce preschool disruptive behavior. *Psychology in the Schools, 44,* 53–63.

Rhode, G., Jensen, W. R., & Reavis, H. K. (1993). *The tough kid book*. Longmont, CO: Sopris West.

Schanding, G., & Sterling-Turner, H. (2010). Use of the Mystery Motivator for a high school class. *Journal of Applied School Psychology, 26,* 38–53.

MYSTERY MOTIVATOR CHART

Monday	Tuesday	Wednesday	Thursday	Friday

TIER

Mystery Motivator: Procedural Integrity Checklist

Age/Grade:	Preschool – High School
Setting:	School, Home, Clinic
Individual or Group:	One or more
Tier:	1, 2, & 3
Desired/ Appropriate Behavior:	Work completion, compliance, keeping hands and feet to self, appropriate language, prepared for class/school, homework completion
Skill Level:	Fluency to generalization

The procedural integrity checklist is completed by a designated adult (e.g., principal, assistant principal, school psychologist, treatment specialist, behavior specialist, counselor, lead teacher) who is familiar with the Mystery Motivator procedures. The designated adult will observe the individual interventionist implementing the Mystery Motivator procedure and provide feedback.

Procedure for Integrity Checklist Observer

1) Complete the Procedural Integrity Checklists (see pages 54-55) information about the teacher, group (class, period), location, date, time, observer name, and signature. The first checklist is for the initial training day for the group of children, and the second checklist is for the daily implementation.
2) Observe the interventionist's initial training for the children using the Initial Training Procedures observation.
3) Observe the interventionist's implementation of the Mystery Motivator procedure. An observation should occur within the first two weeks of implementing the Mystery Motivator procedure so that feedback can be provided to the interventionist early in the implementation.
4) Observe the interventionist for the presence of behaviors on the Checklist and mark Yes if present or No if not present. If there was not an opportunity to observe a behavior, then mark N/O for not observed.
5) Count the number of behaviors marked Yes and write the number on the line for "Number of behaviors marked Yes."
6) Write the total number of behaviors observed (i.e., the total behaviors marked Yes or No).
7) Calculate the percent marked Yes. A chart is provided for determining the percent marked Yes. If fewer than four behaviors are marked Yes, then feedback should be provided to the interventionist immediately and another observation completed the next day or as soon as possible.
8) Write any constructive feedback comments in addition to any notations made beside any individual behavior in the "Feedback" section.
9) Provide the interventionist, at an appropriate time, with oral feedback regarding the implementation of the intervention, starting with positive behaviors observed, and a copy of the Mystery Motivator: Procedural Integrity Checklist. *The feedback should be provided the same day of the observation.*

10) Observe the interventionist implementing the Mystery Motivator procedure approximately every other week or twice a month after the initial observation.

Mystery Motivator: Procedural Integrity Checklist
Initial Training Procedures

Interventionist: ______________________ Date: __________ Time: __________

Group: ______________________ Observer: ______________________

Location: ______________________ Signature: ______________________

N/O = Not Observed

Behaviors to Observe	Yes	No	N/O	Comments
1) Time of day for Mystery Motivator to be conducted is determined.				
2)Target behaviors are defined in clear, observable, measureable terms.				
3)Baseline data are collected for at least 3 days prior to implementation.				
4) Suitable daily or weekly rewards are determined.				
5) Game is introduced in a whole group discussion.				
6) Examples of acceptable and unacceptable behaviors are reviewed and practiced with the group.				
7) Clear schedule is created for times the MM will be in effect.				

Number of behaviors marked Yes = _____ out of _____ = ______ %

Percent
1 out of 7 = 14%
2 out of 7 = 29%
3 out of 7 = 43%
4 out of 7 = 57%
5 out of 7 = 71%
6 out of 7 = 86%
7 out of 7 = 100%

Feedback:

Mystery Motivator (MM) Procedural Integrity Checklist
Daily Intervention Procedures

Interventionist: ______________________ Date: __________ Time: __________

Group: ______________________ Observer: ______________________

Location: ______________________ Signature: ______________________

N/O = Not Observed

Behaviors to Observe	Yes	No	N/O	Comments
1) Interventionist introduces/reminds the group of the target behaviors at the beginning of the time period.				
2) Interventionist reminds the children about rewards and about how the Mystery Motivator chart works.				
3) Interventionist acknowledges appropriate behaviors throughout the instructional period and provides feedback to encourage success.				
4) The Mystery Motivator chart is clearly visible in the room.				
5) Interventionist appropriately documents if appropriate behaviors occurred during small groups, if applicable, and acknowledges appropriate behaviors at the conclusion of the group.				
6) Interventionist gives feedback to encourage success.				
7) At the end of the allotted time period, select a child to color in the Mystery Motivator chart, if the children have engaged in the target behaviors.				
8) If the Mystery is revealed, provide the reward or give an explanation about when the reward will be provided that day (e.g., extra recess or free time at end of day).				

Number of behaviors marked Yes = _____ out of _____ = ______ %

Percent
1 out of 8 = 13%
2 out of 8 = 25%
3 out of 8 = 38%
4 out of 8 = 50%
5 out of 8 = 63%
6 out of 8 = 75%
7 out of 8 = 88%
8 out of 8 = 100%

Feedback:

Math Interventions

Additive Interspersal Technique

Age/Grade: Preschool – High School

Setting: School, Home, Clinic, In-patient

Individual or Group: Individual

Tier: 1, 2, & 3

Desired/ Appropriate Behavior: Independent seatwork, task completion, on-task, homework completion, etc.

Skill Level: Fluency to maintenance

Rationale & Research Support

The additive interspersal procedure is an assignment modification strategy that does not involve reducing assignment demands, items, or opportunities to respond to target tasks, unlike some assignment strategies that reduce the amount of work or shorten the assignment. With this procedure, no target items, assigned items, are removed. Instead, brief and easier items are additively interspersed among items that require more time to complete (Cates & Skinner, 2000). Several studies have examined the impact of the additive interspersal procedure on assignment perceptions and choice (e.g., Logan & Skinner, 1998; Meadows & Skinner, 2005; Skinner, Hall-Johnson, Skinner, Cates, Weber, & Johns, 1999; Skinner, Robinson, Johns, Logan, & Belfiore, 1996; Wildmon, Skinner, McCurdy, & Sims, 1999; Wildmon, Skinner, & McDade, 1998; Wildmon, Skinner, Watson, & Garrett, 2004). Cates and Skinner (2000) found that the additive interspersal procedure/technique increased problem completion rates. In addition, they found that children preferred the additive interspersal technique over the control or "traditional" assignments. Children completed significantly more total problems on each interspersal assignment (i.e., 0%, 20%, 40% additional problems) than on the "traditional" assignment. Children indicated that each interspersal assignment (i.e., 0%, 20%, 40% additional problems) required less time and less effort and was less difficult to complete as compared to each control assignment. However, the 20% additional problems appeared to be the most effective. This technique is not to be used for students/children who are acquiring the new skill but rather for children who need to increase their fluency and/or maintenance of skills.

Materials

1) Selected targeted items, problems, and tasks are grade level or instructional level. A target item may be a homework assignment given by the teacher or any other assignment given by the teacher to the child.
2) Additive Interspersal items are the items selected that are easier in difficulty level, more quickly answered, or briefer. Examples of less difficult items are brief math problems, circling items instead of writing the answers, spelling words that are a few grade levels below, etc. If the assignment is 24 target problems, then 8 more additive interspersal problems are added. The ratio should be 70% target problems and 30% additive interspersal problems. Therefore, for 20 target items to complete, 6 more additive interspersal items are added.

Procedure for Interventionist

1) Select your target items. These are the items that are grade level or instructional level. If these are homework items, then they are already selected for you.
2) Select 30% additive interspersal items. These items are supposed to be easier ones and/or ones that can be answered more quickly, etc.
3) If you are designing the homework or independent seatwork assignment, start with a first set of target items and then add one additive interspersal item. For example, based on 24 target items and 8 additive interspersal items, the layout of the assignment will be 4 target items, one additive interspersal item, 4 more target items, another additive interspersal item, etc. Repeat this layout until all items, target and interspersal, are included.
4) Tell the child to start the work and complete as many items as possible without skipping any problems.
5) Once the child has completed the assignment, the person grading the items should first score for number of problems completed (not grading for accuracy) and then score the number of problems correct.

Adjustments/Modification

Some children may find it difficult to start with instructional (target items) before working with the additive interspersal items. In this case, all the interspersal items can be presented at the beginning of the assignment with the target items coming after them. For example, for an assignment with 24 target items and 8 interspersal items, the 8 interspersal items would be presented first and followed by the 24 target items.

If the child is having difficulty with the target items, these items may not be instructional items in that the items may be too difficult for the child to complete without help. This additive interspersal intervention is designed for instructional level material, not new material the child is acquiring. A discussion with the teacher may be necessary about the level of the material in the homework assignment. For this intervention, teachers must understand that if the child cannot complete the target items without assistance, those items are too hard; the teacher should assign other more appropriate instructional target items.

References

Cates, G. L., & Skinner, C. H. (2000). Getting remedial mathematics students to prefer homework with 20% and 40% more problems: An investigation of the strength of the interspersal procedure. *Psychology in the Schools*, *37,* 1–9.

Logan, P., & Skinner, C. H. (1998). Improving students' perceptions of a mathematics assignment by increasing problem completion rates: Is problem completion a reinforcing event? *School Psychology Quarterly*, *13,* 322–331.

Meadows, S. F., & Skinner, C. H. (2005). Causing students to choose more Language Arts work: Enhancing the validity of the Additive Interspersal Procedure. *Journal of Behavior Education, 14,* 227-247.

Skinner, C. H., Hall-Johnson, K., Skinner, A. L., Cates, G., Weber, J., & Johns, G. (1999). Enhancing perceptions of mathematics assignments by increasing relative rates of problem completion through the interspersal technique. *Journal of Experimental Education*, *68,* 43–59.

Skinner, C. H., Robinson, S. L., Johns, G. A., Logan, P., & Belfiore, P. J. (1996). Applying Herrstein's Matching Law to influence students' choice to complete difficult academic tasks. *The Journal of Experimental Education*, *65,* 5–17.

Wildmon, M. E., Skinner, C. H., McCurdy, M., & Sims, S. (1999). Improving secondary students' perception of the "dreaded mathematics word problem assignment" by giving them more word problems. *Psychology in the Schools*, *36,* 319–325.

Wildmon, M., Skinner, C. H., & McDade, A. (1998). Interspersing additional brief, easy problems to increase assignment preference on mathematics reading problems. *Journal of Behavioral Education*, *8,* 337–346.

Wildmon, M. E., Skinner, C. H.,Watson, T. S., & Garrett, L. S. (2004). Enhancing assignment perceptions in students with mathematics learning disabilities by including more work: An extension of interspersal research. *School Psychology Quarterly*, *19,* 106–120.

5

Additive Interspersal Technique: Procedural Integrity Checklist

Age/Grade:	Preschool – High School
Setting:	School, Home, Clinic, In-patient
Individual or Group:	Individual
Tier:	1, 2, & 3
Desired/ Appropriate Behavior:	Independent seatwork, task completion, on-task, homework completion, etc.
Skill Level:	Fluency to maintenance

The Additive Interspersal procedure is an assignment modification strategy that does not involve reducing assignment demands, items, or opportunities to respond to target tasks, unlike some assignment strategies that reduce the amount of work or shorten the assignment.

Procedure for Integrity Checklist Observer

1) Complete the Procedural Integrity Checklist (see page 63) information about the interventionist, child, location, date, time, observer name, and observer signature.
2) Assess the interventionist's implementation of the Additive Interspersal procedure. An initial observation should occur within the first couple of weeks of an interventionist's implementing the Additive Interspersal procedure so that feedback can be provided to the interventionist early in the implementation.
3) Observe the interventionist for the presence of behaviors 1-4 on the Checklist and mark Yes if present or No if not present. Mark N/O if the behavior is not observed.
4) Count the number of behaviors marked Yes and write the number on the line for "Number of behaviors marked Yes."
5) Write the total number of behaviors observed (i.e., the total behaviors marked Yes or No).
6) Calculate the percent marked Yes. A chart is provided for determining the percent marked Yes. If less than 80% of behaviors are marked Yes, then provide feedback immediately to the interventionist and conduct another observation the next day or as soon as possible.
7) Write any constructive feedback comments in addition to any notations made beside any individual behavior in the "Feedback" section.
8) Provide the interventionist, at an appropriate time, with oral feedback regarding the implementation of the intervention, starting with positive behaviors observed, and a copy of the Additive Interspersal: Procedural Integrity Checklist. *The feedback should be provided the same day of the observation.*
9) Observe the interventionist implementing the Additive Interspersal procedure approximately every other week or twice a month after the initial observation.

Additive Interspersal Technique Procedural Integrity Checklist

Interventionist: ____________________ Date: __________ Time: __________

Child: ____________________ Observer: ____________________

Location: ____________________ Signature: ____________________

N/O = Not Observed

Behaviors to Observe	Yes	No	N/O	Comments
1) Review the materials to ensure that 70% of items are target items (instructional level) and 30% are Additive Interspersal items.				
2) The interventionist told the child to begin working the items or problems.				
3) Once the child has completed the items, the interventionist scores the items for items completed.				
4) The interventionist then scores for accuracy.				

Number of behaviors marked Yes = _____ out of _____ = ______ %

Percent
1 out of 4 = 25%
2 out of 4 = 50%
3 out of 4 = 75%
4 out of 4 = 100%

Feedback:

Folding-In Math

Age/Grade:	Preschool – High School
Setting:	School, Home, Clinic, In-patient
Individual or Group:	Individual
Tier:	1, 2, & 3
Desired/ Appropriate Behavior:	Fluency with a variety of math facts
Skill Level:	Acquisition to maintenance

Rationale & Research Support

Research has supported the importance of rehearsal or repetition to move knowledge from acquisition to maintenance. Gates (1930) found that a typical child needs approximately 35 repetitions to achieve mastery of knowledge; however, some children need even more repetitions, and some above average children may need fewer repetitions to achieve mastery. Folding-In is a technique designed to maximize the number of repetitions of new knowledge within a short period of time (Shapiro, 1996). Gickling and Rosenfield (1995) found that the optimum ratio of known to unknown facts for practice was 70%-85% known facts to 15%-30% unknown facts. Roberts, Turco, and Shapiro (1991) and later Roberts and Shapiro (1996) found that retention of learned words was highest when the ratio of known to unknown words was 80%-90% to 10-20% unknown. Repetition techniques have been found to be effective with single digit multiplication facts, simple word problems, and fractions and with children with a learning disability (Burns, 2005; Codding, Archer, & Connell, 2010). The Folding-In intervention can also be used to support learning words. Folding-In Sight Words is found on page 119.

Materials

1) Math flash cards or index cards for writing the target math knowledge (e.g., addition, multiplication, fractions)
2) Math Fact Mastery Tracking Form
3) Folding-In Data Chart

Procedure for Interventionist

This intervention involves "folding in," or slowly incorporating, unknown math facts to known ones. This intervention is typically implemented one-on-one with an interventionist (e.g., interventionist, paraprofessional, parent) and a child. The procedure is typically implemented twice a week and takes approximately 20 minutes to complete (Burns, 2005; Codding et al., 2010).

Pre-assessment Phase

1) Mix up the math flash cards (e.g., addition 0-12).
2) Present each flash card to the child. Allow the child up to 3 seconds to respond. If the child provides the correct answer, then place the flash card in a stack of "known" facts. If the child

provides an incorrect answer, cannot answer within 3 seconds, or indicates he/she does not know the answer, then place the flash card in a stack of "unknown" facts.

3) Make a list of the unknown math facts on the Math Fact Mastery Tracking Form on page 69. This form is used to track mastery during the instructional phase (see Step 10 below).

Instructional Phase

1) Direct the child to select seven cards from his or her pile of pre-assessed **known** facts.
2) Direct the child to select three cards from his or her pile of pre-assessed **unknown** facts.
3) Inform the child that he or she will have 20 minutes to complete the intervention.
4) Present the first **unknown** fact to the learner by reading the stimulus (e.g., 2 X 3, 28 ÷ 7) and providing the answer.
5) Direct the child to write the fact on a piece of paper 3 times while saying it aloud to himself or herself three times and then to turn over the piece of paper.
6) Present a **known** fact, followed by the **unknown** fact, with the child providing the answer to each fact.
7) Present the **first known** fact, the **unknown** fact, and another **known** fact. Repeat this process with the addition of one new **known** fact at the end of the sequence until all seven known facts have been presented and folded-in among the one unknown fact.
8) Shuffle the group of eight facts (one unknown and seven known). The **second unknown** fact is then presented as in Steps 4 and 5. Then, the **second unknown** fact is folded-in as in Steps 6 and 7. These steps are repeated again for the **third unknown** fact. See the Sequence for Presenting Unknown and Known Facts on page 68 for the complete sequence.
9) If the child hesitates more than 3 seconds or is incorrect on any fact, tell the child the correct answer and have him/her write the fact three times. Then, present the fact to the child again.
10) After all the facts have been folded in, present the entire group of 10 facts three times. Each time the packet of flash cards is shuffled to ensure the child is not just memorizing the sequence of responses. The **unknown** facts are marked correct or incorrect on the Math Fact Mastery Tracking Form on page 69. Once an **unknown** fact is correctly answered *three consecutive times*, it becomes a **new known** fact.
11) **New known** facts are included in the stack of **known** facts and are the *first of the seven* cards selected from the **known** facts stack the next time the folding-in intervention is conducted. If the child hesitates for more than 3 seconds or provides an incorrect response for a **known** fact:
    a) Tell the child the correct response and have him/her write the fact three times.
    b) Present the fact to the child again.
    c) At the end of the Folding-In session, add the fact to the **unknown** stack.
    d) Add the fact to the Math Fact Mastery Tracking Form or if the fact is already on the Math Fact Mastery Tracking Form, erase or strikethrough the "Mastered?" column to indicate the fact is not yet mastered.
12) Have the child graph the number of new facts learned using the Folding-In Data Chart on page 127 following the last folding-in intervention session each week.

Adjustments/Modifications

Folding-In can be also be implemented with a pair of peers with each child taking a turn in the interventionist role and the child role. Folding-In has also been successfully implemented as a self-administered intervention (Hulac, Wickerd, & Vining, 2013). Children must be taught the interventionist role and child/student role prior to implementation, and integrity checks of the children implementing the intervention using the Folding-In Math: Procedural Integrity Checklist should be conducted every two weeks.

References

Burns, M. K. (2005). Using incremental rehearsal to increase fluency of single-digit multiplication facts with children identified as learning disabled in mathematics computation. *Education and Treatment of Children, 28(3),* 237-249.

Codding R.S., Archer J., & Connell, J. (2010). A systematic replication and extension using incremental rehearsal to improve multiplication skills: An investigation of generalization. *Journal of Behavioral Education, 19,* 93-105.

Gates, A. (1930). *Interest and ability in reading*. New York: Macmillan.

Gickling, E.E. & Rosenfield, S. (1995). Best practices in curriculum-based measurement. In A. Thomas & J. Grimes (Eds.), *Best practices in school psychology III* (587-95). Bethesda, MD: National Association of School Psychologists.

Hulac, D.M., Wickerd, G., & Vining, O. (2013). Interventions: An application of the self-administered folding-in technique. *Rural Special Education Quarterly, 32(2),* 31-36.

Roberts, M. L., Turco, T., & Shapiro, E. S. (1991). Differential effects of fixed instructional ratios on student's progress in reading. *Journal of Psychoeducational Assessment, 9*, 308-318.

Roberts, M.L. & Shapiro, E.S.(1996). Effects of instructional ratios on students' reading performance in a regular education program. *Journal of School Psychology, 34(1),* 73-91.

Shapiro, E.S. (1996). *Academic skills problems: Direct assessment and intervention* (2nd ed.). New York: The Guilford Press.

6

Sequence for Presenting Unknown and Known Facts

U= Unknown Fact; 1U = 1st Unknown Fact, 2U = 2nd Unknown Fact, 3U = 3rd Unknown Fact, etc.

K= Known Fact; 1K = 1st Known Fact, 2K = 2nd Known Fact, 3U = 3rd Known Fact, etc.

Round	Sequence of Presentation
1	1U (Child writes the fact on a piece of paper 3 times while saying it aloud to himself or herself three times and then turns over the piece of paper.) 1K
2	1U 1K 2K
3	1U 1K 2K 3K
4	1U 1K 2K 3K 4K
5	1U 1K 2K 3K 4K 5K
6	1U 1K 2K 3K 4K 5K 6K
7	1U 1K 2K 3K 4K 5K 6K 7K
8	Shuffle all 8 flash cards.
9	2U (Child writes the fact on a piece of paper 3 times while saying it aloud to himself or herself three times and then turns over the piece of paper.) 1K (1st flash card in the group of shuffled flash cards.)
10	2U 1K 2K
11	2U 1K 2K 3K
12	2U 1K 2K 3K 4K
13	2U 1K 2K 3K 4K 5K
14	2U 1K 2K 3K 4K 5K 6K
15	2U 1K 2K 3K 4K 5K 6K 7K
16	2U 1K 2K 3K 4K 5K 6K 7K 8K
17	Shuffle all 9 flash cards.
18	3U (Child writes the fact on a piece of paper 3 times while saying it aloud to himself or herself three times and then turns over the piece of paper.) 1K (1st flash card in the group of shuffled flash cards.)
19	3U 1K 2K
20	3U 1K 2K 3K
21	3U 1K 2K 3K 4K
22	3U 1K 2K 3K 4K 5K
23	3U 1K 2K 3K 4K 5K 6K
24	3U 1K 2K 3K 4K 5K 6K 7K
25	3U 1K 2K 3K 4K 5K 6K 7K 8K
26	3U 1K 2K 3K 4K 5K 6K 7K 8K 9K
27	Shuffle all 10 flash cards. Present all 10 flash cards and mark correct or incorrect on the Math Fact Mastery Tracking Form.
28	Shuffle all 10 flash cards. Present all 10 flash cards and mark correct or incorrect on the Math Fact Mastery Tracking Form.
29	Shuffle all 10 flash cards. Present all 10 flash cards and mark correct or incorrect on the Math Fact Mastery Tracking Form.

Name: ______________________

Math Fact Mastery Tracking Form

This form is used to track the unknown math facts the child is attempting to master and the child's performance on the unknown math facts when presented in the set of known and unknown math facts in Step 9 of the Folding-In intervention procedures.

Date	Unknown Math Fact	Number of Times Answered Correctly	Mastered? (Answered correctly 3 times)

Folding-In Data Chart

Name: ____________________________________ Grade: ___________

Interventionist: _______________________________

Week	Date	# of Known Facts	Week	Date	# of Known Facts	Week	Date	# of Known Facts
1			7			13		
2			8			14		
3			9			15		
4			10			16		
5			11			17		
6			12			18		

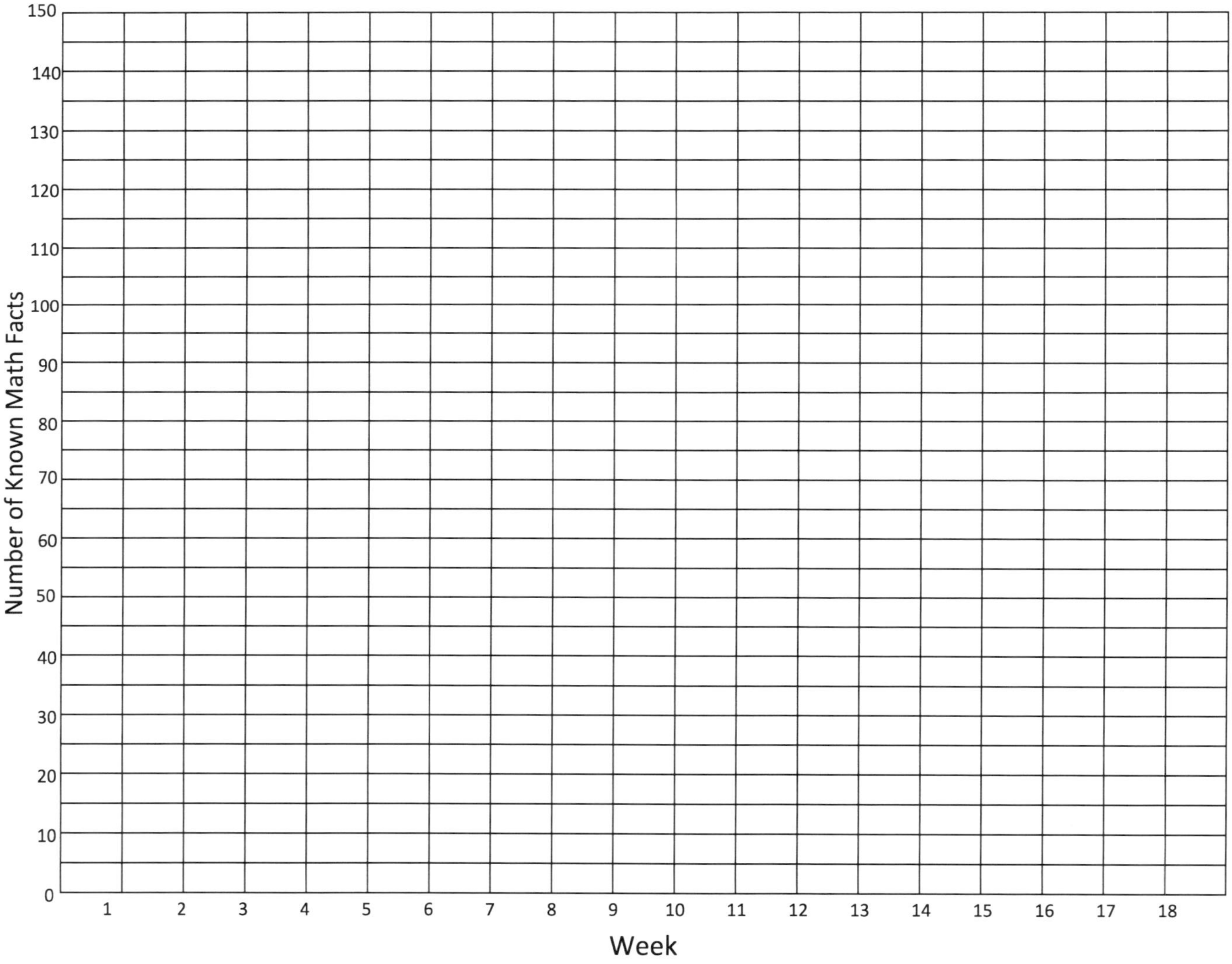

Folding-In Math: Procedural Integrity Checklist

Age/Grade:	Preschool – High School
Setting:	School, Home, Clinic, In-patient
Individual or Group:	Individual
Tier:	1, 2, & 3
Desired/ Appropriate Behavior:	Fluency with a variety of math facts
Skill Level:	Acquisition to maintenance

The procedural integrity checklist is completed by an observer (e.g., principal, assistant principal, school psychologist, treatment specialist, behavior specialist, counselor, lead teacher) who is familiar with the Folding-In Math procedure. The observer will observe the interventionist implementing the Folding-In procedure and provide feedback. The Folding-In intervention is designed to maximize the number of repetitions of new knowledge within a short period of time (Shapiro, 1996).

Procedure for Integrity Checklist Observer

1) Complete the Procedural Integrity Checklist (see page 73) information about the interventionist, child, location, date, time, observer name, and observer signature.
2) Assess the interventionist's implementation of the Folding-In procedure. An initial observation should occur within the first couple of weeks of an interventionist's implementing the Folding-In procedure so that feedback can be provided to the interventionist early in the implementation.
3) Observe the interventionist for the presence of behaviors 1-9 on the Checklist and mark Yes if present or No if not present. Mark N/O if the behavior is not observed.
4) Observe and mark the behaviors for 7-9 on the checklist *only if the child hesitates for more than 3 second or provides an incorrect response* in response to the flash card presented. If the child makes an error on a flash card, mark Yes to indicate that an error was observed and then observe for the behaviors listed in 7-9. Otherwise, mark No. If a child makes an error during the Folding-In procedure, the maximum number of behaviors that may be marked Yes is 9; otherwise the maximum number of behaviors marked is 6.
5) Count the number of behaviors marked Yes and write the number on the line for "Number of behaviors marked Yes."
6) Write the total number of behaviors observed (i.e., the total behaviors marked Yes or No).
7) Calculate the percent marked Yes. A chart is provided for determining the percent marked Yes. If less than 80% of behaviors are marked Yes, then provide feedback immediately to the interventionist and conduct another observation the next day or as soon as possible.
8) Write any constructive feedback comments in addition to any notations made beside any individual behavior in the "Feedback" section.
9) Provide the interventionist, at an appropriate time, with oral feedback regarding the implementation of the intervention, starting with positive behaviors observed, and a copy of the Folding-In Math: Procedural Integrity Checklist. *The feedback should be provided the same day of the observation.*

10) Observe the interventionist implementing the Folding-In – Math procedure approximately every other week or twice a month after the initial observation

Folding-In Math: Procedural Integrity Checklist

Interventionist: ______________________ Date: __________ Time: __________

Child: ______________________ Observer: ______________________

Location: ______________________ Signature: ______________________

N/O = Not Observed

Behaviors to Observe	Yes	No	N/O	Comments
1) The child selects 3 flash cards from his or her pile of pre-assessed unknown facts and 7 flash cards from his or her pile of pre-assessed known facts.				
2) The interventionist presents a new unknown fact to the learner, each time reading the stimulus and providing the answer.				
3) The child writes each new unknown fact on a piece of paper 3 times while saying it aloud and then turns over the piece of paper.				
4) The interventionist presents the unknown fact and the known facts following the Sequence for Presenting Unknown and Known Facts (page 68).				
5) The interventionist marks the unknown facts as correct or incorrect on the Math Fact Mastery Tracking Form.				
6) Evidence is available that the child is graphing the number of new facts learned using the Folding-In Data Chart.				
If the child hesitates for more than 3 seconds or provides an incorrect response: Was this observed? __Yes __No				
7) The interventionist tells the child the correct answer.				
8) The child writes the stimulus and the correct answer 3 times.				
9) The interventionist presents the flash card to the child again.				

Number of behaviors marked Yes = _____ out of _____ = ______ %

Feedback:

Percent

1 out of 6 = 17%	1 out of 9 = 11%
2 out of 6 = 33%	2 out of 9 = 22%
3 out of 6 = 50%	3 out of 9 = 33%
4 out of 6 = 67%	4 out of 9 = 44%
5 out of 6 = 83%	5 out of 9 = 56%
6 out of 6 = 100%	6 out of 9 = 67%
	7 out of 9 = 78%
	8 out of 9 = 89%
	9 out of 9 = 100%

Cover Copy Compare Math

Age/Grade:	Elementary – Middle School
Setting:	School, Home, Clinic, In-patient
Individual or Group:	Individual
Tier:	1, 2, & 3
Desired/ Appropriate Behavior:	Accuracy and fluency in math skills with two or more steps to complete
Skill Level:	Acquisition to maintenance

Rationale & Research Support

Cover Copy Compare (CCC) Math is an efficient, self-administered intervention in which a child studies a model math problem, covers the problem, writes the problem from memory, uncovers the model problem, and compares the problem written from memory to the model problem. CCC employs the evidence-based instructional practices of modeling, active child responding, and immediate corrective feedback. CCC has been used to improve performance on addition, subtraction, multiplication, and division problems (Joseph et al., 2012).

CCC has been studied extensively as documented by a 2012 meta-analysis, which found positive results for CCC for spelling, math, and other subjects (Joseph et al., 2012). CCC has been found to be effective with elementary and secondary children, general education children, and a variety of children with disabilities (Joseph et al., 2012; Moser, Fishley, Konrad, & Hessler, 2012; Zielinski, McLaughlin, & Derby, 2012). CCC math has been demonstrated to improve accuracy (number of correct digits), fluency (number of correct digits per minute), and maintenance up to eight months after intervention (Bolich, Kavon, McLaughlin, Williams, & Urlacher, 1995; Ozaki, Williams, & McLaughlin, 1996; Poncy, Skinner, & Jaspers, 2007; Skinner, Bamberg, Smith, & Powell, 1993; Skinner, Ford, & Yunker, 1991). Codding et al. (2007) found CCC was more effective with children starting at frustration level (i.e., fewer than 10 digits correct per minute) than children at instructional level (i.e., 10-19 digits correct per minute). While CCC is primarily used as an intervention for spelling or math (see CCC Spelling on page 131), Smith, Dittmer, and Skinner (2002) report on its effective use in science, and Skinner, Belfiore, and Pierce (1992) report on its effective use in geography.

Daily implementation of the CCC Math intervention is recommended. The duration of the intervention will vary depending on the target skill and a child's skill level; however, the daily procedure is generally 10 to 15 minutes in length.

Materials

1) Three **assessment probes** with 20-30 problems on the target skill (e.g., single digit addition, two-digit by two-digit subtraction with regrouping, two-digit by one-digit multiplication with no regrouping): These three assessment probes will be used to determine a child's baseline performance. One of the three assessment probes will be the basis for creating a child worksheet and for progress monitoring.
2) A **worksheet** of ten problems addressing the target skill with the problems and answers listed down the left side of the worksheet for each child in the intervention. The ten problems are randomly

taken from the one of the assessment probes. Also write the total possible digits correct for the ten problems in the top right corner of the worksheet with a slash or line above the number. The child will write the number of correct digits above this number and will calculate and record the percent of accuracy. See the Example CCC Math Worksheet on page 83.

3) CCC Data Chart

4) Cover Copy Compare Prompt Sheet (optional)

5) Index card or blank piece of paper to cover words (optional)

Some possible resources for assessment probes and worksheets are listed below:

- AIMSweb
- Accelerated Math™
- Math Resource Studio http://www.schoolhousetech.com/Math/
  Math Resource Studio addresses a wide variety of topics across the five strands of math.
- Math Worksheet Generator http://www.interventioncentral.org/tools/math-worksheet-generator
  This free site allows you to create Cover Copy Compare worksheets for addition, subtraction, multiplication, and division skills with 1-digit to multiple-digit (5-7) numbers.

Procedure for Interventionist

Prior to starting intervention

1) Count the total possible digits correct on the assessment probe.

Examples of Counting Digits Correct		
$\begin{array}{r} 11 \\ +4 \\ \hline 15 \end{array}$	$\begin{array}{r} 12 \\ \times 12 \\ \hline 144 \end{array}$	$\begin{array}{r} 12 \\ \times 0.12 \\ \hline 1.44 \end{array}$
2 possible digits correct	3 possible digits correct	4 possible digits correct (the decimal is counted)

2) Administer the first assessment probe to the child.

3) Score the assessment probe by counting the number of digits correct and dividing by the total possible digits correct to get a percent correct (accuracy).

4) Repeat steps 2 and 3 over the next two days so that the child has three separate scores on the three different assessment probes.

5) Obtain the median digits correct for the child's three assessments. The median digits correct will serve as the baseline for progress monitoring.

6) Prepare an example worksheet with problems and answers listed down the left side of the worksheet and blank space on the right side of the worksheet to write the corresponding problem and answer. The example worksheet needs to contain only 4-5 problems. The example worksheet should contain problems that the child should be able to complete with ease.

7) On a section of the board, on a poster, or on an index card, write the four Cover Copy Compare steps.
    a) Study and think through the model problem and answer.
    b) Cover (hide) the model problem and answer.
    c) Write the corresponding problem and answer from memory.
    d) Compare the completed problem to the model problem and answer.
8) Plan for a) when and where the child will complete the CCC intervention and b) how the child will keep track of the materials. One suggested method is to use pocket folders. Place the progress monitoring graph in the left pocket and the CCC worksheet in the right pocket. A week's worth of worksheets could be placed in the right pocket to begin. After a child completes a worksheet and records the percent of digits correct on the graph, the completed worksheet will be placed behind the graph with the most recently complete worksheet being the first sheet behind the graph.

Introducing the procedure

Modeling

1) Inform the child you will be teaching a method, Cover Copy Compare (CCC), for practicing and improving skill in math. For example, you might say, "I will be teaching you a new method called Cover Copy and Compare to improve your math skills."
2) Provide the child with the example CCC Worksheet.
3) Say to the child, "I am going to demonstrate how to complete a Cover Copy Compare worksheet." Say to the child, "This is an example worksheet, which has only five problems for practice. Your actual worksheet will have ten math problems."
4) Show the child the first problem.
5) Say to the child, "The first step is to look at the model problem and to think through the problem and answer." Say to the child, "I am going to say out loud what you need to be thinking or saying to yourself silently as you review the problem and answer. You may move your lips without making a sound if that helps you."
6) Demonstrate thinking through the problem. For example, if the problem is "11 + 4 = 15," then model saying, "Eleven plus four equals fifteen."
7) Say to the child, "The second step is cover or hide the problem and answer on the left side of the paper." In advance, decide if the child will fold the worksheet to cover the model problem and answer on the left side of the worksheet or use an index card to cover the problem. If the child will be folding the worksheet, show the child how to properly fold the worksheet to cover the model problem before moving on to the next step.
8) Demonstrate covering or hiding the problem and answer.
9) Say to the child, "The third step is to complete the problem that was just reviewed."
10) Demonstrate completing the problem.

11) Say to the child, "The fourth step is to compare the problem you completed to the covered or hidden problem and answer to verify that the problem you wrote and answered is the same as the model problem and answer."
12) Demonstrate completing comparing the completed problem and answer to the model problem and answer.

Guided Practice

1) Say to the child, "You are going to complete the next problem with my guidance."
2) Ask the child, "What is the first step?" Affirm the correct response and restate the first step. For example, you might say, "That's correct. The first step is to study and think through the problem and answer." If the child does not provide the correct first step, then state the first step for the child and have the child say the step out loud. If the child is having difficulty remembering the steps, then consider using the Cover Copy Compare Prompt Sheet on page 86 to aid the child in remembering the steps.
3) Ask the child to say what he or she is thinking as the problem is being studied.
4) Ask the child, "What is the second step?" Again affirm the correct response and restate the second step or use the procedure in step 2 to remind the child of the appropriate step.
5) Say to the child, "Complete the second step using the example worksheet."
6) Ask the child, "What is the third step?" Again affirm the correct response and restate the third step or use the procedure in step 2 to remind the child of the appropriate step.
7) Say to the child, "Complete the third step using the example worksheet."
8) Ask the child, "What is the fourth step?" Again affirm the correct response and restate the fourth step or use the procedure in step 2 to remind the child of the appropriate step.
9) Say to the child, "Complete the fourth step using the example worksheet."

Modeling a Problem Completed Incorrectly

1) Say to the child, "Now I am going to demonstrate what to do if you make an error when you are using a problem on the example worksheet."
2) Demonstrate thinking through the problem.
3) Demonstrate covering or hiding the problem and answer.
4) Demonstrate completing the problem, including at least one error.
5) Demonstrate comparing the completed problem and answer to the model problem and answer and identifying the error made. Say to the child, "I am going to circle any digit that is incorrect."
6) Demonstrate circling the incorrect digit(s).
7) Say to the child, "If you make an error, you are going to attempt completing the problem one more time, repeating the four steps."
8) Demonstrate thinking through the problem. Talk out loud what you are thinking as you think through the model problem and answer, giving specific attention to the part of the solution where the error was made.

9) Demonstrate covering or hiding the problem and answer.

10) Say to the child, "If you have to write the problem and answer again, you will complete the problem and answer on the back of worksheet."

11) Demonstrate writing and completing the problem.

12) Demonstrate comparing the second attempt of completed problem to the model problem and answer.

13) Say to the child, "If you make an error the second time you complete the problem and answer, you do not have to repeat the steps again. Just move to the next model problem and answer."

Independent Practice

1) Say to the child, "Now you are going to complete the next problem on your own." Say to the child when to begin.

2) Observe to see that the child is completing the steps in the correct order. Provide immediate corrective feedback for any step that the child is not completing in the correct sequence. Provide positive feedback to child as the steps are completed correctly.

Teaching How to Score the Worksheet

Note: The interventionist may have to complete the following steps for younger children.

1) Say to the child, "Now I am going to demonstrate how to score the worksheet."

2) Say to the child, "You are going to count the number of digits correct for each problem."

3) Demonstrate counting the number of digits correct for the first problem. Write the number of correct digits in the right-hand margin.

4) Say to the child, "Count the number of digits correct with me for the second problem." Write the number of correct digits in the right-hand margin.

5) Repeat this process with the third problem.

6) Repeat this process with the fourth problem, being sure to emphasize that the incorrect digits that are circled are not counted.

7) Say to the child, "Next you will sum the number of digits correct written in the right margin."

8) Demonstrate summing the number of digits correct.

9) Say to the child, "The next step is to write the total number of digits correct above the total possible digits correct provided in the top right corner of the worksheet."

10) Say to the child, "Then you calculate the percent of digits correct."

11) Demonstrate how to calculate the percent of digits correct, either manually or using a calculator. Use of a calculator should be determined based on the needs of the child, consistency with regular classroom instruction, curriculum requirements, and any other relevant considerations.

7

Teaching How to Record the Score

Review the Exampled CCC Scored Worksheet on page 84 before teaching how to record the score.

Note: The interventionist may have to complete the following steps for younger children.

1) Say to the child, "Now I am going to demonstrate how to record the score so that you can keep track of your progress."
2) Show the child the CCC Math Data Chart on page 85.
3) Say to the child, "The y-axis [point to the y-axis] represents the percent of digits correct, and the x-axis [point to the x-axis] represents each day that a worksheet is completed and a score is calculated."
4) Demonstrate how to record the percent of digits correct from the example worksheet on the CCC Math Data Chart.
5) Say to the child, "I am going to show you how you will record additional scores for a few more days. I am just pretending I have scores so that I can provide you an example."
6) Demonstrate recording additional scores for the next three days in this sequence: 80, 85, 82, 85.
7) Say to the child, "You will connect each score on the graph using a line to make a line graph." Demonstrate connecting the data points with a line to make a line graph.
8) Say to the child, "If you are absent on a day when you were supposed to do CCC, write an 'A' for absent on for that day on the graph. Put the 'A' at the same place on the graph as your last percent of digits correct. For example, if you were absent today and the day before your percent of digits correct was 85, then you would write an 'A' at 85 for today."
9) Demonstrate recording an absence on the graph by writing an 'A' at 85 and connecting the point with a line.

Teaching Daily Classroom Procedures

1) Tell the child how to start and end the CCC session and manage the CCC materials each day.
2) Demonstrate the procedure previously determined in step 8 under Prior to Starting the Intervention above. Demonstrate how to get materials, where to complete the intervention, and how to prepare for the next day. Be sure to include instructions for what the child should do if he or she completes the CCC worksheet and graphing prior to the end of the intervention time period. For example, the child might work on homework or read a book silently.

Daily Procedure

1) Monitor the child to make sure the daily procedures are being followed. Prompt or cue the child as appropriate when needed. Randomly praise the child for following the procedures. Make sure you are providing praise more frequently than prompting or cueing. If you are finding it difficult to praise more than prompt or cue, then consider re-instructing the child on the daily procedures or providing the child with the Cover Copy Compare Prompt Sheet on page 86.
2) Check the child's CCC worksheet and CCC Math Data Chart to make sure each is being completed correctly. Initially check these forms each day. Provide feedback to the child as necessary. As the

child demonstrates accuracy in completing the forms, then you may conduct checks less frequently; however, at a minimum, check at least once a week.

3) When a child achieves 90% or better on three consecutive attempts for the same CCC worksheet, then provide the child with a worksheet with a new set of ten problems based on a different assessment probe.

Adjustments/Modifications

If a child is not demonstrating at least 90% mastery of the problems practiced during the CCC Math intervention after three attempts on the same CCC worksheet, then consider modifying the intervention. If the child had fewer than 10 digits correct on the assessment probes (frustration level), then consider moving to a lower level skill. For example, if the CCC intervention focused on two-digit by two-digit addition with carryover, then administer probes with two-digit by two-digit addition without carryover and determine if the child scored above the frustration level. For some children, a modified variation of CCC (MCCC) may be more effective; in this procedure a child copies a model problem and answer while looking at the model before proceeding to cover, copy, and compare. While Grafman and Cates (2010) found children's fluency scores were higher using CCC compared to MCCC, both methods resulted in increased fluency.

CCC plus error drill is an effective modification of the basic CCC procedure (Becker, McLaughlin, Weber, & Gower, 2009). With this approach, an extra error drill is added to the CCC procedure. After the child completes the CCC worksheet, the interventionist reviews the errors made by the child. The interventionist correctly models the incorrect math problems. The child then says the complete problem and answer out loud several times before writing it on separate sheet of paper. After completing these steps for each incorrect problem, the child says out loud all problems written on the separate sheet of paper.

Another effective modification is to add a goal for the digits correct (Codding, Chan-Iannetta, Palmer, & Lukito, 2009). With this approach, a child is presented with the CCC Math Data Chart before completing the CCC Worksheet. Previous performance is presented on the chart along with a goal for the current CCC session. The interventionist sets a goal for digits correct that represents a one-problem increase over the most recent score. The goal is indicated on the chart along with the actual number.

References

Becker, A., McLaughlin, T. F., Weber, K. P., & Gower, J. (2009). The effects of copy, cover, and compare with and without error drill on multiplication fact fluency and accuracy. *Electronic Journal of Research in Educational Psychology, 18,* 747-760.

Bolich, B., Kavon, N., McLaughlin, T. F., Williams, R. L., & Urlacher, S. (1995). The effects of Copy, Cover, Compare procedure and a token economy on the retention of basic multiplication facts by two middle school students with ADD and ADHD. *B.C. Journal of Special Education, 19,* 1-10.

Codding, R. S., Chan-Iannetta, L., Palmer, M., & Lukito, G. (2009). Examining a class-wide application of cover-copy-compare with and without goal setting to enhance mathematics fluency. *School Psychology Quarterly, 24,* 173-185.

Codding, R. S., Shiyko, M., Russo, M., Birch, S., Fanning, E., & Jaspen, D. (2007). Comparing math interventions: Does initial level of fluency predict intervention effectiveness? *Journal of School Psychology, 45,* 603-617.

Grafman, J. M., & Cates, G. L. (2010). The differential effects of two self-managed math instruction procedures: Cover, copy, and compare versus copy, cover, and compare. *Psychology in the Schools, 47,* 153-165.

Joseph, L. M., Konrad, M., Cates, G., Vajcner, T., Eveligh, E. & Fishley, K. M. (2012). A meta-analytic review of the cover-copy-compare and variations of this self-management procedure. *Psychology in the Schools, 49,* 122-136.

Moser, L.A., Fishley, K.M., Konrad, M., & Hessler, T. (2012). Effects of the copy-cover-compare strategy on acquisition, maintenance, and generalization of spelling sight words for elementary students with attention deficit/hyperactivity disorder. *Child & Family Behavior Therapy, 34(2),* 93-110.

Ozaki, C., Williams, R. L., & McLaughlin, T. E. (1996). Effects of a copy/cover/compare drill and practice procedure for multiplication facts mastery with a sixth grade student with learning disabilities. *B.C. Journal of Special Education, 20,* 65-73.

Poncy, B. C., Skinner, C. H., & Jaspers, K. E. (2007). Evaluating and comparing interventions designed to enhance math fact accuracy and fluency: Cover, copy and compare versus taped problems. *Journal of Behavioral Education, 16,* 27-37.

Skinner, C. H., Bamberg, H.W., Smith, E. S., & Powell, S. S. (1993). Cognitive cover, copy and compare: Subvocal responding to increase rates of accurate division responding. *Remedial and Special Education, 14,* 49-56.

Skinner, C. H., Belfiore, P. J., & Pierce, N. (1992). Cover, copy, and compare: Increasing geography accuracy in students with behavior disorders. *School Psychology Review, 21,* 73-81.

Skinner, C. H., Ford, J.M., & Yunker, B.D. (1991). A comparison of instructional response requirements on the multiplication performance of behaviorally disordered students. *Behavioral Disorders, 17,* 56-65.

Smith, T. J., Dittmer, K. I., & Skinner, C. H. (2002) Enhancing science performance in students with learning disabilities using cover, copy, and compare: A student shows the way. *Psychology in the Schools, 39,* 417-427.

Zielinski, K., McLaughlin, T.F., & Derby, K.M. (2012). The effect of "Cover, Copy, and Compare" on spelling accuracy of high school students with learning disabilities. *American Secondary Education 41(1),* 78-95.

7

Name: ______________________

Example CCC Math Worksheet

/30 = _____%

Date: ______________________

Copy

1) $\begin{array}{r} 2 \\ +\ 3 \\ \hline 5 \end{array}$

2) $\begin{array}{r} 7 \\ +\ 1 \\ \hline 8 \end{array}$

3) $\begin{array}{r} 5 \\ +\ 4 \\ \hline 9 \end{array}$

4) $\begin{array}{r} 3 \\ +\ 3 \\ \hline 6 \end{array}$

5) $\begin{array}{r} 3 \\ +\ 5 \\ \hline 8 \end{array}$

6) $\begin{array}{r} 2 \\ +\ 2 \\ \hline 4 \end{array}$

7) $\begin{array}{r} 2 \\ +\ 1 \\ \hline 3 \end{array}$

8) $\begin{array}{r} 5 \\ +\ 4 \\ \hline 9 \end{array}$

9) $\begin{array}{r} 4 \\ +\ 2 \\ \hline 6 \end{array}$

10) $\begin{array}{r} 3 \\ +\ 0 \\ \hline 3 \end{array}$

Fold

7

Name: ____________________

Example Scored CCC Math Worksheet

27/30 = 90 %

Date: ____________________

	Problem	Copy	Score
1)	2 + 3 = 5	2 + 3 = 5	3
2)	7 + 1 = 8	7 + 1 = 8	3
3)	3 + 3 = 6	3 + 3 = 6	3
4)	2 + 7 = 9	2 + 7 = (8)	2
5)	3 + 5 = 8	3 + 5 = 8	3
6)	2 + 2 = 4	2 + 2 = 4	3
7)	2 + 1 = 3	(1) + (2) = 3	1
8)	4 + 3 = 7	4 + 3 = 7	3
9)	4 + 2 = 6	4 + 2 = 6	3
10)	3 + 0 = 3	3 + 0 = 3	3

Fold

CCC Math Data Chart

Name: ______________________________ Grade: __________

Interventionist: ______________________________

DAY#	DATE	SCORE	DAY #	DATE	SCORE	DAY#	DATE	SCORE
1			13			25		
2			14			26		
3			15			27		
4			16			28		
5			17			29		
6			18			30		
7			19			31		
8			20			32		
9			21			33		
10			22			34		
11			23			35		
12			24			36		

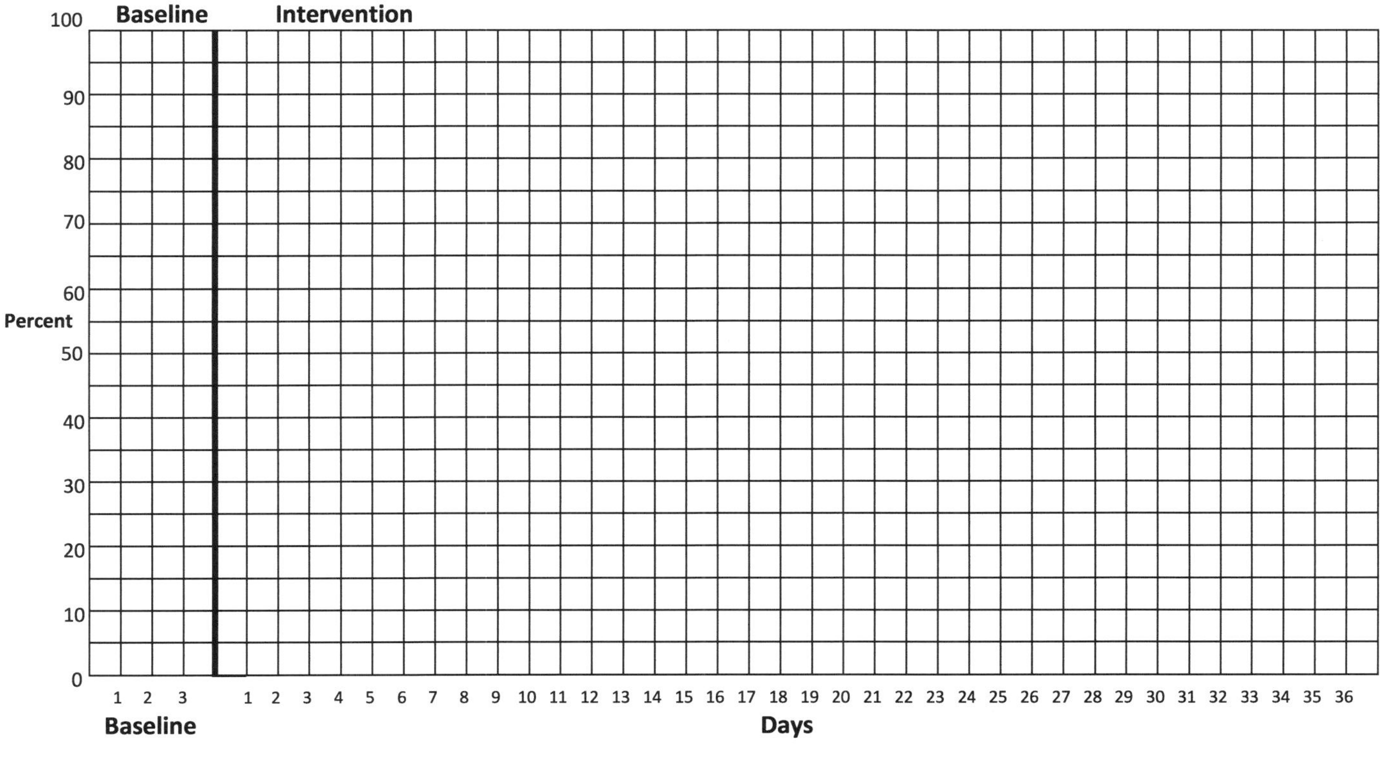

Cover Copy Compare Prompt Sheet

If folders are used to hold child materials, this prompt sheet can be taped or pasted to the back of the folder so that the child can refer to the steps as need.

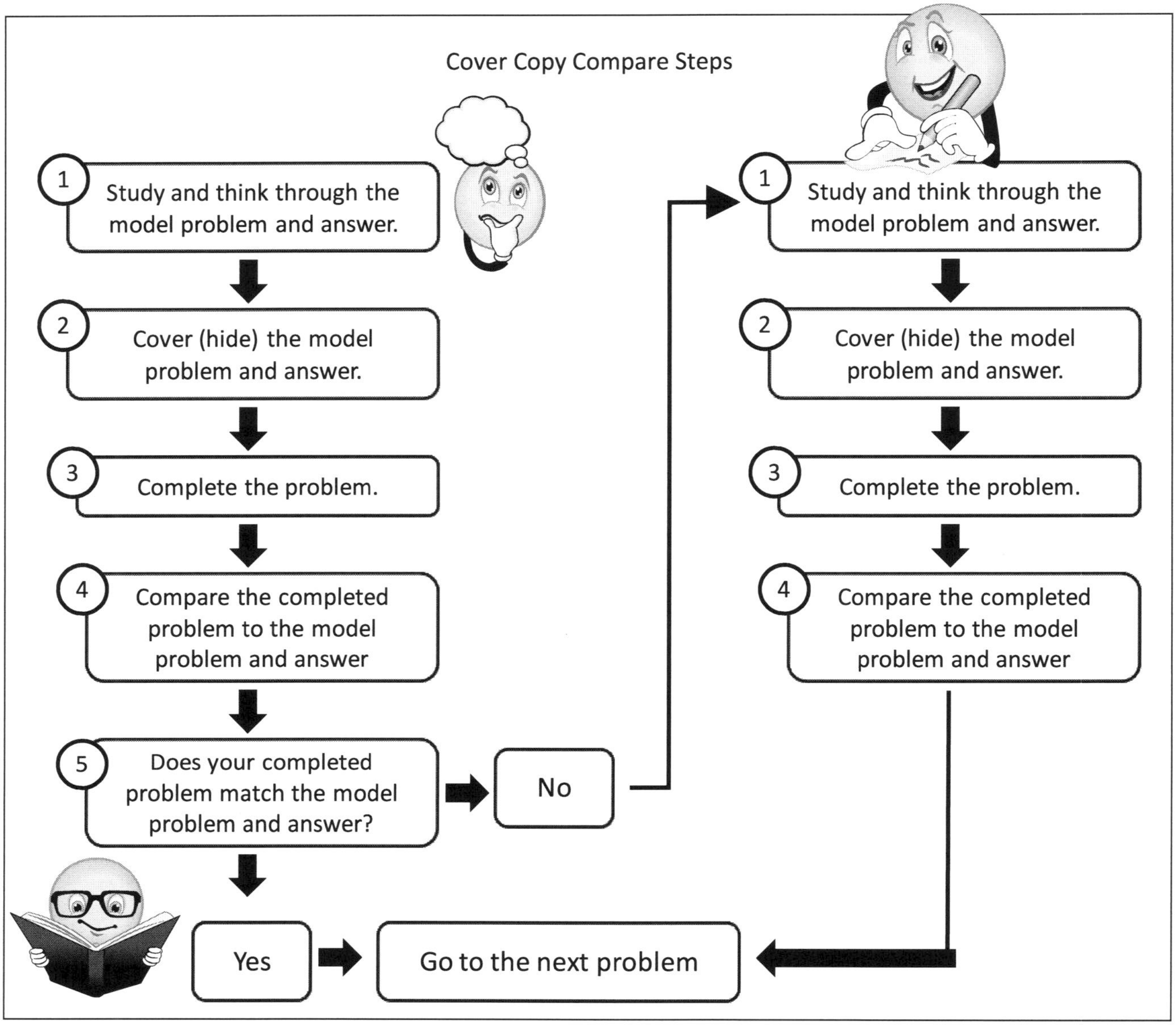

Images used with permission from Microsoft.

Cover Copy Compare Math: Procedural Integrity Checklist

Age/Grade:	Elementary – Middle School
Setting:	School, Home, Clinic, In-patient
Individual or Group:	Individual
Tier:	1, 2, & 3
Desired/ Appropriate Behavior:	Accuracy and fluency in math skills with two or more steps to complete
Skill Level:	Acquisition to maintenance

The procedural integrity checklist is completed by an observer (e.g., principal, assistant principal, school psychologist, treatment specialist, behavior specialist, counselor, lead teacher) who is familiar with the Cover Copy Compare (CCC) procedure. The observer will observe the interventionist implementing the CCC procedure and provide feedback. CCC Math is an efficient, self-administered intervention in which a child studies a model math problem, covers the problem, writes the problem from memory, uncovers the model problem, and compares the problem written from memory to the model problem.

Procedure for Integrity Checklist Observer

1) Complete the Procedural Integrity Checklist (see page 88) information about the interventionist, child, location, date, time, observer name, and observer signature.
2) Assess the interventionist's implementation of the CCC procedure. An initial observation should occur within the first couple of weeks of an interventionist's implementing the CCC procedure so that feedback can be provided to the interventionist early in the implementation.
3) Observe for the presence of behaviors 1-7 on the Checklist and mark Yes if present or No if not present. Mark N/O if the behavior is not observed.
4) Count the number of behaviors marked Yes and write the number on the line for "Number of behaviors marked Yes."
5) Write the total number of behaviors observed (i.e., the total behaviors marked Yes or No). Do not include any of the behaviors marked N/O in the total.
6) Calculate the percent marked Yes. A chart is provided for determining the percent marked Yes. If less than 80% of behaviors are marked Yes, then provide feedback immediately to the interventionist and conduct another observation the next day or as soon as possible.
7) Write any constructive feedback comments in addition to any notations made beside any individual behavior in the "Feedback" section.
8) Provide the interventionist, at an appropriate time, with oral feedback regarding the implementation of the intervention, starting with positive behaviors observed, and a copy of the Cover Copy Compare Math: Procedural Integrity Checklist. *The feedback should be provided the same day of the observation.*
9) Observe implementation of the CCC Math procedure approximately every other week or twice a month after the initial observation.

Cover Copy Compare Math: Procedural Integrity Checklist

Interventionist: ______________________ Date: __________ Time: __________

Child: ______________________ Observer: ______________________

Location: ______________________ Signature: ______________________

N/O = Not Observed

Behaviors to Observe	Yes	No	N/O	Comments
1) The child obtains materials for and starts CCC without prompting by the interventionist.				
2) The child takes time to look at the model problem.				
3) The child covers each model problem before copying the problem from memory.				
4) The child circles any digit that is incorrect.				
5) Evidence is available that the child or interventionist scores the CCC worksheet correctly.				
6) Evidence is available that the child or interventionist is graphing the percent of correct digits using the CCC Math Data Chart.				

Number of behaviors marked Yes = _____ out of _____ = ______ %

Feedback:

Percent
1 out of 6 = 17%
2 out of 6 = 33%
3 out of 6 = 50%
4 out of 6 = 67%
5 out of 6 = 83%
6 out of 6 = 100%

Accelerated Math[1]

Age/Grade: 2nd Grade – 8th Grade

Setting: School

Individual or Group: Individual or group of fewer than 15 children is recommended

Tier: 2 & 3

Desired/ Appropriate Behavior: Fluency in math skills

Skill Level: Acquisition to maintenance

Rationale & Research Support

Accelerated Math is a software program designed to deliver individualized assignments based on interventionist assignment and child performance. The learning objectives are aligned to state and Common Core State Standards. The program provides children with immediate feedback and new assignments based on performance. The program also assists an interventionist in tracking the performance and progress of each child individually (Renaissance Learning, 2013). Studies of Accelerated Math have generally shown higher performance and gains for children in grades 2-8 participating in Accelerated Math compared to children not participating in Accelerated Math (Caputo, 2007; Nunnery & Ross, 2007; Schepens, 2012; Ysseldyke, Betts, Thill, & Hannigan, 2004; Ysseldkye & Bolt, 2007; Ysseldyke, Spicuzza, Kosciolek, & Boys, 2003; Ysseldyke, & Tardrew, 2007). Although a number of studies indicate higher performance and gains for children participating in Accelerated Math compared to children not participating, few studies meet the What Works Clearinghouse (WWC) evidence standards. The WWC (2008, 2010) has rated Accelerated Math as having mixed effects at the elementary level and as having no discernible effects at the middle grades level. However, Slavin and Lake (2007) found the median effect size for Accelerated Math was larger than the median effect size for curriculum studies. There was a wide variance in the implementation of Accelerated Math in the research, which is generally employed as a supplement to mathematics instruction in the general education classroom. This procedure provides a standardized implementation of Accelerated Math designed specifically for children in need of Tier 2 or Tier 3 intervention.

Materials

1) Accelerated Math*
2) STAR Math*
3) AccelScan* scanner and scan cards, Renaissance Responders*, or computers for scoring Accelerated Math diagnostic, practice, exercise, and test assignments
4) Access to computers for STAR Math* assessments
5) Computer for the interventionist managing the intervention

---

[1] Accelerated Math, STAR Math, AccelScan, Renaissance Responder, and NEO2 are products and trademarks of Renaissance Learning, Inc.

6) Printer and paper for printing out child assignments or computers for children to access assignments (children may still need paper for working out problems)

7) Printer and paper for printing out child reports

Procedure for Interventionist

These procedures describe the implementation of Accelerated Math as a Tier 2 intervention in 25-30 minute periods. Accelerated Math practices and tests are implemented for four consecutive days, and on the fifth day children are administered a STAR Math assessment. If you are unfamiliar with the functions and features of STAR Math, refer to *Getting the Most out of STAR Math* and *Getting Results with Accelerated Math Live,* available at http://www.renlearn.com/training/app/gettingresults.aspx

Prior to starting intervention

1) Establish a child's baseline performance on the STAR Math assessment by having the child complete at least three STAR Math assessments over three consecutive weeks. There should be a minimum of one week between STAR Math assessments. The median score (or the middle STAR Math assessment score result when the scores are put in rank order) will serve as the starting test score in Step 2.

2) Set a goal in STAR Math for each child assigned to intervention. For children in Tier 2, the Goal End date should be set to 10 school weeks from *when the intervention will start*. Enter "Accelerated Math Intervention __ Minutes" as the name of the intervention, inserting the number of minutes the intervention is conducted in the blank. A Tier 2 intervention of Accelerated Math should be 25-30 minute in length.

   Set the starting test as the STAR Math assessment associated with the median score identified in Step 1. The starting test will serve as the baseline assessment for the purpose of progress monitoring. If a child enters another intervention or the goal is increased, then a new starting test should be selected. Begin children with a moderate goal. Based on a child's progress at the time of review, the goal can be changed and/or the goal rate (type) can be changed from moderate to ambitious. Note: The baseline period will need to be indicated on the STAR Math Student Progress Monitoring Report. See Step 12 for instructions.

   Refer to pages 22-25 of the *Getting the Most out of STAR Math* for the procedures for setting a goal in STAR Math.

3) Assign children receiving intervention to a group or groups in Accelerated Math. A single group is sufficient for most situations, but if an interventionist has more than one period of time for intervention and/or with different children (i.e., Tier 2 and Tier 3 children), then it may be helpful to group children by time period.

4) Create an objectives list for children.

   a) **Tier 2 children** (i.e., generally children within one grade level of their current grade placement as indicated by STAR Math reports): Create a new objectives list that contains all the objectives for one grade below the current grade placement and all the objectives for the current grade placement. The purpose in creating a new objectives list with all the objectives for the two grades is so that children can work in the intervention and progress seamlessly on objectives from one grade to the next. Having one objective list also simplifies the task of making assignments to children from only one list rather than managing two or more lists.

b) **Tier 3 children** (i.e., generally children more than one grade level below their current grade placement as indicated by STAR Math reports):

   i) Determine the lowest grade level or Accelerated Math library using STAR Math reports for the group of Tier 3 children and create a new objectives list starting one grade below the lowest grade level library for any child indicated by STAR Math.

   ii) Add all the objectives from the starting lowest grade level determined in step i) to the current grade level of children, keeping only the *core* objectives (i.e., those objectives marked by a circle within Accelerated Math). The non-core objectives can be deleted as objectives from each grade level as that level is added to the list, or they can be deleted after the entire list is created. (Hint: One list of core objectives can be created for an entire school and shared by creating a core list from the lowest grade level performance to the highest grade represented in the school. A shared list needs to be created by someone with administrator rights for the school or district so that it can be shared across interventionists.)

   Refer to pages A3-A5 of the *Getting Results with Accelerated Math Live* for the procedures for assigning objectives and creating objective lists.

5) Assign objectives to the children. In Accelerated Math, click the Assignment Book to assign the appropriate list created in step 4 to the respective group of children.

6) Prior to implementing Accelerated Math for the first time, develop a procedure for quickly and efficiently distributing the materials to children. Distributing materials or children accessing materials on their own should take less than 1 minute. Also, plan to frequently praise children (individually or as group) for following procedures.

Starting intervention

1) Assign objectives to each child for diagnostic testing.

   a) **Tier 2 children**: Use each child's STAR Math Instructional Planning Report to identify the skills at which a child may be ready to work. Initially, assign children objectives that are <u>below</u> those indicated on the Instructional Planning Report so that a child will likely experience some success; starting at this point is also likely to more clearly identify on which skill(s) a child begins to struggle. To identify starting objectives, identify where the skills on the Instructional Planning Report rank on the objectives list and then look for the lower level objectives that logically precede the skills on the Instructional Planning Report. For example, if the Instructional Planning Report identified that a child was ready to work on two-digit by two-digit subtraction with borrowing, then you would look for skill objectives that logically precede that skill such as two-digit by two-digit subtraction without borrowing. Assign <u>no more than two or three</u> objectives at a time for diagnostic testing. Although the Instructional Planning Report provides information about skills in all math domains, the numbers and operations domain should be the primary source of information for the purpose of identifying the objectives to assign for diagnostic testing. For a 25-30 minute intervention, a diagnostic assessment of medium length as defined in Accelerated Math will be appropriate for most children.

b) **Tier 3 children**: Use each child's STAR Math Instructional Planning Report to identify the skills at which is a child may be ready to work. Initially, assign children objectives that are one grade level below those indicated on the Instructional Planning Report so that a child will likely experience some success; starting at this point is also more likely to more clearly identify on which skill(s) a child begins to struggle. To identify starting objectives, identify where the skills on the Instructional Planning Report rank on the objectives list and then look for the lower level objectives that logically precede the skills on the Instructional Planning Report. For example, if the Instructional Planning Report identified a child was ready to work on two-digit by two-digit subtraction with borrowing, then you would look for skill objectives that logically precede that skill such as two-digit by two-digit subtraction without borrowing. If few or no core objectives are identified on the Instructional Planning Report, you may have to look at the objectives list for the appropriate grade level to identify the appropriate core objectives to assign initially. Assign no more than two or three objectives at a time for diagnostic testing. Although the Instructional Planning Report provides information about skills in all math domains, the numbers and operations domain should be the primary source of information for the purpose of identifying the objectives to assign for diagnostic testing. For a 25-30 minute intervention, a diagnostic assessment of medium length will be appropriate for most children.

2) Review the diagnostic tests results for each child and identify the objectives on which he or she does not reach success (less than 80% correct). These objectives will be assigned to the child for practice (Step 8). Refer to page A4 of the *Getting Results with Accelerated Math Live* for the procedures for assigning objectives to children.

   If a child demonstrates mastery on all of the assigned objectives, then continue with diagnostic testing with the next two or three objectives in the objectives list. Continue this process until a child does not demonstrate success and then move to Step 8.

3) Assign practice tests to children. Based on a child's objectives identified as unsuccessful (i.e., less than 80% correct), assign the objectives for a child to practice. Assign children no more than two or three objectives to practice at a time. Assign practice tests of medium or long duration (i.e., 20-30 items) as defined in Accelerated Math. The practice should take children most of the 25- to 30-minute intervention to complete. Adjust the length of the practice test based on the needs of the child. Prior to children attempting a first practice test on new objectives, they should be provided some direct instruction. The Accelerated Math libraries provide sample items for each objective that can be used for direct instruction. Children working on the same objectives can be grouped together for instruction. Print the Accelerated Math Student Group Report to identify which children are working on the same objectives.

Daily Procedure

1) Once children start practice tests, then guide children through the practice test, regular test, and diagnostic test cycle. Refer to pages 50-58 of the *Getting Results with Accelerated Math Live* for guidance in implementing the practice-regular-diagnostic test cycle on a daily basis. Use the Accelerated Math Status of the Class Report daily to keep track of children's progress and to keep up with which children need an intervention, are ready for a regular test, or are ready for additional diagnostic testing. Be sure to customize this report by selecting the "Include Group Data" and "Include assignments printed section" boxes before viewing and printing this report. Hint:

Managing the practice-regular-diagnostic test cycle in Accelerated Math requires daily attention. Plan on spending a few minutes each day outside of the intervention to the reports and checking whether children need to be assigned new objectives for practice, regular, or diagnostic testing for period.

2) Children will complete work in the practice-regular-diagnostic test cycle for four consecutive school days. On the fifth school day, children will take a STAR Math assessment for the purpose of progress monitoring. All children in an intervention group can work on the same four-day Accelerated Math and one-day STAR Math assessment schedule, or the children can be arranged in groups so that some groups are working on Accelerated Math while another is completing the STAR Math assessment. The latter arrangement may be necessary in cases where the number of computers available is not sufficient for all children in intervention to be administered STAR Math at the same time or to accommodate fewer children who will need to receive instruction and feedback on a daily basis.

Decision Making

1) After a child completes five weeks of the four-day Accelerated Math and one-day STAR Math assessment schedule, evaluate a child's progress by reviewing the Student Progress Monitoring Report.
    a) If a child's trend line trajectory is close to or above the goal line, then the child continues with the intervention as currently implemented.
    b) If a child's trend line trajectory is below the goal line, then provide corrective feedback to the child on the previous practice or exercise prior to each new practice test and exercise.
2) After a child completes ten weeks of the four-day Accelerated Math and one-day STAR Math assessment schedule, evaluate a child's progress by reviewing the Student Progress Monitoring Report. Draw a vertical line (also called a phase line) on Student Progress Monitoring Report to indicate the date a child started the Accelerated Math intervention. Label the area to the left of the vertical line as "Baseline" and the area to the right of the vertical line as "Intervention." This step is important since the Accelerated Math intervention for a child may not begin until two or more weeks *after* the median STAR Math assessment score that is used as the baseline for setting the goal. If the phase line is not drawn on the Student Progress Monitoring Report, then other interventionists, a problem-solving team, administrator, parent, or other user of the report may incorrectly assume that intervention began on the same date as the baseline STAR Math assessment score.
    a) If a child's
        - trend line is above the goal line,
        - three most recent scores are above the goal line, <u>and</u>
        - current level of performance is in the On Watch range based on School Benchmarks as reported on the STAR Math Instructional Planning Report or Screening Report, then
            (i) continue the intervention based on other child considerations such as grades in math, classroom performance, or motivation or
            (ii) recommend to the school problem-solving team that the child exit Tier 2 or Tier 3.

b) If a child's trend line is above the goal line but the three most recent scores are not above the goal line or the child's current level is not in the On Watch range based on School Benchmarks as reported on the STAR Math Instructional Planning Report or Screening Report, then the child continues with the intervention as currently implemented.

c) If a child's trend line is below the goal line, then refer the child to the school problem-solving team to consider modifying the duration or frequency of the intervention, adding to the intervention, or changing the intervention.

References

Caputo, M. T. (2007). A comparison of the effects of the *Accelerated Math* program and the Delaware procedural fluency workbook program on academic growth in grade six at X middle school. (Doctoral dissertation, Wilmington University, Wilmington). *Dissertation Abstracts International* 68 (09A).

Nunnery, J. A., & Ross, S. M. (2007). The effects of the School Renaissance program on student achievement in reading and mathematics. *Research in the Schools, 14(1),* 40–59.

Renaissance Learning (2013). *Getting results with Accelerated Math Live*. Wisconsin Rapids, Wisconsin: Author.

Schepens, S.B. (2012). The impact of accelerated mathematics: Leadership initiatives to close the ethnic achievement gaps among children. *Dissertation Abstracts International* 72(11-A).

Slavin, R. E. & Lake, C. (2007, February). Effective programs in elementary mathematics: A best-evidence synthesis. Baltimore, MD: Johns Hopkins University, Center for Data-Driven Reform in Education. Retrieved from http://www.bestevidence.org/word/elem_math_Feb_9_2007.pdf

What Works Clearinghouse. (2010). *Accelerated Math*. Washington, DC: U.S. Department of Education. Retrieved from http://ies.ed.gov/ncee/wwc/pdf/intervention_reports/wwc_accelmath_091410.pdf

What Works Clearinghouse. (2008). *Accelerated Math*. Washington, DC: U.S. Department of Education. Retrieved from http://ies.ed.gov/ncee/wwc/pdf/intervention_reports/wwc_accelmath_093008.pdf

Ysseldyke, J., Betts, J., Thill, T., & Hannigan, E. (2004). Use of an instructional management system to improve mathematics skills for children in Title I programs. *Preventing School Failure, 48(4),* 10-14.

Ysseldyke, J., & Bolt, D. M. (2007). Effect of technology-enhanced continuous progress monitoring on math achievement. *School Psychology Review, 36(3)*, 453–467.

Ysseldyke, J., Spicuzza, R., Kosciolek, S., & Boys, C. (2003). Effects of a learning information system on mathematics achievement and classroom structure. *Journal of Educational Research, 96(3)*, 163–173.

Ysseldyke, J., & Tardrew, S. (2007). Use of a progress monitoring system to enable teachers to differentiate mathematics instruction. *Journal of Applied School Psychology, 24(1),* 1–28.

Accelerated Math: Procedural Integrity Checklist

Age/Grade:	2nd Grade – 8th Grade
Setting:	School
Individual or Group:	Individual or group of less than 15 children is recommended
Tier:	2 & 3
Desired/ Appropriate Behavior:	Fluency in math skills
Skill Level:	Acquisition to maintenance

Accelerated Math is a software program designed to deliver individualized assignments based on interventionist assignment and child performance. The procedural integrity checklist is completed by an observer (e.g., principal, assistant principal, school psychologist, treatment specialist, behavior specialist, counselor, lead teacher) who is familiar with the Accelerated Math procedure. The checklist is divided into two parts. Part one of the checklist is used to conduct observations in the classroom while the intervention is being conducted. Part two of the checklist addresses evidence that the interventionist is conducting assessment with the appropriate frequency and is providing feedback to children. The evidence for part two is gathered by looking at interventionist documentation or other evidence sources (e.g., computer-based assessments). The observer will observe the individual interventionist implementing the Accelerated Math procedure and provide feedback.

Procedure for Integrity Checklist Observer

1) Complete the Procedural Integrity Checklist (see page 97) information about the interventionist, child, location, date, time, observer name, and observer signature.
2) Assess the interventionist's implementation of the Accelerated Math procedure. An initial observation should occur within the first couple of weeks of an interventionist's implementing the Accelerated Math procedure so that feedback can be provided to the interventionist early in the implementation.
3) Observe the interventionist for the presence of behaviors under Part 1: Daily Procedures on the Checklist and marks Yes if present or No if not present.
4) Evaluate the presence of products under Part 2: Assessment on the Checklist and marks Yes if present or No if not present. Evaluation of Part 2 is based on interventionist documentation, child folders, review of STAR Math™ reports on line, or interviews. Part 2 of the checklist may be completed before or after the Part 1 observation.
5) Count the number of behaviors marked Yes on Part 1 and Part 2 and write the number on the line for "Number of behaviors marked Yes."
6) Calculate the percent marked Yes. A chart is provided for determining the percent marked Yes. If fewer than four behaviors are marked Yes, then provide feedback immediately to the interventionist and conduct another observation the next day or as soon as possible.
7) Write any constructive feedback comments in addition to any notations made beside any individual behavior in the "Feedback" section.

8) Provide the interventionist, at an appropriate time, with oral feedback regarding the implementation of the intervention, starting with positive behaviors observed, and a copy of the Accelerated Math: Procedural Integrity Checklist. *The feedback should be provided the same day of the observation.*

9) Observe the interventionist implementing the Accelerated Math procedure approximately every other week or twice a month after the initial observation.

Accelerated Math: Procedural Integrity Checklist

Interventionist: ______________________ Date: __________ Time: __________

Child: ______________________ Observer: ______________________

Location: ______________________ Signature: ______________________

Part 1: Daily Procedures – Behaviors to Observe	Yes	No	Comments
1) The interventionist has a quick, efficient procedure for distributing materials for the day (i.e., distributing materials takes no class time or less than 1 minute).			
2) The interventionist praises children (individually or as group) for following procedures.			
3) The interventionist moves around the room to check that children are completing the Accelerated Math assignment.			
4) The interventionist provides children with specific, descriptive praise about their performance as she moves about the room.			
5) *All* children work for at least 20 minutes on the Accelerated Math™ assignment.			

Feedback:

Part 2: Assessment – Products to Observe	Yes	No	Comments
6) There is evidence children are being assessed on STAR Math™ every 5th day of intervention.			
7) There is evidence the STAR Math™ results are provided to children.			
8) There is evidence children know their STAR Math™ goal and their current level of performance. Gather this information by interviewing at least two children at random at an appropriate time (e.g., when the Accelerated Math assignment is completed).			

Feedback:

Daily Procedures & Assessment (Part 1 and Part 2) Number of behaviors marked Yes = _____ out of 8 = ______ %	1 out of 8 = 12% 2 out of 8 = 25% 3 out of 8 = 38% 4 out of 8 = 50% 5 out of 8 = 63% 6 out of 8 = 75% 7 out of 8 = 88% 8 out of 8 = 100%

Look, Ask, Pick (LAP)

Age/Grade:	4th Grade – High School
Setting:	School, Home, Clinic, In-patient
Individual or Group:	Individual
Tier:	2 & 3
Desired/ Appropriate Behavior:	Adding and subtracting like and unlike fractions
Skill Level:	Acquisition to maintenance

Rationale & Research Support

As one of the only examples of assessing the effectiveness of a fraction intervention through single-case design technology, researchers (Everett, Harsy, Hupp, & Jewell, in press; Test & Ellis, 2005) employed a first-letter mnemonic, LAP, for solving addition and subtraction of like and unlike fractions. LAP reminds child of the three steps:

> **L**ook at the sign and denominator,
>
> **A**sk yourself the question, "Will the smallest denominator divide into the largest denominator an even number of times?" and
>
> **P**ick your fraction type" (p. 4).

Mnemonic strategies, defined as memory aids used to assist in the recall of facts, steps, or processes (Manalo, Bunnell, & Stillman, 2000), have been employed in differing math interventions (e.g., Cade & Gunter 2002; Joseph & Hunter, 2001).

Materials

1) LAP mnemonic flashcards (See flashcards following the procedure.)
2) 18-problem CBM math probes containing only addition and subtraction of like and unlike fractions problems
3) LAP Intervention Data Chart
4) LAP quiz that asks seven questions about the mnemonic and its use (The quiz is provided following the procedure.)
5) 7-problem Curriculum-based Measurement (CBM) math probes containing only addition and subtraction of like and unlike fractions problems
6) Stopwatch

Procedure for Interventionist

Before Implementing the Intervention

1) Create and review LAP mnemonic flashcards. Create LAP mnemonic flashcards so that one letter (i.e., L, A, or P) of the procedure appears on one side of the card, with the corresponding action associated with the letter appearing on the other. Review the flashcards with a child by having the child read the flashcards orally while you offer verbal guidance on each component of the mnemonic.

2) Create a 7-problem practice CBM probe that contains at least one addition and one subtraction problem of each fraction type. The three types of fraction problems (Everett, et al., 2013; Test & Ellis 2005) are as follows:

   Type 1 fractions – addition and subtraction of fractions with like denominators.

   Type 2 fractions – addition and subtraction of fractions with unlike denominators where one denominator divides evenly into the other denominator.

   Type 3 fractions – addition and subtraction of fractions with unlike denominators where one denominator does not divide evenly into the other denominator.

3) Create 18-problem CBM probes that contain at least 3 addition and 3 subtraction problems for each of the three fraction types. Use several probes with different problems for each day of intervention and progress monitoring (at a minimum once a week for progress monitoring). Therefore, each fraction type will have a total of 6 fraction problems, 3 addition and 3 subtraction (Everett, et al., 2013; Test & Ellis 2005). The three types of fraction problems (Everett, et al., 2013; Test & Ellis 2005) are:

   Type 1 fractions – addition and subtraction of fractions with like denominators.

   Type 2 fractions – addition and subtraction of fractions unlike denominators where one divides evenly into the other.

   Type 3 fractions – fractions with unlike denominators where one does not divide evenly into the other.

4) Collect baseline data and set the initial goal before starting the intervention.

   a) Administer three 18-problem CBM probes.

   b) For a minimum of 3 days or sessions, administer the probe as follows.

      Say to the child:

      "You're going to take a 3-minute math test. I want you to write your answers to these fraction problems. Some are addition, and some are subtraction. Look at each problem carefully before you answer it. When I say 'BEGIN' write your answer to the first problem (demonstrate by pointing) and work across the page. Then go to the next row. Try to work each problem. If you come to one you really don't know how to do, put an 'X' through it and go to the next one."

      Then say, "**Are there any questions?"** (Pause for the child to respond.)

      Say **"Begin"** and start your stopwatch/timer.

      When the stopwatch reaches three minutes say, "**Stop and put your pencil down.**"

   c) Score the probe. Each correct digit that a child writes is marked with an underline and counted as a digit. The fraction sign (i.e., /) is also counted. For example, if the correct answer is 3/5 and the child's response is 3/5, then the child has three digits correct, the 3, the forward slash symbol (/), and the 5. If the child incorrectly responded 6/5 to this same problem, then the child has two digits correct: the forward slash symbol (/) and the 5. Sum the total number of correct digits and divide by 3. This will give you Digits Correct Per Minute (DCPM).

d) Set the baseline. Take the median score of the three probes that were administered under the timed condition. The median will be the baseline value. A sample LAP Intervention Data Chart is provided below.

e) Set the goal for child. The goal should be set as 110% of the baseline value. For children in Tier 2, the goal end date should be set to 10 school weeks from when the intervention begins. An example is provided below:

- Median DCPM earned by child during baseline = 21
- 110% of 21 = 1.10 X 21 = 23.1
- Round to the nearest whole number, if necessary. In this case 23.1 would be rounded to 23.
- Initial Goal = 23 DCPM
- On the child's progress monitoring graph, mark the median DCPM as the starting point, and then at the point on the graph representing ten weeks from the starting point, mark the goal DCPM. Connect the starting DCPM and goal DCPM with a straight line and label it as the goal.

Daily Implementation of the Intervention

1) Begin the intervention session with the child reviewing the LAP mnemonic using the LAP flash cards. If the child has not been previously introduced to the LAP flash cards, present each card to the child initial-only side first and then turn the card over and state what step is associated with the initial. Present the LAP flash cards in the order of the problem-solving steps L-A-P. Direct the child to look at the side of the flash cards with the initials L, A, and P and ask the child to state the problem-solving steps outlined by the LAP mnemonic. If the child states an incorrect response or hesitates for 3 seconds, then immediately give him or her corrective feedback. Mnemonic skill building is facilitated at the beginning of each intervention session through flash card review and then the LAP quiz.

2) Give the LAP quiz and score immediately. Provide the child feedback on the quiz performance.

3) Administer the child the 7-problem LAP CBM probe following completion of the LAP review and LAP quiz. Require the child to verbally explain the steps of the LAP technique while solving each individual problem. To ensure the child practices correct problem completion when making errors, you will help the child complete the problem while verbally explaining the appropriate LAP rule reminders. The child then independently attempts to solve the missed problem again verbally explaining the LAP steps while solving the problem. If the child misses another step, the interventionist will stop the child and verbally explain the missing step. The child will then again attempt to independently solve problem. Repeat the steps as necessary to aid the child's learning and until the child correctly solves the problem.

   For example, to correctly complete the problem 1/6 + 1/2 (a Type 2 problem), a child should provide an explanation similar to the following. "L: I *look* at the sign and denominator and know the fraction is an addition problem with unlike denominators. A: I *ask* myself the question, 'Will the smallest denominator divide into the largest denominator an even number of times?' Yes, two will divide into six an even number of times. P: So, I *pick* a Type 2 fraction." In addition to describing the mnemonic, the child will also describe the steps required to solve the problem. As this example refers to a Type 2 addition problem, the correct explanation would include something similar to the following. "I know that 2 is smaller than 6, so I'm going to keep the 6 on the bottom. I know that 2 can go into 6 three times, so I multiply the 2 by 3 and get another 6 on the bottom. Now, I multiply the 1 on top by three to get a new fraction (i.e., 3/6). Now, I add the top numbers (i.e., 1 + 3) to get the top of the answer, and I keep the 6 on the bottom."

In mathematical notation, the solution for this as described is as follows:

1/6 + 1/2 = 1/6 + (1/2 *3/3) = 1/6 + 3/6 = **4/6.**

Although only one example solution is currently included for illustration purposes, such explanations are required all problems on the 7-problem probes (regardless of whether the probes are addition or subtraction problems of Type 1, 2, or 3). Again, any mistakes made by the child related to either verbal explanation of the LAP mnemonic or its use to arrive at the correct problem solution require that you immediately correct the error and appropriately model the correction.

During the first intervention session, your modeling (using verbal explanations of the type provided above) precedes the child's attempts so that you can teach correct problem-solving techniques for all three types of addition and subtraction problems.

For all other intervention sessions, the child solves the 7-problem probe immediately following LAP quiz completion. Then, you model the correct mnemonic usage and problem solving only when needed (i.e., when a child's errors make modeling necessary).

4) Direct the child, following completion of the 7-problem probe, to complete independent practice on a separate 18-problem probe that contains three addition and three subtraction problems for each type (as created in step 3 above). The child completes fraction problems without the verbal explanation of the solutions required on the 7-problem probe. The child works silently on probe completion with the exception that, if needed, he or she may ask for assistance, at which point you would model correct LAP usage/problem solution. The child has 5 minutes to work on the 18-problem probe. Time the child using a stopwatch or other appropriate device. The 18-problem probe is used each day the intervention is implemented.
5) Score the 18-problem probe and provide feedback to the child.
6) Progress monitor twice a week on a new 18-problem probe. Follow the same directions in Steps 4 b) and c) for administering and scoring. Note that the student has only 3 minutes to complete the probe for progress monitoring.

Adjustments/Modification

For a child in Tier 3, the goal end date should be set to a longer time period (e.g., 16 weeks) from when the intervention begins. Review the child's progress every four weeks to determine if the child's performance trend is improving and if the child is likely to reach the goal by the end date.

References

Cade, T. & Gunter, P.L. (2002). Teaching students with severe emotional or behavioral disorders to use a musical mnemonic technique to solve basic division calculations. *Behavioral Disorders, 27(3)*, 208-14.

Everett, G. E., Harsy, J. D., Hupp, S. D.A., & Jewell, J. D. (in press). An Investigation of the Look-Ask-Pick Mnemonic to Improve Fraction Skills. *Education and Treatment of Children.*

Joseph, L.M. & Hunter, A.D. (2001). Differential application of a cue card strategy for solving fraction problems: exploring instructional utility of the cognitive assessment system. *Child Study Journal, 31(2)*, 123-36.

Manalo, E., Bunnell, J. K., & Stillman, J. A. (2000). The use of process mnemonics in teaching students with mathematics learning disabilities. *Learning Disability Quarterly, 23(2)*, 137–156.

Test, D. W., & Ellis, M. F. (2005). The effects of LAP fractions on addition and subtraction of fractions with students with mild disabilities. *Education and Treatment of Children, 28,* 11-24.

Look at the sign and denominator

Look at the sign and denominator

Look at the sign and denominator

TIER www.evidencebasedreform.com

TIER www.evidencebasedreform.com

A

A

A

Ask yourself the question, "Will the smallest denominator divide into the largest denominator an even number of times?"

Ask yourself the question, "Will the smallest denominator divide into the largest denominator an even number of times?"

Ask yourself the question, "Will the smallest denominator divide into the largest denominator an even number of times?"

TIER www.evidencebasedreform.com

TIER www.evidencebasedreform.com

TIER www.evidencebasedreform.com

P

P

P

Pick
your fraction
type

TIER www.evidencebasedreform.com

Pick
your fraction
type

TIER www.evidencebasedreform.com

Pick
your fraction
type

TIER www.evidencebasedreform.com

LAP Intervention Data Chart

Student Name: ______________________ **Grade:** __________

Intervention Teacher: ____________________ **Beginning Date of Intervention:** ____________________

	A	B	C	D		A	B	C	D		A	B	C	D
Day	Digits Correct 3 min.	Digits Correct 1 min.	Digits Incorrect 3 min.	Digits Incorrect 1 min.	Day	Digits Correct 3 min.	Digits Correct 1 min.	Digits Incorrect 3 min.	Digits Incorrect 1 min.	Day	Digits Correct 3 min.	Digits Correct 1 min.	Digits Incorrect 3 min.	Digits Incorrect 1 min.
1					13					25				
2					14					26				
3					15					27				
4					16					28				
5					17					29				
6					18					30				
7					19					31				
8					20					32				
9					21					33				
10					22					34				
11					23					35				
12					24					36				

Column B = Column A number divided by 3. Column D = Column C number divided by 3

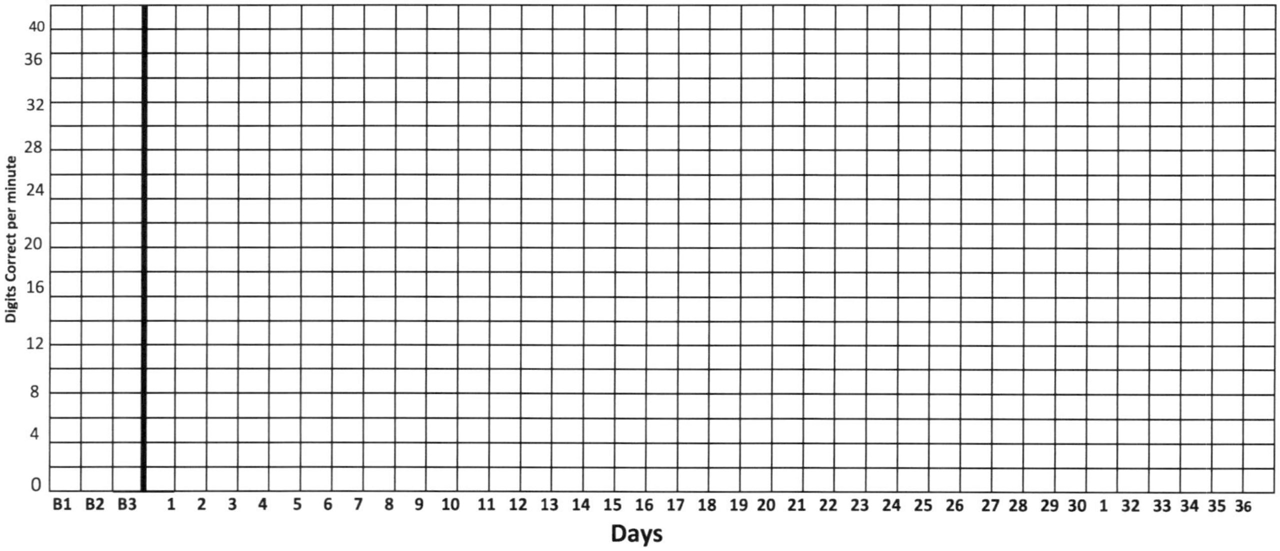

TIER

LAP Quiz

1. What does L stand for and suggest you do?

2. What does A stand for and suggest you do?

3. What does P stand for and suggest you do?

4. What number is the denominator for 7/9 or $\frac{7}{9}$?

5. What type of fraction is 1/4 + 2/4?

6. What type of fraction is 1/6 + 1/2?

7. What type of fraction is 1/5 + 2/7?

LAP Quiz

Answer Key

1. What does L stand for and suggest you do?

   Look at the sign and denominator

2. What does A stand for and suggest you do?

   Ask myself the question, "Will the smallest denominator divide into the largest denominator an even number of times?"

3. What does P stand for and suggest you do?

   Pick the fraction type

4. What number is the denominator for 7/9 or $\frac{7}{9}$?

   9

5. What type of fraction is 1/4 + 2/4?

   A Type 1 fraction – fractions with like denominators

6. What type of fraction is 1/6 + 1/2?

   A Type 2 fraction – fractions with unlike denominators where one denominator divides evenly into the other denominator

7. What type of fraction is 1/5 + 2/7?

   A Type 3 fraction – fractions with unlike denominators where one denominator does not divide evenly into the other denominator

Look, Ask, Pick (LAP): Procedural Integrity Checklist

Age/Grade:	4th Grade – High School
Setting:	School, Home, Clinic, In-patient
Individual or Group:	Individual
Tier:	2 & 3
Desired/ Appropriate Behavior:	Adding and subtracting like and unlike fractions
Skill Level:	Acquisition to maintenance

The procedural integrity checklist is completed by an observer (e.g., principal, assistant principal, school psychologist, treatment specialist, behavior specialist, counselor, lead teacher) who is familiar with the LAP procedure. The observer will observe the interventionist implementing the LAP procedure and provide feedback. The LAP intervention was developed as an efficient Tier 2 or 3 intervention for children struggling with adding and subtracting like and unlike fractions.

Procedure for Integrity Checklist Observer

1) Complete the Procedural Integrity Checklist (see page 115) information about the interventionist, child, location, date, time, observer name, and observer signature.
2) Assess the interventionist's implementation of the LAP procedure. An initial observation should occur within the first couple of weeks of an interventionist's implementing the LAP procedure so that feedback can be provided to the interventionist early in the implementation.
3) Observe the interventionist for the presence of behaviors 1-7 on the Checklist and mark Yes if present or No if not present. Mark N/O if the behavior is not observed.
4) Observe and mark the behaviors for 6a and 6b on the checklist *only if the child makes an error* on th*e 7*-problem LAP CBM probe. If the child makes an error on the 7-problem LAP CBM probe, mark Yes to indicate that an error was observed and then observe for the behaviors listed in 6a and 6b. Otherwise, mark No and move on to behavior 7. If a child makes an error on the 7-problem LAP CBM probe, the maximum number of behaviors that may be marked Yes is 9; otherwise the maximum number of behaviors marked is 7.
5) Count the number of behaviors marked Yes and write the number on the line for "Number of behaviors marked Yes."
6) Write the total number of behaviors observed (i.e., the total behaviors marked Yes or No).
7) Calculate the percent marked Yes. A chart is provided for determining the percent marked Yes. If fewer than four behaviors are marked Yes, then provide feedback immediately to the interventionist and conduct another observation the next day or as soon as possible.
8) Write any constructive feedback comments in addition to any notations made beside any individual behavior in the "Feedback" section.

9

9) Provide the interventionist, at an appropriate time, with oral feedback regarding the implementation of the intervention, starting with positive behaviors observed, and a copy of the LAP: Procedural Integrity Checklist. *The feedback should be provided the same day of the observation.*

10) Observe the interventionist implementing the LAP procedure approximately every other week or twice a month after the initial observation.

Look, Ask, Pick (LAP): Procedural Integrity Checklist

Interventionist: ______________________ Date: __________ Time: __________

Child: ______________________ Observer: ______________________

Location: ______________________ Signature: ______________________

N/O = Not Observed

Behaviors to Observe	Yes	No	N/O	Comments
1) The child reviews the LAP mnemonic using the LAP flashcards at the beginning of the instructional period.				
2) The interventionist provides immediate corrective feedback on the LAP flashcards if the child stated an incorrect response or hesitates for 3 seconds				
3) The interventionist administers the LAP quiz.				
4) The interventionist scores the LAP quiz immediately and provides feedback to the child.				
5) The interventionist administers the 7-problem LAP CBM probe.				
6) The child verbally explains to the interventionist the steps of the LAP technique while solving each individual problem on the 7-problem LAP CBM probe.				
If the child made an error on the 7-problem LAP CBM probe:	Was this observed? __Yes __No			
6a) The interventionist explains the appropriate LAP rule reminder to the child.				
6b) The child independently attempts to solve the missed problem until solving it correctly.				
7) The interventionist administers the 18-problem LAP CBM probe.				

Number of behaviors marked Yes = _____ out of _____ = ______ %

Feedback:

Percent

1 out of 7 = 14%	1 out of 9 = 11%
2 out of 7 = 29%	2 out of 9 = 22%
3 out of 7 = 43%	3 out of 9 = 33%
4 out of 7 = 57%	4 out of 9 = 44%
5 out of 7 = 71%	5 out of 9 = 56%
6 out of 7 = 86%	6 out of 9 = 67%
7 out of 7 = 100%	7 out of 9 = 78%
	8 out of 9 = 89%
	9 out of 9 = 100%

Reading or Reading Related Interventions

Folding-In Sight Words/Vocabulary

Age/Grade:	Preschool – High School
Setting:	School, Home, Clinic, In-patient
Individual or Group:	Individual
Tier:	1, 2, & 3
Desired/ Appropriate Behavior:	Fluency with a variety of sight words or sight vocabulary
Skill Level:	Acquisition to maintenance

Rationale & Research Support

Research has supported the importance of rehearsal or repetition to move knowledge from acquisition to maintenance. Gates (1930) found that a typical child needs approximately 35 repetitions to achieve mastery of knowledge; however, some children need even more repetitions, and some above average children may need fewer repetitions to achieve mastery. Folding-In is a technique designed to maximize the number of repetitions of new knowledge within a short period of time (Shapiro, 1996). Gickling and Rosenfield (1995) found that the optimum ratio of known to unknown words for practice was 70%-85% known words to 15%-30% unknown words. Roberts, Turco, and Shapiro (1991) and later Roberts and Shapiro (1996) found that retention of learned words was highest when the ratio of known to unknown words was 80%-90% to 10-20% unknown. Repetition techniques have been found to be effective for teaching words and vocabulary (Burns, Dean, & Foley, 2004; MacQuarrie, Tucker, Burns, & Hartman, 2002).

Any word can be a sight word for an individual student. However, the definition of a sight word is a high frequency word or commonly used word that children are encouraged to memorize as a whole by sight so that they can automatically recognize the word in print without having to use any strategies to decode. Sight words account for a large percentage (up to 75%) of the words used in beginning children's print materials (Kear & Gladhart, 1983). Although sight words are considered high frequency words, sight vocabulary is also very important. Sight vocabulary is often confused with sight words (high frequency or commonly used words). Sight vocabulary is defined as each individual's own bank of vocabulary words that the individual recognizes instantly without having to decode.

This intervention can be used in reading, language arts, science, social studies, or any other subject that requires reading. Folding-In can be used to build fluency and maintenance for letter naming, letter sound correspondence, and phonemes. The Folding-In intervention can also be used to support learning math words. Folding-In Math is found on page 65.

Materials

1) Flash cards or index cards for writing the target words
2) Sight Word/Vocabulary Mastery Tracking Form
3) Folding-In Data Chart

Procedure for Interventionist

This intervention involves "folding in," or slowly incorporating, unknown words to known ones. This intervention is typically implemented one-on-one with an interventionist (e.g., interventionist, paraprofessional, or parent) and a child. The procedure is typically implemented twice a week and takes approximately 20 minutes to complete (Burns, 2005; Codding, Archer, & Connell, 2010).

Pre-assessment Phase

1) Select words for the child to learn. Choose either sight word assessment or sight vocabulary assessment based on the needs and goal of the child.
   a) Sight word assessment
      i) Select an appropriate list of sight words on which to assess the child. The words may be drawn from a word list such as Dolch, Fry, or Zeno.
      ii) Create or use a set of flash cards with one word from the selected list on each card.
      iii) Tell the child that you are going to present a flash card with a word on it and that you want the child to do his or her best to read the word.
      iv) Present each flash card to the child. Allow the child up to 3 seconds to respond. If the child provides the correct response, then place the flash card in a stack of "known" words. If the child cannot respond within 3 seconds, provides an incorrect response, or indicates he/she does not know the word, place the flash card in a stack of "unknown" words.
   b) Sight vocabulary assessment
      i) Vocabulary list assessment
         (1) Select an appropriate list of sight words on which to assess the child. The words may be drawn from a word list such as EDL Core Vocabularies or vocabulary words identified in a textbook.
         (2) Create or use a set of flash cards with one word from the selected list on each card.
         (3) Tell the child that you are going to present a flash card with a word on it and that you want the child to do his or her best to read the word.
         (4) Present each flash card to the child. Allow the child up to 3 seconds to respond. If the child provides the correct response, then place the flash card in a stack of "known" words. If the child cannot respond within 3 seconds, provides an incorrect response, or indicates he/she does not know the word, place the flash card in a stack of "unknown" words.
      ii) Text passage assessment
         (1) Select a text passage for the child to read. Typically, the text is one that the child is currently reading in class.
         (2) Mark or highlight each of the key words in the text; typically, these words are the verbs and nouns required to comprehend the text. Refer to this marked copy of the text while the child reads an unmarked copy of the same text in the next step.
         (3) To assess the child, present the child with an unmarked copy of the text and ask the child to do his or her best to read the entire text. The child should know at least 50% or more of the words presented in the text. As the child reads, mark any words – key words or other words – on which the child hesitates for 3 seconds. Do not assist the

child with any of the words. If the child hesitates for more than 3 seconds on any word or stops reading before reading to the end of the text, ask the child to continue reading. (If the child cannot independently read more than 40% of the words in the sentences, stop and find a new text or passage.) The words on which the child hesitated will become the list of "unknown" words. The key words that were read correctly by the child will become list of "known" words. If the child hesitated for 3 seconds on more than 50% of the key words in the text, then you must select another text passage to use to assess the child's sight vocabulary.

(4) Create a set of flash cards with one word per card. Separate the flash cards into "known" and "unknown" words.

2) Make a list of the unknown words on the Sight Word/Vocabulary Mastery Tracking Form on page 126. This form is used to track mastery during the instructional phase (see Step 10 below).

Instructional Phase

1) Direct the child to select seven cards from his or her pile of pre-assessed **known** words.
2) Direct the child to select three cards from his or her pile of pre-assessed **unknown** words.
3) Inform the child that he or she will have 20 minutes to complete the intervention.
4) Present the first **unknown** word to the learner by reading the flash card and saying the word.
5) Direct the child to write the word on a piece of paper 3 times while saying it aloud three times and then to turn over the piece of paper.
6) Present a **known** word, followed by the **unknown** word, with the child saying each word.
7) Present the **first known** word, the **unknown** word, and another **known** word. Repeat this process with the addition of one new **known** word at the end of the sequence until all seven known words have been presented and folded-in among the one unknown word.
8) Shuffle the group of eight words (one unknown and seven known). The **second unknown** word is then presented as in Steps 4 and 5. Then the **second unknown** word is folded-in as in Steps 6 and 7. These steps are repeated again for the **third unknown** word. See the Sequence for Presenting Unknown and Known Words on page 123 for the complete sequence.
9) If the child hesitates more than 3 seconds or is incorrect on any word, tell the child the correct response by saying the word and have him/her write the word three times. Then present the word to the child again.
10) After all the words have been folded in, present the entire group of 10 words three times. Each time the packet of flash cards is shuffled to ensure the child is not just memorizing the sequence of responses. The **unknown** words are marked correct or incorrect on the Sight Word/Vocabulary Mastery Tracking Form on page 126. Once an **unknown** word is said correctly *three consecutive times*, it becomes a **new known** word.
11) **New known** words are included in the stack of **known** words and are the *first of the seven* cards selected from the **known** words stack the next time the Folding-In intervention is conducted. If the child hesitates for more than 3 seconds or provides an incorrect response for a **known** word, follow the steps below:
    a) Tell the child the correct response and have him/her write the word three times.
    b) Present the word to the child again.
    c) At the end of the Folding-In session, add the word to the **unknown** stack.

d) Add the word to the Sight Word/Vocabulary Mastery Tracking Form or, if the word is already on the Sight Word/Vocabulary Mastery Tracking Form, erase or strikethrough the "Mastered?" column to indicate the word is not yet mastered.

12) Have the child graph the number of new words learned using the Folding-In Data Chart on page 127 following the last Folding-In intervention session each week.

Sequence for Presenting Unknown and Known Words

U= Unknown Word; 1U = 1st Unknown Word, 2U = 2nd Unknown Word, 3U = 3rd Unknown Word, etc.

K= Known Word; 1K = 1st Known Word, 2K = 2nd Known Word, 3U = 3rd Known Word, etc.

Round	Sequence of Presentation
1	1U (Child writes the word on a piece of paper 3 times while saying it aloud three times and then turns over the piece of paper.) 1K
2	1U 1K 2K
3	1U 1K 2K 3K
4	1U 1K 2K 3K 4K
5	1U 1K 2K 3K 4K 5K
6	1U 1K 2K 3K 4K 5K 6K
7	1U 1K 2K 3K 4K 5K 6K 7K
8	Shuffle all 8 flash cards.
9	2U (Child writes the word on a piece of paper 3 times while saying it aloud three times and then turns over the piece of paper.) 1K (1st flash card in the group of shuffled flash cards.)
10	2U 1K 2K
11	2U 1K 2K 3K
12	2U 1K 2K 3K 4K
13	2U 1K 2K 3K 4K 5K
14	2U 1K 2K 3K 4K 5K 6K
15	2U 1K 2K 3K 4K 5K 6K 7K
16	2U 1K 2K 3K 4K 5K 6K 7K 8K
17	Shuffle all 9 flash cards.
18	3U (Child writes the word on a piece of paper 3 times while saying it aloud three timesand then then turns over the piece of paper.) 1K (1st flash card in the group of shuffled flash cards.)
19	3U 1K 2K
20	3U 1K 2K 3K
21	3U 1K 2K 3K 4K
22	3U 1K 2K 3K 4K 5K
23	3U 1K 2K 3K 4K 5K 6K
24	3U 1K 2K 3K 4K 5K 6K 7K
25	3U 1K 2K 3K 4K 5K 6K 7K 8K
26	3U 1K 2K 3K 4K 5K 6K 7K 8K 9K
27	Shuffle all 10 flash cards. Present all 10 flash cards and mark correct or incorrect on the Sight Word/Vocabulary Mastery Tracking Form.
28	Shuffle all 10 flash cards. Present all 10 flash cards and mark correct or incorrect on the Sight Word/Vocabulary Mastery Tracking Form.
29	Shuffle all 10 flash cards. Present all 10 flash cards and mark correct or incorrect on the Sight Word/Vocabulary Mastery Tracking Form.

Adjustments/Modifications

Providing a picture with a word has been found to be even more effective than presenting the word alone. A picture or drawing that represents the word is presented to the right of each word on the flash card. The use of a picture with a word has resulted in faster acquisition with maintenance for three weeks following the intervention compared to a phonics intervention (Baranek, Fienup, & Pace, 2011).

Folding-In can be also be implemented with a pair of peers with each child taking a turn in the interventionist role and the child role. Folding-In has also been successfully implemented as a self-administered intervention (Hulac, Wickerd, & Vining, 2013). Children must be taught the interventionist role and child/student role prior to implementation, and integrity checks of the children implementing the intervention using the Folding-In Sight Words/Vocabulary: Procedural Integrity Checklist should be conducted every two weeks.

References

Baranek A., Fienup D.M., & Pace G. (2011). Brief experimental analysis of sight word interventions: A comparison of acquisition and maintenance of detected interventions. *Behavior Modification, 35(1),* 78-94.

Burns, M. K. (2005). Using incremental rehearsal to increase fluency of single-digit multiplication words with children identified as learning disabled in mathematics computation. *Education and Treatment of Children, 28(3),* 237-249.

Burns, M.K., Dean, V.J., & Foley, S. (2004). Preteaching unknown key words with incremental rehearsal to improve reading fluency and comprehension with children identified as reading disabled. *Journal of School Psychology, 42,* 303-314.

Codding R.S., Archer J., & Connell, J. (2010). A systematic replication and extension using incremental rehearsal to improve multiplication skills: An investigation of generalization. *Journal of Behavioral Education, 19,* 93-105.

Gates, A. (1930). *Interest and ability in reading*. New York: Macmillan.

Gickling, E.E. & Rosenfield, S. (1995). Best practices in curriculum-based measurement. In A. Thomas & J. Grimes (Eds.), *Best practices in school psychology III* (587-95). Bethesda, MD: National Association of School Psychologists

Hulac, D.M., Wickerd, G. & Vining, O. (2013). Interventions: An application of the self-administered folding-in technique. *Rural Special Education Quarterly, 32(2),* 31-36.

Kear, D. J. & Gladhart, M. A. (1983). Comparative study to identify high-frequency words in printed materials. *Perceptual and Motor Skills,* 57 (3): 807.

MacQuarrie, L. L., Tucker, J. A., Burns, M. K., & Hartman, B. (2002). Comparison of retention rates using traditional, drill sandwich, and incremental rehearsal flash card methods. *School Psychology Review, 31(4),* 584–595.

Roberts, M. L., Turco, T., & Shapiro, E. S. (1991). Differential effects of fixed instructional ratios on student's progress in reading. *Journal of Psychoeducational Assessment, 9,* 308-318.

Roberts, M.L. & Shapiro, E.S.(1996). Effects of instructional ratios on students' reading performance in a regular education program. *Journal of School Psychology, 34(1),* 73-91.

Shapiro, E.S. (1996). *Academic skills problems: Direct assessment and intervention* (2nd ed.). New York: The Guilford Press.

Child: ______________________

Sight Word/Vocabulary Mastery Tracking Form

This form is used to track the words the child is attempting to master and the child's performance on the unknown words when presented in the set of known and unknown words in the Folding-In intervention procedures.

Date	Unknown Word	Number of Times Responded Correctly	Mastered? (Responded correctly 3 times)

Folding-In Data Chart

Child Name: ______________________________ Grade: __________

Interventionist: ______________________________

Week	Date	# of Known Words	Week	Date	# of Known Words	Week	Date	# of Known Words
1			7			13		
2			8			14		
3			9			15		
4			10			16		
5			11			17		
6			12			18		

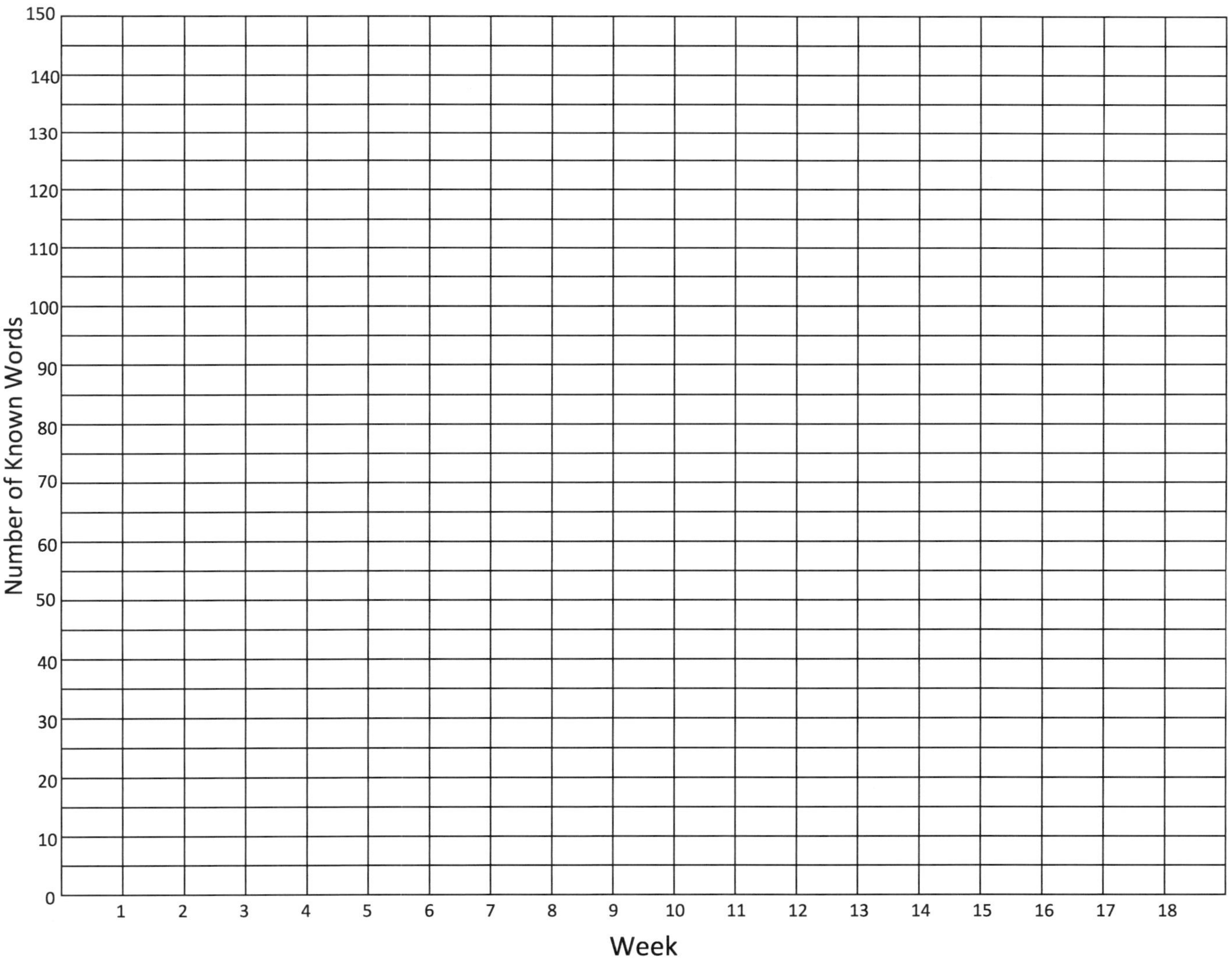

Folding-In Sight Words/Vocabulary: Procedural Integrity Checklist

Age/Grade:	Preschool – High School
Setting:	School, Home, Clinic, In-patient
Individual or Group:	Individual
Tier:	1, 2, & 3
Desired/ Appropriate Behavior:	Fluency with a variety of sight words or sight vocabulary
Skill Level:	Acquisition to maintenance

The procedural integrity checklist is completed by an observer (e.g., principal, assistant principal, school psychologist, treatment specialist, behavior specialist, counselor, lead teacher) who is familiar with the Folding-In Sight Words/Vocabulary procedure. The observer will observe the interventionist implementing the Folding-In procedure and provide feedback. The Folding-In intervention is designed to maximize the number of repetitions of new knowledge within a short period of time (Shapiro, 1996).

Procedure for Integrity Checklist Observer

1) Complete the Procedural Integrity Checklist (see page 130) information about the interventionist, child, location, date, time, observer name, and observer signature.
2) Assess the interventionist's implementation of the Folding-In procedure. An initial observation should occur within the first couple of weeks of an interventionist's implementing the Folding-In procedure so that feedback can be provided to the interventionist early in the implementation.
3) Observe the interventionist for the presence of behaviors 1-6 on the Checklist and mark Yes if present or No if not present. Mark N/O if the behavior is not observed. Marking N/O indicates that the child or the interventionist had the opportunity but did not complete the step.
4) Observe and mark the behaviors for 7-9 on the checklist *only if the child hesitates for more than 3 seconds or provides an incorrect response* in response to the flash card presented. If the child makes an error on a flash card, observe for the behaviors listed in 7-9.
5) Count the number of behaviors marked Yes and write the number on the line for "Number of behaviors marked Yes." If a child makes an error during the Folding-In procedure, the maximum number of behaviors that may be marked Yes is 9; otherwise the maximum number of behaviors marked is 6.
6) Write the total number of behaviors observed (i.e., the total behaviors marked Yes or No) in steps 1-9.
7) Calculate the percent marked Yes. A chart is provided for determining the percent marked Yes. If less than 80% of behaviors are marked Yes, then provide feedback immediately to the interventionist and conduct another observation the next day or as soon as possible.
8) Write any constructive feedback comments in addition to any notations made beside any individual behavior in the "Feedback" section.
9) Provide the interventionist, at an appropriate time, with oral feedback regarding the implementation of the intervention, starting with positive behaviors observed, and a copy of the Folding-In Sight Words/Vocabulary: Procedural Integrity Checklist. *The feedback should be provided the same day of the observation.*

10) Observe the interventionist implementing the Folding-In Sight Words/Vocabulary procedure approximately every other week or twice a month after the initial observation.

Folding-In Sight Words/Vocabulary: Procedural Integrity Checklist

Interventionist: ______________________ Date: __________ Time: __________

Child: ______________________ Observer: ______________________

Location: ______________________ Signature: ______________________

N/O = Not Observed

Behaviors to Observe	Yes	No	N/O	Comments
1) The child selects 3 flash cards from the pile of pre-assessed unknown words and 7 flash cards from the pile of pre-assessed known words.				
2) The interventionist presents a new unknown word to the child, each time by reading the word on the flash card aloud.				
3) The child writes each new unknown word on a piece of paper 3 times while saying it aloud and then turns over the piece of paper.				
4) The interventionist presents the unknown word and the known words following the Sequence for Presenting Unknown and Known Words (page 123).				
5) The interventionist marks the unknown words as correct or incorrect on the Sight Word/Vocabulary Mastery Tracking Form.				
6) Evidence is available that the child is graphing the number of new words learned using the Folding-In Data Chart.				
Only if the child hesitates for more than 3 seconds or provides an incorrect response, mark a response for steps 7 - 9:				
7) The interventionist tells the child the correct response.				
8) The child writes the word 3 times.				
9) The interventionist presents the flash card to the child again.				

Number of behaviors marked Yes = _____ out of _____ = ______ %

Feedback:

Percent

1 out of 6 = 17%	1 out of 9 = 11%
2 out of 6 = 33%	2 out of 9 = 22%
3 out of 6 = 50%	3 out of 9 = 33%
4 out of 6 = 67%	4 out of 9 = 44%
5 out of 6 = 83%	5 out of 9 = 56%
6 out of 6 = 100%	6 out of 9 = 67%
	7 out of 9 = 78%
	8 out of 9 = 89%
	9 out of 9 = 100%

Cover Copy Compare Spelling

Age/Grade:	Elementary – High School
Setting:	School, Home, Clinic, In-patient
Individual or Group:	Individual
Tier:	1, 2, & 3
Desired/ Appropriate Behavior:	Accuracy in spelling words
Skill Level:	Acquisition to generalization

Rationale & Research Support

Cover Copy Compare (CCC) Spelling is an efficient, self-administered intervention in which a child studies a model word, covers the word, writes the word from memory, uncovers the word, and compares the model word to the word as written from memory. CCC employs the evidence-based instructional practices of modeling, active child responding, and immediate corrective feedback. CCC has been found more effective than traditional spelling instruction such as writing a word multiple times (Grskovic & Belfiore, 1996; Hubbert, Weber, & McLaughlin, 2000; Wirtz & Gardner, 1996).

CCC has been studied extensively as documented by a 2012 meta-analysis which found positive results for CCC for spelling, math, and other subjects (Joseph et al., 2012). CCC has been found to be effective with elementary and secondary children, general education children, and a variety of children with disabilities (Joseph et al., 2012; Moser, Fishley, Konrad, & Hessler, 2012; Zielinski, McLaughlin, & Derby, 2012). In addition to acquisition and maintenance of word spelling, CCC has been found to support generalization to spelling words in sentences (Cuvo, Ashley, Marso, Zhang, & Fry, 1995) and reading words in sentences (Cates et al. 2007; Moser, Fishley, Konrad, & Hessler, 2012). While CCC is primarily used as an intervention for spelling or math (see CCC Math on page 75), Smith, Dittmer, and Skinner (2002) report on its effective use in science and Skinner, Belfiore, and Pierce (1992) report on its effective use in geography.

Daily implementation of the CCC Spelling intervention is recommended.

Materials

1) CCC Word Mastery Tracking Form
2) CCC Worksheet
3) CCC Data Chart
4) Index card or blank piece of paper to cover words (optional)

Procedure for Interventionist

Before starting intervention

1) Select words for the child to learn. Write the words on the CCC Word Mastery Tracking Form on page 137. The child will complete 5 to 10 words each day of the CCC intervention. An additional

word from the CCC Word Mastery Tracking Form will be added each time a word is mastered. Therefore, the CCC Word Mastery Tracking Form should list more words than the number the child will be expected to complete each day of the CCC intervention. A word is mastered when the child spells the word correctly on three separate days using the CCC procedure.

2) Prepare an example CCC Worksheet (see page 138) with words written down the left side of the worksheet under the Word column. The example worksheet needs to have only 5 words. The example worksheet should contain words that the child should be able to complete with ease.
3) Prepare a CCC Word Mastery Tracking Form (see page 137) and a CCC Data Chart (see page 139) to use in conjunction with the example CCC Worksheet prepared in step 2.
4) Determine the number of words the child will complete on the CCC Worksheet during the intervention. A total of 5-10 words per day is recommended.
5) Plan for a) when and where the child will complete the CCC intervention and b) how the child will keep track of the materials. One suggested method is to use pocket folders. Place the CCC Data Chart and CCC Word Mastery Tracking Form in the left pocket and ready-to-complete CCC Worksheets in the right pocket. A week's worth of CCC Worksheets could be placed in the right pocket to begin. After a child completes a CCC Worksheet, the completed worksheet can be placed behind the data chart and mastery form in the left pocket with the most recently complete worksheet being the first sheet behind the data chart.

Introducing the procedure

Modeling

1) Inform the child you will be teaching a method, Cover Copy Compare (CCC), for practicing and improving skill in spelling. For example, you might say, "I will be teaching you a new method called Cover Copy and Compare to improve your spelling skills."
2) Provide the child with the example CCC Worksheet.
3) Say to the child, "I am going to demonstrate how to complete a Cover Copy Compare worksheet." Say to the child, "This is an example worksheet, which has only five words for practice. Your actual worksheet will have ____ spelling words."
4) Show the child the first word.
5) Say to the child, "The first step is to look at the model word in the Word column and to say the word aloud and think about how the word is spelled." Say to the child, "I am going to talk out loud so that you will hear me say what you need to be thinking or saying to yourself silently as you review the word. You may move your lips without making a sound if that helps you."
6) Demonstrate thinking through the problem. For example, if the word is "boat," then model saying the word sounding out the phonemes (b ō t) and then saying the letters (b-o-a-t).
7) Say to the child, "The second step is cover or hide the word in the Word column." In advance, decide if the child will fold the worksheet along the line indicated on the worksheet or use an index card to cover the word. If the child is going to fold the worksheet, before the next step show the child the way to properly fold the worksheet to cover the word in the Word column.
8) Demonstrate covering or hiding the word.

9) Say to the child, "The third step is to write the word from memory in the column labeled Copy."

10) Demonstrate writing the word.

11) Say to the child, "The fourth step is to compare the completed spelling word to the covered or hidden word to verify that the word is spelled like the model word. If the word written in the Copy column matches the model word exactly, then make a check mark in the Compare column."

12) Demonstrate writing at least one word matching the model word exactly and making a check mark in the Compare column.

13) Say to the child, "If the word written in the Copy column does not match the model word, then put an X mark in the Compare column and write the word correctly in the Correction column. After you have finished comparing the word and making any correction, then you can move to the next word on the list."

14) Demonstrate writing at least one word that does not match the model word and making an X mark in the Compare column and writing the word in the Correction column by copying the model word in the Word column.

Guided Practice

Continue into guided practice using the example CCC used for modeling.

1) Say to the child, "You are going to complete the next word with my guidance."

2) Ask the child, "What is the first step?" Praise the child for providing the correct response and affirm the first step. For example, you might say, "That's correct. The first step is to say the word and think about how the word is spelled." If the child does not provide the correct step, then state the step again and have the children say the step out loud.

3) Ask the child to say what he or she is thinking as the word is being studied.

4) Ask the child, "What is the second step?" Praise the child for providing the correct response and affirm the response by restating it. If the child do not provide the correct response, then state the step again and have the child say the step out loud.

5) Say to the child, "Complete the second step using the example worksheet."

6) Ask the child, "What is the third step?" Again affirm the correct response and restate the third step.

7) Say to the child, "Complete the third step using the example worksheet."

8) Ask the child, "What is the fourth step?" Again affirm the correct response and restate the fourth step.

9) Say to the child, "Complete the fourth step using the example worksheet."

Independent Practice

1) Say to the child, "Now you are going to complete the next word on your own." Tell the child when to begin.

2) Observe to see that the child is completing the steps in the correct order. Provide immediate corrective feedback for any step the child is not completing in the correct sequence. Provide positive feedback to the child as the steps are completed correctly.

11

Teaching How to Track Progress and Prepare for the Next CCC Session

Using the example CCC used for modeling and guided practice for the following steps.
Note: The interventionist may have to complete the following steps for younger children.

1) Say to the child, "Now I am going to demonstrate how to track your progress."

2) Say to the child, "After you have completed your CCC Worksheet, then you will mark each of the words that has a check mark in the Compare column as correct in the Number of Times Correct column on the CCC Word Mastery Tracking Form. The first time you have a check mark in the Compare column for a word, you will make a check mark in the '1' column. The second time you have a check mark in the Compare column for a word, you will make a check mark in the '2' column. And the third time you have a check mark in the Compare column for a word, you will make a check mark in the '3' column and then write the date that you put a check mark in column 3."

3) Demonstrate reviewing the CCC Worksheet for check marks in the Compare column and putting a check mark in the 1 column on the CCC Word Mastery Tracking Form.

4) Demonstrate making a check mark in the 2 column and the 3 column and writing the date the check mark is made in the 3 column. Explain that the child will to complete at least three separate CCC Worksheets before all three columns will have a check mark.

5) Say to the child, "Now I am going to demonstrate how to prepare for the next time you will do CCC. After you have completed the CCC Worksheet and marked the CCC Word Mastery Tracking Form, you will write the words on a new CCC Worksheet for the next time you will do CCC."

   a) Say, "First, cross through any word in the Word column which was mastered." Demonstrate striking through a word that is mastered.

   b) Say, "Second, write any words that are not crossed out on your current CCC Worksheet on your new CCC worksheet." Demonstrate writing the words that are not crossed out on the current CCC Worksheet on a new CCC Worksheet.

   c) Say, "Third, if your new CCC worksheet has fewer than ___ (insert pre-determined number of words the child will have each CCC session), then add a new word or several new words from the CCC Word Mastery Tracking Form." Demonstrate finding a new word on the CCC Word Mastery Tracking Form and adding the word to the CCC Worksheet.

6) Say to the child, "Now I am going to demonstrate how to chart your progress." Show the child the CCC Data Chart on page 139.

7) Say to the child, "At the end of each week you will count the number of words you mastered that week and write that number on the chart along with the date you record the information on the chart."

8) Demonstrate counting the number of words using the Date Mastered column of the CCC Word Mastery Tracking Form and writing the number of words mastered for a week and the date on the CCC Data Chart. Demonstrate this task for three example weeks, being sure to use appropriate dates for each week.

9) Say to the child, "Next you will mark the number of words mastered on the chart. The y-axis (pointing to the vertical axis) represents the number of mastered words for the week, and the x-axis (pointing to the horizontal axis) represents the number of the week."

10) Demonstrate marking the number of words mastered on the chart for week 1, week 2, and week 3.

11) Demonstrate making a vertical bar from the x-axis to the point marking the number of words mastered for a week. Demonstrate making one or two vertical bars and allow the child to make at least one on the example data chart.

Teaching Daily Classroom Procedures

1) Tell the child how to start and end the CCC session and manage the CCC materials each day.

2) Demonstrate the procedure previously determined in step 4 under Prior to Starting the Intervention above. Demonstrate how to get materials, where to complete the intervention, and how to prepare for the next day. Be sure to include instructions for what the child should do if the CCC worksheet, CCC Word Mastery Tracking Form, and CCC Data chart are completed prior to the end of the intervention time period. For example, the child might work on homework or read a book silently.

Daily Procedure

1) Monitor the child to make sure the daily procedures are being followed. Prompt or cue the child as appropriate if needed. Randomly praise the child for following the procedures. Make sure you are providing praise more frequently than prompting or cueing. If you are finding it difficult to praise more than to prompt or cue, then consider re-instructing the child on the daily procedures.

2) Check the child's CCC worksheet, CCC Word Mastery Tracking Form, and CCC Data Chart to make sure each is being completed correctly. Initially check these forms each day. Provide feedback to the child as necessary. As the child demonstrates accuracy in completing the forms, checks may be conducted less frequently, but at a minimum check once a week.

Adjustments/Modifications

If a child is not demonstrating at least 80% mastery of the words practiced during the CCC Spelling intervention on spelling tests or spelling in sentences, then consider increasing the number of days each word is minimally practiced to at least five. For some children, a variation of CCC in which a child copies a word while looking at the model word before proceeding to cover, copy, and compare may be more effective. Initially copying the word may force a child who is trying to rush through the process to think about the word and letter sequence while directly copying the model word before attempting to write the word from memory. While Erion, Davenport, Rodax, Scholl, & Hardy (2009) found no overall difference been found between rewriting a word during correction once versus three times, one child did show higher rates of retention with rewriting a word three times during correction, so this modification might be implemented for a child not demonstrating at least 80% mastery.

References

Cates, G. L., Dunne, M., Erkfritz., K. N., Kivisto, A., Lee, N., & Wierzbicki, J. (2007). Differential effects of two spelling procedures on acquisition, maintenance, and adaptation to reading. *Journal of Behavioral Education, 16,* 71-82.

Cuvo, A. J., Ashley, K. M., Marso, K. J., Zhang, B. L., & Fry, T. A. (1995). Effect of response practice variables on learning spelling and sight vocabulary. *Journal of Applied Behavior Analysis, 28,* 155-173.

Erion, J., Davenport, C., Rodax, N., Scholl, B., & Hardy, J. (2009). Cover-copy-compare and spelling: One versus three repetitions. *Journal of Behavioral Education, 18,* 319-330.

Grskovic, J. A., & Belfiore, P. J. (1996). Improving the spelling performance of students with disabilities. *Journal of Behavioral Education, 6,* 343-354.

Hubbert, E. R., Weber, K. P., & McLaughlin, T. F. (2000). A comparison of Copy, Cover, and Compare and a traditional spelling intervention for an adolescent with a conduct disorder. *Child & Family Behavior Therapy, 22,* 55-68.

Joseph, L. M., Konrad, M., Cates, G., Vajcner, T., Eveligh, E. & Fishley, K. M. (2012). A meta-analytic review of the cover-copy-compare and variations of this self-management procedure. *Psychology in the Schools, 49,* 122-136.

Moser, L.A., Fishley, K.M., Konrad, M., & Hessler, T. (2012). Effects of the copy-cover-compare strategy on acquisition, maintenance, and generalization of spelling sight words for elementary students with attention deficit/hyperactivity disorder. *Child & Family Behavior Therapy, 34(2),* 93-110.

Skinner, C. H., Belfiore, P. J., & Pierce, N. (1992). Cover, copy, and compare: Increasing geography accuracy in students with behavior disorders. *School Psychology Review, 21,* 73-81.

Smith, T. J., Dittmer, K. I., & Skinner, C. H. (2002) Enhancing science performance in students with learning disabilities using cover, copy, and compare: A student shows the way. *Psychology in the Schools, 39,* 417-427.

Wirtz, C. L. & Gardner, R. (1996). Using self-correction to improve the spelling performance of low achieving third graders. *Remedial and Special Education, 17,* 48-59.

Zielinski, K., McLaughlin, T.F., & Derby, K.M. (2012). The effect of "Cover, Copy, and Compare" on spelling accuracy of high school students with learning disabilities. *American Secondary Education 41(1),* 78-95.

CCC Word Mastery Tracking Form

Name: ______________________

Date: ______________________

This form is used to track the words the child is attempting to master and the child's performance on the words when using the CCC procedures.

Word	Number of Times Correct			Date Mastered
	1	2	3	

CCC Worksheet

Name: ______________________

Date: ______________________

	Word	Copy	Compare	Correction
1)				
2)				
3)				
4)				
5)				
6)				
7)				
8)				
9)				
10)				

Fold

TIER

CCC Data Chart

Name: ______________________________ Grade: __________

Interventionist: ______________________________

Week	Date	# of Mastered Words	Week	Date	# of Mastered Words	Week	Date	# of Mastered Words
1			7			13		
2			8			14		
3			9			15		
4			10			16		
5			11			17		
6			12			18		

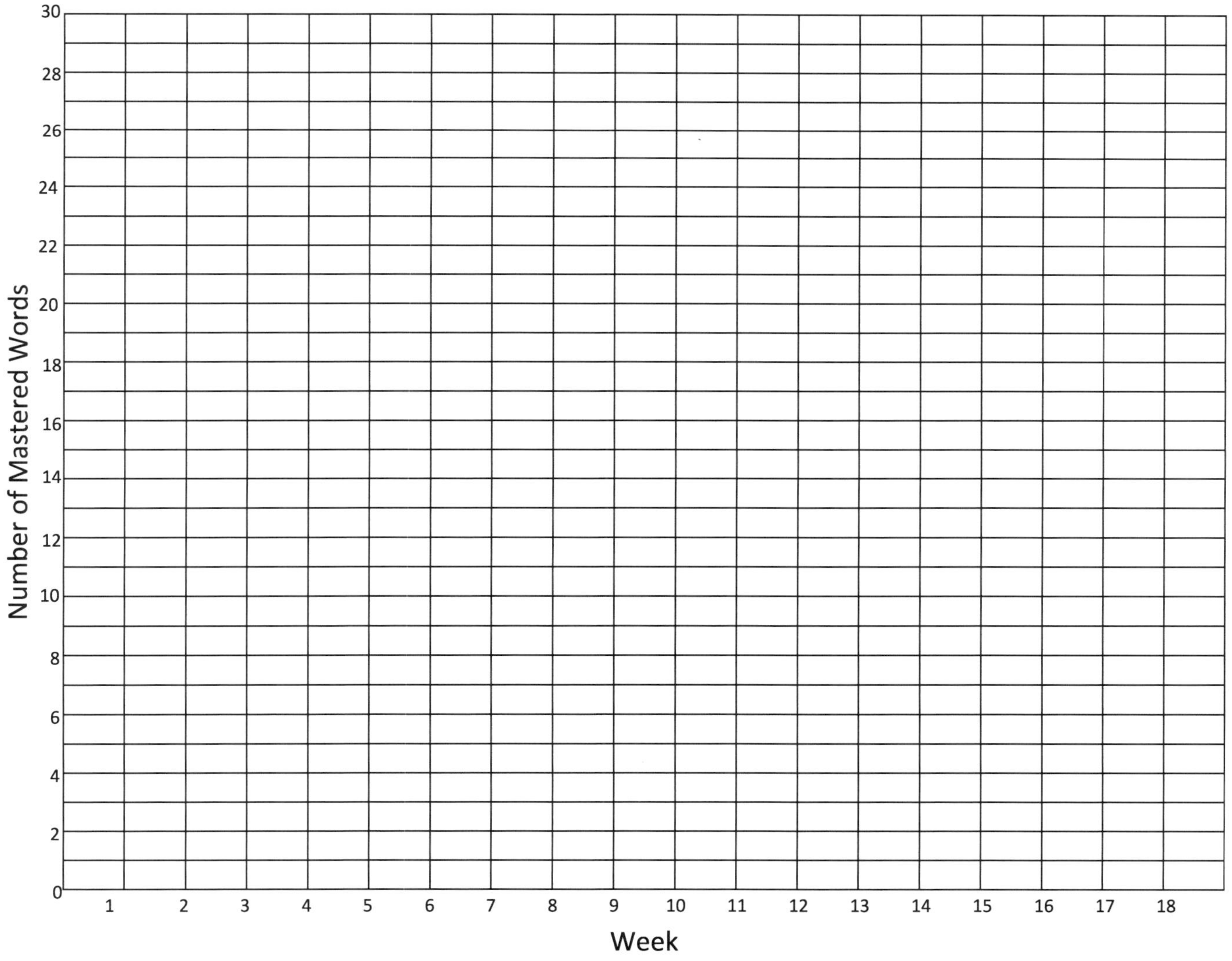

Cover Copy Compare Spelling: Procedural Integrity Checklist

Age/Grade:	Elementary – High School
Setting:	School, Home, Clinic, In-patient
Individual or Group:	Individual
Tier:	1, 2, & 3
Desired/ Appropriate Behavior:	Accuracy in spelling words
Skill Level:	Acquisition to generalization

The procedural integrity checklist is completed by an observer (e.g., principal, assistant principal, school psychologist, treatment specialist, behavior specialist, counselor, lead teacher) who is familiar with the Cover Copy Compare (CCC) Spelling procedure. The observer will observe the interventionist implementing the CCC procedure and provide feedback. CCC Spelling is an efficient, self-administered intervention in which a child studies a target word, covers the word, writes the word from memory, uncovers the word, and compares the target word to the word as written from memory.

Procedure for Integrity Checklist Observer

1) Complete the Procedural Integrity Checklist (see page 141) information about the interventionist, child, location, date, time, observer name, and observer signature.
2) Assess the interventionist's implementation of the CCC procedure. An initial observation should occur within the first couple of weeks of an interventionist's implementing the CCC procedure so that feedback can be provided to the interventionist early in the implementation.
3) Observe for the presence of behaviors 1-7 on the Checklist and mark Yes if present or No if not present. Mark N/O if the behavior is not observed.
4) Count the number of behaviors marked Yes and write the number on the line for "Number of behaviors marked Yes."
5) Write the total number of behaviors observed (i.e., the total behaviors marked Yes or No).
6) Calculate the percent marked Yes. A chart is provided for determining the percent marked Yes. If less than 80% of behaviors are marked Yes, then provide feedback immediately to the interventionist and conduct another observation the next day or as soon as possible.
7) Write any constructive feedback comments in addition to any notations made beside any individual behavior in the "Feedback" section.
8) Provide the interventionist, at an appropriate time, with oral feedback regarding the implementation of the intervention, starting with positive behaviors observed, and a copy of the Cover Copy Compare Spelling: Procedural Integrity Checklist. *The feedback should be provided the same day of the observation.*
9) Observe implementation of the CCC Spelling procedure approximately every other week or twice a month after the initial observation.

Cover Copy Compare Spelling: Procedural Integrity Checklist

Interventionist: ______________________ Date: __________ Time: __________

Child: ______________________ Observer: ______________________

Location: ______________________ Signature: ______________________

N/O = Not Observed

Behaviors to Observe	Yes	No	N/O	Comments
1) The child obtains materials for and starts CCC without prompting by the interventionist.				
2) The child takes time to look at the model word.				
3) The child covers each word before copying the word from memory.				
4) The child compares each word copied from memory to the model word and puts a check mark in the Compare column of the CCC Worksheet if the copied word matches the model word or an X mark if the copied word does not match the model word.				
5) The child copies the model word in the Correction column of the CCC Worksheet if an X is marked in the Compare column.				
6) Evidence is available that the child or interventionist marks the word(s) copied correctly on the CCC Word Mastery Tracking Form.				
7) Evidence is available that the child or interventionist is using the CCC Data Chart to graph the number of new words mastered each week.				

Number of behaviors marked Yes = _____ out of _____ = ______ %

Percent
1 out of 7 = 14%
2 out of 7 = 29%
3 out of 7 = 43%
4 out of 7 = 57%
5 out of 7 = 71%
6 out of 7 = 86%
7 out of 7 = 100%

Feedback:

Word and Sentence Repeat

Age/Grade:	1st-5th Grades
Setting:	School, Home, Clinic, In-patient
Individual or Group:	Individual
Tier:	1, 2, & 3
Desired/ Appropriate Behavior:	Reading with accuracy and fluency; reading comprehension
Skill Level:	Fluency to maintenance

Rationale & Research Support

In Word and Sentence Repeat intervention, when a child hesitates on a word, substitutes, or omits a word, the correct word is provided immediately by an interventionist (also known as immediate corrective feedback), the child repeats the correct word, completes reading the sentence, and then rereads the entire sentence. Reading fluency has been shown to improve reading comprehension (Sindelar, Monda, & O'Shea, 1990). This procedure was found to be more effective than only providing word correction in improving reading accuracy and comprehension. Word and Sentence Repeat has been found to be an effective intervention for children with disabilities (Singh, 1990). Providing children with feedback on their reading behavior improves their task completion (Kastelen, Nickel, & McLaughlin, 1984). Immediate feedback improves motivation of children to perform reading tasks and decreases their frustration (Cottingham, 1993). Word and Sentence Repeat is a one-on-one intervention. This intervention should be conducted each school day for 20 minutes.

Materials

1) Instructional reading level text (i.e., passage, book)
2) Word and Sentence Repeat Interventionist's Checklist
3) Inspect It (I^2) card

Procedure for Interventionist

Prior to Starting Intervention

1) Identify the instructional reading material to use with the child. Use a standardized assessment such as AIMSweb, DRA2, or STAR Reading to aid in identifying a child's instructional level. An instructional level reading text is one in which a child can read 93-97% of the words. Being able to read less than 93% of the words in a text is a frustrational level text and being able to read more than 97% of the words in a text is an independent level text (Gickling & Armstrong, 1978). Reading material should be selected based on the child's reading level and should be of sufficient length to support the child reading for 20 minutes. In most cases, a book will be the best text for this purpose. The text may be fiction or non-fiction. Allow the child to choose reading material in which the child has an interest *and* which is within the child's instructional reading level. Although allowing a child to self-select text based on interest supports motivation and engagement (Johnson

& Blair, 2003; Schraw, Flowerday, & Reisetter, 1998), a child may limit choices without support (Kelley & Clausen-Grace, 2006; Stahl, 2004). Also, reading from a variety of texts increases reading competencies (Kuhn & Stahl, 2000). To support interest and variety, a child will need guidance (Reutzel, Jones, & Newman, 2010; Kelley & Clausen-Grace, 2010). Use of a topic and genre inventory can support identification of a variety of texts that may be of interest to a child (Kelley & Clausen-Grace, 2010). If the child finishes reading a book before meeting the goal level of oral reading fluency, then have the child pick another high-interest book within the child's instructional reading level.

2) Introduce the child to the intervention. Use the Detectives Checklist on page 147 as a reference.
   a) Say to the child, "You are going to read out loud while I follow along. I want you to try to do your best reading. If you come to a word that you do not know, I will help you with it. First, I will tell you the correct word while you listen and point to the word. Second, I want you to repeat the word five times and then read the rest of the sentence. Third, I want you to read the sentence again."
   b) Pause and ask the child to state the three steps.
   c) Then say, "If you make a reading error such as substituting a word or skipping a word, then I will tap the Inspect It card (demonstrate tapping on the card). If you respond by saying the correct word, then you will read the rest of the sentence. If you do not know the word, then I will ask you to do the three steps: 1) listen and point to the word while I say it, 2) repeat the word five times and read the rest of the sentence, and 3) reread the sentence again."
   d) Say to the child, "Try your best to read accurately."
   e) Note that research indicates that child's acquisition of a word is improved by the child saying the word repeatedly. Research indicates that repeating the word five times is the optimal number of times a child should repeat a word (Worsdell, Iwata, Dozier, Johnson, Neidert, & Thomason, 2005).

Intervention

1) Place the Inspect It card facing the child and within the child's visual field (e.g., just above or to the side of the text).
2) Follow along with the text while the child reads out loud. Having a copy of the text to read as the child reads will make following along easier.
3) If the child asks for help with a word or hesitates for 5 seconds, take the following steps:
   a) Say the correct word while the child listens and points to the word in the text.
   b) Prompt the child to repeat the word correctly five times and read the rest of sentence.
   c) Have the child reread the sentence again (prompt if necessary).
   d) Have the child continue reading.
4) When the child substitutes or omits a word, immediately prompt the child to correct the error by tapping the Inspect It card. Point to the word if the child needs assistance in identifying the substituted or omitted word.
   a) *If the child says the correct word*, then the child continues reading.

b) *If the child does not know the word*, take the following steps:

i) Say the correct word while the child listens and points to the word in the text.

ii) Prompt the child to repeat the word correctly five times and read the rest of sentence.

iii) Have the child reread the sentence again (prompt if necessary).

iv) Have the child continue reading.

5) Frequently offer feedback and praise for correct reading.

a) Praise should be specific and descriptive of the task just completed

Examples: Good job! You read all the words correctly.

That was a tough paragraph/page/etc. You did a good job of working through it.

b) Praise should NOT be vague or embarrassing.

Examples: That was good! [Problem: Not specific about what was good]

You tried but you stumbled on a lot of words. [Problem: This statement focuses on the problem the child had rather than on the positive things that the child may have done.]

Adjustments/Modifications

Sometimes a child may ask for help or hesitate on every word that appears "challenging" in order to escape attempting to read the word. If a child frequently asks for help or hesitates in order to have the word provided, then a) increase the amount of time for the hesitation (i.e., wait time), b) remind the child to use reading strategies (e.g., sounding out, context clues, etc.) and attempt the word, or c) a combination of a) and b).

References

Cottingham, B.J. (1993). *An evaluation of immediate corrective feedback in the reading to read intervention*. (Unpublished doctoral dissertation). University of Southern Mississippi, Hattiesburg.

Gickling, E. E. & Armstrong, D. L. (1978). Levels of instructional difficulty as related to on-task behavior, task completion, and comprehension. *Journal of Learning Disabilities, 11,* 559–566.

Johnson, D. & Blair, A. (2003). The importance and use of student self-selected literature to reading engagement in an elementary reading curriculum. *Reading Horizons, 43(3),* 181-202.

Kastelen, L., Nickel, M., & McLaughlin, T. F. (1984). A performance feedback system: Generalization of effects across tasks and time with eighth-grade English students. *Education and Treatment of Children, 7,* 141–155.

Kelley, M.J. & Clausen-Grace, N. (2006). R^5 : The sustained silent reading makeover that transformed readers. *The Reading Teacher, 60(2),* 148–157.

Kelley, M.J. & Clausen-Grace, N. (2010). R^5: A sustained silent reading makeover that works. In E.H. Hiebert & D.R. Reutzel (Eds.), *Revisiting silent reading: New directions for teachers and researchers* (pp. 168-180). Newark, DE: International Reading Association.

Kuhn, M.R. & Stahl, S.A. (2000). *Fluency: A review of developmental and remedial practices.* Ann Arbor, MI: Center for the Improvement of Early Reading Achievement.

Reutzel, D.R., Jones, C.D., & Newman, T.L. (2010). Scaffolded silent reading: Improving the conditions of silent reading practice in classrooms. In E.H. Hiebert & D.R. Reutzel (Eds.), *Revisiting silent reading: New directions for teachers and researchers* (pp. 129-150). Newark, DE: International Reading Association.

Schraw, G., Flowerday, T., & Reisetter, M. (1998). The role of choice in reader engagement. *Journal of Educational Psychology, 90,* 705–714.

Sindelar, P. T., Monda, L., & O'Shea, L. (1990). Effects of repeated readings on instructional- and mastery-level readers. *Journal of Educational Research, 83,* 353–363.

Singh, N.N. (1990). Effects of two error-correction procedures on oral reading errors. Word supply versus sentence repeat. *Behavior Modification, 14(2),* 188-99.

Stahl, S. (2004). What do we know about fluency? In P. McCardle & V. Chhabra (Eds.), *The voice of evidence in reading research* (pp. 187–211). Baltimore: Paul H. Brookes.

Worsdell, A.S., Iwata, B.A., Dozier, C.L., Johnson, A.D., Neidert, P.L., & Thomason, J.L. (2005). Analysis of response repetition as an error-correction strategy during sight-word reading. *Journal of Applied Behavior Analysis, 38(4),* 511-527.

Detective's Checklist

1. Listen to the Reader and follow along in the text.

2. If the Reader asks for help with a word or hesitates for 5 seconds, then…

OR

2. When the Reader substitutes a word or skips a word, then…

Tap the I^2 card

If the Reader does not know the word, then…

If the reader says the correct word, then…

3. Detective Holmes prompts the Reader to continue reading. The Reader continues reading.

3. Detective Holmes says the correct word while the Reader listens and points to the word in the text.
4. Detective Holmes prompts the Reader to repeat the word correctly five times and read the rest of sentence.
5. The Reader rereads the sentence again (prompt if necessary).
6. The Reader continues reading.

TIER

Inspect It (I^2) Card

Directions: Copy this Inspect It (I2) card template on two a piece of paper or card stock and cut out a card for each interventionist. Laminate the card to make the card last longer.

I^2 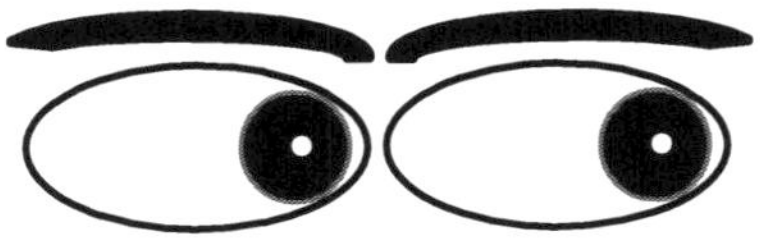 Inspect It	I^2 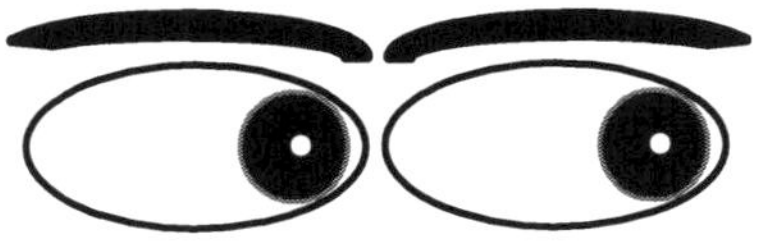 Inspect It
I^2  Inspect It	I^2  Inspect It

TIER

Word and Sentence Repeat: Procedural Integrity Checklist

Age/Grade:	1st-5th Grades
Setting:	School, Home, Clinic, In-patient
Individual or Group:	Individual
Tier:	1, 2, & 3
Desired/ Appropriate Behavior:	Reading with accuracy and fluency; reading comprehension
Skill Level:	Fluency to maintenance

The procedural integrity checklist is completed by an observer (e.g., principal, assistant principal, school psychologist, treatment specialist, behavior specialist, counselor, lead teacher) who is familiar with the daily Word and Sentence Repeat procedure. The observer will observe the interventionist implementing the Word and Sentence Repeat procedure and provide feedback. Word and Sentence Repeat is a one-on-one intervention to improve reading fluency. Improved reading fluency has been shown to affect reading comprehension.

Procedure for Integrity Checklist Observer

1) Complete the Procedural Integrity Checklist (see page 151) information about the interventionist, child, location, date, time, observer name, and observer signature.
2) Assess the interventionist's implementation of the Word and Sentence Repeat procedure. An initial observation should occur within the first couple of weeks of an interventionist's implementing the Word and Sentence Repeat procedure so that feedback can be provided to the interventionist early in the implementation.
3) Observe the interventionist for the presence of behaviors 1-9 on the Checklist and mark Yes if present or No if not present. At a minimum, behaviors 1, 2, and 9 will be observed.
4) Observe and mark the behaviors for 3-6 on the checklist *only if the child asks for help with a word or hesitates for more than 5 seconds*. If the child asks for help or hesitates, mark Yes to indicate that this situation was observed and then observe for the behaviors listed in 3-6. Otherwise, mark No.
5) Observe and mark the behaviors for 7-8 on the checklist *only if the child omits or substitutes a word*. If the child omits or substitutes a word, mark Yes to indicate that this situation was observed and then observe for the behaviors listed in 7-8. Otherwise, mark No.
6) Count the number of behaviors marked Yes and write the number on the line for "Number of behaviors marked Yes."
7) Write the total number of behaviors observed (i.e., the total behaviors marked Yes or No).
8) Calculate the percent marked Yes. A chart is provided for determining the percent marked Yes. If less than 80% of behaviors are marked Yes, then provide feedback immediately to the interventionist and conduct another observation the next day or as soon as possible.
9) Write any constructive feedback comments in addition to any notations made beside any individual behavior in the "Feedback" section.

10) Provide the interventionist, at an appropriate time, with oral feedback regarding the implementation of the intervention, starting with positive behaviors observed, and a copy of the Word and Sentence Repeat: Procedural Integrity Checklist. *The feedback should be provided the same day of the observation.*

11) Observe the interventionist implementing the Word and Sentence Repeat procedure approximately every other week or twice a month after the initial observation.

Word and Sentence Repeat: Procedural Integrity Checklist

Interventionist: ____________________ Date: ____________________

Child: ____________________ Time: ____________________

Location: ____________________ Observer Signature: ____________________

Behaviors to Observe	Yes	No	Comments
At Beginning of Intervention			
1) The interventionist has a quick, efficient procedure for accessing the reading materials for the day (i.e., accessing materials takes less than 1 minute).			
2) The interventionist follows along with the text while the child reads out loud.			
If the child asks for help with a word or hesitates for 5 seconds: Was this observed? __Yes __No			
3) The interventionist says the correct word while the child listens and points to the word in the text.			
4) The interventionist prompts the child to repeat the word correctly five times.			
5) The interventionist prompts the child to read the rest of sentence.			
6) The interventionist prompts (if necessary) the child to reread the sentence again.			
If the child commits a reading error (substitution or omission): Was this observed? __Yes __No			
7) The interventionist prompts the child to correct the error by tapping the Inspect It card.			
8) If the child says the word, the child continues reading. **OR** If the child does not know the word, then the interventionist follows steps 3-6 above			
During or at End of Intervention			
9) The interventionist offers *appropriate, specific, and descriptive* praise for correct reading at least once.			
Observation Totals			
Sum of *numbered* behaviors (1-9) marked Yes			
Sum of *numbered* behaviors Observed (total marked Yes **and** No).			

Number of behaviors marked Yes = _____ out of _____ = ______ %

Feedback:

Percent
1 out of 9 = 11%
2 out of 9 = 22%
3 out of 9 = 33%
4 out of 9 = 44%
5 out of 9 = 56%
6 out of 9 = 67%
7 out of 9 = 78%
8 out of 9 = 89%
9 out of 9 = 100%

Partner Reading

Age/Grade: Elementary – High School

Setting: School, Home, Clinic, In-patient

Individual or Group: Group (2-3 children)

Tier: 1, 2, & 3

Desired/ Appropriate Behavior: Reading fluency; secondary benefits may include increased accuracy, increased reading level, increased vocabulary, and increased comprehension

Skill Level: Fluency

Rationale & Research Support

Partner Reading is a peer-assisted intervention in which children take turns reading and providing support to each other. Partner reading has been utilized as a part of a number of literacy programs including Cooperative Integrated Reading and Composition, Successful for All, Fluency-Oriented Reading Instruction, Peer-Assisted Learning Strategies, and Classwide Peer Tutoring (Fuchs, Fuchs, Mathes, & Simmons, 1997; Madden, Stevens, & Slavin, 1986; Simmons, Fuchs, Fuchs, Hodge, & Mathes, 1994; Slavin & Madden, 2000; Stahl, Holubec, & Crammond, 1997). A number of studies have found positive outcomes associated with partner reading for struggling readers. Positive outcomes associated with partner reading include improved reading accuracy, improved fluency, increased reading level, increased vocabulary, and increased comprehension (Eldredge, 1990; Eldredge & Quinn 1988, MacDonald, 2010; Vaughn et al., 2000). Elbaum, Vaughn, Hughes, Moody, and Schumm (2000) found that pairing children with learning disabilities with peers was more effective than whole class instruction. Partner reading has other benefits such as greater attention, involvement, collaboration, and on-task behavior (Griffin, 2002; Meisinger, Schwanenflugel, Bradley & Stahl, 2004). The time spent in partner reading is generally between 30-40 minutes per session.

Materials

4) Role Cards
5) Inspect It (I^2) card
6) Detective's Checklist

Procedure for Interventionist

Prior to Implementing Intervention

1) Identify the instructional reading material to use with the children performing partner reading. The level of the text will be determined by the level of the lower performing child in each pair. Use a standardized assessment such as AIMSweb, DRA2, or STAR Reading to aid in identifying a child's instructional level. An instructional level reading text is one in which a child can read 93-97% of the words. A text in which a child is able to read less than 93% of the words is a frustrational level text, whereas a text in which a child is able to read more than 97% of the words is an independent level

text (Gickling & Armstrong, 1978). Reading material should be selected based on the child's reading level and of sufficient length to support the child reading for 30-40 minutes depending on the age of the child. In most cases, a book will be the best text for this purpose. The text may be fiction or non-fiction. Allow the reading partners to choose reading material in which they have an interest, if possible, *and* which is within the lower performing child's instructional reading level. Although allowing children to self-select text based on interest supports motivation and engagement (Johnson & Blair, 2003; Schraw, Flowerday, & Reisetter, 1998), children may limit their choices without support (Kelley & Clausen-Grace, 2006; Stahl, 2004). Also, reading from a variety of texts increases reading competencies (Kuhn & Stahl, 2000). To support interest and variety, a child will need guidance (Reutzel, Jones, & Newman, 2010; Kelley & Clausen-Grace, 2010). Use of a topic and genre inventory can support identification of a variety of texts that may be of interest to a child (Kelley & Clausen-Grace, 2010).

2) Pair a higher performing child with a lower performing child based on the standardized assessment used in Step 1 or a similar universal screening measure. For the purpose of the intervention, a higher performing child is one whose reading level is in the top half of the class or group. Research has found that there is greater cooperation when children are allowed to choose a partner rather than being assigned a partner (Meisinger et al., 2004). If you allow partner choice, the lower performing child should choose. You can limit the choice of higher performing children based on which children are most likely to work well together with the lower performing child. Also, be sensitive to children with special learning, social, or emotional needs when assigning pairings.

3) Prepare to assign children to their roles. Each day one child will quietly read the text out loud (the "Reader") while the other child listens and gives assistance and feedback and praise (the "Detective Holmes"). Then the children will switch roles. Each day the first child to serve as Reader will be the higher performing of the pair, and the child serving as Detective Holmes will be the lower performing. The trigger for switching roles should be determined before introducing the intervention to the children and should be based on the age and developmental needs of the children. The trigger for switching roles could be a sentence, a paragraph, a page, or a specified amount of time (generally 5-10 minutes). If using a specified amount of time, use a timer or countdown clock with a bell or other sound to signal children to change roles. Use the role cards provided starting on page 161 to assist switching and monitoring the roles.

   When you have an odd number of children during the regularly scheduled class or when a child is absent, create a group of three children ("triad") for the partner reading. When forming a triad, pair a lower performing child with two higher performing children. When a triad is formed, the first Reader will still be the highest performing of the three children. The teacher will designate the lower performing child to initially serve as Detective Holmes and the other high performing child to serve as Watson. The child in the Watson role will follow the reading of the text and help Detective Holmes, if Holmes does not know a word. Choose the members for the triad carefully to make sure it is a cohesive group. The partner reading cycle for a triad is as follows:

Partner Reading Schedule for Three Children

Child	Role (The roles start over after the 3rd trigger for changing roles.)		
	1st	2nd	3rd
1st Child	Reader	Watson	Detective Holmes
2nd Child	Detective Holmes	Reader	Watson
3rd Child	Watson	Detective Holmes	Reader

It may be helpful to copy this schedule and provide it to the triad or post it for reference for the days when a triad is required.

If the intervention group has an odd number of children, then one triad will be necessary when all children are present. However, because partners or pairs are preferred to triads, the child whose first role is Watson should be designated a "Roving Reader"; the Roving Reader will partner with another child whose partner reader is absent that day. When the Roving Reader leaves the original triad, the two children left in the triad will become partner readers. Choose a "Roving Reader" who can adjust to working with a different partner or group from day to day.

4) Select another adult or a child with which to model the intervention to other children. If selecting a child, a high performing reader would be a good choice. Practice modeling the intervention with the selected individual before modeling the intervention for children participating in the Partner Reading intervention. Before the practice modeling, determine on which words the person playing the Reader will stumble; the Reader will either a) ask for help, b) hesitate for 5 seconds, c) substitute another word, or d) omit the word. Read the Modeling the Procedure section below ahead of time to aid in preparation. For modeling purposes, all the children for whom the modeling is being performed should be able to see the text being used. Projecting the text may be most effective for this purpose.

5) Plan for a) when and where the children will complete the Partner Reading, b) how children will know who starts as the Reader each session, and c) how the children will keep track of the text, role cards, Inspect It (I^2) cards, and Detective's Checklist materials. One suggested method is to use pocket folders to keep the text and Detective's Checklist on one side and role cards and Inspect It (I^2) Cards on the other.

6) Prepare materials for modeling the intervention and for distributing to the participating children. Role cards (starting on page 161), Inspect It (I^2)cards (page 164), and the Detective's Checklist (page 165) will be needed.

Modeling the Procedure

1) Inform the children you will be teaching a method, Partner Reading, for practicing and improving skill in reading. For example, you might say, "I will be teaching you a new method called Partner Reading to improve your reading skills."

Say, "______________ (name of adult or child assisting with modeling) will be helping me demonstrate Partner Reading."

2) Say and hold up or point to the materials, "You will be using the following materials for Partner Reading: role cards, Inspect It cards, and the Detective's Checklist."

3) Say, "Most of the time you will work as a pair with one person being the Reader (point to or show the Reader role card) and one person being Detective Holmes (point to or show the Detective Holmes role card). The Reader's job is to read his or her best. The Detective Holmes' role is to assist the Reader if he or she asks for help with a word, hesitates for 5 seconds, substitutes a word, or omits a word. If there is third person in your group, then that person will have the role of Watson (point to or show the Watson role card), and his or her job will be to help Detective Holmes."

4) Say, "_______________ (name of adult or child assisting with modeling) and I are going to model Partner Reading for you. _____________ will be the Reader, and I will be Detective Holmes. The Reader will read the text doing his/her best. If the Reader comes to an unknown word and asks for help or gets stuck and hesitates for 5 seconds on a word, I, Detective Holmes, will help with the word. First, I will tell the Reader the correct word while the Reader listens and points to the word. Second, the Reader will repeat the word five times and then read the rest of the sentence. Third, the Reader will read the sentence again."

Note that research indicates that child's acquisition of a word is improved by the child saying the word repeatedly. Research indicates that repeating the word five times is the optimal number of times a child should repeat a word (Worsdell, Iwata, Dozier, Johnson, Neidert, & Thomason, 2005).

5) Pause and ask the children being trained, "What are the three steps when the Reader comes to an unknown word?" The children should chorally respond with something like, "First, the Reader listens and points to the word while Detective Holmes says the word. Second, the Reader repeats the word five times and reads the rest of the sentence. Third, the Reader reads the sentence again." Praise children for providing the correct response and affirm the three steps. For example, you might say, "That's correct. "First, the Reader listens and points to the word while Detective Holmes says the word. Second, the Reader repeats the word five times and reads the rest of the sentence. Third, the Reader reads the sentence again." If the children do not provide the correct steps, then state the steps again and have the children say the steps out loud. For younger children or if the children are having difficulty remembering the steps, then consider providing the Detective's Checklist on page 165 to aid the children in remembering the steps.

6) Demonstrate the procedure with the adult or child serving as the Reader reading the text and asking for help with an unknown word and hesitating for five seconds on a word. The Reader should not demonstrate asking for help and hesitating for 5 seconds using consecutive sentences.

7) Say, "If the Reader makes a reading error such as substitutes a word or skips a word, then I will tap the Inspect It (I^2) card (demonstrate tapping on the card). If the Reader responds by saying the correct word, then the Reader will read the rest of the sentence. If the Reader does not know the word, then I, Detective Holmes, will ask the Reader to do the three steps: 1) listen and point to the word while I say it; 2) repeat the word five times and read the rest of the sentence; and 3) reread the sentence."

8) Pause and ask the children being trained, "What does Detective Holmes do if the Reader substitutes or skips a word?" The children should respond with something like, "Detective Holmes taps the Inspect It (I^2) card, and the Reader tries to correct the mistake." Praise children for providing the correct response and affirm the response by restating it. If the children do not provide the correct

response, then state the steps again and have the children say the steps out loud after each step. For younger children or if the children are having difficulty remembering the steps, then consider providing the Detective's Checklist on page 165 to aid the children in remembering the steps.

9) Demonstrate the procedure with the adult or child serving as the Reader reading the text and substituting or skipping a word. Do not demonstrate substituting and skipping words using consecutive sentences.

10) Say, "Now we are going to demonstrate switching roles. When the Reader reaches __________ (state the trigger for switching roles that was predetermined in Step 3 of Prior to Starting Intervention), we will switch roles. When we switch roles, we will also switch roles cards like this _________ (demonstrate switching role cards in a way that is quick and quiet such as sliding the cards on the desk or table)."

11) Demonstrate the procedure with the adult or child serving as the Reader reading the text and then switching roles with Detective Holmes when the trigger is reached. Demonstrate switching roles 2-3 times depending on the duration until the next trigger.

12) Say, "Remember, most of the time you will work as a pair with one person being the Reader and one person being Detective Holmes. Sometimes you may be in a group of three. In a a group of three, the third person will have the role of Watson, and his or her job will be to help Detective Holmes. I will show you how to switch roles if you are in a group of three."

13) Say, "Partners also need to give each other feedback and praise for correct reading. When the Reader reaches _____________ (the end of a page, end of five minutes of reading, etc.), then Detective Holmes will provide specific praise and positive feedback. Specific praise and positive feedback should be specific and descriptive of the task just completed."

"An example of praise is 'Good job! You read all the words correctly.'"

An example of positive feedback is 'That was a tough paragraph/page/etc. You did a good job of working through it.'"

"Praise should NOT be vague or embarrassing."

"An example of vague praise is 'That was good!'" (Problem: Praise was not specific about what was good).

"An example of negative feedback is 'You tried, but you stumbled on a lot of words.'" (Problem: This statement focuses on the problem the Reader had rather than on the positive things that the Reader may have done.)

Ask the children being trained, "Can you provide an example of specific praise or positive feedback?" Affirm correct examples provided by any children. If a child provides a non-example of praise or feedback, then praise the child for trying and, if possible, either ask the children how the praise or feedback could be specific and positive or restate the praise or feedback so that it is specific and positive.

Daily Procedure

Monitor the partners to make sure the Partner Reading procedures are being followed. Prompt or cue the children as appropriate if needed. Randomly praise children for following the procedures. Make sure you are providing praise more frequently than prompting or cueing. If you are finding it difficult to praise more than prompt or cue, then consider re-instructing the children on the procedures.

Adjustments/Modifications

1) Sometimes the Reader child may ask for help or hesitate on every word that appears "challenging" in order to escape attempting to read the word. If the Reader child frequently asks for help or hesitates in order to have the word provided, then instruct the child with the Detective Holmes role to a) increase the amount of time for the hesitation (i.e., wait time), b) remind the Reader to use reading strategies (e.g., sounding out, context clues, etc.) and attempt the word, or c) a combination of a) and b).
2) If increasing comprehension is a concern, then introduce a time for asking questions into the procedure. The trigger for the question time could be a sufficient amount of text, such as a page or two, or an amount of time, such as 5 or 10 minutes). The question time should be 2-5 minutes in length. During question time, the child with the Detective Holmes role will ask the Reader who, what, where, when, and why questions. Below are some examples of questions children might ask each other:

    What do you think the main idea is?

    How would you summarize what we read in one sentence?

    Who are the characters in the story? Describe each one.

    What did you think would happen, or what did you think the text would be about before we started reading based upon the title, pictures, etc.?

    What was the order of events in the text that was read today?

    What do you think will happen next?

    Why do you like or not like this part of the story/article?

   Consider leading children in brainstorming general questions that they can use following the reading. These questions should then be posted some place that is easily visible for all children to reference.

If reading accuracy is a greater concern than fluency, introduce a word acquisition component into the procedure. MacDonald (2010) describes such a procedure. In such a procedure, unknown words are studied, and word features such as vowel blends, prefixes, suffixes or tenses are discussed. Unknown words are recorded on a worksheet in the first column, and then the word is written, broken into syllables in the second column, and then the Reader practices orally saying each part of the word and then putting all the parts together. The worksheet has ten additional columns to record each time the Reader reads the word. If an unknown word is read correctly, a check mark is made; if a word is read incorrectly, an X is made. A few minutes before the end of the intervention session, the worksheet of unknown words is reviewed. If the Reader has read an unknown word correctly five times consecutively, that word is considered known and is no longer tracked. If the Reader was not able to read a word correctly five times consecutively out of ten possible attempts, the word is placed on a new unknown word worksheet and tracked for another ten attempts. Alternatively, unknown words could be made part of a Folding-In Sight Words/Vocabulary intervention (see page 119) to supplement the

Partner Reading. It may be helpful to provide children with a reference sheet of common vowel blends, prefixes, and suffixes.

References

Elbaum, B., Vaughn, S., Hughes, M., Moody, S. W., & Schumm, J. S. (2000). How reading outcomes of students with disabilities are related to instructional grouping formats: A meta-analytic review. In R. Gersten, E. Schiller, & S. Vaughn (Eds.), *Contemporary special education research* (pp. 105-135). Mahwah, NJ: Erlbaum.

Eldredge, J. L. (1990). Increasing the performance of poor readers in the third grade with a group-assisted strategy. *Journal of Educational Research, 84 (2),* 69-77.

Eldredge, J. L. & Quinn, D.W. (1988). Increasing reading performance of low-achieving second graders with dyad reading groups. *Journal of Educational Research, 82(1),* 40-46.

Fuchs, D., Fuchs, L.S., Mathes, P.G., & Simmons, D.C. (1997). Peer-assisted learning strategies: Classrooms more responsive to diversity. *American Educational Research Journal, 34(1),* 174-206

Gickling, E. E., & Armstrong, D. L. (1978). Levels of instructional difficulty as related to on-task behavior, task completion, and comprehension. *Journal of Learning Disabilities, 11,* 559–566.

Griffin, M. L. (2002). Why don't you use your finger? Paired reading in first grade. *The Reading Teacher, 55,* 766-774.

Johnson, D. & Blair, A. (2003). The importance and use of student self-selected literature to reading engagement in an elementary reading curriculum. *Reading Horizons, 43(3),* 181-202.

Kelley, M., & Clausen-Grace, N. (2006). R^5 : The sustained silent reading makeover that transformed readers. *The Reading Teacher, 60(2),* 148–157.

Kelley, M.J. & Clausen-Grace, N. (2010). R^5: A sustained silent reading makeover that works. In E.H. Hiebert & D.R. Reutzel (Eds.), *Revisiting silent reading: New directions for teachers and researchers* (pp. 168-180). Newark, DE: International Reading Association.

Kuhn, M.R. & Stahl, S.A. (2000). *Fluency: A review of developmental and remedial practices.* Ann Arbor, MI: Center for the Improvement of Early Reading Achievement.

Madden, N. A., Stevens, R. J., & Slavin, R. E. (1986, November). *Reading instruction in the mainstream: A cooperative learning approach* (Technical Report No. 5). Baltimore, MD: Johns Hopkins University, Center for Research on Elementary and Middle Schools.

McDonald, P. (2010). Paired reading: A structured approach to raising attainment in literacy. *Support for Learning, 25(1),* 16-23.

Meisinger, E.B., Schwanenflugel, P.J., Bradley. B.A., & Stahl, S.A. (2004). Interaction quality during partner reading. *Journal of Literacy Research, 36(2),* 111-140

Reutzel, D.R., Jones, C.D., & Newman, T.L. (2010). Scaffolded silent reading: Improving the conditions of silent reading practice in classrooms. In E.H. Hiebert & D.R. Reutzel (Eds.), *Revisiting silent reading: New directions for teachers and researchers* (pp. 129-150). Newark, DE: International Reading Association.

Schraw, G., Flowerday, T., & Reisetter, M. (1998). The role of choice in reader engagement. *Journal of Educational Psychology, 90,* 705–714.

Simmons, D. C., Fuchs, D., Fuchs, L. S., Hodge, J. P., & Mathes, P. G. (1994). Importance of instructional complexity and role reciprocity to classwide peer tutoring. Learning Disabilities Research and Practice, 9, 203-212.

Slavin, R. E., & Madden, N. A. (2000). Research on achievement outcomes of Success for All: A summary and response to critics. *Phi Delta Kappan, 82,* 38-40, 59-66.

Stahl, S. (2004). What do we know about fluency? In P. McCardle & V. Chhabra (Eds.), *The voice of evidence in reading research* (pp. 187–211). Baltimore: Paul H. Brookes.

Stahl, S. A., Holubec, K., & Crammond, B. (1997). *Fluency oriented reading instruction* (Reading Report No. 79). Athens, GA: National Reading Research Center, University of Georgia.

Vaughn, S., Chard, D. J., Bryant, D. P., Coleman, M., Tyler, B., Linan-Thompson, S., & Kouzekani, K. (2000). Fluency and comprehension interventions for third-grade students. Remedial and Special Education, 21, 325-335.

Worsdell, A.S., Iwata, B.A., Dozier, C.L., Johnson, A.D., Neidert, P.L., & Thomason, J.L. (2005). Analysis of response repetition as an error-correction strategy during sight-word reading. *Journal of Applied Behavior Analysis, 38(4),* 511-527.

Role Cards - Reader

Directions: Copy the role cards using a different color for each role: Reader, Holmes, and Watson. Cut out the cards for use by the reading partners. Few or no "Watson" cards may be needed. Laminate the cards to make the cards last longer.

Reader

Reader

Reader

Reader

Role Cards – Detective Holmes

Detective

Holmes

Detective

Holmes

Detective

Holmes

Detective

Holmes

Image used with permission from Microsoft.

Role Cards – Watson

Watson

Watson

Watson

Watson

Image used with permission from Microsoft.

Inspect It (I^2) Card

Directions: Copy this Inspect It (I^2) card template onto a piece of paper or card stock and cut out a cards. Laminate the card to make the card last longer.

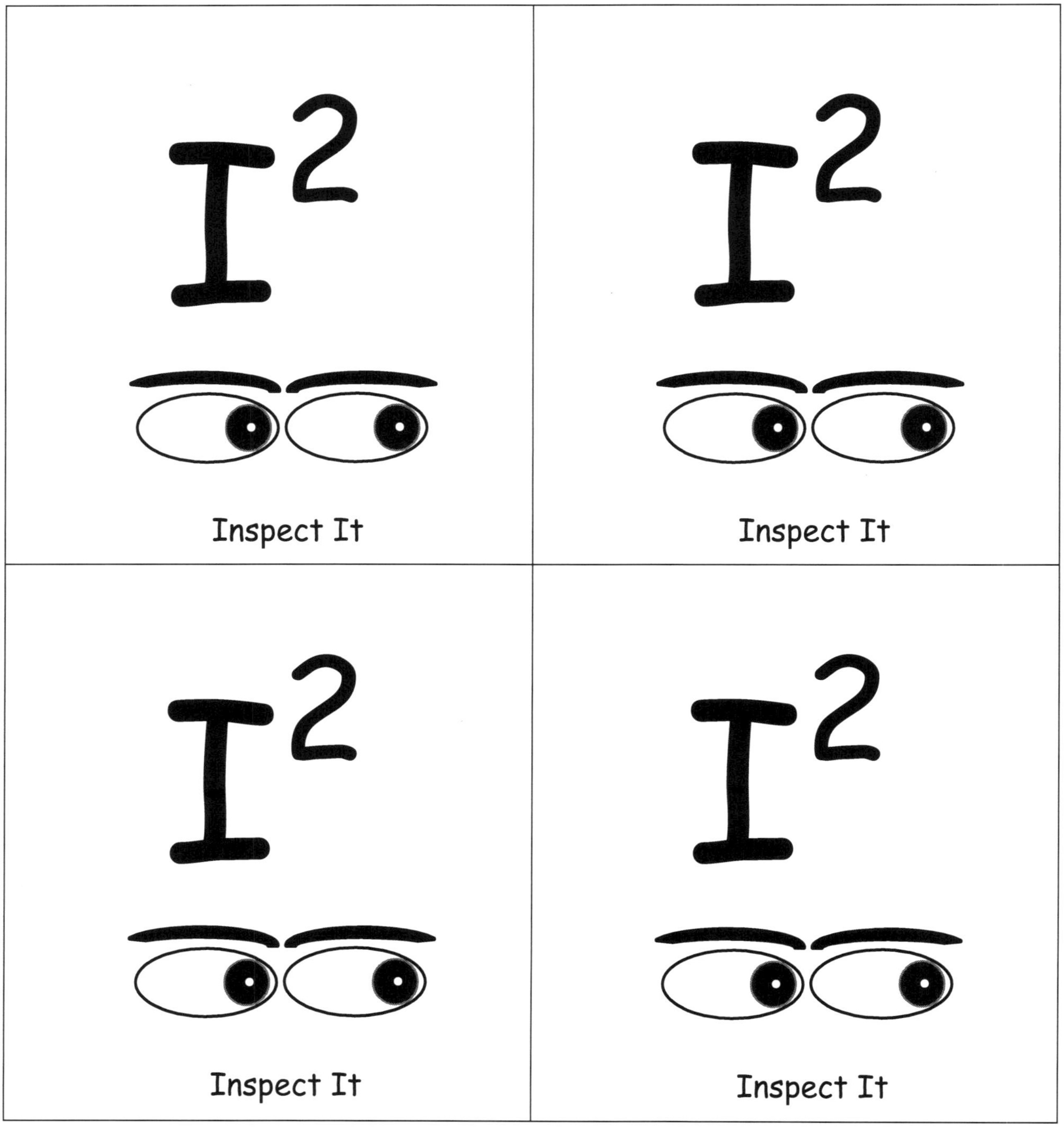

Detective's Checklist

2. Listen to the Reader and follow along in the text.

2. If the Reader asks for help with a word or hesitates for 5 seconds, then...

OR

2. When the Reader substitutes a word or skips a word, then...

Tap the I^2 card

If the Reader does not know the word, then...

If the reader says the correct word, then...

3. Detective Holmes prompts the Reader to continue reading. The Reader continues reading.

3. Detective Holmes says the correct word while the Reader listens and points to the word in the text.
4. Detective Holmes prompts the Reader to repeat the word correctly five times and read the rest of sentence.
5. The Reader rereads the sentence again (prompt if necessary).
6. The Reader continues reading.

Partner Reading: Procedural Integrity Checklist

Age/Grade:	Elementary – High School
Setting:	School, Home, Clinic, In-patient
Individual or Group:	Group (2-3 children)
Tier:	1, 2, & 3
Desired/ Appropriate Behavior:	Reading fluency; secondary benefits may include increased accuracy, increased reading level, increased vocabulary, and increased comprehension
Skill Level:	Fluency

The procedural integrity checklist is completed by an observer (e.g., principal, assistant principal, school psychologist, treatment specialist, behavior specialist, counselor, lead teacher) who is familiar with the Partner Reading procedure. The observer will observe the interventionist and children implementing the Partner Reading procedure and provide feedback. Partner Reading is peer-to-peer intervention to improve reading fluency. Improved reading fluency has been shown to affect reading comprehension.

Procedure for Integrity Checklist Observer

1) Complete the Procedural Integrity Checklist (see page 168) information about the interventionist, child, location, date, time, observer name, and observer signature.
2) Assess the interventionist's implementation of the Partner Reading procedure. An initial observation should occur within the first couple of weeks of an interventionist's implementing the Partner Reading procedure so that feedback can be provided to the interventionist early in the implementation.
3) Observe the interventionist for the presence of behaviors 1-9 on the Checklist and mark Yes if present or No if not present. At a minimum, behaviors 1, 2, and 9 will be observed.
4) Observe and mark the behaviors for 3-6 on the checklist *only if a child asks for help with a word or hesitates for more than 5 seconds*. If a child asks for help or hesitates, mark Yes to indicate that this situation was observed and then observe for the behaviors listed in 3-6. Otherwise, mark No.
5) Observe and mark the behaviors for 7-8 on the checklist *only if a child substitutes or skips a word*. If a child substitutes or skips a word, mark Yes to indicate that this situation was observed and then observe for the behaviors listed in 7-8. Otherwise, mark No.
6) Count the number of behaviors marked Yes and write the number on the line for "Number of behaviors marked Yes."
7) Write the total number of behaviors observed (i.e., the total behaviors marked Yes or No).
8) Calculate the percent marked Yes. A chart is provided for determining the percent marked Yes. If less than 80% of behaviors are marked Yes, then provide feedback immediately to the interventionist and conduct another observation the next day or as soon as possible.
9) Write any constructive feedback comments in addition to any notations made beside any individual behavior in the "Feedback" section.

10) Provide the interventionist, at an appropriate time, with oral feedback regarding the implementation of the intervention, starting with positive behaviors observed, and a copy of the Partner Reading: Procedural Integrity Checklist. *The feedback should be provided the same day of the observation.*

11) Observe the interventionist and children implementing the Partner Reading procedure approximately every other week or twice a month after the initial observation.

Partner Reading: Procedural Integrity Checklist

Interventionist: ______________________ Date: ______________________

Group: ______________________ Time: ______________________

Location: ______________________ Observer Signature: ______________________

Behaviors to Observe	Yes	No	Comments
At Beginning of Intervention			
1) The interventionist has a quick, efficient procedure for children to access the Partner Reading materials for the day (i.e., accessing materials takes less than 1 minute).			
2) The child designated as Detective Holmes (or Watson) with a role card follows along with the text while the child designated as the Reader reads out loud.			
If the Reader asks for help with a word or hesitates for 5 seconds: Was this observed? __Yes __No			
3) The Detective Holmes (or Watson) says the correct word while the Reader listens and points to the word in the text.			
4) The Reader repeats the word correctly five times.			
5) The Reader reads the rest of sentence.			
6) The Reader rereads the sentence again.			
If the child commits a reading error (substituting or skipping): Was this observed? __Yes __No			
7) The Detective Holmes (or Watson) prompts the Reader to correct the error by tapping the Inspect It (I^2) card.			
8) If the Reader says the word, the Reader continues reading. **OR** If the Reader does not know the word, then Detective Holmes (or Watson) follows steps 3-6 above			
During or at End of Intervention			
9) The child designated as Detective Holmes (or Watson) offers *appropriate, specific, and descriptive* praise for correct reading or positive feedback at least once.			
Observation Totals			
Sum of *numbered* behaviors (1-9) marked Yes			
Sum of *numbered* behaviors Observed (total marked Yes **and** No).			

Number of behaviors marked Yes = _____ out of _____ = ______ %

Feedback:

Percent
1 out of 9 = 11%
2 out of 9 = 22%
3 out of 9 = 33%
4 out of 9 = 44%
5 out of 9 = 56%
6 out of 9 = 67%
7 out of 9 = 78%
8 out of 9 = 89%
9 out of 9 = 100%

Semantic Mapping

Age/Grade:	3rd Grade – High School
Setting:	School, Home, Clinic, In-patient
Individual or Group:	One or more people
Tier:	1, 2, & 3
Desired/ Appropriate Behavior:	Concept and vocabulary development , support for reading fluency and comprehension
Skill Level:	Acquisition to maintenance

Rationale & Research Support

Research supports the use of explicit vocabulary instruction for children in all grade levels and content areas (Kamil et al., 2008). In fact, research indicates that children may learn only about 15 percent of vocabulary through reading (Swanborn & de Glopper, 1999). Relating a new word to existing words positively influences the speed of learning vocabulary (Hoover & Storkel, 2005).

Semantic mapping is a visual strategy for vocabulary expansion and extension of knowledge by displaying words related to one another in categories. Semantic mapping is an adaptation of concept definition mapping but builds on children's prior knowledge. While semantic mapping draws on prior knowledge, it recognizes important components and shows the relationships among the components. Semantic mapping is a very dynamic process, one that the teacher should model first before using it as an intervention. Semantic mapping may be used before, during, and after reading to promote reading comprehension.

Materials

1) Semantic Map handout
2) Key vocabulary/concept word(s)
3) Expository or informational text, dictionary, thesaurus (optional)

Procedure for Interventionist

Prior to Lesson

1) Select words from a text that reflect the concepts to be learned prior to the lesson (e.g., a vocabulary word or concept that is foundational to future knowledge or can be easily generalized to other words or concepts).
2) Determine whether the selected word or concept is one that will be new to children or one for which they are likely to have prior knowledge. If the selected word or concept is new, then follow the **During the Lesson – New Word or Concept** (starting on page 170). If the selected word or concept is one for which children likely have prior knowledge, then follow the lesson procedure for **During the Lesson – Prior Knowledge Word or Concept** (starting on page 171).

3) Review the appropriate blank semantic map (page 175 or 176). When modeling the steps, determine if the semantic map will be drawn on the board or projected or otherwise shown to children.

4) Identify which steps might be difficult with your struggling children. Write down how you are going to modify (differentiate) the steps, word, concept, and/ or activities for your children as needed.

During the Lesson – New Word or Concept

1) **Model** the following steps.
    a) Write the target word on the board or other visual image of the map (see page 175 for example).
    b) Provide children with a copy of the semantic map.
    c) Explain and/or give children a written copy of the steps involved in completing the map. Ask children to complete their map as you model the steps for them.
    d) Model writing the definition of the word or concept.
    e) Model identifying and/or defining the part of speech and writing it in the appropriate location on the map. Children should have been introduced to parts of speech prior to implementing this intervention. If introducing a word using a part of speech new to children, provide direct instruction on the part of speech before using the word with semantic mapping.
    f) Model brainstorming as many synonyms as you can for the target word. You may also ask for input from children.
    g) Model brainstorming as many antonyms as you can for the target word. You many also ask for Input from children.
    h) Model writing a sentence using the target word.
    i) Model drawing a picture to represent the target word.
2) Provide **guided practice** using the following steps.
    a) Write the target word on the board or other visual image of the map.
    b) Provide children with a copy of the semantic map (see page 175 for example). Ask children to complete their map as the group completes the map together.
    c) Ask children to describe the steps involved in completing the semantic map. At a minimum, their responses should include the following steps.
        i) Writing the target word
        ii) Defining the word
        iii) Identifying the part of speech
        iv) Identifying synonyms
        v) Identifying antonyms
        vi) Drawing a picture to represent the target word
    d) Aid the children in writing the definition of the target word or concept.

e) Ask children to identify the part of speech for the target word.

f) Ask children to think of synonyms for the target word. Write the words provided by children in a list separate from the semantic map. Review the list of words. If any of the words are not synonyms, provide children feedback as to why the word is not an appropriate synonym and cross it off the list. Copy the final list of synonyms to the synonyms box on the map.

g) Ask children to think of antonyms for the target word. Write the words provided by children in a list separate from the semantic map. Review the list of words. If any of the words are not antonyms, provide children feedback as to why the word is not an appropriate antonym and cross it off the list. Copy the final list of antonyms to the antonyms box on the map.

h) Ask children to think of a sentence in which they could use the target word. Allow approximately 20-30 seconds for children to think. Children may need to write the sentence to aid them. Ask a child to share her sentence by calling on a volunteer or by random selection. If a child shares a sentence that incorrectly uses the target word, provide children feedback as to why the sentence is not appropriate and either show to change the sentence to make the sentence correct or call on another child.

i) Ask children to think of a way to visually represent the target word. Allow approximately 20-30 seconds for children to think. Ask a child to share an idea for a visual representation, calling on a volunteer or randomly selecting a child. Ask the child to explain the why she chose the visual representation.

j) Discuss with children how semantic mapping might be used prior, during, or after reading a text.

3) Provide **independent practice** using the following steps.

a) Put children in groups to construct a semantic map for a target word that they will be encountering in text or other materials later in the period or in the near future. Groups should be composed of a high performing child, a low performing child, and two middle performing children.

b) Provide children with a semantic map (see page 175 for example) or provide a visual template for them to copy. All children should complete a semantic map to have for individual reference following the group independent practice session.

c) Encourage children to use their own knowledge to complete the semantic map. Let children know what resources they may access in their group if they need help in completing the map.

d) As groups work, move around the room to monitor work. Provide modeling or guided practice to the groups as necessary to insure the children are correctly completing the semantic map.

e) After the groups have had an appropriate amount of time to complete the map, call on groups to present their map or parts of their map to the group.

f) Discuss with the children how the semantic map might be expanded or revised to reflect new information they learned.

During the Lesson – <u>Prior Knowledge</u> Word or Concept

1) **Model** the following steps.

a) Write the target word on the board or other visual image of the map (see page 176 for example of a bubble map).

b) Provide children with a copy of the semantic bubble map.

c) Explain and/or give children a written copy of the steps involved in completing the map. Ask children to complete their map as you model the steps for them.

d) Model brainstorming and writing a list of as many related or associated words as you can for the target word. You may also ask for input from children.

e) Put the words into categories (e.g., body parts, food, enemies, properties, forms, etc.) grouped into bubbles around the target word. Label the category for each bubble. Check or strikethrough the words on the brainstormed list as they are placed into a category bubble.

f) Review the target word and each of the bubbles. Add any words that should be added to a category.

g) Review the categories. Add any category that should be included. Add any associated words for the new category.

2) Provide **guided practice** using the following steps.

a) Write the target word on the board or other visual image of the bubble map (see page 176 for example).

b) Provide children with a copy of the semantic bubble map. Ask children to complete their map as the class completes the map together.

c) Ask the children to describe the steps involved in completing the semantic map. At a minimum, responses should include the following steps.

i) Writing the target word

ii) Brainstorming related or associate words

iii) Placing the words into categories

iv) Review the bubble map to see if there are any words or categories to be added

d) Ask children to brainstorm as many related or associated words as they can for the target word. Write the words provided by children in a list separate from the semantic bubble map. Review the list of words. If any of the words are not related, provide children feedback as to why the word is not an appropriate related or associated word and cross it off the list.

e) Ask children to assist in categorizing the words. Start with the first word on the list and ask children in which category they would the put the word. Provide the children guidance in naming the category if necessary. Write the word in one of the bubbles and write the category for the bubble. Check or strikethrough the word on the brainstormed list.

f) Ask children if they can find other words on the list that fit in the same category. Write any of the appropriate words from the list in the category bubble and check or strikethrough each word on the list as words are added to the bubble. Once children exhaust words to add to the category, move to the next step.

g) Move to the first word on the list that has not been crossed off and ask children in which category they would the put the word. Provide the children guidance in naming the category if necessary. Write the word in one of the bubbles and write the category for the bubble. Check or strikethrough the word on the list.

h) Repeat steps 6 and 7 until all words are checked or struck through on the list.

i) Ask children to review the target word and each of the bubbles. Ask children if any words should be added to any of the categories (allow children 20-30 seconds to think). Add any appropriate words provided by the children to the appropriate category.

j) Ask children if any categories should be added to the map (allow children 20-30 seconds to think). If the category is appropriate, add a bubble for the category and ask children for words related to the target word that belongs in that category. If a category suggested by children is not appropriate, provide children feedback as to why the category is not appropriate.

k) Ask children to review their map and to make sure they have updated their copy of the map to reflect the complete work of the class.

l) Discuss with children how semantic mapping might be used prior, during, or after reading a text.

3) Provide **independent practice** using the following steps.

a) Put children in groups to construct a semantic bubble map. Groups should be composed of a high performing child, a low performing child, and two middle performing children.

b) Ask children to work together in one of these two ways:

i) Work as a group to complete a semantic bubble map for an assigned target word that they will be encountering in text or other materials later in the class period or in the near future.

OR

i) Work as group to read an assigned text.

ii) Identify key words in the text.

iii) Create a semantic bubble map for each key word.

c) Provide children with a semantic bubble map (see page 176 for example) or provide a visual template for them to copy. All children should complete a semantic bubble map that they will have for individual reference following the class session.

d) Encourage children to use their own knowledge to complete the semantic map. Let children know what resources they may access in their group if they need help in completing the map.

e) As groups work, move around the room to monitor work. Provide modeling or guided practice to the groups as necessary.

f) After the groups have had an appropriate amount of time to complete the map, call on groups to present their map or parts of their map to the group.

g) Discuss with the children how the semantic map might be expanded or revised to reflect new information they learn.

References

Kamil, M. L., Borman, G. D., Dole, J., Kral, C. C., Salinger, T., & Torgesen, J. (2008). *Improving adolescent literacy: Effective classroom and intervention practices: A Practice Guide* (NCEE #2008-4027). Washington, DC: National Center for Education Evaluation and Regional Assistance, Institute of Education Sciences, U.S. Department of Education. Retrieved from http://ies.ed.gov/ncee/wwc.

Hoover, J.R. & Storkel, H.L. (2005). Understanding word learning by preschool children: Insights from multiple tasks, stimulus characteristics, error analysis. *ASHA Perspectives on Language Learning and Education, 12(3),* 8-12.

Swanborn, M. S. L. & de Glopper, K. (1999). Incidental word learning while reading: A meta-analysis. *Review of Educational Research, 69(3),* 261–85.

Semantic Map
New Word or Concept

Definitions

Part of speech

Draw a picture to represent the **target word**

Target Word

Synonyms

Use the **target word** in a sentence

Antonyms

Semantic Map

Prior Knowledge
Word or Concept

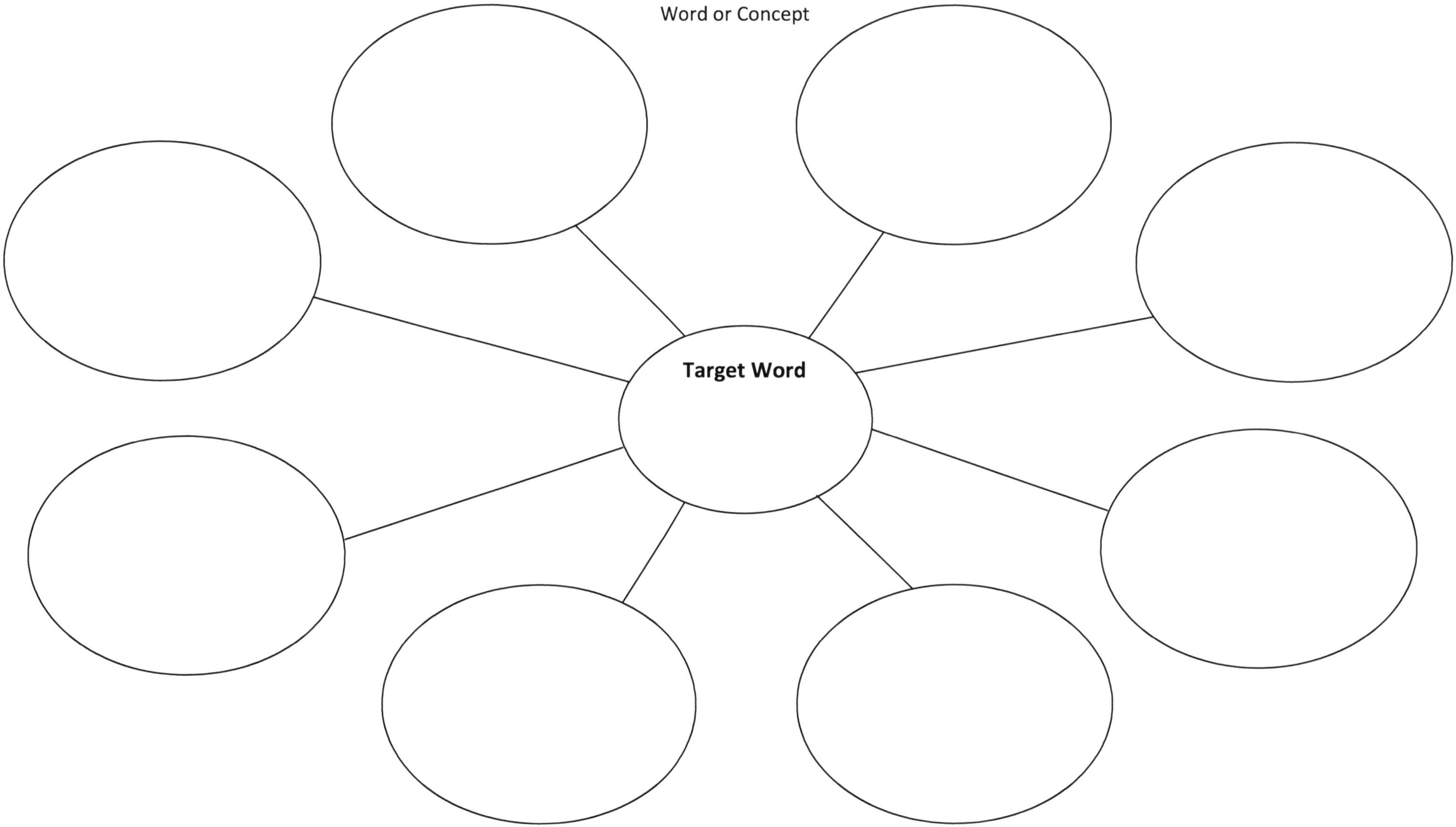

TIER

Semantic Mapping: Procedural Integrity Checklist

Age/Grade:	3rd grade – High School
Setting:	School, Home, Clinic, In-patient
Individual or Group:	One or more people
Tier:	1, 2, & 3
Desired/ Appropriate Behavior:	Concept and vocabulary development , support for reading fluency and comprehension
Skill Level:	Acquisition to maintenance

Semantic mapping is a visual strategy for vocabulary expansion and extension of knowledge by displaying words related to one another in categories. The procedural integrity checklist is completed by an observer (e.g., principal, assistant principal, school psychologist, treatment specialist, behavior specialist, counselor, lead teacher) who is familiar with the Semantic Mapping procedure. The observer will observe the individual interventionist implementing the Semantic Mapping procedure and provide feedback. Separate checklists are used, one for semantic mapping of a new word or concept and one for semantic mapping of a prior knowledge word or concept.

Procedure for Integrity Checklist Observer

1) Select the appropriate Procedural Integrity Checklist for the observation. Select either the checklist for New Word or Concept or Prior Knowledge Word or Concept (see page 179 or 180).
2) Determine a time to observe when the interventionist will be *modeling* the Semantic Mapping procedure.
3) Complete the Procedural Integrity Checklist information about the interventionist, group, location, date, time, observer name, and signature.
4) Assess the interventionist's modeling of the Semantic Mapping procedure. An initial observation should occur within the first of week of an interventionist's implementing the Semantic Mapping procedure so that feedback can be provided to the interventionist early in the implementation.
5) Observe the interventionist for the presence of behaviors on the appropriate Checklist and mark Yes if present or No if not present.
6) Count the number of behaviors marked Yes and write the number on the line for "Number of behaviors marked Yes."
7) Write the total number of behaviors observed (i.e., the total behaviors marked Yes or No).
8) Calculate the percent marked Yes. A chart is provided for determining the percent marked Yes. If less than 80% of behaviors are marked Yes, then provide feedback immediately to the interventionist and conduct another observation the next day or as soon as possible.
9) Write any constructive feedback comments in addition to any notations made beside any individual behavior or in the "Feedback" section.

10) Provide the interventionist, at an appropriate time, with oral feedback regarding the implementation of the intervention, starting with positive behaviors observed, and a copy of the Procedural Integrity Checklist. *The feedback should be provided the same day of the observation.*

Semantic Mapping: Procedural Integrity Checklist
New Word or Concept

Interventionist: ______________________ Date: __________ Time: __________

Group: ______________________ Observer: ______________________

Location: ______________________ Signature: ______________________

Behaviors to Observe	Yes	No	Comments
1) The interventionist writes the target word/concept for the children to see.			
2) The interventionist provides a semantic map handout or models construction of the map for the children.			
3) The interventionist explains the semantic map steps to the children.			
4) The interventionist writes the definition of the word or concept on the map.			
5) The interventionist models identifying and/or defining the part of speech and writes it in the appropriate location on the map.			
6) The interventionist models brainstorming synonyms for the target word. Input from children also may be solicited.			
7) The interventionist models brainstorming antonyms for the target word. Input from children also may be solicited.			
8) The interventionist models writing a sentence using the target word.			
9) The interventionist models drawing a picture to represent the target word.			

Number of behaviors marked Yes = _____ out of _____ = ______ %

Feedback:

Percent
1 out of 9 = 11%
2 out of 9 = 22%
3 out of 9 = 33%
4 out of 9 = 44%
5 out of 9 = 56%
6 out of 9 = 67%
7 out of 9 = 78%
8 out of 9 = 89%
9 out of 9 = 100%

Semantic Mapping: Procedural Integrity Checklist

Prior Knowledge Word or Concept

Interventionist: ______________________ Date: __________ Time: __________

Group: ______________________ Observer: ______________________

Location: ______________________ Signature: ______________________

Behaviors to Observe	Yes	No	Comments
1) The interventionist writes the target word/concept for the children to see.			
2) The interventionist provides a semantic map handout or models construction of the map for the children.			
3) The interventionist explains the semantic map steps to the children.			
4) The interventionist models brainstorming and/or asks children to think of words associated with the target word/concept.			
5) The interventionist guides children in grouping the associated words into categories on the semantic map. The interventionist labels each category.			
6) The interventionist guides children in reviewing the target word/concept and each of categories (bubbles). The interventionist adds words to categories or categories to the map as appropriate.			

Number of behaviors marked Yes = _____ out of _____ = ______ %

Feedback:

Percent
1 out of 6 = 17%
2 out of 6 = 33%
3 out of 6 = 50%
4 out of 6 = 67%
5 out of 6 = 83%
6 out of 6 = 100%

Behavior Interventions

Active Supervision of Non-Structured Settings

Age/Grade:	Preschool – High School
Setting:	School, In-patient
Individual or Group:	Group
Tier:	1
Desired/ Appropriate Behavior:	Increase in pro-social behaviors, appropriate behaviors in unstructured settings
Skill Level:	Fluency to maintenance

Rationale & Research Support

While much attention is paid to classroom management or group management as well as individual children, non-classroom settings and other transition settings are also crucial with regard to child behavior. Non-classroom and transition settings include such locations as the hallway, cafeteria, playground, gym, bus, and other areas where children transition or gather. These settings are typically characterized by a large number of children with few adult supervisors; they are unstructured in nature and typically characterized by an abundance of social interaction (Sugai & Horner, 2002). Based on these characteristics, it is not surprising that 50% of problem behavior in schools occurs in non-classroom areas. The research on active supervision and pre-correction appear to effectively reduce problem behavior in non-classroom settings (Colvin, Sugai, Good, & Lee, 1997; De Pry & Sugai, 2002; Lewis, Colvin, & Sugai, 2000).

Procedure for Interventionist

There are seven components of active supervision that have been adapted by Johnson-Gros, Lyons, and Griffin (2008).

1) Arrive at the designated post on time. *Arriving at a designated post on-time* is defined as the interventionist and/or other personnel (teachers, assistants, assistant principals, etc.) should be at the designated post (e.g., right outside the door in the hallway, at designated location) within 20 seconds after the designated prompt (e.g., bell) or time (e.g., 7:50 a.m.). It is good practice to have a backup person assigned to each post in the event of an individual's absence.
2) Be present at the designated post throughout the transition. *Present at a post* is defined as the interventionist being present in the post area for the duration of the transition/supervision time.
3) Move towards congregating groups of children as needed. *Moving towards congregating groups of children* is defined as the interventionist physically moving into proximity of a group of children (i.e., within 2-4 feet) without leaving designated post area.
4) Escort children through the areas as necessary. *Escorting* is defined as personnel accompanying or guiding children through the area. Escorting can be accomplished by physical prompts such as moving arms along or verbal prompts such as, "Keep moving."
5) Scan the area as children move through. *Scanning* is defined as the interventionist turning their head and looking back and forth over the area to be supervised.
6) Interact positively with children. *Positive interacting* is defined as brief positive nonverbal and verbal interactions with children (e.g., smiling, greetings, gestures, and prompting). The goal at all

times is to have more positive interactions with children than negative or corrective interactions. At the beginning of the day, it is especially important that children are greeted with enthusiasm and that the interventionist strives to create an atmosphere of "we are excited that you are here today."

- Greeting can include statements such as “Good morning!,” “Good day!,” “Glad to see you!,” “Welcome” (etc.)
- Gesture can include physical gestures to indicate to children to keep moving such as thumbs up, etc.
- Prompting includes brief verbal interactions such as statements about appropriate behaviors (e.g., “Thank you for walking.”).
- Refrain from asking questions as questions will increase interactions and decrease other important behaviors (i.e., scanning, escorting, etc.).
- Physical interaction (e.g., pat on the back, handshake) should be kept to a minimum since this increases interaction and impedes movement.

7) If interaction with other adults is necessary, the interaction should be brief. *Interacting briefly with other adults* is defined as the interventionist remaining in their post area without lengthy interactions with other adults walking through the area. Brief communication (approximately 5 –10 seconds) is acceptable.

References

Colvin, G., Sugai, G., Good, R. H., & Lee, Y. (1997). Using active supervision and pre-correction to improve transition behaviors in an elementary school. *School Psychology Quarterly, 12,* 344-363.

De Pry, R. L. & Sugai, G. (2002). The effect of active supervision and pre-correction on minor behavioral incidents in a sixth grade general education classroom. *Journal of Behavioral Education, 11,* 255-267.

Johnson-Gros, K. N., Lyons, E. A., & Griffin, J. R. (2008). Reducing excessive tardies using PBS in a high school. *Education and Treatment of Children,31,*39-53.

Lewis, T. J., Colvin, G., & Sugai, G. (2000). The effects of pre-correction and active supervision on the recess behavior of elementary students. *Education and Treatment of Children, 23*, 109-121.

Sugai, G. & Horner, R. (2002). The evolution of discipline practices: School-wide positive behavior supports. *Psychology in the Schools, 24,* 23-50.

Active Supervision of Non-Structured Settings: Procedural Integrity Checklist

Age/Grade:	Preschool – High School
Setting:	School, In-patient
Individual or Group:	Group
Tier:	1
Desired/ Appropriate Behavior:	Increase in pro-social behaviors, appropriate behaviors in unstructured settings.
Skill Level:	Fluency to maintenance

Active Supervision was designed as a preventive approach to the management of non-classroom or transition setting behaviors. The checklist is designed to take one minute for each person observed. Depending on the layout of the building or grounds, more than one person could be observed during a transition period (e.g., arrival of children to school, class change, moving of children from one location to another etc.). One checklist is provided that can be used to observe up to four individuals during one observation. A second checklist is provided that can be divided into two for providing individual observations and feedback.

Procedure for Interventionist

All seven components of active supervision are measured during each integrity check. Use the checklist to record these observations.

1) Choose a location for observation (e.g., hallway, cafeteria, playground, etc.) either based on data that indicate a "trouble" spot or general facility-wide implementation. In the general school-wide or facility-wide implementation, the observer can randomly choose a particular location to observe.
2) Obtain a list of the personnel and their designated posts and backup personnel in case of absences for the targeted location.
3) Select personnel (teachers, assistants, assistant principals, supervisors, direct care staff, etc.) for observation. The number of personnel selected for observation is based upon the transition time or the location. The observer can randomly choose the personnel. For example, a school has four hallways and a breezeway where children can be observed moving during class changes. Each hallway has eight staff, and the breezeway has four staff. The observer may have randomly chosen the second hallway. Because there are eight personnel to observe, the observer must randomly choose the four staff to observe.
4) An observer who is familiar with the procedures (e.g., principal, assistant principal, school psychologist, treatment specialist, behavior specialist, counselor, lead teacher) completes the Procedural Integrity Checklist (see page 187) information about the location, date, time, and observer's name.
5) List the names of personnel on the integrity checklist.
6) Stand in or near the location (i.e., hallway, playground, break area, and cafeteria) in view of the personnel to be observed during the transition.
7) When the defined prompt is signaled (e.g., bell finishes ringing for class to be dismissed), start the timing device (e.g., stopwatch) to assess the component, *On-Time*. Circle "Y" for Yes, the individual was on time. Circle "N" for No, the individual was not on time.

8) After the first 20 seconds when the observation for arriving at the designated post on-time is complete for all personnel being observed, use a momentary time sampling procedure (see Conducting Direct Observations) in one minute increments for each person until the allotted time or the activity is over (e.g., bell to end class change, recess, lunch).

   At the beginning of each one minute interval, the observer looks for the components for that one person being observed and marks which components are present or not. For example, the observer is observing four personnel during transition from one class period to the next. The transition period is 5 minutes. The observer observes in the first 20 seconds after the defined signal (e.g. bell ringing) the four personnel to see if they arrive at their post within the 20 seconds. Then, after the first minute is up, the observer observes the first person on the integrity checklist. The observer looks up at the beginning of the second minute and observes the remaining six components (i.e., at post, escorting, moving, scanning, and interacting) and circles "Y" for Yes or "N" for No. Two components may not be observed because they were not necessary: Moves to Groups and Interacting Briefly with Adults. If one or both of these components is not observed because the component was not necessary, then the observer circles "N/O" for Not Observed. Then, the observer repeats the steps at the next minute for the next person until all four personnel observations have been conducted.

9) Count the number of behaviors marked Yes and write the number on the line for "Number of behaviors marked Yes."

10) Write the total number of behaviors observed (i.e., the total behaviors marked Yes and No).

11) Calculate the percent marked Yes. A chart is provided for determining the percent marked Yes. If less than 80% of behaviors are marked Yes, then provide feedback immediately to the interventionist and conduct another observation the next day or as soon as possible.

12) Write any constructive feedback comments in addition to any notations made beside any individual behavior in the "Feedback" section.

13) Provide the personnel, at an appropriate time, with oral feedback regarding the implementation of the intervention, starting with positive behaviors observed, and a copy of the Active Supervision: Procedural Integrity Checklist. *The feedback should be provided the same day of the observation.*

14) Observe personnel implementing the Active Supervision approximately every other week or twice a month after the initial observation. At an appropriate time following each observation, provide the personnel individually with oral feedback regarding their active supervision, starting with positive behaviors observed, and a copy of the Procedural Integrity Checklist data. *The feedback should be provided the same day of the observation.*

    An individual feedback report is provided. Note that the page is formatted to provide two individual feedback reports per page to conserve paper. The individual feedback report can be used to conduct the observation if the observer is observing only one or two individuals at a time.

15) After the initial observation, if the observer finds an individual is correctly implementing all components of active supervision, then the observer should observe that individual implementing the active supervision of non-classroom settings on the regularly scheduled observation. If the observer finds that an individual is not correctly implementing all components of active supervision, then the observer should conduct another observation as soon as possible, preferably the next day to provide additional feedback.

Active Supervision of Non-Structured Settings

Procedural Integrity Checklist

Location: ______________________ Date: ____________ Time: ____________

Observer: ______________________ Signature: ______________________

N/O = Not Observed

Personnel Name	Post On Time	At Post	Moves to Groups	Escorting	Scanning	Positive Interaction w/ Children	Interacting Briefly with Adults
	Y N	Y N	Y N N/O	Y N	Y N	Y N	Y N N/O
Personnel Name	**Post On Time**	**At Post**	**Moves to Groups**	**Escorting**	**Scanning**	**Positive Interaction w/ Children**	**Interacting Briefly with Adults**
	Y N	Y N	Y N N/O	Y N	Y N	Y N	Y N N/O
Personnel Name	**Post On Time**	**At Post**	**Moves to Groups**	**Escorting**	**Scanning**	**Positive Interaction w/ Children**	**Interacting Briefly with Adults**
	Y N	Y N	Y N N/O	Y N	Y N	Y N	Y N N/O
Personnel Name	**Post On Time**	**At Post**	**Moves to Groups**	**Escorting**	**Scanning**	**Positive Interaction w/ Children**	**Interacting Briefly with Adults**
	Y N	Y N	Y N N/O	Y N	Y N	Y N	Y N N/O

Notes:

Active Supervision of Non-Classroom Settings

Procedural Integrity Checklist – Individual Feedback Report

Location: ______________________ Date: __________ Time: __________

Observer: ______________________ Signature: ______________________

N/O = Not Observed

Personnel Name	Post On Time	At Post	Moves to Groups	Escorting	Scanning	Positive Interaction w/ Children	Interacting Briefly with Adults
	Y N	Y N	Y N N/O	Y N	Y N	Y N	Y N N/O

Feedback:

Active Supervision of Non-Classroom Settings

Procedural Integrity Checklist – Individual Feedback Report

Location: ______________________ Date: __________ Time: __________

Observer: ______________________ Signature: ______________________

N/O = Not Observed

Personnel Name	Post On Time	At Post	Moves to Groups	Escorting	Scanning	Positive Interaction w/ Children	Interacting Briefly with Adults
	Y N	Y N	Y N N/O	Y N	Y N	Y N	Y N N/O

Feedback:

Behavior Contract

Age/Grade:	Preschool – High School
Setting:	Home, School, Clinic, In-patient
Individual or Group:	One or more people
Tier:	1, 2, & 3
Desired/ Appropriate Behavior:	Homework completion, academic performance, reduction in office referrals, home responsibilities (e.g., chores)
Skill Level:	Fluency to maintenance

Rationale & Research Support

A behavior contract is a document that describes in writing the relationship between completed behaviors or tasks of one or two parties and the delivery or access to a predetermined reinforcer or reward to the person(s) for the occurrence or nonoccurrence of the behaviors or tasks. Behavior contracts have a long established history of increasing a myriad of academic performance-related behaviors across many age groups (Bristol & Sloane, 1974; Kelley & Stokes, 1982, 1984; Wilkson, 2003). Welch and Holborn (1988) also demonstrated that caregivers, if given good procedures, could implement behavior contracts and experience good outcomes (increase in home related behaviors) for adolescents.

Materials

1) Self-Identification of Possible Tasks (List 1)
2) Group Identification of Possible Tasks (List 2)
3) Self-Identification of Possible Rewards (List 3)
4) Contract

Procedure for Interventionist

These procedures are adapted and modified from the works of Cooper, Heron, and Heward (2007) and Miltenberger (2008). In writing a behavior contract, one needs to consider several things. First, all parties need to consider what type of contract will be developed, either a one party or two party contract. A detailed explanation of the types of contracts is provided below. Second, the behavior contract has three required components: 1) behavior/tasks, 2) rewards, 3) record of behavior/tasks. Finally, when developing a contract, all parties need to be able to negotiate the "terms" of the contract. If only one party draws up the contract and expects the other party to agree without any negotiation, then the document is not by definition a contract. For the best likelihood that the negotiation will be successful, follow the steps outlined below.

Contract Types

As previously stated, there are two types of contracts, one party contracts and two party contracts. In a *one party contract*, one person (contractor) desires to change behavior(s) of another party (contractee) and designs rewards or punishers with a contract manager, who implements the consequences. Generally, the goal is to increase an appropriate or desirable behavior or decrease an inappropriate or undesirable behavior of one person. The contract manager is the person who will deliver or provide access to the reward or punisher. The contract manager cannot gain anything from the contractual obligations. In addition, when the contract manager is someone who is personally involved with the contractee, it may be difficult to implement or deliver the consequences because the manager and/or contractee may have negative emotional responses from the interaction. Either manager or contractee may be upset or angry when the person either has to deliver a punishing consequence or withhold a reward. Therefore, the recommendation is that, if possible, the manager be someone who does not have a personal relationship with the contractee.

Two party contracts exist when two people (e.g., siblings, parent-child, spouses, coworkers, etc.) want to identify/change (increasing or decreasing) behaviors or tasks and agree upon the related consequences, rewards and/or punishers. The two types of two party contracts are *quid pro quo* contracts and parallel contracts. A *quid pro quo* contract simply states that one person will do something in return for the other person doing something. Problems may arise when one person does not display desired behavior(s) or complete the task(s) and the other person does. Thus, the two parties can decide to develop a parallel contract, which entails identifying behaviors or tasks and consequences that are not interrelated. For example, one party can complete his or her behavior(s) successfully and obtain his or her reward while the other party does not complete his or her behavior(s) successfully and does not obtain his or her reward. Each person's behavior is not contingent on the other person's behavior.

Components

The three essential components to a behavior contract are the behaviors/tasks, rewards, and a record of the behaviors/tasks.

1) The behaviors/tasks part of the contract consists of four elements listed below.
    a) Specify who will or will not perform the behavior/task (i.e., usually the contractee but it may be both the contractee and the contractor).
    b) Identify the behavior/task that will be performed or that will not be performed.
    c) Specify a beginning and end for the behavior/task. For example, how long should the behavior occur or how much time should pass without the occurrence of the behavior? By when does the behavior/task have to be demonstrated?
    d) Determine how well the task(s) or behavior(s) should be performed; that is, provide a criterion or criteria for what is means to "perform" the behavior or task. A checklist may be useful in presenting the behaviors or tasks in a sequential order such as a task analysis or a checklist with the criterion for successful completion.

Example of a Task Analysis or Checklist

Getting Ready for Math Class (Circle 1 for Excellent, 2 for Good, and 3 for Poor)

Day/Task	Clear your desk of unnecessary items.			Place your math book, a pencil, and your calculator on your desk.			Wait quietly for the instructor to begin class.		
Monday	1	2	3	1	2	3	1	2	3
Tuesday	1	2	3	1	2	3	1	2	3
Wednesday	1	2	3	1	2	3	1	2	3
Thursday	1	2	3	1	2	3	1	2	3
Friday	1	2	3	1	2	3	1	2	3

2) The reward part of the contract consists of four elements listed below.

   a) Identify the person who will evaluate the completion of the task(s) or behavior(s).

   b) Identify the reward or punishment.

      i) Positive Reinforcement: If an appropriate or desirable behavior is displayed/performed, then a reward is provided to increase the likelihood of the behavior recurring.

      ii) Negative Reinforcement: If an appropriate or desirable behavior is displayed/performed, then an aversive task, event, etc. is removed or prevented to increase the likelihood of the behavior recurring.

      iii) Positive Punishment: If an inappropriate or undesirable behavior is displayed/performed, then a punisher is provided to decrease the likelihood of the behavior recurring.

      iv) Negative Punishment: If an inappropriate or undesirable behavior is displayed/performed, then a reward is lost to decrease the likelihood of the behavior recurring.

   c) Determine when the reward or punishment will be delivered or given. The reward needs to be delivered *as soon as it is feasible to do so* but after the task(s) or behavior(s) have been successfully completed.

   d) Determine the amount or duration of the reward or punishment. For example, if free time is the reward, then specify the amount of free time (e.g., 15 minutes).

3) The completion of the behavior(s) or task(s) and the delivery of the reward(s) must be recorded on an official task record. The task record can be a checklist if multiple behaviors or tasks are to be completed. The task record can also display multiple time periods (hourly, morning/afternoon, class periods, or daily) if the behavior or task must be exhibited during multiple time periods for the reward to be given. An example of a task record is provided below.

Example Task Record 1: John will be ready (standing by the front door) at 7:40am at 100% for 4 out of 5 days.

	Monday	Tuesday	Wednesday	Thursday	Friday
Out of bed by 7:00am					
Eat breakfast					
Brush teeth					
Brush hair					
Get dressed					
Have all materials for school					
Are all tasks completed on time?	Yes No	Yes No	Yes No	Yes No	Yes No

Example Task Record 2: John will have all homework completed to show his teacher by the end of 1st period (5 minutes before the bell rings) at an 80% completion rate for the week.

	Monday	Tuesday	Wednesday	Thursday	Friday
Homework	Yes No	Yes No	Yes No	Yes No	Yes No

Steps

Five steps must be followed in developing a behavior contract. These steps are designed to help in the negotiation process. When working with a child, an adult (e.g., teacher, caregiver, parent, etc.) can make all the decisions without any input from the child. However, if all parties can agree to the terms of the contract and can see the benefits from the contract, then adherence and integrity to the contract is more likely if all parties participate in developing the contract. Therefore, older children and adolescents can frequently engage in the negotiation process. The steps outlined below were first described by Dardig and Heward (1981). The contract manager will lead the parties through these steps.

1) The team holds a meeting. All parties (the team) that will be a part of the contract will meet, including the contract manager, contractor, and contractee(s). In the meeting the participants will discuss how the contract works, what the components of the contract are, and how each person can help others to achieve goals. The contract manager is the lead in the contract negotiations. The contract manager is also the person who checks to ensure fidelity of the contract. The team can consist of the contractor (e.g., parent, teacher, etc.), the contractee (i.e., the child), and the contract manager. As another example, the team might consist of the contractor who would like to contract with a group of children (e.g., his or her children, a group of children, etc.).

2) The contractee complete List 1 (see page 196), which is designed to help identify those behavior(s) or task(s) that he or she can perform/complete within the context of the contract. List 1 is a self-identification list for the contractee to complete possible task(s)/behavior(s) that could be considered for the contract. See example List 1 below.

Example List 1

Name: Lisa

Things I do to complete my classwork:	Other ways I could complete my classwork:
1) bring my pencil to class	1) start my work when told
2) bring paper to class	2) ignore distractions
3) complete some homework	3) check my work

3) The contractor completes List 2 (see page 197) while the contractee is completing List 1. List 2 helps identify behaviors or tasks of the contactor that may be used in the contract. Once the contractee completes List 1, then the contractee passes his or her List 1 to the contractor to add ideas about him or her onto List 1. For example, Lisa is the contractee who completed List 1 above. The contractor, Lisa's teacher, Rachel, completed List 2. After each one of them is done with List 1 and List 2, the contractor, Rachel, will write on the contractee's, Lisa, List 1 to give her ideas about Lisa's behaviors. The rationale of this step is to understand what each group member believes that he or she is doing currently toward the goal behavior and ways to improve the goal behavior. This also allows for any disagreement to be resolved before the contract is written.

Example List 2

Name: Rachel

Things Lisa does to complete classwork:	Other ways Lisa could complete classwork:
1) listen to directions	1) keep all her class materials organized
2)	2) start working when told
3)	3) ask questions if she doesn't understand

4) Have each contractee complete List 3 (see page 198). This list is designed to identify appropriate rewards or punishers for the contract. The recommendation most often given is that the team use rewards prior to using punishers. Each contractee identifies potential rewards he or she would like to earn. List 3 should include everyday items and activities and some special items the contractee has wanted for a while.

5) The team resolves any disagreements identified during the process of completing and exchanging Lists 1 and 2 between the contractor and contractee. Once everyone has agreed to the lists and any disagreements have been resolved, the team writes the contract.

6) The contract manager writes the contract (see blank contract template on page 199). The team begins with the behavior(s) or task(s) of each contractee (one person or several). When writing each behavior or task, the team must make sure that it adheres to the components of the task outlined above (Component 1) including who, what, when, and how well. Once each task is written, then the team should refer to List 3 to write the consequences. Again, the team must refer to the components that are essential to write a good consequence (see Component 2 above). A contract template is provided in the materials below.

7) The team decides when the contractor and contractee will start implementing the contract.

8) The implementation of the contract begins. The contractor and contractee are responsible for behaviors/tasks written in the contract. The contract manager is responsible for

a. giving the rewards for meeting the goals specified in the contract, and
b. keeping a record of progress (i.e., how frequently the contractee is completing the behaviors/tasks and receiving a reward).

In some cases the contractor may be responsible for A and B above, but having the contractor manager be responsible is preferred.

9) The team adjusts the contract as needed. After the contract has been implemented for several weeks (four is the recommended minimum), if the contractee is being successful consistently in completing the behaviors/tasks and receiving rewards, then the team should consider another meeting with all parties with the contractor and contractee to adjust the contract to increase the behaviors/tasks or length of time before the contractee receives a reward. These adjustments should be working toward the goal of phasing out and eventually ending the contract because the contractee is able to maintain the behaviors/tasks. If the contractee is not being successful or is highly inconsistent in completing behaviors/tasks, then the team should meet with all parties to revise the contract to improve success. The adjustments and modifications discussed below will serve as guidance in this process.

Adjustments/Modification

This section is provided for adjustments or modifications that may be needed to increase the success of the behavior contract.

1) Build in several layers of rewards if needed. Contracts can include bonus rewards for exceeding the goal or beating the best day, week, time period, etc.
2) Add a response cost contingency if needed. Sometimes it is necessary to build in a removal of rewards if the agreed upon task or behavior is not completed. This contingency is much like losing privileges. The loss of a privilege needs to fit the behavior.
3) Put the contract in a location that is visible for the contractee to be provided a prompt in completing/displaying the behavior(s) or task(s). For example, place the contract in a clear sheet protector and put it in the front of the contractee's notebook.
4) Renegotiate the contract. If any party is unhappy with any element of the contract, consider revamping it. If one party is consistently unhappy, the contract's success is unlikely. For example, if one party believes that one person has to work harder than the other person or the reward is too little for the effort, then the person will become dissatisfied with the contract. However, that a child does not earn a reward one day and is unhappy for that day does not provide sufficient reason to renegotiate the contract.
5) Keep all aspects of the contract age appropriate and also bear in mind the reading level of the participants. If a child does not have a high reading level, use clip art to visibly depict the tasks and rewards; use smiley faces for level of completion.
6) In the case where there are multiple contractees, then each contractee will complete a List 1 for himself/herself and a List 2 for each of the other contractees. When there are multiple contractees, each contractee is also a contractor to the other contractees. Once all the contractees have completed List 1 for themselves, they complete a List 2 for each of the other contractees. Then each contractee passes his or her List 1 around to the other contractees (who will serve as contractors to

the contractee) to add their ideas about him or her onto List 1. For example, Lisa, José, and Terence are contracting as a group. After each one of them is done with List 1 and List 2, Lisa will write on José's and Terry's List 1 to give her ideas about their behaviors. This process continues until everyone has completed putting their ideas on each contractee's List 1. Again, the rationale of this step is to understand what each group member believes that he or she is doing currently toward the goal behavior and ways to improve the goal behavior. This also allows for any disagreement to be resolved before the contract is written.

References

Bristol, M. M., & Sloane, H. N. (1974). Effects of contingency contracting on stufy rate and test performance. *Journal of Applied Behavior Analysis, 7,* 271-285.

Cooper J.O, Heron T.E, Heward W.L. (2007) Applied behavior analysis (2nd ed.) Upper Saddle River, NJ: Pearson.

Dardig, J. C., & Heward, W. L. (1981). Sign here: A contracting book for children and their parents (2nd ed.). Bridgewater, NJ: Fournies.

Kelley, M. L. & Stokes, T. T. (1982). Contingency contracting with disadvantages youths: Improving classroom performance. *Journal of Applied Behavior Analysis, 15,* 447-454.

Kelley, M. L. & Stokes, T. T. (1984). Student-teacher contracting with goal setting for maintenance. *Behavior Modification, 8,* 223-244.

Miltenberger, Raymond G. (2008). Behavior Modification Principles and Procedures, 4th edition. California: Thomson Higher Education.

Welch, S. J., & Holborn, S. W. (1988). Contingency contracting with delinquents: Effects of a brief training manual on staff contract negotiation and writing skills. *Journal of Applied Behavior Analysis, 21,* 357-368.

Wilkinson, L. A. (2003). Using behavioral consultation to reduce challenging behavior in the classroom. *Preventing School Failure, 47(3),* 100-105.

List 1 – Self-Identification of Possible Tasks

Directions:

1) The contract manager writes the name of the contractee, date, and completes the "Things I do now to" and "Other ways I could" statements.
2) The contractee writes down what he or she already does in the first column. In the second column, the contractee writes what he or she could do improve the behavior.

Name: ______________________________ Date: ______________________________

Things I do now to ____________________	Other ways I could ____________________
1) ______________________________ ______________________________	1) ______________________________ ______________________________
2) ______________________________ ______________________________	2) ______________________________ ______________________________
3) ______________________________ ______________________________	3) ______________________________ ______________________________
4) ______________________________ ______________________________	4) ______________________________ ______________________________
5) ______________________________ ______________________________	5) ______________________________ ______________________________
6) ______________________________ ______________________________	6) ______________________________ ______________________________
7) ______________________________	7) ______________________________

List 2 – Group Identification of Possible Tasks

Directions:

1) The contract manager writes the name of the contractor, date, and completes the "Things _____ does to" and "Other ways ________ could __________" statements.
2) The contractor writes down what he or she already does in the first column. In the second column, the contractor writes what he or she can do to improve the behavior.

Name: ________________________________ Date: ________________________________

Things __________ does to: _________________ Other ways __________ could ______________

1) ______________________________	1) ______________________________
______________________________	______________________________
2) ______________________________	1) ______________________________
______________________________	______________________________
3) ______________________________	3) ______________________________
______________________________	______________________________
4) ______________________________	4) ______________________________
______________________________	______________________________
5) ______________________________	5) ______________________________
______________________________	______________________________
6) ______________________________	6) ______________________________
______________________________	______________________________
7) ______________________________	7) ______________________________

List 3 – Self-Identification of Possible Rewards

Directions:

1) The contract manager writes the name of the contractee and date.
2) The contractee writes down his or her favorite things, activities, and special events or items that may serve as potential rewards.

Name: ____________________ Date: ____________________

My favorite things, activities, and special things to do or get!

1) ____________________

2) ____________________

3) ____________________

4) ____________________

5) ____________________

6) ____________________

7) ____________________

8) ____________________

9) ____________________

10) ____________________

11) ____________________

12) ____________________

Contract

TASK	REWARD
Who: ______________________	Who: ______________________
What: ______________________	What: ______________________
______________________	______________________
______________________	______________________
______________________	______________________
______________________	______________________
When: ______________________	When: ______________________
How well: ______________________	How much:______________________
______________________	______________________
______________________	______________________
______________________	______________________
______________________	______________________
______________________	______________________
Contractee Signature:	Contractor Signature:
______________________	______________________
Date: ______________________	Date: ______________________
	Contract Manager Signature:
	______________________
	Date: ______________________

Behavior Contract: Procedural Integrity Checklist

Age/Grade:	Preschool – High School
Setting:	Home, School, Clinic, In-patient
Individual or Group:	One or more people
Tier:	1, 2, & 3
Desired/ Appropriate Behavior:	Homework completion, academic performance, reduction in office referrals, home responsibilities (e.g., chores)
Skill Level:	Fluency to maintenance

A behavior contract is a document that describes in writing the relationship between completed tasks or behaviors of one or two parties and the delivery or access to a predetermined reinforcer or reward for the occurrence or nonoccurrence of the behavior(s) or task(s) to the person(s). Five steps must be followed in developing a behavior contract. These steps are designed to help in the negotiation process. When working with a child, an adult (e.g., teacher, caregiver, parent, etc.) can make all the decisions without any input from the child. However, if all parties can agree to the terms of the contract and can see the benefits from the contract, then adherence and integrity to the contract is more likely. The following steps outlined below were first described by Dardig and Heward (1981).

The Procedural Integrity Checklist–Contract Development is completed by an observer who *is not* the contract manager, contractor, or contractee. The observer will assess the process of the contract manager, contractor, and contractee developing and completing the behavior contract. The *Contract Implementation* Procedural Integrity Checklist is also completed by an observer who *is not* the contract manager, contractor, or contractee. The purpose of the Contract Implementation Procedural Integrity Checklist is to assess the tracking of behavior/task completion, the giving of rewards for meeting the goals specified in the contract, and the recording of progress being made by the contractee.

Procedure for Integrity Checklist Observer

Contract Development

1) Arrange to be at the meeting to develop the behavior contract. All parties that will be a part of the contract will attend, including the contract manager, contractor, and contractee(s).
2) Complete the Contract Development Procedural Integrity Checklist (see page 203) information about the contract manager, contractor, contractee, date, time, observer name, and observer signature.
3) Observe for behaviors 1-6. The contract manager should explain how the contract works, what the components of the contract are, and how each person can help others to achieve goals.
    a) Observe the contractee completing List 1 and contractor completing List 2.
    b) Observe the contractee and contractor pass the respective Lists 1 and 2 around to each other to add their ideas about the other onto each list. The respective List 1 and 2 are returned to the respective contractee and contractor. The contract manager may facilitate this process.
    c) Observe the contract manager resolve any disagreements between the items on List 1 and List 2 after the lists have been returned to the contractee and contractor.

d) Observe the contractee complete List 3. This list is designed to identify appropriate rewards or punishers for the contract. The recommendation most often given is that the team use rewards prior to using punishers. List 3 should include everyday items and activities and some special items the child has wanted for a while.

4) Observe that the team writing the behavior contract addresses procedural checklist items 7-9. The team should begin with the task(s) or behavior(s) of each contractee, whether it is one person or several.

5) Observe for the four elements of the task/behaviors part of the contract. This part of the contract should be based on Lists 1 and 2.

6) Observe for the four elements of the reward part of the contract. This part of the contract should be based on List 3.

7) Observe for the creation of a task record that provides for a record of behavior/task completion and delivery of the reward.

8) Count the number of behaviors marked Yes and write the number on the line for "Number of behaviors marked Yes."

9) Write the total number of behaviors observed (i.e., the total behaviors marked Yes or No).

10) Calculate the percent marked Yes. A chart is provided for determining the percent marked Yes.

11) Write any constructive feedback comments in addition to any notations made beside any individual behavior in the "Feedback" section.

12) Provide the contract manager, at an appropriate time, with oral feedback regarding the implementation of the intervention, starting with positive behaviors observed, and a copy of the Behavior Contract: Procedural Integrity Checklist – Contract Development. *The feedback should be provided the same day of the observation.*

Contract Implementation

Once the behavior contract has been developed, then the implementation phase is introduced.

1) Determine a time to observe the contractor, contractee, and contract manager at a time when the behavior contract is being implemented. The contractor, contractee, and contract manager should not be notified of the observation. Review a copy of the behavior contract prior to conducting the observation. Have a copy of the behavior contract available for reference during the observation.

2) Complete the Contract Implementation Procedural Integrity Checklist (see page 204) information about the contract manager, contractor, contractee, date, time, observer name, and observer signature.

3) Observe for behaviors 1-4 on the Checklist and mark Yes if present or No if not present. If there is not an opportunity to observe a behavior, then mark N/O for not observed.

4) Count the number of behaviors marked Yes and write the number on the line for "Number of behaviors marked Yes."

5) Write the total number of behaviors observed (i.e., the total behaviors marked Yes or No).

6) Calculate the percent marked Yes. A chart is provided for determining the percent marked Yes.

7) Write any constructive feedback comments in addition to any notations made beside any individual behavior in the "Feedback" section.

8) Provide the contractor and contract manager, at an appropriate time, with oral feedback regarding the implementation of the intervention, starting with positive behaviors observed, and a copy of the Behavior Contract: Procedural Integrity Checklist – Contract Implementation. *The feedback should be provided the same day of the observation.*

9) Observe the contractor, contractee, and contract manager implementing the behavior contract approximately every other week or twice a month after the initial observation.

Behavior Contract: Procedural Integrity Checklist
Contract Development

Contract Mgr: ______________________ Date: __________ Time: __________

Contractor(s): ______________________ Observer: ______________________

Contractee: ______________________ Signature: ______________________

N/O = Not Observed

Behaviors to Observe	Yes	No	N/O	Comments
1) All parties meet to develop the behavior contract.				
2) The contract manager explains how the contract works, what the components of the contract are, and how each person can help others to achieve goals.				
3) The contractee completes List 1.				
4) The contractor completes List 2.				
5) The contract manager resolves any disagreements between the contractee (List 1) and contractor (List 2).				
6) The contractee completes List 3.				
7) The tasks/behaviors part of the contract consists of four elements:				
a) The person (or persons) who will perform the behavior is documented.				
b) The behavior (or behaviors) that must be performed or demonstrated is documented.				
c) The contract identifies/sets a clear beginning and end.				
d) This criterion (or criteria) for how well the behavior has to be performed is stated				
8) The reward part of the contract consists of four elements:				
a) The person who will evaluate the completion of the task(s) or behavior(s) is identified.				
b) The reward or punisher is stated.				
c) The time at which or time frame in which the reward will be delivered or given to the person is stated.				
d) The amount of the reward is stated.				
9) The task record provides a record of completion of the behavior(s) or task(s) AND the delivery of the reward(s).				

Number of behaviors marked Yes = _____ out of _____ = ______ %

Feedback:

Percent

1 out of 15 = 7%	9 out of 15 = 60%
2 out of 15 = 13%	10 out of 15 = 67%
3 out of 15= 20%	11 out of 15 = 73%
4 out of 15 = 27%	12 out of 15 = 80%
5 out of 15 = 33%	13 out of 15 = 87%
6 out of 15 = 40%	14 out of 15 = 93%
7 out of 15= 47%	15 out of 15 = 100%
8 out of 15 = 53%	

Behavior Contract: Procedural Integrity Checklist
Contract Implementation

Contract Mgr: ______________________ Date: __________ Time: __________

Contractor(s): ______________________ Observer: ______________________

Contractee(s): ______________________ Signature: ______________________

N/O = Not Observed

Behaviors to Observe	Yes	No	N/O	Comments
1) The contractor or contractee completes the task record at the time of completion of the behavior or task.				
2) The contract manager (or contractor) gives the reward within the contract time frame.				
3) The contractor manager maintains a record of rewards given for goals met.				
4) The contract manager maintains a record of progress (how frequently the contractee is completing the behaviors/tasks and receiving a reward).				

Number of behaviors marked Yes = _____ out of _____ = ______ %

Feedback:

Percent
1 out of 4 = 25%
2 out of 4 = 50%
3 out of 4 = 75%
4 out of 4 = 100%

Daily Behavior Report Card

Age/Grade:	Preschool – High School
Setting:	School, Home, Clinic
Individual or Group:	Individual
Tier:	2 & 3
Desired/ Appropriate Behavior:	Work completion, compliance, keeping hands and feet to self, appropriate language, prepared for class/school, homework completion
Skill Level:	Fluency to generalization. Children who are at acquisition of the behaviors described above must be taught the behaviors before trying to build fluency with this intervention.

Rationale & Research Support

Daily Behavior Report Cards (DBRC) have been widely used and accepted across multiple settings and situations (Chafouleas, Riley-Tillman, Sassu, LaFrance, & Patwa, 2007). They are used to intervene with generally disruptive, challenging behaviors as well as to improve academic performance and work completion (Vannest, Davis, Davis, Mason, & Burke, 2010). Daily behavior report cards may also be called a school note, home-school note, or good behavior note; however, regardless of the title of the intervention, the purpose is to rate behaviors on a daily basis and provide feedback of those ratings to the child/adolescent. The ratings can be sent home to parents for parent-delivered consequences/ rewards or can be used in the classroom/clinic for adult-delivered consequences/rewards (Palcic, Jurbergs, & Kelley, 2009).

Materials

1) Daily behavior report card
2) List of rewards

Procedure for Interventionist

1) Clearly define the target behaviors.
   a) Name no more than 3-5 target behaviors.
   b) Choose one behavior that is considered a "give-me" behavior or a behavior that the child performs well and will provide more opportunities for positive feedback.
   c) Operationally define all target behaviors so that they are clear, observable, and measureable. Examples are as follows:
      - **On-task:** Child's eyes are oriented towards teacher/adult. Child is working on assignments, moving around in the room in order to put up work or gather materials that are to be used for current assignment, speaking to adult or other children as given permission and for the purpose of completing current assignment, or using materials in an appropriate fashion.
      - **Speaks only with permission:** Child raises a hand to speak or speaks during a time designated by the teacher/adult and all individuals have permission to speak (e.g., a teacher poses questions and children are allowed to call out answers). Any incident of talking out loud without the permission of the teacher/adult or unauthorized

vocalization (e.g., shouts, whistles, grunts, noises) is not considered speaking with permission, and the child would not earn a point for that time period.

2) Create the behavior report card.

   a) Separate the day or observation period into approximate equal intervals (e.g., equal class periods, 30-minute intervals, etc.).

   b) List the target behaviors defined in step 1 above on the report card.

   c) For each behavior and observation period, provide a rating. Ratings can be No – Sometimes – Yes or 0 – 1 – 2. The purpose is to indicate that the behavior did not occur at all during the time period, occurred periodically throughout the time period, or occurred for the entire time period. If using No – Sometimes – Yes, a number value (e.g., 0 – 1 – 2) must be assigned to each rating in order to calculate total points earned for the day.

3) Collect baseline data and set an initial goal.

   - Use the report card created in order to collect baseline data.
   - For a minimum of 3 days, collect data without the knowledge of the child. Calculate the percentage of points earned each day by dividing the total number of points earned by the total number of possible points. If 13 points out of 30 possible points were earned, the daily percentage of points would be 43%.
   - Calculate the average of the points earned during baseline. If the three days of baseline yielded 57%, 43%, and 50% of points, respectively, the average percentage earned during baseline is 50% [(57+43+50)/3].
   - Set the initial goal at an increase of 10% of the baseline percentage and add to the average points the child earned during the baseline period. Start with a daily goal. For example:
     - Average points earned by child during baseline (3 days) = 17, 13, 15
     - Daily possible points = 30
     - Daily percentage for the 3 days: 17/30 = 57%, 13/30 = 43%, 15/30 = 50%
     - Baseline percentage = (57+ 43 + 50)/3 = 50
     - 10% of 50 = 5
     - 50 + 5 = 55
     - Initial Daily Goal = 55% or an average of 16.5, which is rounded to the next whole number of 17, out of 30 possible points (0.55 X 30 = 16.5)

4) Review target behaviors and procedure with student.

   a) Once the goal is determined, review the Daily Behavior Report Card and procedure with the child.

   b) Discuss target behaviors and provide examples and non-examples of the behaviors.

   c) Review these behaviors at the beginning of each day with the child.

d) Determine if rewards will be provided at school or at home. If rewards are to be provided at school, create a list of rewards that the child would like to earn on each day the goal is met.

5) Begin Use of Daily Behavior Report Card (DBRC)

a) Remind child of target behaviors at the beginning of each day.

b) At the end of each observation period (e.g., equal class periods, 30-minute intervals, etc.), provide feedback to the child regarding whether or not behavior was exhibited during that time period and indicate the points earned on the DBRC by circling the appropriate indicator or points.

c) At the end of each day, calculate the percentage of points earned. Document on the DBRC whether the child met or exceeded the goal and send a copy of the DBRC home for parents. If the reward is being provided at school/clinic, deliver the pre-determined reward. If the child does not meet the daily goal, then the child receives feedback, starting with feedback on what the child did well followed by constructive feedback on what to improve. If the child does not meet the daily goal, the child does not receive a reward.

6) Progress monitor and set a goal each week.

a) Use the DBRC data for the week to monitor progress and set a new goal if appropriate.

b) If the child *did not attain* the goal set for the week, the goal should be kept at the goal set for the previous week.

c) If the child *did attain* the goal set for the week, calculate the daily points and average the points for the week. At the end of the week, change the daily goal by determining 10% of the average and adding that to the average points for the week.

- Average points earned by child for the week = 18
- Daily possible points = 30
- Average percentage for the week = 18/30 = 60%
- 10% of 60 = 6
- 60 + 6 = 66
- New Daily Goal = 66% or an average of 19.8, which is rounded to the next whole number of 20, out of 30 possible points (0.66 X 30 = 16.5)

Adjustments/Modification

For Tier 2, the DBRC can be used as described above. At this level, the DBRC is the only aspect of the intervention that is being implemented. For Tier 3, modifications to the DBRC can be put into place that provide more opportunities for feedback and reinforcement by having shorter increments of the day to earn points (e.g., 30-minute intervals or 15-minute intervals). Another modification is to use unknown rewards with a "Grab Bag" to aid in the motivation for access to the reward. Overall, the DBRC can be one part of a more extensive Behavior Intervention Plan (BIP) that is implemented following the development of a Functional Behavior Assessment (FBA).

If the child is consistently meeting the daily DBRC goal at a desired level (e.g., $\geq$ 80%), then consider adjusting the DBRC with a goal of fading out and eventually ending the DBRC intervention. To fade out the DBRC, the goal could be changed from a daily goal to a goal that must be met for two consecutive days. Once the child is meeting the goal for two consecutive days, the goal then might be changed to meeting a weekly average goal. Never go straight from a daily goal to a weekly goal. The child should be consistently meeting the goal for a period of at least four weeks before ending the DBRC intervention.

References

Chafouleas, S.M., Riley-Tillman, T.C., Sassu, K.A., LaFrance, M.J.,& Patwa, S.S. (2007). Daily behavior report cards: An investigation of consistency of on-task data across raters and methods. *Journal of Positive Behavior Interventions*, *9*, 30-37.

Palcic, J.L., Jurbergs, N., & Kelley, M.L. (2009). A comparison of teacher and parent delivered consequences: Improving classroom behavior in low-income children with ADHD. *Child & Family Behavior Therapy*, *31*, 117-133.

Vannest, K.J., Davis, J.L., Davis, C.R., Mason, B.A., & Burke, M.D. (2010). Effective intervention for behavior with a daily behavior report card: A meta-analysis. *School Psychology Review*, *39*, 654-672.

Daily Behavior Report Card (DBRC) Procedural Integrity Checklist

Age/Grade:	Preschool-High School
Setting:	School, Home, Clinic
Individual or Group:	Individual
Tier:	2 & 3
Desired/ Appropriate Behavior:	Work completion, compliance, keeping hands and feet to self, appropriate language, prepared for class/school, homework completion
Skill Level:	Fluency to generalization. Children who are at acquisition of the behaviors described above must be taught the behaviors before trying to build fluency with this intervention.

The procedural integrity checklist is completed by an observer (e.g., principal, assistant principal, school psychologist, treatment specialist, behavior specialist, counselor, lead teacher) who is familiar with the Daily Behavior Report Card (DBRC) procedure. The observer will observe the individual interventionist implementing the DRBC procedure and provide feedback. The DBRC program was developed as an efficient Tier 2 or Tier 3 intervention for reducing problem behavior. The DBRC was designed as an approach to the management of classrooms behaviors that rewards children for displaying appropriate, on-task behaviors.

Procedure for Integrity Checklist Observer

1) Completes the Procedural Integrity Checklist (see page 211) information about the interventionist, group (class, period), location, date, time, observer name, and observer signature.

2) Observe the interventionist's training of the child on the DBRC procedure using the DBRC Procedural Integrity Checklist – Initial Training Procedure. This observation will occur on the first day of the intervention.

3) Observe the interventionist's implementation of the DBRC procedure using the DBRC Procedural Integrity Checklist – Daily Intervention Procedure. A Daily Intervention Procedure observation should occur within the first two weeks of implementing the DBRC procedure so that feedback can be provided to the interventionist early in the implementation.

4) Observe the interventionist for the presence of behaviors on the Checklist and mark Yes if present or No if not present. If there is not an opportunity to observe a behavior, then mark N/O for not observed.

5) Count the number of behaviors marked Yes and write the number on the line for "Number of behaviors marked Yes."

6) Write the total number of behaviors observed (i.e., the total behaviors marked Yes or No).

7) Calculate the percent marked Yes. A chart is provided for determining the percent marked Yes. If less than 80% of behaviors are marked Yes, then provide feedback immediately to the interventionist and conduct another observation the next day or as soon as possible.

8) Write any constructive feedback comments in addition to any notations made beside any individual behavior in the "Feedback" section.

9) Provide the interventionist, at an appropriate time, with oral feedback regarding the implementation of the intervention, starting with positive behaviors observed, and a copy of the DBRC: Procedural Integrity Checklist. *The feedback should be provided the same day of the observation.*

10) Observe the interventionist implementing the DBRC procedure approximately every other week or twice a month after the initial observation.

Daily Behavior Report Card: Procedural Integrity Checklist
Initial Training Procedure

Interventionist: ______________________ Date: __________ Time: __________

Child: ______________________ Observer: ______________________

Location: ______________________ Signature: ______________________

N/O = Not Observed

Behaviors to Observe	Yes	No	N/O	Comments
1) The interventionist defines target behaviors that are clear, observable, and measureable.				
2) The interventionist collected baseline data for at least 3 days prior to implementation.				
3) The interventionist set an Initial goal based on baseline data.				
4) The interventionist introduces the DBRC to the child and target behaviors are explained using examples and non-examples.				
5) The interventionist selects suitable rewards for the child.				

Number of behaviors marked Yes = _____ out of _____ = ______ %

Feedback:

Percent
1 out of 5 = 20%
2 out of 5 = 40%
3 out of 5 = 60%
4 out of 5 = 80%
5 out of 5 = 100%

Daily Behavior Report Card: Procedural Integrity Checklist
Daily Intervention Procedure

Interventionist: ______________________ Date: __________ Time: __________

Child: ______________________ Observer: ______________________

Location: ______________________ Signature: ______________________

N/O = Not Observed

Behaviors to Observe	Yes	No	N/O	Comments
1) The interventionist introduces the target behaviors at the beginning of the instructional period.				
2) The interventionist encourages the student to have a good day and earn the daily points.				
3) At the end of each period/interval, the interventionist provides the child with feedback on target behaviors and circles the corresponding item on the DBRC.				
4) If the child exhibits appropriate behavior, interventionist provides praise and encouragement. If the child does not exhibit appropriate behavior, interventionist minimizes criticism and encourages the child to earn points for the next period.				
5) The interventionist writes only positive comments on the DBRC.				
6) The interventionist calculates the Daily Points correctly and provided feedback to the child.				
7) The interventionist provides the reward at the appropriate time (if reward is being provided at school).				
8) The interventionist sends a copy of the DBRC home to parents.				
9) At the end of the week, the interventionist reviews the DBRC data and sets a new goal for the next week, if appropriate.				

Number of behaviors marked Yes = _____ out of _____ = ______ %

Feedback:

Percent
1 out of 9 = 11%
2 out of 9 = 22%
3 out of 9 = 33%
4 out of 9 = 44%
5 out of 9 = 56%
6 out of 9 = 67%
7 out of 9 = 78%
8 out of 9 = 89%
9 out of 9 = 100%

Check In Check Out (CICO) Procedures

Age/Grade: 3rd. – High School

Setting: School

Individual or Group: Individual

Tier: 2 & 3

Desired/ Appropriate Behavior: Homework completion, academic performance, reduction in office referrals

Skill Level: Fluency to generalization

Rationale & Research Support

The CICO program was developed as an efficient Tier 2/3 intervention for reducing problem behavior. CICO was designed to increase feedback and positive adult attention (Crone, Horner, & Hawken, 2004). Previous research has shown that CICO is an easy-to-implement behavioral strategy, effective to decrease Office Discipline Referrals (Hawken & Horner, 2003; March & Horner, 2002) and to increase appropriate behavior (Todd, Campbell, Meyer, & Horner, 2008). CICO has been shown to be a relatively simple and inexpensive Tier 2 intervention (Hawken, MacLeod, & Rawlings, 2007). CICO has also been shown to have relatively high levels of teacher and staff acceptability. Todd et al. (2008) has shown that typical school personnel were able to effectively implement the CICO intervention. Finally, Mong, Johnson, and Mong (2011) also found that CICO can increase academic progress for children.

Materials

1) Daily Behavior Report Card (DBRC)
2) Folder to keep the DBRC
3) Rewards

Procedure for Interventionist

The CICO program is based on a daily protocol in which a child checks in with a designated adult (e.g., someone with whom the child has a good relationship or who is an ideal candidate to develop a relationship with the child) in the morning. During the initial check in, the adult and child review his or her behavioral goals for the day, discuss strategies he or she can use to obtain those goals, and then review his or her target points required on the Daily Behavior Report Card (DBRC; DBRC protocol procedures) to gain access to reinforcement (i.e., a reward) at the end of the day. The DBRC is carried by the child throughout the day. During natural transitions (i.e., changing subjects), teachers provide feedback by filling out the child's DBRC.

At the end of the school day, children take the DBRC to the identified adult to check out for the day. The child's percentage of points for the day is calculated, and the child receives praise and rewards if he or she meets the daily point goal. If the child does not meet his or her daily goal, the designated adult provides information on how to achieve the goal the following school day. The child then brings the DBRC home to obtain parent/guardian signature. Parents are instructed to provide rewards for meeting daily goals at home and are encouraged to review strategies to help the child improve his or her behavior the following day.

Before Implementing CICO

1) Develop a DBRC (see DBRC procedures on page 205).
2) Give a copy of the DBRC to each teacher who instructs and/or supervises the child, including others such as special area teachers, to rate the child for one week without the child knowing that he or she is being rated.
3) Collect all DBRC's after one week to determine the baseline performance.
4) Set goals for the first week. Generally, the goal is set at 10% more than baseline for the first week. If the child has met the weekly goal, then the goal is increased another 10%. Repeat the procedure each week as the child meets the goal.
5) Identify a designated adult, or mentor, within the school for the child to meet with for Check In and Check Out daily.
    a) This person should be someone who can be available every morning and afternoon.
    b) The designated adult, or mentor, should also be someone with whom the child has a relationship or someone who can develop a relationship with the child.
    c) The adult selected should be someone who can be a "mentor" rather than someone who disciplines the child, such as an administrator.
    d) The staff should also identify one or two backup designated adults, or mentors, in case of absences, etc.
6) Meet with the child to discuss the DBRC.
    a) Ask the child what rewards he or she is willing to work for or give the child a preference assessment.
    b) Ask the child who he or she would like to meet with to Check In or Check Out, if feasible. If there are only a couple of choices, then allow the child to choose. If only one person is available, then discuss with the child about meeting with the designated adult.
7) Ensure that the designated adult meets with the child prior to the implementation to discuss where the child should go every morning and afternoon, time, and alternative designated adult in case of absences.
8) Meet with the parent(s) or guardians before implementing the procedure to discuss the behaviors on the DBRC, the goal, and the rewards at school.
    a) The educational staff should also talk to the parent(s) or guardian(s) about reviewing the DBRC when the child brings it home. The staff should explain to parents that they should discuss the good behaviors rated as well as inappropriate behaviors. The staff should discuss with the parents strategies to review with his or her child to improve inappropriate behaviors.
    b) In addition, the staff should discuss with the parent(s) or guardian(s) rewards that can be used at home to reward and reinforce the school efforts.

Implementing CICO

1) Children are required to check in with the designated adult, or mentor, before school.
    a) The adult/mentor asks
        1) if the child has the DBRC from the previous day,
        2) if the DBRC from the previous day is signed by the parent or guardian,
        3) if the child has his or her materials for the day.
    b) The adult/mentor provides the child with a new blank DBRC form to be taken to class for feedback throughout the day.

c) The child is prompted to identify daily goals.
   For example, if the child received a lower score on the DBRC for an identified behavior in a certain setting or class, the adult can say, "What can you do today to improve your on-task in reading?"
d) The adult gives feedback to encourage success. For example, the adult can say, "You have displayed such GOOD on-task behavior so you can do it!"
e) The child receives praise for checking in. For example, the adult can say, "Thank you for (coming in, remembering, etc.) and talking to me this morning! I appreciate you working (with me, so hard)!"

2) At specified times of the day (e.g., generally at the end of class period, content area, or after transitions), the child approaches the teacher with the DBRC, and the teacher provides the child with feedback about the child's behavior by rating the child.
   a) Teachers provide immediate verbal praise for a child who met behavioral expectations for that time period.
   b) Teachers provide corrective feedback if the child did not meet the expectations.
3) At the end of the school day, the child takes the DBRC to the designated adult to check out.
   a) The percentage of points earned for the day is calculated.
   b) The child receives verbal praise and rewards if the child met the daily point goal.
   c) The child can choose from among specific rewards predetermined prior to CICO being implemented, including pencils, time with a preferred adult, or extra recess time the following day.
   d) If the child did not meet his or her daily goal, the designated adult provides information on what the child needs to work on for the following school day.
4) The child then takes his or her DBRC home to be signed by a parent/guardian.
5) The DBRC must be signed by a parent/guardian and returned the following morning.

Adjustments/Modification

For children in Tier 2, this is the exact procedure to follow as this is the intervention that will be implemented. For children in Tier 3, this procedure is included within the Behavior Intervention Plan (BIP). Thus, this is one intervention that is individualized and part of a larger plan. Generally, a child in Tier 3 has had a Functional Behavior Assessment (FBA) conducted prior to the BIP being developed.

References

Crone, D.A., Horner, R.H., & Hawken, L. (2004). *Responding to problem behavior in the school: The behavior education program*. New York: Guilford.

Hawken, L.S. & Horner, R.H. (2003). Evaluation of a targeted intervention within a schoolwide system of behavior support. *Journal of Behavioral Education, 12*, 225-240.

Hawken, L.S. MacLeod, K.S., & Rawlings, L. (2007). Effects of the behavior education program (BEP) of office discipline referrals of elementary school students. *Journal of Positive Behavior Interventions, 9(2)*, 94-101.

March, R.E. & Horner, R.H. (2002). Feasibility and contributions of functional behavior assessments in schools. *Journal of Emotional and Behavioral Disorders, 10(3)*, 158-170.

Mong, M. D., Johnson, K. N., & Mong, K. W. (2011). Effects of Check-in/Checkout on Behavioral Indices and Mathematics Generalization. *Behavioral Disorders* Retrieved February 19, 2012 from HighBeam Research: http://www.highbeam.com/doc/1P3-2469557481.html

Todd, A.W., Campbell, A.L., Meyer, G.G., & Horner, R.H. (2008). The effects of a targeted interventions to reduce problem behaviors: elementary school implementation of check in-check out. *Journal of Positive Behavior Interventions, 10(1)*, 46-55.

Check In Check Out (CICO): Procedural Integrity Checklist

Age/Grade:	3rd. – High School
Setting:	School
Individual or Group:	Individual
Tier:	2 & 3
Desired/ Appropriate Behavior:	Homework completion, academic performance, reduction in office referrals
Skill Level:	Fluency to generalization

This document provides the procedure for checking the implementation integrity of CICO procedure and a procedural checklist. The CICO procedure is described in a separate document. The CICO program was developed as an efficient Tier 2/3 intervention for reducing problem behavior. CICO was designed to increase feedback and positive adult attention.

Procedure for Integrity Checklist Observer

1) The designated adult (e.g., assistant principal, lead teacher) completes the Procedural Integrity Checklist (see page 218) information about the interventionist (e.g., teacher, mentor, etc), group (class, period), location, date, time, and observer name.
2) The designated adult observes the interventionist's implementation of CICO procedure. An initial observation of the procedures should occur within the first couple of weeks of implementing the CICO procedure so that feedback can be provided to the designated adult early in the implementation.
3) The designated adult observes the interventionist or child for the presence of behaviors 1-17 on the Checklist and puts a checkmark under "Yes" if the behavior present or "No" if the behavior is not present.
4) At the completion of the observation, the designated adult counts the number of behaviors check marked Yes and writes the number on the line for "Number of behaviors marked Yes."
5) The designated adult writes the total number of behaviors observed and the percent check marked Yes.
6) The designated adult writes any constructive feedback comments in addition to any notations made beside any individual behavior in the "Feedback" section.
7) At an appropriate time following each observation, the designated adult provides the interventionist with oral feedback regarding the implementation of the intervention, starting with positive behaviors observed, and a copy of the CICO Procedural Integrity Checklist. *The feedback should be provided the same day of the observation.*
8) After the initial observation, the designated adult should observe the interventionist implementing the CICO procedure 2-8 times, depending on the length of the implementation.

Check In Check Out (CICO): Procedural Integrity Checklist

Interventionist: ______________________ Date: __________ Time: __________

Child: ______________________ Observer: ______________________

Location: ______________________ Signature: ______________________

N/O = Not Observed

Behaviors to Observe	Yes	No	N/O	Comments
1) Child arrived to check in with the designated adult before school.				
2) The designated adult received the DBRC from the previous day.				
3) The designated adult checked to ensure the parent or guardian signed the DBRC.				
4) The designated adult checked to ensure the child had his or her materials for the day.				
5) The designated adult provided the child with a new blank Daily Behavior Report Card(DBRC) form to take to class for feedback throughout the day.				
6) The designated adult prompted the child to identify daily goals.				
7) The designated adult gave feedback to encourage success.				
8) The designated adult praised the child for checking in.				
9) At the end of the school day, the child took the DBRC to the designated adult to check out.				
10) The designated adult calculated the percentage of points the child earned for the day.				
11) The designated adult gave the child verbal praise and rewards if the child met his or her daily point goal.				
12) The child chose from specific rewards.				
13) If the child did not meet his or her daily goal, the designated adult provided information on what the child should work on for the following school day				
14) The designated adult reminded the child to takes his or her DBRC home to be signed by a parent/guardian				

Number of behaviors marked Yes = _____ out of _____ = ______ %

Feedback:

Percent
1 out of 14 = 7%
2 out of 14 = 14%
3 out of 14 = 21%
4 out of 14 = 28%
5 out of 14 = 36%
6 out of 14 = 43%
7 out of 14 = 50%
8 out of 14 = 57%
9 out of 14 = 64%
10 out of 14 = 73%
11 out of 14 = 79%
12 out of 14 = 86%
13 out of 14 = 93%
14 out of 14 = 100%

PreCorrection

Age/Grade: Preschool – High School

Setting: School, Home, Clinic, In-patient

Individual or Group: Individual or Group

Tier: 1 & 2

Desired/ Appropriate Behavior: Homework completion, academic performance, reduction in office referrals, general appropriate behavior, home responsibilities (e.g., chores)

Skill Level: Fluency to maintenance

Rationale & Research Support

PreCorrection is a systematic way to anticipate and address problem behaviors that occur in the school (Crosby, Jolivette, & Patterson, 2006). Preventive disciplinary techniques should be used in order to encourage prosocial behaviors and discourage antisocial behaviors and/or discipline problems (Baer, Cavalier, & Manning, 2002). Precorrection provides opportunities to practice skills or to be prompted about expected behaviors prior to the situation in which the behaviors typically occur (Colvin, Sugai, Patching, 1993). PreCorrection has been used in classroom and non-classroom settings, such as hallways, playground, and cafeterias to improve inappropriate behaviors (Lewis, Colvin, & Sugai, 2000; Lewis, Sugai, & Colvin, 1998). This intervention is made up of eight steps and provides little disruption to the classroom routine (Crosby et al.).

Procedure for Interventionist

1) Identify the context and predictable behaviors of concern. These behaviors can be academic or behavioral in nature. For example, the behavior of concern may be a reading fluency deficit when the child is presented with high frequency of unknown words. Another example could be pushing peers during unstructured routines such as lining up in the hallway or during recess.
2) Define target, expected behaviors in positive terms. That is, define the behavior that is expected rather than stating the behavior that is inappropriate (e.g., Walk quietly on the right side of the hall in a single file line. When you come to a word you do not know, stop and sound it out, say the word, and then continue reading).
3) Collect baseline data. Determine how many children should be targeted (e.g., one student, small group, or entire class). If one student is the target, collect data by observing the target behavior for that student at the time and in the context in which the behaviors typically occur. If the target is a small or large group, observe a random selection of the target children using a Momentary Time Sampling procedure (e.g., 15-second intervals or a one-minute interval) to determine baseline levels of the target behaviors. Baseline Data Collection procedures and a Momentary Time Sampling Observation Form are provided below.
4) Modify the context in order to increase the likelihood of the appropriate, desirable behavior. Some examples include making instructional, task, or activity accommodations or altering the method of instruction, activity, scheduling, or even seating arrangement.
   - Example 1: The problem behavior is that while children enter the classroom from PE, they are talking loudly and pushing one another. To change the context, the teacher waits at the door

and reminds them to get in line quietly. The teacher waits for appropriate behavior prior to allowing the children enter the room.

- Example 2: A child has trouble asking for help when having difficulty with an academic task. To modify the context, the interventionist provides a cue card that the child turns over when help is needed. This use of the card is explained and practiced with the child and allows the child to indicate the need for help without having to raise a hand.

5) Conduct behavior rehearsals of the expected behavior. Have children practice the expected behaviors with guidance or independently. Have the children independently practice the expected behaviors at different times during the day.

6) Provide strong reinforcement for expected behaviors. Reinforcement can be in the form of praise (e.g., Good job!, a thumbs up), or it can be a preferred activity or a tangible reward (e.g., treasure box prize).

7) Prompt expected behaviors before performance. Prior to the context or situation in which the behaviors typically occur, provide a verbal reminder of the expected behaviors. For example, when children are about to enter the hallway to go to the cafeteria, the verbal reminder might be, "Walk quietly on the right side of the hall in a single file line."

8) Monitor the plan. Determine if specific target behaviors of an individual student or a group of children as defined in step 2 above have increased expected behaviors or decreased unwanted behaviors. Continue to use the procedure used in step 3 above to compare behaviors and determine effectiveness.

References

Baer, G. G., Cavalier, A. R., & Manning, M. A. (2002). Best practices in school discipline. In A. Thomas & J. Grimes (Eds.), *Best Practices in School Psychology* (4th Ed.) (pp. 977-991). Bethesda, MD: National Association of School Psychologists.

Colvin, G., Sugai, G., & Patching, B., (1993). Precorrection: An instructional approach for managing predictable problem behaviors. *Intervention in School and Clinic, 28(3),* 143-150.

Crosby, S., Jolivette, K., & Patterson, D. (2006). Using Precorrection to Manage Inappropriate Academic and Social Behaviors. *Beyond Behavior, 16,* 14-17.

Lewis, T. J., Colvin, G., & Sugai, G. (2000). The effects of pre-correction and active supervision on the recess behavior of elementary students. *Education and Treatment of Children, 23*, 109-121.

Lewis, T., Sugai, G., & Colvin, G. (1998). Reducing problem behavior through a schoolwide system of effective behavioral support: Investigation of a schoolwide social skills training program and contextual interventions. *School Psychology Review, 27*, 446-460.

PreCorrection: Procedural Integrity Checklist

Age/Grade:	Preschool – High School
Setting:	School, Home, Clinic, In-patient
Individual or Group:	One or more people
Tier:	1 & 2
Desired/ Appropriate Behavior:	Homework completion, academic performance, reduction in office referrals, home responsibilities (e.g., chores)
Skill Level:	Fluency to maintenance

The procedural integrity checklist is completed by a designated adult (e.g., principal, assistant principal, school psychologist, treatment specialist, behavior specialist, counselor, lead teacher) who is familiar with the PreCorrection procedures. The observer will observe the individual interventionist implementing the PreCorrection procedure and provide feedback.

Procedure for Integrity Checklist Observer

1) An observer who is familiar with the procedures (e.g., principal, assistant principal, school psychologist, treatment specialist, behavior specialist, counselor, lead teacher) completes the Procedural Integrity Checklist (see page 222) information about the adult, group (class, period, etc.), location, date, time, observer name, and signature.
2) The observer observes the person implementing the PreCorrection procedure. An initial observation should occur early during implementation so that feedback can be provided to the interventionist as early as possible.
3) The observer watches the interventionist for the presence of behaviors on the Checklist and marks Yes if present or No if not present. If there is not an opportunity to observe some of the behaviors, then the observer marks N/O for not observed. For example, if the interventionist is implementing only the first phase of the intervention, the sections for the following phases will be considered "not observed."
4) At the completion of the observation, the observer counts the number of behaviors marked Yes and writes the number on the line for "Number of behaviors marked Yes."
5) Then the observer writes the total number of behaviors observed (i.e., the total behaviors marked Yes or No) and the percent marked Yes.
6) The observer should write any constructive feedback comments in addition to any notations made beside any individual behavior in the "Feedback" section.
7) At an appropriate time following each observation, the observer provides the interventionist with oral feedback regarding the implementation of the intervention, starting with positive behaviors observed, and a copy of the PreCorrection: Procedural Integrity Checklist. The feedback should be provided the same day of the observation.
8) Observe the interventionist implementing the PreCorrection procedure approximately every other week or twice a month after the initial observation.

PreCorrection: Procedural Integrity Checklist
Daily Intervention Procedures

Interventionist: ______________________ Date: __________ Time: __________

Group: ______________________ Observer: ______________________

Location: ______________________ Signature: ______________________

N/O = Not Observed

Behaviors to Observe	Yes	No	N/O	Comments
1) Interventionist identifies the context in which the problem behavior typically occurs.				
2) The interventionist defined target behaviors in positive terms.				
3) The interventionist ensured the collection of baseline data for target behaviors.				
4) The interventionist modified the context in which problem behaviors typically occurred.				
5) Behavioral rehearsals of the expected behavior occur daily.				
6) The interventionist gives feedback and reinforcement to encourage success.				
7) The interventionist prompted expected behaviors prior to the context or situation in which they typically occurred.				
8) The interventionist monitors progress of target behaviors weekly.				

Number of behaviors marked Yes = _____ out of _____ = ______ %

Feedback:

Percent
1 out of 8 = 13%
2 out of 8 = 25%
3 out of 8 = 38%
4 out of 8 = 50%
5 out of 8 = 63%
6 out of 8 = 75%
7 out of 8 = 88%
8 out of 8 = 100%

Time In

Age/Grade:	Preschool – High School
Setting:	School, Home, Clinic, In-patient
Individual or Group:	One or more people
Tier:	1, 2, & 3
Desired/ Appropriate Behavior:	Compliance, on-task, generally appropriate classroom behavior
Skill Level:	Fluency to maintenance

Rationale & Research Support

Do you have students or children who engage in various disruptive behaviors in order to get attention? Time-In (TI) is considered an antecedent management that provides attention for general, appropriate behavior. TI was defined by Christophersen (1988) as the attention a child receives in the form of verbal praise, smiles, and appropriate physical contact contingent upon generally appropriate behavior. TI is designed to provide a child with an enriched environment through the delivery of reinforcement for appropriate behavior. TI can be delivered verbally or physically. Verbal TI includes statements such as "I like the way you are sitting quietly." and "Good job doing your homework." Physical TI includes light pats on the hand, arm, shoulder, or head. Researchers have shown that providing verbal and/or physical TI to a child prior to presenting the child a command increases compliance levels (Ford, Olmi, Edwards, & Tingstrom, 2001; Mandal, 2001).

It is important, when delivering praise to children for generally appropriate behavior, to use behavior-specific praise that identifies the student's specific desirable behavior. This type of praise has been most effective in promoting appropriate behavior (Chalk & Bizo, 2004). The use of behavior-specific praise has also been correlated to on-task behavior. Specifically, as the use of behavior-specific praise increased in a classroom of children with emotional and behavior disorders, on-task behavior also increased (Sutherland, Wehby, & Copeland, 2000).

Materials

1) MotivAider® (for use as a timer to indicate when Time-In should be delivered)
2) List of methods (physical and verbal) of Time-In

Procedure for Interventionist

1) Define target, expected behaviors in positive terms. That is, define the behavior that is expected rather than stating behavior that is inappropriate (e.g., Walk quietly on the right side of the hall in a single file line. When you come to a word you do not know, stop and sound it out, say the word and then continue reading.).
2) Determine the ways in which Time-In (positive attention) will be delivered. Also important is determining a variety of methods to use when giving attention.

3) Determine how frequently attention will be given and during which time of day or class period to emphasize the use of Time-In as an intervention.
   a) TI should be delivered every 3 minutes for children who typically engage in a negative behavior every 3-5 minutes.
   b) TI should be delivered during a time of day that the child typically engages in the negative behavior (e.g., if the behavior occurs most often during the afternoon, deliver TI more often at that time).
   c) TI should be delivered throughout the day for children who typically engage in negative behavior frequently throughout the day.
4) Use Time-In based on the schedule that has been determined. If setting a MotivAider® or using a timer, deliver positive attention (either verbally or physically using the list made in the first step) when the timer goes off. If the child is engaged in appropriate behavior, provide brief praise that is behavior specific (if verbal). If the child is not engaged in appropriate behavior when the timer goes off, ignore the behavior. Wait for the next interval to determine if TI is warranted at the next interval. If the child exhibits negative behavior, either ignore the behavior or briefly redirect the child in a neutral manner.

Adjustments/Modification

1) For use at a Tier 1 intervention due to overall inappropriate behaviors (e.g., off-task, talking out, etc.) classwide or groupwide, the target behaviors should first be defined and then observed during the set time of day that the intervention will be used. Children should be randomly selected for observation to determine the overall engagement in target behaviors in the classroom.
2) For use as a Tier 2 or 3 intervention to target specific children, their target behaviors should be defined. Using a 10-second Momentary Time Sampling procedure, baseline data should be collected during the designated time of day that Time-In will be implemented. Once the intervention begins, data should continue to be collected using the same observation to compare baseline to intervention.
3) If using Time-In throughout the day, rather than using a timer, delivering praise using a more frequent schedule and later fading into a less frequent schedule is encouraged (Wallace, Iwata, Hanley, Thompson, & Roscoe, 2012). For example, the interventionist may start with a schedule of non-contingent praise or Time-In every 30 seconds. The schedule should gradually change to a less frequent use of TI to reach a schedule of every 5 minutes or more.

References

Chalk, K., & Bizo, L.A. (2004). Specific praise improves on-task behavior and numeracy enjoyment: A study of year four pupils engaged in the numeracy hour. *Educational Psychology in Practice, 20,* 335–351.

Christophersen, E. (1988). *Beyond discipline: Parenting that lasts a lifetime.* Kansas City, MO: Westport.

Ford, A. D., Olmi, D. J., Edwards, R. P., & Tingstrom, D. H. (2001). The sequential introduction of compliance training components with elementary-aged children in general education classroom settings. *School Psychology Quarterly, 16,* 142-157.

Mandal, R. L. (2001). *Evaluation of a compliance training package from a single component to successive components.* Unpublished doctoral dissertation. University of Southern Mississippi, Hattiesburg.

Sutherland, K.S., Wehby, J.H., & Copeland, S.R. (2000). Effect of varying rates of behavior-specific praise on the on-task behavior of students with EBD. *Journal of Emotional and Behavioral Disorders, 8,* 2–8.

Wallace, M. D., Iwata, B. A., Hanley, G. P., Thompson, R. H., & Roscoe, E. M. (2012). Noncontingent reinforcement: A further examination of schedule effects during treatment. *Journal of Applied Behavior Analysis, 45*, 709-719.

Time-In: Procedural Integrity Checklist

Age/Grade:	Preschool – High School
Setting:	School, Home, Clinic, In-patient
Individual or Group:	One or more people
Tier:	1, 2, & 3
Desired/ Appropriate Behavior:	Compliance, on-task, generally appropriate classroom behavior
Skill Level:	Fluency to maintenance

The procedural integrity checklist is completed by a designated adult (e.g., principal, assistant principal, school psychologist, treatment specialist, behavior specialist, counselor, lead teacher) who is familiar with the Time-In procedures. The designated adult (observer) will observe the individual interventionist implementing the Time-In procedure and provide feedback.

Procedure for Integrity Checklist Observer

1) An observer who is familiar with the procedures (e.g., principal, assistant principal, school psychologist, treatment specialist, behavior specialist, counselor, lead teacher) completes the Procedural Integrity Checklist (see page 228) information about the adult, group (class, period, etc.), location, date, time, observer name, and signature.
2) The observer observes the person implementing the Time-In procedure. An initial observation should occur early during implementation so that feedback can be provided to the interventionist as early as possible.
3) The observer watches the interventionist for the presence of behaviors on the Checklist and marks Yes if present or No if not present. If there was not an opportunity to observe some of the behaviors, then the observer marks N/O for not observed. For example, if the interventionist is implementing only the first phase of the intervention, the sections for the following phases will be considered "not observed."
4) At the completion of the observation, the observer counts the number of behaviors marked Yes and writes the number on the line for "Number of behaviors marked Yes."
5) Then the observer writes the total number of behaviors observed (i.e., the total behaviors marked Yes or No) and the percent marked Yes.
6) The observer should write any constructive feedback comments in addition to any notations made beside any individual behavior in the "Feedback" section.
7) At an appropriate time following each observation, the observer provides the interventionist with oral feedback regarding the implementation of the intervention, starting with positive behaviors observed, and a copy of the Time-In: Procedural Integrity Checklist. The feedback should be provided the same day of the observation.

8) Observe the interventionist implementing the Time-In procedure approximately every other week or twice a month after the initial observation.

Time-In: Procedural Integrity Checklist

Interventionist: ______________________ Date: __________ Time: __________

Group: ______________________ Observer: ______________________

Location: ______________________ Signature: ______________________

N/O = Not Observed

Behaviors to Observe	Yes	No	N/O	Comments
1) The interventionist reminds children of target behaviors and reviews definitions.				
2) The interventionist has a timer or MotivAider® to indicate the appropriate time to deliver Time-In.				
3) When the timer reaches 0:00 or goes off, if a student is engaged in appropriate behavior, the interventionist delivers either verbal or physical Time-In.				
4) When the timer reaches 0:00 or goes off, if a child is not engaged in appropriate behavior, the interventionist either ignores the behavior or briefly redirects in a neutral manner.				

Number of behaviors marked Yes = _____ out of _____ = ______ %

Feedback:

Percent

1 out of 4 = 25%
2 out of 4 = 50%
3 out of 4 = 75%
4 out of 4 = 100%

TIER

Compliance Training

Age/Grade:	Preschool – 5th grade
Setting:	School, Home, Clinic
Individual or Group:	Individual
Tier:	1, 2, & 3
Desired/ Appropriate Behavior:	Compliance
Skill Level:	Fluency to generalization

Rationale & Research Support

Noncompliance is often viewed as a child's problem, but teaching appropriate skills and techniques to parents, caregivers, and teachers can often improve a child's noncompliant behavior quickly and relatively easily. A child's education may be hindered if compliance levels fall below 40%, resulting in fewer opportunities for instruction (Ford, Olmi, Edwards, & Tingstrom, 2001; Rhode, Jenson, & Reavis, 1993). According to Ford et al. and Martens and Kelly (1993), compliance with teacher instructions is necessary for effective learning. The use of Time In, Effective Instruction Delivery, and Contingent Praise have been shown to be effective either independently or in combination in increasing childhood compliance (Benoit, Edwards, Olmi, Wilczynski, &Mandal, 2001; Ford et al.; Marlow, Tingstrom, Olmi, & Edwards, 1997). Studies show increases of 40-60% in compliance when all three components are implemented with fidelity (Benoit, et al.; Ford et al.; Mandal, Olmi, Edwards, Tingstrom, & Benoit, 2000; Marlow et al., 1997; Olmi, Sevier, & Nastasi, 1997).

The two types of compliance are Initiated Compliance and Completion Compliance. The three major positive components to compliance training are Time In, Effective Instruction Delivery, and Contingent Praise. Time In is a procedure in which all appropriate behaviors are reinforced through verbal or physical praise. Effective Instruction Delivery is giving commands in such a way that children are more likely to comply with the instructions they have been given. Contingent Praise is a form of positive praise (verbal or physical contact), which is contingent on the child's compliance with the commands given.

Materials

1) MotivAider®

Procedure for Interventionist

Prior to Starting Intervention

Note: Each step may not be completed by the interventionist. However, it is the primary responsibility of the interventionist to ensure the completion of the step.

1) Ensure the collection of baseline performance data (see explanation of baseline data in Conducting Direct Observations) on the child and the interventionist working with the child using the Compliance Training Observation Form. These observations should be completed by an observer who is someone other than the interventionist working with the child on the intervention

(e.g., school psychologist, behavior specialist, or other adult). The child behaviors being observed include Initiated Compliance and Completion Compliance. The interventionist behaviors being observed include Time In (Positive Attention), Effective Instruction Delivery, Contingent Praise, and Negative Attention. Negative Attention is any attention given to the child by the interventionist in the form of an inappropriate facial or gestural prompt toward the student and/or verbal reprimand or redirection. The purpose of observing Negative Attention is to determine a rate for both positive and negative on the observation form. Specific definitions of the interventionist behaviors are included with each phase of the intervention. However, no changes in behavior should occur at this point. This data collection is to determine pre-intervention use of interventionist behaviors (i.e., Time-In, Effective Instruction Delivery, and Contingent Praise) as well as child compliance.

2) Ensure the collection of baseline data for at least three different observations at times when the child has difficulty complying with directions. The observations for baseline data are conducted by an observer other than the interventionist (see step 1). During the observation, the interventionist should give at least 10 instructions within a 10-15 minute period in the same manner in which instructions are always given. The interventionist should not change any behaviors at this point. The observer should document the use of the interventionist behaviors on the observation form and the child's Initiated Compliance and Completion Compliance.

    a) Initiated Compliance (IC) is defined as the child starting the instruction (e.g., moving towards, redirecting body parts, etc.) within 5 seconds of the end of the instruction.

    b) Completion Compliance (CC) is defined as any time the child completes the entire instruction.

3) Review baseline data to examine the child's behavior and the interventionist's behavior. The observer and the interventionist (along with anyone else involved in the intervention such as the school psychologist, behavior specialist, counselor, etc.) should be involved in the review of the data. The data to be reviewed should include all data collected during the observations (i.e., baseline rates of Time In, Effective Instruction Delivery, Contingent Praise, Initiated Compliance, Completion Compliance, and the positive to negative attention ratio).

Intervention Implementation

1) Implement Time In (TI) as the first phase of the intervention (see page 223). TI is any verbal praise, physical gesture, or appropriate physical contact when the child behaves appropriately, or differential reinforcement for appropriate behavior which is the use of reinforcement for appropriate behavior or correct responses and no reinforcement when there is inappropriate behavior. TI should be delivered at a rate that equals or exceeds 1 per minute. See the Compliance Training Observation Form for the description of how to determine rate of TI.

    a) The interventionist should deliver random praise for appropriate behavior throughout the day. This praise should take the form of verbal praise or physical gestures and/or contact.

        - For verbal praise, the interventionist could say "I like the way you are sitting so quietly."
        - For physical gestures, the interventionist could give a "thumbs up" or a smile.
        - For physical contact, the interventionist could give a "high five," a pat on the back, or a pat on the head.

b) The interventionist should deliver TI at a rate of approximately 5 positives for each negative statement. To determine the positive/negative rate, use the baseline data collection. Specifically, if 3 negative statements are delivered during a 10-minute observation, then the interventionist should deliver approximately 15 positives during that 10-minute period.

c) The interventionist should ensure that observations, using the Compliance Training Observation form, are conducted at a minimum of twice per month. Observations may be conducted weekly or bi-weekly if possible. The second intervention phase should not be implemented until a minimum of 3 observations have occurred.

d) The interventionist working with the child should practice and give feedback with another staff member (e.g., school psychologist, behavior specialist, another interventionist) using TI until the rate per minute equals 1 or more on at least 3 observations. See the Compliance Training Observation form for a description of how to calculate rate per minute.

e) The second phase of this intervention should not be implemented until the interventionist has been observed delivering TI and achieved a rate per minute that equals or exceeds 1 during three consecutive observations.

2) Implement Effective Instruction Delivery (EID) is the second phase of the intervention. EID is giving commands in such a way that children are more likely to comply with instructions they have been given. The main components associated with EID are eye contact, directive statements, descriptive wording, close proximity, and a 5-second wait for initiated compliance. TI should continue to be utilized while EID is added to the intervention.

a) The Interventionist should use the following methods for delivering instructions to the child.

i) Deliver instructions in close proximity (2-4 feet).

(1) Avoid yelling commands across the room. Giving commands across the room leads to ambiguity regarding the target of the command. Giving commands from too great a distance from the child also gives the child an opportunity to pretend not to hear.

(2) When possible, use a bending position or kneeling position when giving a direction; research shows that using this posture increases the likelihood of the child's compliance.

ii) Deliver the instruction with eye contact. Make sure that the child's attention is gained prior to giving the instruction.

iii) Break complex instructions down and avoid compound requests.

(1) Give commands one at a time.

- Example: "Sarah, go wash your hands."
- Non-Example: "Go to the bathroom and wash your hands, brush your teeth, and comb your hair."
- Example: "Sam, put your toys in the box."
- Non-Example: "Clean your room." This command requires multiple actions and steps in order to comply.

iv) Deliver instructions as directives.

(1) Tell the child what to do rather than asking for compliance.

(2) Giving instructions in the form of a question allows the child to test the limits or make the choice to not comply.

- Example: “Sally, put your teddy bear in your toy box.”
- Non-example: “Sally, will you put your teddy bear away please?”
- Example: “Blake, put the car in the toy box.”
- Non-Example: “Let’s clean up now, okay?

v) Use a quiet-toned, neutral voice. Be matter-of-fact and non-emotional when addressing problem behavior.

- Example: “Jenna, come and sit in the circle with the group.”
- Non-Example: “COME HERE NOW!”

vi) Be descriptive in the instruction.

(1) Make sure your expectations for the child are clear.

- Example: “Kristin, put your feet firmly on the ground.”
- Non-Example: “Get down!”
- Example: “Timmy, put the blocks in the red container.”
- Non-example: “Timmy, put your toys away!”

vii) Use more “start” instructions than “stop” instructions.

(1) Be sure to tell children what TO DO rather than just what NOT to do.

- Example: “Trent, draw a picture with the crayon.”
- Non-example: “Don’t put that crayon in your nose!”

viii) Give a 5-second wait period before reissuing the instruction or delivering consequences for noncompliance.

(1) Allow the child the opportunity to process the instructions and comply.

b) Continue the use of the Compliance Training Observation throughout the implementation of EID to determine the child’s response (i.e., percentage compliance) as well as the interventionist’s use of EID.

c) The third and last phase of this intervention should not be implemented until the interventionist has delivered instructions with an 85% accuracy rate during three consecutive observations. Specifically, the percentage of each of the interventionist’s behaviors calculated on the observation form should be 85% or higher. If 20 commands are given during the observation, then each component of EID should be given at least 17 of the 20 commands. See steps 4-6 on the observation form for specific guidelines on calculating the percentage of each behavior.

3) Implement Contingent Praise (CP) as the last phase of the intervention. Contingent Praise (CP) is positive praise (verbal or physical contact) that is contingent on the child complying with the instructions given.

   a) Deliver praise to the child contingent upon compliance to instructions.

   b) Deliver verbal and appropriate physical praise immediately (within 5 seconds of completed compliance) to a child whenever the child complies with a specific instruction.

      - For example, if the interventionist tells a child to "Hand me the blue ball" and the child complies with the instruction, the interventionist might say "Great job!" or "Thank you for handing me the ball!"

   c) Contingent praise can be paired with positive physical gesture and/or positive touch.

      - For example, when the interventionist says "Great job putting away materials," he or she can also give a high five at the same time.

Adjustments/Modification

Tier 1

For Tier 1, the interventionist can plan to use the procedures described above for the entire classroom. The interventionist should plan to deliver Time In to various and random children throughout the classroom approximately every 2 minutes (a MotivAider® can be used for reminders throughout the day). The purpose of compliance training at Tier 1 is not to address noncompliance in a specific child; rather it is used to create general compliance and appropriate behavior throughout the class or group of children.

Tier 2

For Tier 2, compliance training procedures are used to respond to an increase in noncompliance from specific, individual children. Time In should be structured and planned specifically for the individual student whose compliance has reached a level of less than 60%. The interventionist should use approximately 5 positive statements/interactions to every negative statement/interaction with that student. Data are collected for individual commands/directives given to that student and for that student's compliance. Effective Instructions are structured and practiced so that they are increasingly used for the individual student. Contingent Praise is increased and used specifically for an individual student.

Tier 3

For Tier 3, compliance training practices are created in a setting outside the classroom. The interventionist administers commands/directives using behavioral momentum. Specifically, behavioral momentum is when the interventionist uses commands that are considered high probability (i.e., commands that are most likely to elicit compliance) followed by commands/directives that are considered low probability (i.e., less likely to elicit compliance). For example, the interventionist may give instructions such as "touch your nose" or "tap your head" followed by "sit down," which has a lower probability of compliance. The interventionist should provide rewards for compliance in these practices and should continue the procedures described above in the classroom setting.

References

Benoit, D. A., Edwards, R. P., Olmi, D. J., Wilczynski, S. M., & Mandal, R. L. (2001). Generalization of a positive treatment package for child noncompliance. *Child & Family Behavior Therapy, 20,* 19-32.

Ford, A. D., Olmi, D. J., Edwards, R. P., &Tingstrom, D. H. (2001).The sequential introduction of compliance training components with elementary-aged children in general education classroom settings.*School Psychology Quarterly, 16,* 142-157.

Mandal. R. L., Olmi, D. J., Edwards, R. P., Tingstrom, D. H., & Benoit, D. A. (2000). Effective instruction delivery and time-in: Positive procedures for achieving child compliance. *Child and Family Behavior Therapy, 22,* 1-12.

Marlow, A. G., Tingstrom, D. H., Olmi, D. J., & Edwards, R. P. (1997). The effects of classroom-based time-in/time-out on compliance rates in children with speech/language disabilities. *Child & Family Behavior Therapy, 19, (2),* 1-15.

Martens, B. K. & Kelly, S. Q. (1993). A behavioral analysis of effective teaching. *School Psychology Quarterly, 8,* 10-26.

Olmi, D. J., Sevier, R. C. & Nastasi, D. F. (1997). Time-in/time-out as a response to noncompliance and inappropriate behavior with children with developmental disabilities: Two case studies. *Psychology in the Schools, 31,* 31-39.

Rhode, G., Jenson, W. R., & Reavis, H. K. (1993). *The tough kid book.* Longmont, CO: Sopris West.

Compliance Training: Procedural Integrity Checklist

Age/Grade:	Preschool – 5th grade
Setting:	School, Home, Clinic
Individual or Group:	Individual
Tier:	1, 2, & 3
Desired/ Appropriate Behavior:	Compliance
Skill Level:	Fluency to generalization

This document provides the procedure for checking the implementation integrity of the Compliance Training procedure and a procedural checklist. The Compliance Training intervention was developed as an efficient Tier 1, 2, or 3 intervention for increasing compliance and reducing problem behavior. Reducing problem behavior was designed as an approach to manage noncompliance behaviors of children by providing interventionists and other adults' antecedent and consequence strategies for delivering instructions and acknowledging compliance. Antecedent strategies are those that require a change of behaviors prior to the child's behavior occurring (e.g., changing instructions prior to the occurrence of compliance or noncompliance). Consequence strategies are those that occur after the behavior occurs (i.e., reinforcement for the occurrence of appropriate behavior).

Procedure for Integrity Checklist Observer

1) An observer who is familiar with the procedures (e.g., principal, assistant principal, school psychologist, treatment specialist, behavior specialist, counselor, lead teacher) completes the Procedural Integrity Checklist (see page 237) information about the adult, group (class, period, etc.), location, date, time, and observer's name. This observer can be the same person using the Compliance Training Observation form or it can be a different person.
2) The observer observes the person implementing the Compliance Training procedure. An initial observation should occur during the training day and then a second observation within the first couple of weeks of implementing the Compliance Training procedure so that feedback can be provided to the designated adult early in the implementation.
3) The observer watches the interventionist for the presence of behaviors on the Checklist and marks Yes if present or No if not present. If there was not an opportunity to observe some of the behaviors, then the observer marks N/O for not observed. For example, if the interventionist is implementing only the first phase of the intervention, the sections for the following phases will be considered "not observed."
4) At the completion of the observation, the observer counts the number of behaviors marked Yes and writes the number on the line for "Number of behaviors marked Yes."
5) Then the observer writes the total number of behaviors observed (i.e., the total behaviors marked Yes or No) and the percent marked Yes.
6) The observer should write any constructive feedback comments in addition to any notations made beside any individual behavior in the "Feedback" section.

7) At an appropriate time following each observation, the observer provides the interventionist with oral feedback regarding the implementation of the intervention, starting with positive behaviors observed, and a copy of the Compliance Training Procedural Integrity Checklist. The feedback should be provided the same day of the observation.

8) After the initial observation, the observer should observe the interventionist implementing the Compliance Training procedure 2-8 times depending on the length of the implementation (i.e., approximately twice a month).

9) Throughout the intervention, the interventionist is instructed to achieve an 85% accuracy rate during 3 consecutive observations before moving to the next phase of the intervention. This accuracy rate is determined by totaling the number of occurrences of each behavior and dividing that by the number of opportunities for that behavior. See the Compliance Training Observation for specific directions and examples for this calculation.

Compliance Training Procedural Integrity Checklist
Baseline and Initial Training Procedures

Interventionist: ______________________ Date: __________ Time: __________

Child: ______________________ Observer: ______________________

Location: ______________________ Signature: ______________________

N/O = Not Observed

Behaviors to Observe	Yes	No	N/O	Comments
1) At least 3 baseline observations of the interventionist and target child have been completed. (These observations include baseline rates of TI, EID, CP and child compliance.)				
2) The interventionist gave 10 instructions within a 10-15 minute period in the manner in which instructions are always given (no changes should be made.)				
3) TI data (i.e., positive to negative attention ratio) are calculated correctly as described in the Observation Form.				
4) EID baseline data are calculated correctly as described in the Observation Form.				
5) CP baseline data are calculated correctly as described in the Observation Form.				
6) Compliance baseline data are calculated correctly as described in the Observation Form.				

Number of behaviors marked Yes = _____ out of _____ = ______ %

Percent
1out of 6 = 17%
2 out of 6 = 33%
3 out of 6 = 50%
4 out of 6 = 67%
5 out of 6 = 83%
6 out of 6 = 100%

Feedback:

Compliance Training: Procedural Integrity Checklist
Daily Intervention Procedures

Interventionist: ______________________ Date: __________ Time: __________

Child: ______________________ Observer: ______________________

Location: ______________________ Signature: ______________________

N/O = Not Observed

Behaviors to Observe	Yes	No	N/O	Comments
1) A designated adult completes observations of the child's compliance and the interventionist's use of the Compliance Training procedures a minimum of twice per month throughout the implementation of the intervention.				
Time In				
2) The interventionist implements Time-In as the first step of the intervention.				
3) The interventionist delivers Time-In at a rate of 1 per minute as determined by the rate calculated on the Compliance Training Observation form.				
4) The interventionist reaches a rate per minute that equals or exceeds 1 at least 3 times prior to implementing the second phase of the intervention.				
Time In Integrity = _____/4 x 100 = _____%				
Effective Instruction Delivery				
5) The interventionist implements Effective Instruction Delivery as the second phase of the intervention.				
6) The interventionist delivers instructions in close proximity (within 2-4 feet) to the child.				
7) The interventionist delivers instructions with eye contact.				
8) The interventionist uses simple requests rather than compound requests.				
9) The interventionist delivers instructions as directives.				
10) The interventionist uses a quiet-toned, neutral voice when delivering instructions.				
11) The interventionist uses instructions that are descriptive.				
12) The interventionist uses more "start" requests than "stop" requests.				
13) The interventionist provides a 5-sec wait period before reissuing an instruction or delivering consequences.				
14) The interventionist reaches an 85% accuracy or integrity rate at least 3 times prior to implementing the third and last phase of the intervention.				

Effective Instruction Delivery Integrity _____/10 = _____%				
Contingent Praise				
15) The interventionist implements Contingent Praise as the third phase of the intervention.				
16) The interventionist delivers praise (verbal or physical) to the child contingent upon compliance to instructions.				
17) The interventionist reaches an 85% accuracy or integrity rate at least 3 times prior during the implementation of this last phase.				
Contingent Praise Integrity ______/3 = ________%				

Number of behaviors marked Yes = _____ out of _____ = ______ %

Feedback:

Time In
1 out of 4 = 25%
2 out of 4 = 50%
3 out of 4 = 75%
4 out of 4 = 100%
Effective Instruction Delivery
1 out of 10 = 10%
2 out of 10 = 20%
3 out of 10 = 30%
4 out of 10 = 40%
5 out of 10 = 50%
6 out of 10 = 60%
7 out of 10 = 70%
8 out of 10 = 80%
9 out of 10 = 90%
10 out of 10 = 100%
Contingent Praise
1 out of 3 = 33%
2 out of 3 = 67%
3 out of 3 = 100%

Total Integrity
1 out of 17 = 6%
2 out of 17 = 12%
3 out of 17 = 18%
4 out of 17 = 24%
5 out of 17 = 29%
6 out of 17 = 35%
7 out of 17 = 41%
8 out of 17 = 47%
9 out of 17 = 53%
10 out of 17 = 59%
11 out of 17 = 65%
12 out of 17 = 71%
13 out of 17 = 77%
14 out of 17 = 82%
15 out of 17 = 88%
16 out of 17 = 94%
17 out of 17 = 100%

Positive Peer Reporting

Age/Grade:	Preschool – High School
Setting:	School, Home, Clinic, In-patient
Individual or Group:	Individual
Tier:	1, 2 & 3
Desired/ Appropriate Behavior:	Increase appropriate prosocial behavior
Skill Level:	Fluency to generalization

Rationale & Research Support

Positive Peer Reporting (PPR) is a group intervention that was first introduced by Grieger, Kaufmann, and Grieger (1976) as a class-wide method to improve social behavior and interactions. PPR was designed to address children that have been socially rejected or children who are socially withdrawn/ isolated. Children in a group atmosphere (i.e., classroom, skills group, and residential home) are given the chance to provide positive comments about the behavior of another child. The children making the comments are provided reinforcement using a token economy for describing positive behaviors that the target child engaged in during a specified time period. Because the positive comments from other children and rewards earned are relevant and important, the target child experiences a change in his/her environment from one that involves either negative or neutral social interactions to one that involves more opportunity for positive social interaction. PPR has been researched with children as young as four to five years old to adolescents (Johnson-Gros & Shriver, 2006; Skinner, Neddenriep, Robinson, Ervin, & Jones, 2002) across school and residential facilities (Bowers, et al., 2009; Ervin, Miller, & Friman, 1996).

Materials

1) Poster or written steps visible for the group on making a positive comment
2) Container and material (e.g., slips of paper) with the children's names written or printed
3) Tokens (e.g., stars, cotton balls, etc.)
4) Container, poster, or other display to place the tokens
5) PPR Behavioral Observation form

Procedure for Interventionist

Before Training the Children and Implementation

1) Select a target time to implement PPR. This designated time can be a class period, recess, lunch, group time, dinner time, etc. The target time should be a time that children are allowed to socially interact as well as a time that children can improve their prosocial skills.
2) Decide how many points (e.g., 100) the group must earn collectively in order to be able to exchange them for a group reward. Children will earn a point every time that they successfully praise a peer when you call on them. When first implementing this intervention, the points the group must earn should be low enough that the reward will be earned within 1-2 days. Once the group is familiar with

the intervention, the points should be increased. Telling the children the goal will change is appropriate when introducing the intervention. When increasing the points explain to the children that they are now familiar with the process and the goal is being increased to reflect their mastery of the intervention. When setting the number of points the group must earn, consider the developmental age of the children and what is an appropriate length of time for a delayed reward.

3) Make a poster or other visual display of the PPR steps. On this poster or visual display are the four PPR steps.

    1. Look at the person.
    2. Smile.
    3. Say something nice or good that the person said or did during the day.
    4. Say something like 'good job' or 'way to go'.

4) Make or gather materials for selecting children. Write the names of the children in the group on slips of paper, popsicle sticks, or some other appropriate material. Place the children's names in a container, box, bag, jar, etc. for selecting a child to be the focus for the positive peer comments. The child that is the focus is given a label such as "star," "bee," "rockstar," or "selected student" of the day and the child's name is written on a board or placed where the other children will see the name.

5) Make or gather materials for keeping track of points the group earns when a peer provides a positive comment about the selected child ("star," "bee," "rockstar," "selected student," etc.). The method of tracking points earned needs to be a visual display such as a clear container with cotton balls or marbles or a poster on which tokens are placed using Velcro. See example tokens for a poster or wall display below.

6) Determine whether the PPR intervention will be implemented for all children or selected children. See Adjustments/Modifications for addition guidance on selecting children.

7) Conduct a baseline observation using the PPR Behavioral Observation instructions and form found in the Conducting Direct Observations section of this book (see page 414). This same observation will be used during implementation of the intervention to track progress and to determine whether or not to modify the intervention.

Training the Group for Implementing PPR

1) Define PPR. PPR can be defined as the opposite of tattling.

   The interventionist (i.e., the person responsible for implementing the intervention such as a teacher, parent, etc.) says: *PPR is the opposite of tattling. Instead of telling something that someone did wrong, I want you to tell me something good or nice that someone did.*

2) Explain the selection process to the group. (e.g., Children's names will be written on strips of paper and placed in a container.) Show the children the selected container.

   The interventionist says: *See this (container, box, bag, etc.)? Everyone's name has been placed in this (container, box, bag, etc.). Each day, I will pick one name out of the (container, box, bag, etc.). That person will be the ("star," "bee," "rockstar," "selected student," etc.) of the day. I will write the (student's, person's, or child's) name on the (board, sheet, etc.) so that everyone remembers who the (person, student, or child) is.*

3) Explain that the rest of the group will have to watch the behavior of the ("star," "bee," "rockstar," "selected student," etc.) during the designated time (class period, recess, lunch, group time, dinner time, etc.) and remember all of the good things the ("star," "bee," "rockstar," "selected student," etc.) did.

   The interventionist says: *The rest of the group will have to watch how the ("star," "bee," "rockstar," "selected student," etc.) behaves during __________ (your selected targeted time such as lunch, recess, dinner time, centers, group work, etc.). Try to watch for nice or helpful things that the ("star," "bee," "rockstar," "selected student," etc.) does for others.*

4) Tell the group that at a designated time during the day, they will all have the opportunity to report specific and genuine examples of what the ("star," "bee," "rockstar," "selected student," etc.) did.

   The interventionist says: *During __________ I will give you the opportunity to tell me and the group something you noticed that the ("star," "bee," "rockstar," "selected student," etc.) did during ________ (your selected targeted area such as lunch, recess, dinner time, centers, group work, etc.).*

5) Teach the group the four steps involved in making positive comments using the poster provided or visual display of the steps. You can change the wording for the steps as needed depending on the children's developmental level. You can also use picture icons for children who are younger or developmentally delayed.

   The interventionist says: *On this poster (point, or hold up) are the four steps that will remind you how to tell the group about what the "star" did. The first step is to (point the step) "Look at the person." The second step is to "Smile." The third step is to "Say something nice or good that the person said or did during the day." And the fourth step is to "Say something like 'good job' or 'way to go'."*

6) Start a discussion with the group, asking for specific examples of nice or helpful things someone might say or do. Start the discussion using this example: *"Billy helped me clean up at recess today. Good job!"* Remember to smile when making these statements. Write examples given by the group on the board (if possible). In addition, include some non-examples. Start with this: *"Jane was nice to me today"* and explain that instead someone would need to say what Jane said or did that was nice.

   The interventionist says: *Here is an example of how to say something about the ("star," "bee," "rockstar," "selected student," etc.): "Billy helped me clean up at recess today." Now that we know all of the steps to help us, who can give me another example of a nice thing that something said or did?*

   (Praise appropriate examples; provide feedback for inappropriate examples.)

   The interventionist says: *It is important to tell the group exactly what you saw the ("star," "bee," "rockstar," "selected student," etc.) doing. If you tell the group "Jane was nice to me today," then we really do not know what the ("star," "bee," "rockstar," "selected student," etc.) did. It would be better to say, "Jane told me I looked nice today. Way to go!"*

7) Explain to the group that when they offer a statement, they will earn a token to put in/on the container/chart. When the group earns a total of __ tokens, they will have earned a prize. Have one example of a group reward acceptable to you in case the children need an example to get them started with ideas for group rewards.

The interventionist says: *Whoever makes a positive statement will receive a token to put in/on container/chart. Now, when the whole group earns a total of __ tokens, the group will earn a reward. But first, we need to come up with some rewards that all of you will enjoy. Who has an idea of a group reward?*

Reward ideas will then be placed on the board and children will vote on the reward they would like best. The adult will guide the group on appropriate awards. For example, the adult can give a list of acceptable rewards or a visual display of rewards. The rewards can change if the children do not find the reward reinforcing.

8) Tell the children that tomorrow morning will be the first day to pick a name out of the container, box, bag, etc.

   The interventionist says: *Today was just practice. Tomorrow will be the first day we pick a name out of the (container, box, bag, etc.)!*

Day 1 Implementation Script

1) On the first day of implementation, you will say first thing in the morning:

   The interventionist says: *From now on during __________, we will be talking about how we act towards each other. Everyone's name is going to be put into a drawing, and each day I will select one person to be the ("star," "bee," "rockstar," "selected student," etc.) of the day. At the end of __________, everyone will have a chance to say something nice or positive to the "star." What you say should describe something that you saw the ("star," "bee," "rockstar," "selected student," etc.) do or say at some point during the day.*

2) Randomly select a child's name. Write the (student's, person's, or child's) name on the (board, sheet, etc.)

3) Tell the children to observe the "star's" behavior.

4) At a designated time, children will have the opportunity to spend approximately 10 minutes making positive comments about the "star."

   At PPR Time:

   The interventionist says: *Now is the time to tell me and the group something you saw the ("star," "bee," "rockstar," "selected student," etc.) do today! Who would like to go first?*

   Use a hand raising procedure or otherwise choosing a child to give feedback. If the children display inappropriate behaviors (e.g., blurting out, getting out or his or her seat), review your procedure with the children. Whoever makes a positive statement will receive a token to put in/on the container/chart. Tally the number of positive comments given and add that number of points toward the group reward. Post the point total earned by the group publicly to generate interest. When the group has met its cumulative point goal, give the group its promised reward and start a new group point chart. Remind the group they must earn collectively in order to be able to exchange the points for a group reward. In addition, the interventionist will want to remind the group how many points they need to earn. The group may not earn the reward the first day.

Adjustments/Modification

At Tier 1, all children's names are put into the selection container and then a name is randomly selected during the specified PPR times. No one child is selected more often than another child. Conduct baseline and intervention implementation observations using the PPR Behavioral Observation form on all children for Tier 1 intervention.

At Tier 2 and Tier 3, the targeted children (no more than 2) are "randomly" selected more often than the rest of the group to be the "star" of the day. However, the interventionist may decide that he or she wants to implement PPR twice a day because some children are having difficulty in one area and some children are having difficulty in another area. For example, the interventionist may select one child who is having difficulty with appropriate interaction during lunch, recess, or dinner time while the other child is having difficulty with appropriate interaction during group activities. Thus, the interventionist can have 2 different PPR times throughout the day. For Tier 2 and Tier 3 intervention, first conduct baseline observations on all children using the PPR Behavioral Observation form. Then collect baseline observations on the selected Tier 2 or Tier 3 students. Conduct intervention implementation observations on the selected Tier 2 or Tier 3 students. Compare the intervention implementation observations for the selected Tier 2 or Tier 3 students to the baseline observations for the same children and to the baseline observations for all children to make decisions about progress.

References

Bowers, F., Cook, C.R., Jensen, M.E., Snyder, T., & Mchearern, A. (2009). Generalization and maintenance of positive peer reporting intervention for peer-rejected youth. *International Journal of Cognitive Behavior Therapy*.

Ervin, R. A., Miller, P.M., & Friman, P. C. (1996). Feed the hungry bee: Using positive peer reports to improve the social interactions and acceptance of a socially rejected girl in residential care. *Journal of Applied Behavior Analysis*, 29, 251-253.

Grieger, T., Kaufmann, J. M., & Grieger, R. M. (1976). Effects of peer reporting on cooperative play and aggression of kindergarten children. *Journal of School Psychology*, 14, 307-313.

Johnson-Gros, K. N. & Shriver, M. (2006). Compliance training and positive peer reporting with a 4-year-old in a pre-school classroom. *Journal of Evidence Based Practice for Schools*, 7, 167-185.

Skinner, C. H., Neddenriep, C. E., Robinson, S. L., Ervin, R., & Jones, K. (2002). Altering educational environments through positive peer reporting: prevention and remediation of social problems associated with behavior disorders. *Psychology in the Schools*, 39, 191-201.

Sample Tokens for Tracking Points Earned by a Group

Images used with permission from Microsoft.

TIER

TIER

TIER

Positive Peer Reporting: Procedural Integrity Checklist

Age/Grade:	Preschool – High School
Setting:	School, Home, Clinic, In-patient
Individual or Group:	Individual
Tier:	1, 2 & 3
Desired/ Appropriate Behavior:	Increase appropriate prosocial behavior
Skill Level:	Fluency to generalization

The procedural integrity checklist is completed by an observer (e.g., principal, assistant principal, school psychologist, treatment specialist, behavior specialist, counselor, lead teacher) who is familiar with the Positive Peer Reporting (PPR) procedure. The observer will observe the individual interventionist implementing the PPR procedure and provide feedback. PPR is a group intervention that was developed as a class-wide method to improve social behavior and interactions. PPR was designed to address children that have been socially rejected or children who are socially withdrawn/isolated. Children in a group atmosphere are given the chance to provide positive comments about the behavior of another child.

Procedure for Integrity Checklist Observer

Initial Group Training

1) Arrange to observe the group when the interventionist is training the group to implement PPR.
2) Complete the PPR Procedural Integrity Checklist – Initial Group Training (see page 253) information about the interventionist, group, location, date, time, observer name, and observer signature.
3) Observe the interventionist for the presence of behaviors 1-13 on the Checklist and mark Yes if present or No if not present. If there is not an opportunity to observe a behavior, then mark N/O for not observed.
4) Count the number of behaviors marked Yes and write the number on the line for "Number of behaviors marked Yes."
5) Write the total number of behaviors observed (i.e., the total behaviors marked Yes or No).
6) Calculate the percent marked Yes. A chart is provided for determining the percent marked Yes. If less than 80% of behaviors are marked Yes, then provide feedback immediately to the interventionist so the checklist items can be addressed by the interventionist.
7) Write any constructive feedback comments in addition to any notations made beside any individual behavior in the "Feedback" section.
8) Provide the interventionist, at an appropriate time, with oral feedback regarding the intervention plan development, starting with positive behaviors observed, and a copy of the Positive Peer Reporting: Procedural Integrity Checklist – Initial Group Training. *The feedback should be provided the same day of the observation.*

Intervention Implementation

1) Determine a time to observe when the PPR intervention is being implemented.
2) Complete the PPR Procedural Integrity Checklist – Intervention Implementation (see page 254) information about the interventionist, group, location, date, time, observer name, and observer signature.
3) Observe the interventionist for the presence of behaviors 1-13 on the Checklist and mark Yes if present or No if not present. If there is not an opportunity to observe a behavior, then mark N/O for not observed.
4) Count the number of behaviors marked Yes and write the number on the line for "Number of behaviors marked Yes."
5) Write the total number of behaviors observed (i.e., the total behaviors marked Yes or No).
6) Calculate the percent marked Yes. A chart is provided for determining the percent marked Yes. If less than 80% of behaviors are marked Yes, then provide feedback immediately to the interventionist so the checklist items can be addressed by the interventionist.
7) Write any constructive feedback comments in addition to any notations made beside any individual behavior in the "Feedback" section.
8) Provide the interventionist, at an appropriate time, with oral feedback regarding the intervention plan development, starting with positive behaviors observed, and a copy of the Positive Peer Reporting: Procedural Integrity Checklist – Intervention Implementation. *The feedback should be provided the same day of the observation.*
9) Observe the interventionist implementing the PPR procedure approximately every other week or twice a month after the initial observation.

Positive Peer Reporting: Procedural Integrity Checklist
Initial Group Training

Interventionist: ______________________ Date: __________ Time: __________

Group: ______________________ Observer: ______________________

Location: ______________________ Signature: ______________________

Behaviors to Observe	Yes	No	Comments
1) PPR is defined as "opposite of tattling."			
2) The selection process is described to group.			
3) The children are told to observe the selected child's behavior throughout the specified time.			
4) The children are told that they will have the opportunity to report positive examples of behavior.			
5) Four steps used to make positive comments are explained to the group.			
6) Poster, jar, etc. is displayed in a visible location.			
7) Examples and non-examples of positive comments are provided.			
8) Children are given the opportunity to provide examples of positive comments.			
9) Process of earning a token after reporting comment is described.			
10) The group is told the criteria (number of points) to earn a reward.			
11) Ideas for rewards are obtained from the group.			
12) The group votes on rewards.			
13) Preferred reward is identified.			

Number of behaviors marked Yes = _____ out of _____ = ______ %

Feedback:

Percent
1 out of 13 = 8%
2 out of 13 = 15%
3 out of 13 = 23%
4 out of 13 = 31%
5 out of 13 = 39%
6 out of 13 = 46%
7 out of 13 = 54%
8 out of 13 = 62%
9 out of 13 = 69%
10 out of 13 = 77%
11 out of 13 = 85%
12 out of 13 = 92%
13 out of 13 = 100%

Positive Peer Reporting: Procedural Integrity Checklist
Intervention Implementation

Interventionist: ______________________ Date: __________ Time: __________

Child: ______________________ Observer: ______________________

Location: ______________________ Signature: ______________________

N/O = Not Observed

Behaviors to Observe	Yes	No	N/O	Comments
Beginning of Time Period				
1) Interventionist states the procedure.				
2) Child's name is selected from the container.				
3) The selected child's name is written in a visible location.				
PPR Time				
4) Interventionist states the procedure.				
5) Children are called on to make comments.				
6) The interventionist praises child for appropriate comments.				
7) The interventionist provides a token for appropriate comments.				
8) Child places the token in the appropriate place.				
9) Intervention time lasts approximately 7-10 minutes.				

Number of behaviors marked Yes = _____ out of _____ = ______ %

Feedback:

Percent
1 out of 9 = 11%
2 out of 9 = 22%
3 out of 9 = 33%
4 out of 9 = 44%
5 out of 9 = 56%
6 out of 9 = 67%
7 out of 9 = 78%
8 out of 9 = 89%
9 out of 9 = 100%

Variable Ratio – Variable Interval Reinforcement

Age/Grade:	Preschool – High School
Setting:	School, Home, In-patient
Individual or Group:	One or more people
Tier:	2 & 3
Desired/ Appropriate Behavior:	On-task, attentive behavior as well as specific targeted appropriate behaviors such as compliance, talking with permission, or remaining in seat or area
Skill Level:	Fluency to maintenance

Rationale and Research Support

Do you have a child who needs frequent reinforcement to be able to maintain appropriate levels of behavior? The schedule of reinforcement is the plan that determines when and how often reinforcement will be delivered for appropriate behavior. When using a ratio schedule, reinforcement is based on the number of responses that occur. The number of responses required prior to reinforcement can remain the same (i.e., fixed ratio), or they can vary (i.e., variable ratio or VR) each time. When using an interval schedule, reinforcement is based on the passing of an interval of time. This interval can remain the same (i.e., fixed interval), or it can vary (i.e., variable interval or VI) each time (Miltenberger, 2001). Houten and Nau (1980) found that when the schedule of reinforcement was variable interval rather than fixed interval, a child exhibited an increase in attentive behavior and a decrease in disruptive behavior and also completed more math problems. Moskowitz (2011) also found that variable ratio and fixed ratio schedules of reinforcement resulted in an increase of the occurrence and stability of the appropriate behavior.

Materials

1) Reinforcement List
2) Timer or MotivAider®
3) Variable Ratio or Variable Interval Reinforcement Charts
4) Rewards and reward pictures for the chart

Procedure for Interventionist

Variable Ratio Schedule

1) Define 1 or 2 target behaviors for the child and the corresponding replacement behavior. To define a target behavior and a replacement behavior, an operational definition of each behavior is needed. An operational definition is one that objective, clear, and observable. An operational definition should pass the Stranger test, meaning that the definition is detailed enough that if a stranger observed the behavior, he or she would be able to accurately identify and record the occurrence of the behavior based on the definition. The operational definition should also pass the Dead Man test in that the behavior should be active not passive. If a dead man can display the behavior, then it is not an active behavior.

a) Target behaviors are the observed behaviors that the interventionist wants to decrease. For example, talking out might be identified as a target behavior. Talking out may be defined as talking out loud without the permission of the interventionist or any occurrence of an unauthorized vocalization (e.g., shouts, whistles, grunts, noises).

b) Replacement behaviors are the positive behaviors the child is expected to exhibit. For example, if a child is having difficulty controlling talking to peers or is talking out in class, a replacement behavior might be "speaks only with permission." The replacement behavior is operationally defined as any time that the child raises his/her hand to speak or speaks during a time that is designated by the interventionist when all children have permission to speak or call out answers.

2) Collect baseline data. Choose a time of day when the target behavior has been observed to occur (e.g., during math instruction). Use the frequency data collection procedure described in the Conducting Direct Observations section of this book to collect data on the frequency of the target behavior. Collect baseline data a minimum of three different days to determine the frequency of the target behavior.

3) Set the schedule for reinforcement. Review the baseline data collection to determine the frequency of the target behavior(s) and to set the reinforcement schedule. For example, if the frequency of the target behavior is every 6 minutes, then the number of minutes to be set on the timer for points (reinforcement) to be earned is every 5 minutes in order to increase the likelihood of the child's successfully displaying the replacement behavior.

4) Explain the procedure to the child. Explain the procedure by showing the child the VR Reinforcement Chart on page 262 or page 263 and explain how points are earned. Describe the replacement behavior that is expected by providing the operational definition as well as examples and non-examples of the behavior.

5) Choose reinforcers and how the child will earn them. The child and the interventionist should develop and negotiate a list of potential rewards for displaying the target behaviors. Document the list of possible rewards on the Reinforcement List on page 261. This list could include any number of items such as edibles (e.g., chips, fruit, favorite snack, etc.), tangibles (e.g., stickers, certificates, small toy, etc.), activities (playing on the computer for a set amount of time, coloring in a coloring book, etc.), and social activities (e.g., free time with a friend, reading a book with a parent, playing a game with friends, etc.). Once the reinforcement list is developed, discuss with the child what amount of the reward should be given for the amount of the displayed behavior.

6) Create or use the VR Reinforcement Chart on page 262 or page 263 to record the replacement behavior and document the earning of rewards. The VR Reinforcement Chart must be visible to the child throughout the day. If a child is able to have the VR Reinforcement Chart on his or her desk without the chart being a distraction, then place it on the desk. If the VR Reinforcement Chart on the desk becomes a distraction, place it somewhere in the child's visual field so that the child can see his or her points throughout the day.

   The VR Reinforcement Chart will include age appropriate symbols for points (e.g., smiley faces for younger children, checkmarks or X's for older children). The VR Reinforcement Chart includes spaces to indicate the earning of a reward, which are designed with "Reward Picture" in the cell.

Have pictures or images available for the child to place in these spaces as the rewards are earned. Pictures or images can be found by using clip art or searching online.

A variable ratio schedule is one that provides a reward for the child following a different number of earned points as the intervention progresses. This schedule relies on pictures of pre-determined rewards being placed throughout the reinforcement chart. For example, the first reward may be provided when the child earns 5 points; however, the second reward could be provided when the child earns 7 points and the third reward following 4 earned points. The number of points required for the child to earn a reward is varied throughout the intervention.

7) Set a timer or MotivAider® for the number of minutes determined for the schedule of reinforcement in step 3. When the time expires, follow the appropriate step below:
   a) If the child has exhibited the replacement behavior(s), either the child or the interventionist fills in the symbol (e.g., smiley face, circle, or circle the X) on the chart. Provide positive attention and praise when the child earns each point. The praise should specifically state what the child did to earn the point (e.g., "I really like the way you raised your hand and waited for me to call on you instead of calling my name without having my permission."). Reset the timer.
   b) If the child exhibits an inappropriate behavior that is in opposition to the replacement behavior (e.g., child yells out rather than raising hand), then give a minor redirection to the child to let the child know that the timer will be reset. For example, say in a calm, quiet voice, "You spoke out without raising your hand, so the timer will be reset."
8) Reward the child when the child earns enough points to reach the picture of the reward. If the reward is a tangible object (e.g., sticker), then provide the reward immediately. If the reward is an activity, then the child can be given a specific amount of time with that activity (e.g., 5 minutes of computer time) immediately. However, if it is not feasible to stop current instruction or work so that the child can engage in the reward activity immediately, give the child a token that represents the reward activity the child will be allowed time for later in the day. For example, give the child a slip of paper that says "I have 5 minutes of computer time" to be turned in later in the day at a predetermined time that does not interfere with instruction.
9) Progress monitor at least twice per week throughout the intervention. Either an outside observer (e.g., school psychologist, behavior specialist, teacher assistant) or the interventionist should observe during the time specified during baseline data collection and refer to the frequency recording observation used in baseline data collection to determine if the frequency of the target behavior has decreased following the implementation of the intervention.

Variable Interval Schedule

1) Define 1 or 2 target behaviors for the child and the corresponding replacement behavior. To define a target behavior and a replacement behavior, an operational definition of each behavior is needed. An operational definition is one that objective, clear, and observable. An operational definition should pass the Stranger test, meaning that the definition is detailed enough that if a stranger observed the behavior, he or she would be able to accurately identify and record the occurrence of the behavior based on the definition. The operational definition should also pass the Dead Man test in that the behavior should be active not passive. If a dead man can display the behavior, then it is not an active behavior.

a) Target behaviors are the observed behavior that the interventionist wants to decrease. For example, talking out might be identified as a target behavior. Talking out may be defined as talking out loud without the permission of the interventionist or any occurrence of an unauthorized vocalization (e.g., shouts, whistles, grunts, noises).

b) Replacement behaviors are the positive behaviors the child is expected to exhibit. For example, if a child is having difficulty controlling talking to peers or is talking out in class, a replacement behavior might be "speaks only with permission." The replacement behavior is operationally defined as any time that the child raises his/her hand to speak or speaks during a time that is designated by the interventionist when all children have permission to speak or call out answers.

2) Collect baseline data. Choose a time of day that the behavior has been observed to occur (e.g., during math instruction). Use the frequency data collection procedure described in the Conducting Direct Observations section in this book to collect data on the frequency of the target behavior. Collect baseline data a minimum of three different days to determine the frequency of the target behavior.

3) Set the reinforcement schedule. Review the baseline data to determine the frequency of the target behavior(s) and to set the variable interval reinforcement schedule using the Variable Interval Schedule of Times on page 266. For example, if the frequency of the target behavior is every 6 minutes, then the interval schedule for reinforcement should be set based on the schedule for 5 minutes using row C of the table.

4) Explain the procedure by showing the child the VI Reinforcement Chart on page 264 or page 265 and explain how points are earned. Describe the replacement behavior that is expected by providing the operational definition as well as examples and non-examples of the behavior.

5) Choose reinforcers and how the child will earn them. The child and the interventionist should develop and negotiate a list of potential rewards for displaying the target behaviors. Document the list of possible rewards on the Reinforcement List on page 261. This list could include any number of items such as edibles (e.g., chips, fruit, favorite snack, etc.), tangibles (e.g., stickers, certificates, small toy, etc.), activities (playing on the computer for a set amount of time, coloring in a coloring book, etc.), and social activities (e.g., free time with a friend, reading a book with a parent, playing a game with friends, etc.). Once the reinforcement list is developed, discuss with the child what amount of the reward should be given for the amount of the displayed behavior.

6) Create or use the VI Reinforcement Chart on page 264 or page 265 to record the replacement behavior and document the earning of rewards. The VI Reinforcement Chart must be visible to the child throughout the day. If the child is able to have the VI Reinforcement Chart on his or her desk without it being a distraction, then place it on the desk. If the VI Reinforcement Chart on the desk becomes a distraction, place it somewhere in the child's visual field so that the child can see his or her points throughout the day. The VI Reinforcement Chart should include age appropriate symbols for points (e.g., smiley faces for younger children, checkmarks or X's for older children). The VI Reinforcement Chart includes pictures of pre-determined rewards at the end of each row on the chart.

A variable interval schedule is one that provides a reward following varying amounts of time as the intervention progresses. For example, the first reward will be provided after the child engages in the appropriate replacement behavior for 5 minutes; however, the second reward will be provided after the child engages in the replacement behavior for 3 minutes and the third reward following 7 minutes. Refer to the Variable Interval Schedule of times on page 266 for the schedule of Variable Interval rates of 3 to 10 minutes.

7) Set a timer or MotivAider® for the variable interval schedule that is selected. For this schedule, the amount of time that passes must average to be a specified amount of time. For example, if using an interval schedule of 3 minutes, the interventionist might reinforce behavior after 2 minutes, then 3 minutes, then 4 minutes, then 1 minute, then 5 minutes, then 2 minutes, and finally 4 minutes (see the Variable Interval Schedule of Times on page 266.) In this example, the interventionist made reinforcement available 7 times over a total interval period of 21 minutes. Thus, on average, three minutes passed before reinforcement was provided ($2 + 3 + 4 + 1 + 5 + 2 + 4 = 21 \div 7 = 3$); therefore, this was a 3 minute interval schedule. When the time expires for each interval, follow the appropriate step below:

    a) If the child has exhibited the replacement behavior(s), either the child or the interventionist fills in the symbol (e.g., smiley face, circle, or circle the X) on the chart. Provide positive attention and praise when the child earns the point. The praise should specifically state what the child did to earn the point (e.g., "I like the way you continued working even when there was noise on the other side of the room.")

    b) If the child exhibits the inappropriate target behavior, then give a minor redirection to the child to let the child know the timer will be reset. For example, the interventionist should say in a calm, quiet voice, "You spoke out without raising your hand, so I will reset the timer."

8) Reward the child when the child earns enough points to reach the last column that indicates "I am working for." If the reward is a tangible object (e.g., sticker), then provide the reward immediately. If the reward is an activity, then the child should be allowed the agreed upon specific amount of time with that activity (e.g., 5 minutes of computer time). However, if it is not feasible to stop current instruction or work so that the child can engage in the reward activity immediately, give the child a token that represents the reward activity the child will be allowed time for later in the day. For example, give the child a slip of paper that says "I have 5 minutes of computer time" to be turned in later in the day at predetermined time that does not interfere with instruction.

9) Progress monitor at least twice per week throughout the intervention. Either an outside observer (e.g., school psychologist, behavior specialist, teacher assistant) or the interventionist should observe during the times that were specified during baseline data collection and refer to the frequency recording observation used in baseline to determine if the frequency of the target behavior has decreased following the implementation of the intervention.

Adjustments/Modifications

For classroom observations, the observation should be conducted by an outside observer to allow the interventionist to interact naturally with the children. However, if no outside observer is available, the interventionist can set a timer and use different methods to determine the frequency of occurrence of the behavior. One method is to use a handheld tally counter. Each time the behavior occurs during the allotted time for the observation, the interventionist simply clicks the button to count another occurrence. Another method is to have pennies or other tokens in a pocket. If the behavior occurs, the interventionist simply moves the penny or token from one pocket to another.

References

Houten, R. V. & Nau, P. A. (1980). A comparison of the effects of fixed and variable ratio schedules of reinforcement on the behavior of deaf children. *Journal of Applied Behavior Analysis, 13,* 13-21.

Miltenberger, R. G. (2001). *Behavior modification: Principles and procedures.* Belmont, CA: Wadsworth Thomson Learning.

Moskowitz, R. (2011). A comparison of variable ratio and fixed ratio schedules of token reinforcement. *Applied Behavioral Analysis Master's Theses. Paper 48.* Retrieved from http://hdl.handle.net/2047/d20000986.

Reinforcer List

Child's Name: ______________________________ Date: ___________________________

Interventionist: ____________________________

Directions: The interventionist and the child should develop a list of potential rewards for displaying the appropriate behaviors. The interventionist and child the child should negotiate this list as well as the amount of the reward (e.g., how many chips, how much time on the computer, etc.)

	Reward		How much?
1.	____________	1.	____________
2.	____________	2.	____________
3.	____________	3.	____________
4.	____________	4.	____________
5.	____________	5.	____________
6.	____________	6.	____________
7.	____________	7.	____________
8.	____________	8.	____________
9.	____________	9.	____________
10.	____________	10.	____________

VR Reinforcement Chart

Name: ____________________ Date: ______________

☺ Initials: _____	☺ Initials: _____	☺ Initials: _____	☺ Initials: _____	REWARD PICTURE Time: _____	☺ Initials: _____	☺ Initials: _____	☺ Initials: _____
☺ Initials: _____	☺ Initials: _____	☺ Initials: _____	REWARD PICTURE Time: _____	☺ Initials: _____	☺ Initials: _____	☺ Initials: _____	☺ Initials: _____
☺ Initials: _____	REWARD PICTURE Time: _____	☺ Initials: _____	☺ Initials: _____	☺ Initials: _____	☺ Initials: _____	REWARD PICTURE Time: _____	☺ Initials: _____
☺ Initials: _____	☺ Initials: _____	REWARD PICTURE Time: _____	☺ Initials: _____	☺ Initials: _____	☺ Initials: _____	☺ Initials: _____	REWARD PICTURE Time: _____

☺ = *Goal 1* (write behavior goal here):

☺ = *Goal 2* (write behavior goal here):

TIER

VR Reinforcement Chart

Name: ______________________ Date: ________________

✓ Initials: _____	✓ Initials: _____	✓ Initials: _____	✓ Initials: _____	REWARD PICTURE Time: ______	✓ Initials: _____	✓ Initials: _____	✓ Initials: _____
✓ Initials: _____	✓ Initials: _____	✓ Initials: _____	REWARD PICTURE Time: ______	✓ Initials: _____	✓ Initials: _____	✓ Initials: _____	✓ Initials: _____
✓ Initials: _____	REWARD PICTURE Time: ______	✓ Initials: _____	✓ Initials: _____	✓ Initials: _____	✓ Initials: _____	REWARD PICTURE Time: ______	✓ Initials: _____
✓ Initials: _____	✓ Initials: _____	REWARD PICTURE Time: ______	✓ Initials: _____	✓ Initials: _____	✓ Initials: _____	✓ Initials: _____	REWARD PICTURE Time: ______

✓ = Goal 1 (write behavior goal here):

✓ = Goal 2 (write behavior goal here):

TIER

VI Reinforcement Chart

Name: ______________________ Date: ______________

Interval 1	Interval 2	Interval 3	Interval 4	Interval 5	Interval 6	Interval 7	I am working for:
☺	☺	☺	☺	☺	☺	☺	REWARD PICTURE Time Reward Earned: ________
☺	☺	☺	☺	☺	☺	☺	REWARD PICTURE Time Reward Earned: ________
☺	☺	☺	☺	☺	☺	☺	REWARD PICTURE Time Reward Earned: ________
☺	☺	☺	☺	☺	☺	☺	REWARD PICTURE Time Reward Earned: ________

☺ =

(Define the behavior(s) here)

TIER

VI Reinforcement Chart

Name: ______________________ Date: ______________

Interval 1	Interval 2	Interval 3	Interval 4	Interval 5	Interval 6	Interval 7	I am working for:
✓	✓	✓	✓	✓	✓	✓	REWARD PICTURE Time Reward Earned: ________
✓	✓	✓	✓	✓	✓	✓	REWARD PICTURE Time Reward Earned: ________
✓	✓	✓	✓	✓	✓	✓	REWARD PICTURE Time Reward Earned: ________
✓	✓	✓	✓	✓	✓	✓	REWARD PICTURE Time Reward Earned: ________

✓ = (Define the behavior(s) here)

23

Variable Interval Schedule Times

Use the table below to set the variable interval reinforcement schedule on the VI Reinforcement Chart. Use baseline data to determine the frequency of the target behavior and to set the variable interval reinforcement schedule. For example, if the frequency of the target behavior is every 6 minutes, then the interval schedule for reinforcement should be set using the schedule for 5 minutes using row C of the table.

Row	Interval Schedule	1st Interval	2nd Interval	3rd Interval	4th Interval	5th Interval	6th Interval	7th Interval
A	3 minutes	2 minutes	3 minutes	4 minutes	1 minute	5 minutes	2 minutes	4 minutes
B	4 minutes	2 minutes	6 minutes	1 minutes	3 minutes	4 minutes	5 minutes	7 minutes
C	5 minutes	3 minutes	7 minutes	4 minutes	6 minutes	5 minutes	2 minutes	5 minutes
D	6 minutes	4 minutes	7 minutes	5 minutes	3 minutes	8 minutes	6 minutes	9 minutes
E	7 minutes	4 minutes	10 minutes	5 minutes	7 minutes	9 minutes	6 minutes	8 minutes
F	8 minutes	5 minutes	7 minutes	6 minutes	11 minutes	8 minutes	9 minutes	10 minutes
G	9 minutes	6 minutes	7 minutes	12 minutes	8 minutes	9 minutes	11 minutes	10 minutes
H	10 minutes	7 minutes	11 minutes	10 minutes	13 minutes	8 minutes	12 minutes	9 minutes

Variable Ratio – Variable Interval: Procedural Integrity Checklist

Age/Grade:	Preschool – High School
Setting:	School, Home, In-patient
Individual or Group:	One or more people
Tier:	2 & 3
Desired/ Appropriate Behavior:	On-task, attentive behavior as well as specific targeted appropriate behaviors such as compliance, talking with permission, or remaining in seat or area.
Skill Level:	Fluency to maintenance

The procedural integrity checklist is completed by an observer (e.g., principal, assistant principal, school psychologist, treatment specialist, behavior specialist, counselor, lead teacher) who is familiar with the Variable Ratio – Variable Interval (VR/VI) procedure. The observer will assess the individual interventionist implementing the procedure and provide feedback. The schedule of reinforcement is the plan that determines when and how often reinforcement will be delivered for appropriate behavior. The use of variable ration or variable interval schedules is based on specific amounts of time or specific number of responses. These schedules can be varied based on the needs and occurrences of behavior exhibited by the children.

Procedure for Integrity Checklist Observer

1) Complete the Variable Ratio – Variable Interval: Procedural Integrity Checklist (see page 269) information about the interventionist, child, location, date, time, observer name, and observer signature.
2) Observe for the presence of behaviors 1-9 on the Checklist and mark Yes if present or No if not present. If there is not an opportunity to observe a behavior, then mark N/O for not observed. An initial observation should occur within the first two weeks of the implementation of the VR/VI procedure so that feedback can be provided to the interventionist early in the implementation.
3) Count the number of behaviors marked Yes and write the number on the line for "Number of behaviors marked Yes."
4) Write the total number of behaviors observed (i.e., the total behaviors marked Yes or No).
5) Calculate the percent marked Yes. A chart is provided for determining the percent marked Yes. If less than 80% of behaviors are marked Yes, then provide feedback immediately to the interventionist and conduct another observation the next day or as soon as possible.
6) Write any constructive feedback comments in addition to any notations made beside any individual behavior in the "Feedback" section.
7) Provide the interventionist, at an appropriate time, with oral feedback regarding the implementation of the intervention, starting with positive behaviors observed, and a copy of the Variable Ratio – Variable Interval: Procedural Integrity Checklist. *The feedback should be provided the same day of the observation.*

8) Observe the interventionist implementing the VR/VI procedure approximately every other week or twice a month after the initial observation.

Variable Ratio – Variable Interval: Procedural Integrity Checklist

Interventionist: ______________________ Date: ______________________

Child: ______________________ Time: ______________________

Location: ______________________ Observer: ______________________

N/O = Not Observed

Behaviors to Observe	Yes	No	N/O	Comments
1) The interventionist reviews definitions with the child and reminds the child of replacement behaviors.				
2) The interventionist places the VR or VI chart in a location that is visible to the child throughout the day.				
3) The chart includes pictures of the rewards that are available.				
4) The interventionist uses a timer to determine when reinforcement will be administered.				
5) *For VR procedures, the interventionist sets the timer for a specific length of time, and the timer stays set for that length of time throughout the designated period or day. *For VI procedures, the interventionist follows the appropriate predetermined interval schedule using a timer for each time interval.				
6) If, during the allotted time, the child engages in inappropriate behavior, the interventionist resets the timer.				
7) When the time expires (for VR or VI), if the child has exhibited the target behavior(s), either the interventionist or the child fills in the symbol on the child's chart.				
8) The interventionist provides labeled praise if the child has earned his/her points.				
9) When the child earns enough points and reaches the reward picture, the interventionist immediately provides the child with his/her reward.				

Number of behaviors marked Yes = _____ out of _____ = ______ %

Feedback:

Percent
1 out of 9 = 11%
2 out of 9 = 22%
3 out of 9 = 33%
4 out of 9 = 44%
5 out of 9 = 56%
6 out of 9 = 67%
7 out of 9 = 78%
8 out of 9 = 89%
9 out of 9 = 100%

Break from Work

Age/Grade:	Preschool – High School
Setting:	School, Home, Clinic, In-patient
Individual or Group:	One or more people
Tier:	1, 2, & 3
Desired/ Appropriate Behavior:	Task completion, on-task, & task accuracy
Skill Level:	Fluency to maintenance

Rationale & Research Support

Many times educators are asked to give praise or rewards (reinforcement) to children when the children are displaying appropriate behaviors. Educators often give praise or rewards randomly. However, the delivery of reinforcement on a Fixed-Time (FT) schedule (sometimes referred to as noncontingent reinforcement or NCR) has been shown to reduce rates of disruption, aggression, and self-injury (Carr et al., 2000). An example of NCR is a teacher giving positive praise every 2 minutes whenever the child displays appropriate behaviors. However, not all of the child's behaviors are reinforced by positive praise.

Sometimes children demonstrate that they want out of a situation such as work, a difficult social situation, or task demands by displaying inappropriate behaviors so that they will be removed from the classroom, sent to in-school suspension, or given out-of-school suspension. This sequence of inappropriate behavior followed by removal from the situation is referred to as escape or negative reinforcement. Negative reinforcement is defined as a removal of aversive stimulus, resulting in the increased probability of the same behavior in the future. For example, a teacher removing a child from the classroom or taking away the child's work increases the probability of inappropriate behaviors in the future, thus providing the child with negative reinforcement. Waller and Higbee (2010) measured the effects of a FT schedule of escape (negative reinforcement), also known as Break from Work, on the disruptive and appropriate academic behaviors of two junior high students in a public school setting. Results demonstrated that FT escape from tasks resulted in a substantial decrease in disruptive behavior and an increase in time engaged in tasks for both participants.

Materials

1) Timer or MotivAider®
2) Visual prompt or cue
3) Chart to monitor progress
4) Break from work chart

Procedure for Interventionist

Before Implementing Break from Work

1) Define 1 or 2 target behaviors for the child and the corresponding replacement behavior. To define a target behavior and a replacement behavior, an operational definition of each behavior is needed.

An operational definition is one that is objective, clear, and observable. An operational definition should pass the Stranger Test, meaning that the definition is detailed enough that if a stranger observed the behavior, he or she would be able to accurately identify and record the occurrence of the behavior based upon the definition. The operational definition should also pass the Dead Man test in that the behavior should be active, not passive. If a dead man can display the behavior, then it is not an active behavior.

c) Target behaviors are the observed behaviors that the interventionist wants to decrease. For example, a target behavior can be identified as talking out. Talking out may be defined as talking out loud without the permission of the interventionist or any occurrence of an unauthorized vocalization (e.g., shouts, whistles, grunts, noises).

d) Replacement behaviors are the positive behaviors the child is expected to display or do. For example, if a child is having difficulty controlling talking to peers or is talking out in class, a replacement behavior might be "speaks only with permission." The replacement behavior might be operationally defined as any time that the child raises his/her hand to speak or speaks during a time that is designated by the interventionist or when all children have permission to speak or call out answers.

2) Collect baseline data. Choose a time of day when the target behavior has been observed to occur (e.g., during math instruction). Use the partial interval recording collection procedure described in the Conducting Direct Observations section of this book to collect data on the percentage of the target behavior. Collect baseline data a minimum of three different days to determine the percentage of the target behavior.

3) Set the schedule for the Break from Work (negative reinforcement). Review the baseline data collection to determine the percentage of the target behavior(s) and to set the schedule. For example, if the percentage of the target behavior is 50% in 20 minutes (using the partial interval observation) and the average number of minutes between each display of the target behaviors is 1 minute, then the number of minutes to be set on the MotivAider® or other timing device for a Break from Work (negative reinforcement) to be earned is every 1 minute (this predetermined time is also called Fixed Time Interval) in order to increase the likelihood of success for the child (Lalli, Casey, & Kates, 1997).

4) Create or use the Break from Work Chart on page 277 to record the replacement behavior and earning of a break. Once a decision has been made about the time interval that will be used, break up the instructional period, study time, etc. into equal intervals. For example, if the child needs a break every 3 minutes based on baseline data, then the divide the instructional period into equal intervals. If the instructional period is 60 minutes and the child needs a break every 3 minutes, then there will be 20 intervals (see Example Break from Work Chart on page 275). Write the number of intervals in which the child needs to display appropriate behavior to meet the goal. Make a slash or other mark in each interval box when the child displays appropriate behavior. At the end of the instructional period or time period, count the number of slashes or marks to determine if the child earned a break based upon the predetermined goal. (In the example based upon 60 instructional minutes with 20 intervals, the interventionist set the MotivAider® to 3 minutes. For every 3-minute interval in which the child displayed the replacement behavior, the interventionist marked a slash in the appropriate interval box. Then, the interventionist

determines if the child met the predetermined goal. Again, please see Example Break from Work Chart on page 275)

5) The Break from Work Chart must be visible to the child throughout the day. If a child is able to leave the chart on his or her desk without the chart being a distraction, then place it on the desk. If the chart on the desk becomes a distraction, place it somewhere else but clearly in the child's visual field so that the child can see the points throughout the day. Use age appropriate symbols for points on the Break from Work Chart (e.g., smiley faces for younger children, checkmarks or X's for older children, etc.).

6) Explain the procedure to the child using the Break from Work Chart on page 277. Then explain how the child will be able to earn points. Describe the replacement behavior that is expected by providing the operational definition as well as examples and non-examples of the behavior.

Implementing Break from Work

7) Set a timer or MotivAider® for the number of minutes determined for the Break from Work schedule in step 3.

    a. At the beginning of each Break from Work session, place two small different color sticky notes on the child's desk; label one "work" (e.g., yellow note) and one "break" (e.g., orange note). At the beginning of each Break from Work session, walk by the child's desk and point to the note labeled "work" as the prompt for the child to begin working. At predetermined time (FT interval), walk by the child's desk and point to the note labeled "break" to cue the child to take an in-seat break from instruction. Use one silent vibrating timer (e.g., MotivAider®) to cue the delivery of escape on the appropriate reinforcement schedule and a second silent vibrating timer to measure the duration of the break. At the end of the break, approach the child's desk and point to the note labeled "work" as a prompt for the child to return to working on the assigned task.

    b. When the time expires, choose the appropriate action below:

        i) If the child exhibited the replacement behavior(s), either the child or the interventionist fills in the symbol (e.g., smiley face, circle, or circle the X) on the chart. Provide positive attention and praise when the child earns the break. The praise should specifically state what was done to earn the break (e.g., "I really like the way you raised your hand and waited for me to call on you instead of calling my name.").

        ii) If the child exhibited an inappropriate behavior that is in opposition to the replacement behavior (e.g., child yells out rather than raising hand), then give a minor redirection to the child to let the child know that the timer will be reset. For example, say in a calm, quiet voice, "You spoke out without raising your hand, so the timer will be reset."

        iii) The negative reinforcement does not have to be given immediately. The interventionist can allow the child to earn a number of seconds or a minute for each interval the child is displaying the replacement behavior. For example, an interventionist might decide that a child can earn 30 seconds of break from work for every 2 minutes the child displays on-task behavior. At the end of a 20-minute Break from Work session composed of ten 2-minute intervals, the child may have earned 2 ½ minutes of break from work because the child was on task five out of the ten 2-minute intervals (30 seconds x 5 intervals equals 150 seconds earned or 2 ½ minutes).

8) Progress monitor at least twice per week throughout the intervention. Either an outside observer (e.g., school psychologist, behavior specialist, teacher assistant) or the interventionist should observe during the times that were specified during baseline data collection and refer to the Partial Interval observation used in baseline data collection to determine if the frequency of the target behavior has decreased following the implementation of the intervention.

Adjustments/Modifications

In classrooms, the observation should be conducted by an outside observer to allow the interventionist to interact naturally with the child. However, if no outside observer is available, the interventionist can set a timer and use different methods to determine the frequency of occurrence of the behavior. One method is to use a handheld tally counter. Each time the behavior occurs during the allotted time for the observation, the interventionist simply clicks the button to count another occurrence. Another method is to have pennies or other tokens in a pocket. If the behavior occurs, the interventionist simply moves the penny or token from one pocket to another.

References

Carr, J. E., Coriaty, S., Wilder, D. A., Gaunt, B. T., Dozier, C. L., & Britton, L. N. (2000). A review of "noncontingent" reinforcement as treatment for the aberrant behavior of individuals with developmental disabilities. *Research in Developmental Disabilities, 21,* 377–391.

Lalli, J. S., Casey, S. D., & Kates, K. (1997). Noncontingent reinforcement as treatment for severe problem behavior: Some procedural variations. *Journal of Applied Behavior Analysis, 30,* 127–137.

Waller, R. D. & Higbee, T. S. (2010). The effects of Fixed-Time escape on inappropriate and appropriate classroom behavior. *Journal of Applied Behavior Analysis, 43,* 149-153.

Example Break from Work Chart

Child Name: ___Tommy_______________________ Date: ______Today____________________

FT Interval (how many minutes are the intervals to earn towards a break): ________________3________________

The goals in the below examples are based on a percentage. The goal for the child in this example is approximately 60%.

Time: 7:30-8:30am

Interval	1	2	3	4	5	6	7	8	9	10
	/	/		/		/		/	/	/
	11	12	13	14	15	16	17	18	19	20
		/	/	/			/	/	/	

Count the number of intervals the child displayed the replacement behavior(s). Then write that number in the total number space. The goal is predetermined based on baseline data or previous data in intervention. However, the goal can change based on the data.

Total number: ___13___/20 Goal is ____12________ If child met goal, BREAK! (The child earns 30 seconds of break for each interval the replacement behavior was displayed.)

Time: 8:30-9:30

Interval	1	2	3	4	5	6	7	8	9	10
	/		/		/	/	/			/
	11	12	13	14	15	16	17	18	19	20
	/	/	/			/	/			

Total number: __11____/20 Goal is: ____12________ If child met goal, BREAK! (The child earns 30 seconds of break for each interval the replacement behavior was displayed.)

Time: 9:35-10:35

Interval	1	2	3	4	5	6	7	8	9	10
	/	/	/	/			/	/		
	11	12	13	14	15	16	17	18	19	20

Total number: __6____/20 Goal is: ___12_________ If child met goal, BREAK! (The child earns 30 seconds of break for each interval the replacement behavior was displayed.)

Time: 10:35-11:15

Interval	1	2	3	4	5	6	7	8	9	10	11	12	13
	/		/	/	/		/		/	/		/	

Total number: __8____/13 Goal is: ______7______ If child met goal, BREAK! (The child earns 30 seconds of break for each interval the replacement behavior was displayed.)

Time: 12:20-12:40

Interval	1	2	3	4	5	6
	/	/			/	/

Total number: ___4___/6 Goal is: _____4_______ If child met goal, BREAK! (The child earns 30 seconds of break for each interval the replacement behavior was displayed.)

Time: 12:40-1:40

Interval	1	2	3	4	5	6	7	8	9	10
	/	/	/		/	/	/		/	
	11	12	13	14	15	16	17	18	19	20
	/	/	/	/	/	/	/			

Total number: ___14___/20 Goal is: _____12_______ If child met goal, BREAK! (The child earns 30 seconds of break for each interval the replacement behavior was displayed.)

1:45-2:00

Interval	1	2	3	4	5
	/	/	/	/	

Total number: ___4___/5 Goal is: ____3________ If met goal, BREAK! (The child earns 30 seconds of break for each interval the replacement behavior was displayed.)

2:40-2:55

Interval	1	2	3	4	5
	/	/	/		

Total number: ___3___/5 Goal is: ____3________ If child met goal, BREAK! (The child earns 30 seconds of break for each interval the replacement behavior was displayed.)

Total for the day: _63_(how many intervals child displayed replacement behaviors)_/109 (total number of intervals) = __58% Goal is: ____65%__________ Did ____Tommy____ meet the goal? YES or NO

Break from Work Chart

Child Name: ______________________________ Date: ______________________________

FT Interval (how many minutes are the intervals to earn towards a break): ______________________________

Time: ________________________

Interval	1	2	3	4	5	6	7	8	9	10

Goal is number: ______/10 Total number met: ______/10 If child met goal, then BREAK!

Time: ________________________

Interval	1	2	3	4	5	6	7	8	9	10

Total number: ______/10 Goal is: ____________ If child met goal, BREAK!

Time: ________________________

Interval	1	2	3	4	5	6	7	8	9	10

Total number: ______/10 Goal is: ____________ If child met goal, BREAK!

Time: ________________________

Interval	1	2	3	4	5	6	7	8	9	10

Total number: ______/10 Goal is: ____________ If child met goal, BREAK!

Time: ________________________

Interval	1	2	3	4	5	6	7	8	9	10

Total number: ______/10 Goal is: ____________ If child met goal, BREAK!

Time: ________________________

Interval	1	2	3	4	5	6	7	8	9	10

Total number: ______/10 Goal is: ____________ If child met goal, BREAK!

Time: ________________________

Interval	1	2	3	4	5	6	7	8	9	10

Total number: ______/10 Goal is: ____________ If child met goal, BREAK!

Time: ________________________

Interval	1	2	3	4	5	6	7	8	9	10

Total number: ______/10 Goal is: ____________ If child met goal, BREAK!

Time: ________________________

Interval	1	2	3	4	5	6	7	8	9	10

Total number: ______/10 Goal is: ____________ If met goal, BREAK!

Total for the day: ______/90. Goal is: ____________ Did (child's name)__________ meet the goal? YES or NO

Break from Work: Procedural Integrity Checklist

Age/Grade:	Preschool – High School
Setting:	School, Home, Clinic, In-patient
Individual or Group:	One or more people
Tier:	1, 2, & 3
Desired/ Appropriate Behavior:	Task completion, on-task, & task accuracy
Skill Level:	Fluency to maintenance

The procedural integrity checklist is completed by an observer (e.g., principal, assistant principal, school psychologist, treatment specialist, behavior specialist, counselor, lead teacher) who is familiar with the Break from Work procedure. The observer will assess the individual interventionist implementing the procedure and provide feedback. The schedule of negative reinforcement (break from work) is the plan that determines when and how often the break from work will be delivered for appropriate behavior. The use of Fixed Time schedules is based on specific amounts of time. These schedules can be varied based on the needs and occurrences of behavior exhibited by the child.

Procedure for Integrity Checklist Observer

1) Complete the Break from Work: Procedural Integrity Checklist (see page 279) information about the interventionist, child, location, date, time, observer name, and observer signature.
2) Observe for the presence of behaviors 1-9 on the Checklist and mark Yes if present or No if not present. If there is not an opportunity to observe a behavior, then mark N/O for not observed. An initial observation should occur within the first two weeks of the implementation of the Break from Work procedure so that feedback can be provided to the interventionist early in the implementation.
3) Count the number of behaviors marked Yes and write the number on the line for "Number of behaviors marked Yes."
4) Write the total number of behaviors observed (i.e., the total behaviors marked Yes and No).
5) Calculate the percent marked Yes. A chart is provided for determining the percent marked Yes. If less than 80% of behaviors are marked Yes, then provide feedback immediately to the interventionist and conduct another observation the next day or as soon as possible.
6) Write any constructive feedback comments in addition to any notations made beside any individual behavior in the "Feedback" section.
7) Provide the interventionist, at an appropriate time, with oral feedback regarding the implementation of the intervention, starting with positive behaviors observed, and a copy of the Break from Work: Procedural Integrity Checklist. *The feedback should be provided the same day of the observation.*
8) Observe the interventionist implementing the Break from Work procedure approximately every other week or twice a month after the initial observation.

Break from Work: Procedural Integrity Checklist

Interventionist: ______________________ Date: ______________________

Child: ______________________ Time: ______________________

Location: ______________________ Observer: ______________________

N/O = Not Observed

Behaviors to Observe	Yes	No	N/O	Comments
1) The interventionist reviews definitions of target behaviors and reminds child of replacement behaviors.				
2) The Break from Work chart is visible to the child throughout the day, either on the child's desk or in an appropriate location in the classroom.				
3) The interventionist uses some sort of visual cue [places two small, different color sticky notes on the child's desk, one labeled "work" (e.g., yellow note) and one labeled "break" (e.g., orange note)] throughout the time period.				
4) The interventionist uses a timing device to be cued of the intervals when the break should be administered.				
5) The interventionist follows the appropriate schedule with the number of minutes on the timer.				
6) If, during the allotted time, the child engages in inappropriate behavior, the interventionist resets the timer.				
7) When the time expires, if the child has exhibited the target behaviors, either the interventionist or child fills in the symbol on the child's chart.				
8) When the time expires, if the child has exhibited the target behaviors, the interventionist provides labeled praise.				
9) The interventionist either allows the break at each interval or the child is given the total time break at the end of the time period.				

Number of behaviors marked Yes = _____ out of _____ = ______ %

Feedback:

Percent
1 out of 9 = 11%
2 out of 9 = 22%
3 out of 9 = 33%
4 out of 9 = 44%
5 out of 9 = 56%
6 out of 9 = 67%
7 out of 9 = 78%
8 out of 9 = 89%
9 out of 9 = 100%

TIER

Structured Breaks

Age/Grade:	Kindergarten – High School
Setting:	School, Home, In-Patient
Individual or Group:	Individual
Tier:	2 & 3
Desired/ Appropriate Behavior:	Appropriate self-removal from difficult situations that have typically resulted in negative, sometimes verbally aggressive behaviors
Skill Level:	Fluency to maintenance

Rationale & Research Support

Do you have a student or a child who seems to become angry at the drop of a hat? Does the child's angry response seem to be out of proportion to the situation? Does the child seem to understand that stepping away from the situation is the only appropriate response and yet cannot make that step? A break card is a visual support that you/an interventionist can use to remind children to utilize communication skills or that children can use as an appropriate way to request escape when they need to step away from a situation that causes anxiety or anger. According to Cihak and Gana (2008), self-management techniques are effective antecedent intervention techniques. The use of this particular type of self-management technique has been called a variety of different names such as "taking a break," "cool down time," or "break cards." Interventions that have focused on self-regulation have shown to cause increases in on-task behavior and compliance (Briesch & Daniels, 2013; Wilkinson, 2005). The use of non-contingent escape from tasks and activities by using break cards has been shown to be an effective way to decrease inappropriate behavior maintained by negative reinforcement (Cihak & Gana, 2008).

Materials

1) Structured Breaks Intervention Worksheet
2) Structured Break Scatterplot
3) Break Cards
4) Reinforcer/Reward List
5) Reinforcers/Rewards

Procedure for Interventionist

1) Review the Structured Breaks Intervention Worksheet and use it to document the specific the target behavior, goal, structured break requirements, and rewards and to support implementation of the intervention.
2) Define target behaviors in observable, measureable terms.

a) Choose no more than 3-5 target behaviors. These behaviors are most often behaviors that need to be decreased. For example, the target behavior can be to decrease verbal outbursts or to decrease the frequency of crying when upset.

b) All target behaviors should be operationally defined so that they are clear, observable, and measureable. Example target behaviors are listed below.

- Crying: to shed tears with an audible sound that can be heard from at least 10 feet away and occurs longer than 30 seconds
- Teasing: to pester, annoy, or upset another by use of jokes, questions, noises, or other verbal/nonverbal means (Other nonverbal means could include making faces or imitating behavioral characteristics of another.)
- Verbal aggression towards peers: to engage in deliberately harmful verbal behavior that is typically both unprovoked and repeated (Other verbal aggression includes an intentional abuse of power such as teasing, taunting, or threatening; this aggression can be initiated by one or more individuals.)
- Verbal outburst: to yell and/or scream at a volume that is above speaking volume (Verbal outburst may be accompanied by crying or physical characteristics such as red face, tensing muscles, or lack of breath.)

3) Collect baseline data on the frequency, duration, and intensity of the target behaviors. Use the Structured Breaks Scatterplot instructions and form found in the Conducting Direct Observations section of this book. An example Scatterplot can also be found in the Conducting Direct Observations section.

4) Determine the requirements for the structured breaks.

a) Determine specific guidelines about where the child will go and what appropriate behavior should be exhibited during the structured breaks. Document these specifics on the Structured Breaks Intervention Worksheet (see the Worksheet on page 288).

i) Some possible locations for a structure break include in a chair in the back of the room or a small area of the room blocked off just for this child, the counselor's office or room, or a mentor's room.

ii) An example of a requirement for appropriate behavior is that the student finishes the allotted time of the break (e.g., 3 minutes) and verbally expresses to the adult the desire to return. If any physical characteristics were present prior to the structured break (e.g., tense muscles or clenched teeth), the student must not have any of the physical characteristics present to return.

b) Determine the specific time limit (e.g., 5 minutes) after which the child is expected to return to class or the appropriate location. The child is to be ready to exhibit appropriate behavior at that time.

An example of determining the specific time limit using the Structured Breaks Scatterplot baseline data on the duration of the target behavior is as follows: If the child cried for 20 minutes on average across 5 incidents of crying during baseline, then initially set the specific time limit a little below the baseline, such as 15 minutes.

c) Determine the number of break cards to be used each day or week by examining the baseline data and the frequency of the target behaviors.

- If the child has one incident of the target behavior per day, then one break card should be made available per day. When the child successfully uses the break card (or no longer needs one per day), then the number of break cards made available should be decreased gradually (e.g., one break card every other day).
- If baseline data indicate that the child engages in two incidents of the target behavior per week, then two break cards should be made available per week.

d) Create break cards. See example break cards on pages 285-287.

e) Determine appropriate daily or weekly rewards (e.g., access to a preferred activity or access to preferred tangible items) for the child for engaging in the replacement behavior of using the break cards to replace the target behavior. Reward the child for using the break card rather than engaging in the target behaviors. (Use the Reinforcement List provided on page 289 to determine possible rewards to use.) Once a list of possible rewards is determined, document the specific rewards to be used for this intervention on the Structured Breaks Intervention Worksheet that must be signed by both the interventionist and the child.

5) Introduce the plan to the child.

a) Use the Structured Breaks Intervention Worksheet to support presentation of the plan to the child.

b) Explain to the child that he/she will have access to break cards to be used when needed to move away from the situation. Explain the purpose of the card is that the child use it at time when the child recognizes the wish to engage in the target behavior. Explain the better choice is for the child to choose to move away from the situation to prevent the occurrence of the target behaviors (e.g., disrespect, verbally aggressive comments towards peers and/or adults).

c) Inform the child of the specific guidelines about where the child will go and what the child should be doing during the break.

d) Inform the child of the specific time limit (e.g., 5 minutes) for the break. Also explain that the child is expected to return to class or the appropriate location and be ready to exhibit appropriate behavior when the break ends.

e) Inform the child of the requirements for earning the reward. Document these requirements on the Structured Breaks Intervention Worksheet.

6) Monitor progress.

a) Determine a review period (e.g., weekly, every 3 weeks). If a child engages in the target behavior one or more times per day, reviews should occur frequently. However, if the child engages in the target behavior once or twice per week, then a review can be held following 3-4 weeks of intervention to determine effectiveness. Following each review period, the number of break cards available for the child should be decreased.

b) Continue to collect data using the Structured Breaks Scatterplot. Specifically, the frequency, duration, and intensity of the target behaviors should be documented using the Scatterplot. Additionally, the appropriate use of break cards should be documented (date and time of occurrence) on the Scatterplot. The goal is to determine if the target behaviors decrease or increase, as intended. Additionally, the goal is to determine if the break cards are being used when an opportunity presents itself.

For example, if the Structured Breaks Scatterplot data indicate that the break cards are being used following an outburst that has already begun, then the child did not appropriately use the break card prior to the behavior occurring. However, if data indicate that break cards are used and not followed by inappropriate behavior or outbursts and the inappropriate behavior continues to decrease, then data indicate the appropriate use of break cards.

Accommodations and Modifications

1) Some children may not be able to identify when they are going to engage in the target behavior or may not be able to appropriately request the break when one is necessary. If this situation occurs, the interventionist should acknowledge when the child needs to take a break and provide the break card to the child. For example, if the child begins to clench his fists and teeth prior to engaging in a verbal outburst, the teacher should deliver a break card to the child upon first observing those behaviors rather than waiting for the outburst to occur.
2) Some children may manipulate the use of the break cards and attempt to stay longer than the time allowed for the break or ask for more break cards than provided. The purpose of the rewards is that the rewards function as reinforcers and increase the use of appropriate replacement behaviors (i.e., break cards). Therefore, if the children do not use the break cards correctly, the recommendation is that the interventionist and child re-visit the list of rewards and modify the options in order to motivate the student to engage in the procedure appropriately.

References

Briesch, A.M. and Daniels, B. (2013). Using self-management interventions to address general education behavioral needs: Assessment of effectiveness and feasibility. *Psychology in the Schools, 50,* 366-381.

Cihak, D. F. and Game, R. I. (2008). Noncontingent escape access to self-reinforcement to increase task engagement for children with moderate to severe disabilities. *Education and Training inDevelopmental Disabilities, 43,* 556-568.

Wilkinson, L. A. (2005). Supporting the inclusion of students with emotional and behavioral disorders: Examples of using conjoint behavioral consultation and self-management. *The International Journal of Special Education, 20,* 73-84.

Example Break Cards

BREAK CARD	BREAK CARD
BREAK CARD	BREAK CARD
BREAK CARD	BREAK CARD

Example Break Cards

 I need a break	 I need a break
 I need a break	 I need a break
 I need a break	 I need a break

Image used with permission from Microsoft.

Example Break Cards

These break cards are to be used when the child does not want to verbally communicate the need for a break or cannot verbally communicate the need for a break. The card should be green on one side and red on the other side. The green side of the card is face up when things are fine. When the child needs to use a break, the child turns the card over to red. Color the side labeled Green with a green crayon, marker, or pencil. Color the side labeled Red with a red crayon, marker, or pencil. Fold the break card in half and glue or tape the halves together so that green is on one side of the card and red on the other side.

GREEN	RED

GREEN	RED

Structured Breaks Intervention Worksheet

Child's Name: ___________________________ Date Worksheet Completed: __________________

Interventionist: _________________________ Date of Implementation: ______________________

1) What behaviors do you want to increase?

____

____

2) What behaviors do you want to decrease?

____

____

3) What rewards are you going to use? ____

____

4) What are the steps that the child should use to deliver the card to the interventionist?

____

____

5) Where will the child go when taking the structured break? (Provide two locations. One location is for primary use; the second is for a backup.)

____

____

6) What behaviors must the child exhibit while taking the break and prior to going back to class? (i.e., describe the procedure for re-entering class.)

____

10) How often will the interventionist review the Structured Breaks intervention? ________________

____

Interventionist Signature: ____

Child's Signature: ____

Reinforcer List

Child's Name: ______________________________ Date: ______________________________

Interventionist: ______________________________

Directions: The interventionist and the child should develop a list of potential rewards for displaying the appropriate behaviors. The interventionist and the child should negotiate this list as well as the amount of the reward (e.g., how many chips, how much time on the computer, etc.)

Reward		How much?	
2.	______________________________	3.	______________________________
4.	______________________________	2.	______________________________
3.	______________________________	3.	______________________________
4.	______________________________	4.	______________________________
5.	______________________________	5.	______________________________
6.	______________________________	6.	______________________________
7.	______________________________	7.	______________________________
8.	______________________________	8.	______________________________
9.	______________________________	9.	______________________________
10.	______________________________	10.	______________________________

Structured Breaks: Procedural Integrity Checklist

Age/Grade:	Kindergarten – High School
Setting:	School, Home, In-Patient
Individual or Group:	Individual
Tier:	2 & 3
Desired/ Appropriate Behavior:	Appropriate self-removal from difficult situations that have typically resulted in negative, sometimes verbally aggressive behaviors
Skill Level:	Fluency to maintenance

The procedural integrity checklist is completed by an observer (e.g., principal, assistant principal, school psychologist, treatment specialist, behavior specialist, counselor, lead teacher) who is familiar with the Structured Breaks procedure. The observer will assess the individual interventionist implementing the Structured Breaks procedure and provide feedback. The Structured Breaks intervention was developed as an efficient Tier 1 or 2 intervention for reducing problem behavior.

Procedure for Integrity Checklist Observer

Intervention Plan Development

1) Arrange to be at the meeting between the interventionist and the child to develop the Structured Breaks intervention plan.
2) Complete the Structured Breaks Procedural Integrity Checklist – Intervention Plan Development (see page 292) information about the interventionist, child, location, date, time, observer name, and observer signature.
3) Observe for behaviors 1-9. The interventionist should explain the target behaviors, the goals, the intervention steps, and the reward to the child.
4) Observe the interventionist for the presence of behaviors on the Checklist and mark Yes if present or No if not present. If there is not an opportunity to observe a behavior, then mark N/O for not observed.
5) Count the number of behaviors marked Yes and write the number on the line for "Number of behaviors marked Yes."
6) Write the total number of behaviors observed (i.e., the total behaviors marked Yes or No).
7) Calculate the percent marked Yes. A chart is provided for determining the percent marked Yes. If less than 80% of behaviors are marked Yes, then provide feedback immediately to the interventionist so the checklist items can be addressed by the interventionist.
8) Write any constructive feedback comments in addition to any notations made beside any individual behavior in the "Feedback" section.
9) Provide the interventionist, at an appropriate time, with oral feedback regarding the intervention plan development, starting with positive behaviors observed, and a copy of the Structured Breaks: Procedural Integrity Checklist – Intervention Plan Development. *The feedback should be provided the same day of the observation.*

Intervention Implementation

1) Determine a time to observe when the child is likely to exhibit the target behaviors. Obtain a copy or review the interventionist's Structured Breaks Scatterplot to aid in identifying the likely time of day or day of the week. If the frequency with which the target behavior occur is low (e.g., once per day, twice per week), then use of the break card is not likely to be observable.
2) Complete the Structured Breaks Procedural Integrity Checklist – Intervention Implementation (see page 293) information about the interventionist, child, location, date, time, observer name, and observer signature.
3) Observe for behaviors 1-9. An initial observation should occur within the first two weeks of the implementation of the Structured Breaks procedure so that feedback can be provided to the interventionist early in the implementation.
4) Observe for the presence of behaviors 1-9 on the Checklist and mark Yes if present or No if not present. If there is not an opportunity to observe a behavior, then mark N/O for not observed.
5) Count the number of behaviors marked Yes and write the number on the line for "Number of behaviors marked Yes."
6) Write the total number of behaviors observed (i.e., the total behaviors marked Yes or No).
7) Calculate the percent marked Yes. A chart is provided for determining the percent marked Yes. If less than 80% of behaviors are marked Yes, then provide feedback immediately to the interventionist and conduct another observation the next day or as soon as possible.
8) Write any constructive feedback comments in addition to any notations made beside any individual behavior in the "Feedback" section.
9) Provide the interventionist, at an appropriate time, with oral feedback regarding the implementation of the intervention, starting with positive behaviors observed, and a copy of the Structured Breaks: Procedural Integrity Checklist – Intervention Implementation. *The feedback should be provided the same day of the observation.*
10) Observe the interventionist implementing the Structured Breaks procedure approximately every other week or twice a month after the initial observation.

Structured Breaks: Procedural Integrity Checklist

Intervention Plan Development

Interventionist: ______________________ Date: __________ Time: __________

Child: ______________________ Observer: ______________________

Location: ______________________ Signature: ______________________

N/O = Not Observed

Behaviors to Observe	Yes	No	N/O	Comments
1) The interventionist introduces the plan to the child. The Structured Breaks Intervention Worksheet is used to support presentation of the plan.				
2) The interventionist reviews with the child the target behaviors to decrease and/or increase.				
3) The interventionist presents the short and long term goals to the child.				
4) The interventionist reviews the steps that the child should use to deliver the card to the interventionist.				
5) The interventionist determines a location and backup location for the breaks and shows these locations to the child.				
6) The interventionist defines the behaviors the child must exhibit while taking the break and prior to going back to class. List the procedure for re-entering class				
7) The interventionist defines the behaviors the child must exhibit for re-entering class.				
8) The interventionist and the child determine and agree upon the rewards.				
9) The interventionist determines when the intervention is reviewed.				

Number of behaviors marked Yes = _____ out of _____ = ______ %

Feedback:

Percent
1 out of 9 = 11%
2 out of 9 = 22%
3 out of 9 = 33%
4 out of 9 = 44%
5 out of 9 = 56%
6 out of 9 = 67%
7 out of 9 = 78%
8 out of 9 = 89%
9 out of 9 = 100%

TIER

Structured Breaks: Procedural Integrity Checklist
Intervention Implementation

Interventionist: ______________________ Date: __________ Time: __________

Child: ______________________ Observer: ______________________

Location: ______________________ Signature: ______________________

N/O = Not Observed

Behaviors to Observe	Yes	No	N/O	Comments
1) The interventionist reminds the child of the Structured Break procedure at the beginning of each day or period.				
2) The interventionist provides the child the allotted break cards at the beginning of the day/period.				
3) The child uses the break card at the appropriate time; or if a modification is being used, the interventionist presents the break card at the appropriate time.				
4) When the child uses the break card, the child is given access to his or her break location for the allotted time.				
5) The child goes to the appropriate structured break location.				
6) The child engages in the pre-determined (as listed on the Structured Breaks Intervention Worksheet) behavior during the structured break.				
7) The child returns from the structured break no later than the pre-determined time.				
8) The child exhibits appropriate behavior upon returning from the structured break.				
9) At the end of the day/period, if the child used the break cards appropriately or if the child did not need to request a break card and did not engage in the negative target behavior, the interventionist provides a predetermined reward. (If the child should have used a break card but did not, then put in comment section)				

Number of behaviors marked Yes = _____ out of _____ = ______ %

Feedback:

Percent
1 out of 9 = 11%
2 out of 9 = 22%
3 out of 9 = 33%
4 out of 9 = 44%
5 out of 9 = 56%
6 out of 9 = 67%
7 out of 9 = 78%
8 out of 9 = 89%
9 out of 9 = 100%

Self-Monitoring

Age/Grade:	2nd grade – High School
Setting:	School, Home, Clinic, In-patient
Individual or Group:	Individual
Tier:	2 & 3
Desired/ Appropriate Behavior:	On-task, task accuracy, task completion, anger management, relaxation, hand raising to ask a question, making appropriate comments, exercising, etc.
Skill Level:	Fluency to generalization

Rationale & Research Support

Self-monitoring, a part of overall self-regulation, is the most common form of self-management strategies taught to children. Self-monitoring requires a variety of prerequisite skills such as self-observation, self-recording, and self-reinforcement (reward) for meeting or exceeding some pre-established goal (Nelson & Hayes, 1981). Self-monitoring has often been thought of as just a measure of the progress of another intervention strategy, but self-monitoring alone can change behaviors. Self-monitoring strategies can decrease dependence on others (e.g., teachers, peers, parents, etc.) to change behavior, thereby increasing the likelihood of the child generalizing the behavior change to new, novel, and/or different settings and/or people (McLaughlin, Krappman, & Welsh, 1985). Several targets are included in self-monitoring, such as monitoring attention, task accuracy, task performance, mood, anxiety, and exercise (Amato-Zech, Hoff, & Doepke, 2006; Lannie & Martens, 2008; Rafferty & Raimondi, 2009).

Materials

1) Self-Monitoring Intervention Worksheet
2) Self-Monitoring Forms
3) Cueing Device (MotivAider®, mp3 audio recording, beep tape, person prompting, alarm, etc.)
4) Reinforcer List

Procedure for Interventionist

Note: Self-monitoring has been mentioned in other interventions as part of the intervention, such as self-management. If using Self-Monitoring as part of another intervention, then all steps apply except choosing/selecting a reward and goal setting.

Prior to Implementing the Intervention

1) Identify the target behavior to self-monitor. The interventionist and the child need to determine if they are going to focus on the behaviors they want to increase or behaviors they want to decrease. However, the recommendation is that the interventionist and child focus on increasing appropriate behaviors. To define a target behavior and a competing behavior, an operational definition of each behavior is needed. An operational definition is one that is objective, clear, and observable. It refers only to the characteristics of the behavior and the environment. An operational definition should pass the Stranger Test, which indicates that the definition should be detailed enough that if a

stranger observed the behavior, he or she would be able to accurately identify and record the occurrence of the behavior based upon the operational definition. Following are examples for some frequent behaviors that have been monitored in the research; however, this list is not exhaustive.

- On-task: The child is seated in a chair or other designated area, with face and eyes oriented towards the person or task, completing the task (i.e., listening to the adult, working on an instructional task).
- Task Accuracy: Accuracy indicates the number of steps to a task that were completed correctly. For example, upon a cue, the child stops working, marks the place where he or she stopped, and checks the work against an answer sheet to record accuracy. Note: Steps in the task that the child has not completed yet are covered (e.g., using a piece of paper to cover problems on a worksheet).
- Task Completion: Completion refers specifically only to the number of tasks completed (not considering accuracy).

Self-Monitoring is a sequence of behaviors in which each behavior in the sequence is matched to the child's instructional hierarchy level. For example, if a child is performing at the acquisition level on a mathematics task, then a Self-Monitoring Intervention that focuses on on-task or task-accuracy may be more appropriate than task completion. (See Instructional Hierarchy in the Introduction for additional background on the instructional hierarchy levels.)

Use the Self-Monitoring Intervention Worksheet on page 300 to record the target and competing behaviors.

2) Select the self-monitoring system that the child will use during the intervention. See the example self-monitoring forms on pages 301-305. The types of self-monitoring systems are a checklist, a rating scale, or a combination of the two. The interventionist can decide to use a checklist of behaviors, which is a list or steps of behaviors that the child should be performing. For example, the interventionist can select to monitor an on-task behavior by using the SLANT (acronym): S = Sit up, L= Look at the person talking, A = Active Thinking, N = Note key information, T = Track the talker. Another example of a behavior with steps to monitor is respect for others, which includes 1) using kind words, 2) keeping hands and feet to self, and 3) asking to use someone else's things.
3) Collect data on a self-monitoring form without any other part of the intervention being implemented or the child being aware of being monitored. The data collected is called baseline (no intervention). The baseline data should be collected for approximately one week before the interventionist and child meet to set the goal.

Design the Intervention

The interventionist meets with the child to discuss ways to improve the child's behavior. The interventionist should discuss the rationale and the advantages for using Self-Monitoring. The interventionist should discuss the target behaviors, self-monitoring form, and baseline data. Once the child understands the intervention, then the following steps should be completed. Document the intervention design conclusions during the meeting with the child using the Self-Monitoring Intervention Worksheet on page 300.

1) Set the schedule to provide cues. Review the baseline data collection to set the schedule. Following are three examples of how to use the baseline data to set the schedule of cues.

- If you want the child to obtain 60% accuracy on a 10-problem worksheet and the child only has 20 minutes to complete the problems, then select every 3 minutes for the child to self-monitor the accuracy (20 minutes ÷ 6 cues for accuracy = 3.33 or 3 minutes between cues).
- If you want the child to increase on-task behavior but the baseline data suggest the child can stay on task for only about 4 minutes on average, then the interventionist can set the MotivAider® for a 4-minute interval to check on-task behavior until the child demonstrates the behavior consistently. At that point, the interventionist can set the MotivAider® to a 5-minute interval.
- If the child experiences anger (e.g., clinched fists, furrowed brow, verbal statements of anger) at least 1 time a day, then the interventionist will want to cue at least 2 times a day.

2) Select a self-monitoring cue to use during the intervention. The selection of the self-monitoring cue is largely determined by the child's needs and the setting in which the intervention will occur. Select a device such as a MotivAider®, mp3 audio recording, beep tape, alarm, or to give the cues. At the beginning at the intervention, aid the child in the self-monitoring to ensure that the child is accurate in the reporting. The cueing device should be unobtrusive to other children who may be around the child using the self-monitoring cue.

3) Choose reinforcers and decide how the child will earn them. Once the target behavior is defined and the self-monitoring system is selected, reinforcers and criteria for earning them are determined. To ensure success when first beginning an intervention, frequent reinforcement is recommended. The interventionist and the child should develop and negotiate a list of potential rewards for displaying the target behaviors. Document the list of possible rewards on the Reinforcer List on page 297. This list could include any number of items such as edibles (e.g., chips, fruit, favorite snack, etc.), tangibles (e.g., stickers, certificates, small toy, etc.), activities (playing on the computer for a set amount of time, coloring in a coloring book, etc.), or social activities (e.g., free time with a friend, reading a book with a parent, playing a game with friends, etc.). Once the Reinforcer List is developed, discuss with the child what amount of the reward should be given for the amount of the displayed behavior.

4) Teach the child how to self-observe.
   a) Describe the target behaviors.
   b) Demonstrate or give examples of inappropriate behaviors.
   c) Ask the child to give examples of the opposing appropriate behaviors.

5) Describe and demonstrate how to use the self-monitoring form to the child.
   a) Allow the child an opportunity to ask questions about the self-monitoring procedures.
   b) Role play with the cueing device and self-monitoring form to ensure the child understands how to self-monitor. If the self-monitoring form uses a checklist, then review the steps with the child at each cueing period to aid in accurate self-observation and monitoring.

6) Set goals for the child.
   a) Review the data with the child to determine if the child's self-monitoring data are consistent across the days of the week. If the child is consistently improving as time goes by, then the child should collect self-monitoring data for another week, and then

you should meet with the child again to review the data. If the child's target behavior is consistent, stable, or starting to decrease, then the interventionist and the child should set a goal (next step).

b) The interventionist and child should set a long-term goal. The long-term goal is the level at which the child should perform the target behavior at the end of the intervention. Then set short-term goals with the child (e.g., either daily or weekly). The goal of the short-term objective is to allow the child to earn reinforcers for performing closer to the long-term goal. In addition, the interventionist should meet the child where he or she is currently functioning.

Here is an example scenario. Janet, the child, has been self-monitoring on-task behavior for a week. The interventionist and Janet meet to review her performance over the past week. Janet started self-monitoring her on-task behavior in reading class. Her performance for Monday through Friday was 50%, 50%, 45%, 40%, and 40%, respectively. The interventionist and the child notice that Janet started to decline in her on-task behavior as the week progressed. They also notice that her average on-task behavior was 45%. Because her on-task behavior declined over time and 45% was not at an acceptable level, they decide to set a long-term goal and short-term goals together. They decide that Janet will have a long-term goal (9 weeks) of 90% on-task behaviors in reading class. Janet and the interventionist decide that to try to have 90% on-task behavior in a week is too high and Janet is not likely to achieve the goal. All goals need to be achievable for the child. They decide that Janet should improve her on-task behavior by 5% each week. The short-term goal is for Janet to display 50% on-task behavior for 5 consecutive days. Once Janet displays 5 consecutive days of 50% or more on-task behavior, the goal will be increased by another 5%. This pattern of setting short-term goals continues until Janet reaches her long-term goal of 90%.

7) Determine how often the intervention will be reviewed for progress and any modifications that may be needed.

Implement the Intervention

1) Implement the intervention.

2) Conduct reliability checks. Compare the child's self-monitoring information to your own observations of the child's behavior. Provide feedback to the child on the accuracy of the self-monitoring data collection. When the child consistently self-monitors with great accuracy (at least 90% of the time), reliability checks can be ended.

3) Reward the child if he or she has met the predetermined goal. The goal, the reward, the amount of the reward, and the location and time of the reward given should have already been specified on the Self-Monitoring Intervention Worksheet on page 300.

4) Fade the role of the interventionist in the intervention. Gradually decrease interventionist prompts and reinforcers as the child exhibits the appropriate behaviors. Interventionist prompts should be faded first. Once the child can display the behavior appropriately and independently at the set criterion (i.e., short-term goal), then either increase the criterion or increase the length of time between rewards. As the child is recording behavior independently and accurately, the interventionist should stop prompting the child to check behaviors and set higher goals for earning reinforcers.

Adjustments/Modification

Modify the self-monitoring forms, self-monitoring directions, and rewards based on the developmental level of the child. For example, a child who is 7 years old may not be able to follow more than 3-5 steps of a behavioral sequence. A young child also may not be able to rate beyond a yes or no. Finally, a young child may not be able to identify anxiety, sadness, or anger accurately. Make these adjustments to the intervention as needed.

References

Amato-Zech, N. A., Hoff, K. E., & Doepke, K. J. (2006) Increasing on-task behavior in the classroom extension of self-monitoring strategies. *Psychology in the Schools, 43,* 211-221.

Lannie, A. L., & Martens, B. K. (2008). Targeting performance dimensions in sequence according to the instructional hierarchy: Effects of children's math work within a self-monitoring program. *Journal of Behavior Education, 17,* 356-375.

McLaughlin, T.F., Krappman, V.F., & Welsh, J.M. (1985). The effects of self-recording for on-task behavior of behaviorally disordered special education students. *Remedial and Special Education, 6,* 42– 45.

Nelson, R.O. & Hayes, S. (1981). Theoretical explanations for reactivity in self-monitoring. *Behavior Modification, 5,* 3–14.

Rafferty, L. A. & Raimondi, S. L. (2009). Self-monitoring of attention versus self-monitoring of performance: Examining the differential effects among students with emotional disturbance engaged in independent math practice. *Journal of Behavior Education, 18,* 279-299.

Self-Monitoring Intervention Worksheet

Child's Name: ______________________ Date of Implementation: ________________

Interventionist: ____________________ Date Completed: ______________________

1) What are the target behaviors do the interventionist and child want to increase?

____

____

____

____

2) What cueing device are the child and/or interventionist going to use?

____

3) Please attach the self-monitoring form.

4) How often is the child going to self-monitor?

____

5) What rewards will the child receive?

____

6) What are the short- and long-term goals?

Short-Term Goal #1:

____

Short-Term Goal #2:

____

Short-Term Goal #3:

____

Long-Term Goal:

____

7) How often will the interventionist review the Self-Monitoring intervention?

____

Interventionist Signature: ______________________

Child Signature: ____________________________

Self-Monitoring Rating Form

Name: ____________________ Week of: ____________________

Interventionist: ____________________ Goal: ____________________

Respect others by:

1) Using kind words
2) Keeping hands and feet to self
3) Asking to use someone else's things

Rating: 3 = I followed all the steps with 0 or 1 reminder. 2 = I followed all the steps with 2 reminders. 1 = I needed 3 or more reminders or did not demonstrate the behaviors.

	Monday	Tuesday	Wednesday	Thursday	Friday
Period 1	3 2 1	3 2 1	3 2 1	3 2 1	3 2 1
Period 2	3 2 1	3 2 1	3 2 1	3 2 1	3 2 1
Period 3	3 2 1	3 2 1	3 2 1	3 2 1	3 2 1
Period 4	3 2 1	3 2 1	3 2 1	3 2 1	3 2 1
Period 5	3 2 1	3 2 1	3 2 1	3 2 1	3 2 1
Period 6	3 2 1	3 2 1	3 2 1	3 2 1	3 2 1
Period 7	3 2 1	3 2 1	3 2 1	3 2 1	3 2 1
Total					

TIER

Name:		
Date:		
Am I doing my work?	Am I doing my work?	Am I doing my work?
☺ Yes ☹ No	☺ Yes ☹ No	☺ Yes ☹ No
☺ Yes ☹ No	☺ Yes ☹ No	☺ Yes ☹ No
☺ Yes ☹ No	☺ Yes ☹ No	☺ Yes ☹ No
☺ Yes ☹ No	☺ Yes ☹ No	☺ Yes ☹ No
☺ Yes ☹ No	☺ Yes ☹ No	☺ Yes ☹ No

Name:		
Date:		
Am I doing my work?	Am I doing my work?	Am I doing my work?
☺ Yes ☹ No	☺ Yes ☹ No	☺ Yes ☹ No
☺ Yes ☹ No	☺ Yes ☹ No	☺ Yes ☹ No
☺ Yes ☹ No	☺ Yes ☹ No	☺ Yes ☹ No
☺ Yes ☹ No	☺ Yes ☹ No	☺ Yes ☹ No
☺ Yes ☹ No	☺ Yes ☹ No	☺ Yes ☹ No

Name:		
Date:		
How many did I get correct?	How many did I get correct?	How many did I get correct?

Name:		
Date:		
How many did I complete?	How many did I complete?	How many did I complete?

Name:		
Date:		
How many did I get correct?	How many did I get correct?	How many did I get correct?

Name:		
Date:		
How many did I get correct?	How many did I get correct?	How many did I get correct?

Self-Monitoring Checklist Form

Name: ______________________ Date: ______________________

Interventionist: ______________________ Goal: ______________________

How many yes's did you get: ______________

SLANT Strategy

S = Sit up

L = Look at the person talking

A = Active Thinking

N = Note key Information

T = Track the Talker

Time: __	**4 minutes**	**8 minutes**	**12 minutes**	**16 minutes**	**20 minutes**	**24 minutes**	**28 minutes**	**32 minutes**	**36 minutes**	**40 minutes**
S	Yes No	Yes No	Yes No	Yes No	Yes No	Yes No	Yes No	Yes No	Yes No	Yes No
L	Yes No	Yes No	Yes No	Yes No	Yes No	Yes No	Yes No	Yes No	Yes No	Yes No
A	Yes No	Yes No	Yes No	Yes No	Yes No	Yes No	Yes No	Yes No	Yes No	Yes No
N	Yes No	Yes No	Yes No	Yes No	Yes No	Yes No	Yes No	Yes No	Yes No	Yes No
T	Yes No	Yes No	Yes No	Yes No	Yes No	Yes No	Yes No	Yes No	Yes No	Yes No
Time: __	**4 minutes**	**8 minutes**	**12 minutes**	**16 minutes**	**20 minutes**	**24 minutes**	**28 minutes**	**32 minutes**	**36 minutes**	**40 minutes**
S	Yes No	Yes No	Yes No	Yes No	Yes No	Yes No	Yes No	Yes No	Yes No	Yes No
L	Yes No	Yes No	Yes No	Yes No	Yes No	Yes No	Yes No	Yes No	Yes No	Yes No
A	Yes No	Yes No	Yes No	Yes No	Yes No	Yes No	Yes No	Yes No	Yes No	Yes No
N	Yes No	Yes No	Yes No	Yes No	Yes No	Yes No	Yes No	Yes No	Yes No	Yes No
T	Yes No	Yes No	Yes No	Yes No	Yes No	Yes No	Yes No	Yes No	Yes No	Yes No

Child Name: ______________________ Week of: ______________________

How angry do I feel right now? Circle one

7	7	7	7	7	7	7	7	7	7
6	6	6	6	6	6	6	6	6	6
5	5	5	5	5	5	5	5	5	5
4	4	4	4	4	4	4	4	4	4
3	3	3	3	3	3	3	3	3	3
2	2	2	2	2	2	2	2	2	2
1	1	1	1	1	1	1	1	1	1
Morning	Afternoon	Morning	Afternoon	Morning	Afternoon	Morning	Afternoon	Morning	Afternoon
Monday		Tuesday		Wednesday		Thursday		Friday	

1……………2……………3……………4……………5……………6……………7

Calm — Mildly Frustrated — Frustrated — Mad — Very Angry

Monday (What do you think caused your mood?): ______________________

Tuesday (What do you think caused your mood?): ______________________

Wednesday (What do you think caused your mood?): ______________________

Thursday (What do you think caused your mood?): ______________________

Friday (What do you think caused your mood?): ______________________

Reinforcer List

Child's Name: ______________________________ Date: __________________________

Interventionist: ____________________________

Directions: The interventionist and the child should develop a list of potential rewards for displaying the appropriate behaviors. The interventionist and child the child should negotiate this list as well as the amount of the reward (e.g., how many chips, how much time on the computer, etc.) after the goals are set.

Reward	**How Much?**
1. ____________________	1. ____________________
2. ____________________	2. ____________________
3. ____________________	3. ____________________
4. ____________________	4. ____________________
5. ____________________	5. ____________________
6. ____________________	6. ____________________
7. ____________________	7. ____________________
8. ____________________	8. ____________________
9. ____________________	9. ____________________
10. ____________________	10. ____________________

Self-Monitoring: Procedural Integrity Checklist

Age/Grade:	2nd grade – High School
Setting:	School, Home, Clinic, In-patient
Individual or Group:	Individual
Tier:	2 & 3
Desired/ Appropriate Behavior:	On-task, task accuracy, task completion, anger management, relaxation, hand raising to ask a question, making appropriate comments, exercising, etc.
Skill Level:	Fluency to generalization

Self-monitoring strategies can decrease dependence on others (e.g., teachers, peers, parents, etc.) to change behavior, thereby increasing the likelihood of the child generalizing the behavior change to new, novel, and/or different settings and/or people (McLaughlin, Krappman, & Welsh, 1985). The procedural integrity checklist is completed by an observer (e.g., principal, assistant principal, school psychologist, treatment specialist, behavior specialist, counselor, lead teacher) who is familiar with the Self-Monitoring procedure. The observer will observe the individual interventionist implementing the Self-Monitoring procedure and provide feedback. The Self-Monitoring: Procedural Integrity Checklist – Intervention Development is completed at the time when the interventionist and the child are completing steps 4-8 of the Self-Monitoring procedure. The Self-Monitoring: Procedural Integrity Checklist – Implementation is completed at the time when the interventionist and the child are implementing the Self-Monitoring procedure.

Procedure for the Integrity Checklist Observer

Intervention Development

1) Arrange to be at the meeting between the interventionist and child to discuss the target behaviors, self-monitoring form, and baseline data.
2) Complete the Self-Monitoring: Procedural Integrity Checklist – Intervention Development information about the interventionist, child, location, date, time, observer name, and observer signature (see page 309).
3) Observe for the presence of behaviors 1-10 on the Checklist and mark Yes if present or No if not present. If there is not an opportunity to observe a behavior, then mark N/O for not observed.
4) Count the number of behaviors marked Yes and write the number on the line for "Number of behaviors marked Yes."
5) Write the total number of behaviors observed (i.e., the total behaviors marked Yes and No).
6) Calculate the percent marked Yes. A chart is provided for determining the percent marked Yes.
7) Write any constructive feedback comments in addition to any notations made beside any individual behavior in the "Feedback" section.
8) Provide the interventionist, at an appropriate time, with oral feedback regarding the session one training, starting with positive behaviors observed, and a copy of the Self-Monitoring: Procedural

Integrity Checklist – Intervention Development. *The feedback should be provided the same day of the observation.*

Implementation

1) Determine a time to observe the interventionist and child at a time when the self-monitoring intervention is being implemented. The interventionist and child should not be notified of the observation. Review a copy of the Self-Monitoring Intervention Worksheet prior to conducting the observation. Have a copy of the Self-Monitoring Intervention Worksheet available for reference during the observation.
2) Complete the Self-Monitoring: Procedural Integrity Checklist – Implementation information about the interventionist, child, location, date, time, observer name, and observer signature (see page 309).
3) Observe for the presence of behaviors 1-4 on the Checklist and mark Yes if present or No if not present. If there is not an opportunity to observe a behavior, then mark N/O for not observed.
4) Count the number of behaviors marked Yes and write the number on the line for "Number of behaviors marked Yes."
5) Write the total number of behaviors observed (i.e., the total behaviors marked Yes and No).
6) Calculate the percent marked Yes. A chart is provided for determining the percent marked Yes. If less than 80% of behaviors are marked Yes, then provide feedback immediately to the interventionist and conduct another observation the next day or as soon as possible.
7) Write any constructive feedback comments in addition to any notations made beside any individual behavior in the "Feedback" section.
8) Provide the interventionist, at an appropriate time, with oral feedback regarding the implementation of the intervention, starting with positive behaviors observed, and a copy of the Self-Monitoring: Procedural Integrity Checklist – Implementation. *The feedback should be provided the same day of the observation.*
9) Observe the interventionist and child implementing the Self-Monitoring procedure approximately every other week or twice a month after the initial observation.

Self-Monitoring: Procedural Integrity Checklist
Prior to Implementation

Interventionist: ____________________ Date: __________ Time: __________

Child: ____________________ Observer: ____________________

Location: ____________________ Signature: ____________________

N/O = Not Observed

Behaviors to Observe	Yes	No	Comments
1) The interventionist has operationally defined the target behavior(s) to increase.			
2) The interventionist has collected baseline data using a self-monitoring form.			
3) The interventionist discusses with the child the target behaviors, self-monitoring form, and baseline data.			
4) The interventionist sets a schedule of cues.			
5) The interventionist and the child select a self-monitoring cue. The decision is documented on the Self-Monitoring Intervention Worksheet.			
6) The interventionist and the child develop a list of possible rewards and document them on the Reinforcer List.			
7) The interventionist and the child discuss what amount of a reward should be given for the amount of the displayed behavior. The decision is documented on the Self-Monitoring Intervention Worksheet.			
8) The interventionist teaches the child how to self-observe a) Describe the target behaviors (appropriate)			
b) Demonstrate or give examples of the inappropriate behaviors			
c) Ask the child to give examples of the appropriate behaviors			
9) The interventionist trains the child to use the self-monitoring form and device and to self-observe by giving examples and non-examples and by role playing.			
10) The interventionist and the child set a long-term goal and a short-term goal. The decision is documented on the Self-Monitoring Intervention Worksheet.			
11) The interventionist determines how often the intervention will be reviewed. The decision is documented on the Self-Monitoring Intervention Worksheet.			

Number of behaviors marked Yes = _____ out of _____ = ______ %

Feedback:

Percent

1 out of 13 = 8%	8 out of 13 = 62%
2 out of 13 = 15%	9 out of 13 = 69%
3 out of 13 = 23%	10 out of 13 = 77%
4 out of 13 = 31%	11 out of 13 = 85%
5 out of 13 = 39%	12 out of 13 = 92%
6 out of 13 = 46%	13 out of 13 = 100%
7 out of 13 = 54%	

Self-Monitoring Procedural Integrity Checklist
Implementation

Interventionist: ______________________ Date: __________ Time: __________

Child: ______________________ Observer: ______________________

Location: ______________________ Signature: ______________________

N/O = Not Observed

Behaviors to Observe	Yes	No	N/O	Comments
1) The child is self-monitoring the behaviors using a self-monitoring form.				
2) The child self-monitors at the appropriate time interval, with or without the assistance of a cue, based on the decision documented on the Self-Monitoring Intervention Worksheet.				
3) The interventionist gives appropriate feedback periodically to the child on the accuracy of the self-monitoring data collection.				
4) The child is rewarded for meeting the goal (evidence may be through an interview or permanent record).				

Number of behaviors marked Yes = _____ out of _____ = ______ %

Feedback:

Percent
1 out of 4 = 25%
2 out of 4 = 50%
3 out of 4 = 75%
4 out of 4 = 100%

Self-Management Procedures

Age/Grade:	2nd Grade – High School
Setting:	School, Home, In-patient
Individual or Group:	Individual
Tier:	2 & 3
Desired/ Appropriate Behavior:	Homework completion, academic performance, on-task behaviors, anger management, exercising, work productivity
Skill Level:	Fluency to generalization

Rationale & Research Support

Self-management at its basic level is an individual engaging in one (more desired) behavior to decrease the occurrence of another (less desired) behavior later in time (Watson & Tharp, 1993). Self-management is a behavioral intervention that teaches children how to recognize their own behavior, to decide which behaviors they want to increase and decrease, to set goals, and to select strategies to meet their goals. Self-management has been demonstrated to be an effective intervention for children with and without disabilities across age ranges in multiple settings (Barry & Santarelli, 2000; Hinshaw & Melnick, 1992; Smith & Sugai, 2000).

Materials

1) Target Behavior, Competing Behavior, and Antecedent Worksheet
2) Problem Situations Awareness Worksheet
3) Reinforcement List
4) Reinforcers/Rewards
5) Self-Monitoring Intervention Worksheet (see Self-Monitoring procedure for interventionist and materials)
6) Index Card
7) Self-Management Intervention Worksheet

Procedure for Interventionist

There are six steps in self-management. The interventionist and child complete the first two steps (decide to use self-management and define behaviors). Then the interventionist and child implement self-monitoring before setting goals and selecting self-management strategies. The first reason for implementing self-monitoring before setting goals and selecting strategies is that self-monitoring can be an effective intervention alone; therefore, self-management may not be needed. The rule of thumb for interventions is that the interventionist implements one or two interventions first. If an interventionist implemented five interventions and the behaviors improved, it is not clear which intervention caused the behavior change. The interventionist has no idea if it is one intervention, two interventions, or five interventions that caused the change. The second reason is the child may see improvements in behavior(s) when implementing the self-monitoring, but either the changes in behavior(s) are not enough or the changes behavior(s) decrease over time. The final reason is the interventionist and child need to be able to determine where the child is currently functioning to set goals and select strategies.

2) Decide to use self-management. The interventionist and child have to decide that self-management would be a good intervention. Self-management requires that the child has learned the prerequisite skills. For example, if the child has never displayed or infrequently displayed anger management, then the first step prior to self-management is teaching anger management. Good practice requires the interventionist to get "buy in" from the child. The ultimate goal is for the child to self-regulate his or her own behavior.

3) Define target behaviors to increase and competing behaviors to decrease. The target behaviors are those behaviors that one wants to increase. Competing behaviors are those behaviors that one wants to decrease. For example, a target behavior might be on-task behavior and a competing behavior might be fidgety behaviors. What does on-task behavior look like? Is it passively sitting in one's desk looking out the window? No! What does fidgety behavior look like? Is fidgety behavior when one uses a body part or an object to make repetitive (3 or more times) movement? Maybe! To define a target behavior and a competing behavior, an operational definition of each behavior is needed. An operational definition is one that is objective, clear, and observable. It refers only to the characteristics of the behavior and the environment (Batsche, Castillo, Dixon, & Forde, 2008; Hintze, Stoner, & Bull, 2000). An operational definition should pass the Stranger Test, which indicates that the definition should be detailed enough that if a stranger observed the behavior, he or she would be able to accurately identify and record the occurrence of the behavior based upon the operational definition. Use the Target Behavior, Competing Behavior, and Antecedent Worksheet on pages 317-318 to record the target and competing behaviors.

   a) Discuss the target behaviors (those behaviors you want the child to increase) and competing behaviors (those behaviors you want the child to decrease) with the child and have the child help define each behavior.

   b) Develop examples and non-examples of the each behavior with the child.

   c) Discuss with the child cues, triggers, signals (i.e., antecedents) that set the occasion for the target behaviors and competing behaviors. For example, if the child states, "I stay more on task if I sit next to a student," then the student may be a trigger to stay on task (the target behavior). Another example is if the child says that he has more difficulty staying on task during the silent reading block (i.e., antecedent or discriminative stimulus), then the silent reading block sets the occasion for off-task behavior (the competing behavior). The antecedents that are identified are used later in the self-management strategies in step 5.

4) Ensure that the child self-monitors. (See the Self-Monitoring procedure for interventionist.)

5) Set goals for the child. Review with the child the data collected on the Self-Monitoring Intervention Worksheet without any other part of the intervention implemented. The data collected is called baseline (no intervention). The baseline data should be collected for approximately one week before meeting with the child to set a goal. Review the data to determine if the child's data are consistent across the days of the week. If the child's target behavior is consistently improving as time goes by, then the interventionist and child should collect another week and meet again. If the child's target behavior is consistent, stable, or starting to decrease, then the interventionist and the child should set a goal. The interventionist and child should set a long-term goal. The long-term goal is the level

at which you want the child to perform the target behavior at the end of the intervention. Then set short-term goals with the child (e.g., either daily or weekly).

Here is an example scenario. Janet, the child, has been self-monitoring on-task behavior for a week. The interventionist and Janet meet to review her performance over the past week. Janet started self-monitoring her on-task behavior in reading class. Her performance for Monday through Friday was 50%, 50%, 45%, 40%, and 40%, respectively. The interventionist and the child notice that Janet started to decline in her on-task behavior as the week progressed. They also notice that her average on-task behavior was 45%. Because her on-task behavior declined over time and 45% was not at an acceptable level, they decide to set a long-term goal and short-term goals together. They decide that Janet will have a long term goal (9 weeks) of 90% on-task behaviors in reading class. Janet and the interventionist decide that to try to have 90% on-task behavior in a week is too high and Janet is not likely to achieve the goal. All goals need to be achievable for the child. They decide that Janet should improve her on-task behavior by 5% each week. Her short-term goal is for Janet to display 50% on-task behavior for 5 consecutive days. Once Janet displays 5 consecutive days of 50% or more on-task behavior, the goal will be increased by another 5%. This pattern of setting short-term goals continues until Janet reaches her long-term goal of 90%.

6) Choose appropriate self-management strategies.

   a) Antecedent manipulation is changing, altering, modifying, removing, and/or presenting cues or signals (discriminative stimuli) to change behavior. An antecedent is a stimulus (cue, signal, trigger, etc.) that precedes a behavior whether it is an appropriate behavior or not. For example, a red stop light is a cue (i.e., antecedent or discriminative stimulus) for you to press your brakes to stop your vehicle (i.e., behavior). Another example is the presentation of a difficult math problem, which is a cue (i.e., antecedent) to display off task behaviors. For final example, a student is removed from a difficult situation (i.e., antecedent or discriminative stimulus); thus, the child displays calmer and more relaxed behaviors. Following are antecedent manipulation strategies.

      i) Present discriminative stimuli or cues to increase target behaviors. The interventionist should go back to the discussion relating to triggers or cues that set the occasion for the target behavior. The question is under what circumstances, during what events, around which people, in what situations, etc. is the target behavior more likely to be displayed? For example, when a child is presented with a book about motorcycles (cue), then the child's reading time increases. Therefore, the interventionist can present motorcycle books when silent independent reading is needed or required. These cues should be implemented in the time frame during which display of the target behavior is desired.

      ii) Remove discriminative stimuli or cues to decrease competing behaviors. The interventionist should go back to the discussion relating to triggers or cues that set the occasion for the competing behavior. The question is under what circumstances, during what events, around which people, in what situations, etc. is the competing behavior more likely to be displayed? When the interventionist has answered these questions, then the interventionist knows the discriminative stimuli or cue that set the occasion to display the competing behavior. These cues or discriminative stimuli that set the occasion for the competing behaviors should be reduced or eliminated. For example, a child is presented with written work (cue) and then displays off-task behavior. Because the interventionist can never eliminate written work, the interventionist can reduce the amount of written work or fold in other tasks that do not have a written component with the writing task.

iii) Increase response effort for the competing behaviors. Generally, competing behaviors are considered more established due to potentially any of the following factors: more reinforcement, more reinforcers (rewards), easier to display (less response effort or can do the behavior effortlessly). When designing a self-management intervention, the interventionist and the child need to develop strategies to increase the response effort. For example, if the child is supposed to be doing homework but the child does homework in the living room with the television, then it is easy for the child to use the remote control to turn on the television. Watching television is a competing behavior to doing homework. Thus the interventionist and the child may decide that sitting at the kitchen table to do homework is a more ideal situation because the child would have to move to the living room to watch television. The idea is to make engaging in the competing behavior more difficult but not necessarily impossible.

iv) Decrease response effort for the target behaviors. Generally, target behaviors can be considered more difficult to establish for a number of reasons: lack of reinforcement, delayed reinforcement, insufficient reinforcement, harder to display, or taking more response effort. For example, a person may want to start exercising but typically sits around and watches television. The person does not get immediate reinforcement for exercising, and it takes more response effort to exercise than to watch television. If the person has to go to the gym to exercise, then even more response effort is required. However, if the person owns a treadmill, the treadmill would help minimize the response effort. Again, the purpose of this strategy is to decrease the response effort, not to make the response effort completely easy.

b) Reinforcement or punishment for behaviors. Always start with reinforcement strategies for the target (desirable) behaviors first. The child and the interventionist should develop and negotiate a list of potential rewards for displaying the target behaviors. Use the Reinforcer List on page 319 to develop the list of potential rewards. This list could include any number of items such as edibles (e.g., chips, fruit, favorite snack, etc.), tangibles (e.g., stickers, certificates, small toy, etc.), activities (playing on the computer for a set amount of time, coloring in a coloring book, etc.), or social activities (e.g., free time with a friend, reading a book with a parent, playing a game with friends, etc.). Once the reinforcement list is developed, discuss with the child what amount of the reward should be given for the amount of the displayed behavior. For example, if the child typically displays 20% on-task behaviors but you have set the first short term goal as 40% on-task behavior, the interventionist and the child could negotiate playing a game for 15 minutes with a peer at the end of the school day, or the parent could read a book to his or her child for 20 minutes at night. If the target behavior is not increasing to the desired levels with reinforcement being given, then punishment should be considered. Positive punishment occurs when an inappropriate or undesirable behavior is displayed/performed and a punisher is provided to decrease the likelihood of the behavior recurring. Negative punishment occurs when an inappropriate or undesirable behavior is displayed/performed and a reward is lost to decrease the likelihood of the behavior reoccurring. Prior to any punishment being considered, problem solve the reinforcement by examining if the reward is enough, if the reward is being given in a timely fashion, etc.

c) Social support is another strategy that aids in the successfulness of self-management. Social support is a person who may be of great benefit to encourage, support, and give praise for the child's effort. The people or person whom the interventionist and child identify should be someone who is available regularly and is willing to check up on the child's progress in order to give encouragement and praise. This person can be an adult (i.e., parent, teacher, grandparent, some other adult), peer (i.e., friend in class, a friend in the neighborhood, etc.), or an older child (i.e., sibling, older child willing to be a support to the child). Having as much social support as the child can have for self-managing the behaviors is helpful for long-term success. If a child can receive support and natural reinforcement (rewards) outside of the programmed reward, the more likely the behaviors will be maintained over time and generalized across people and settings.

d) Self-instructions are a way in which the child can verbalize vocally or sub-vocally instructions to walk through a situation. Self-instructions have three steps.

   i) Identify the situations that are the most problematic and identify the most appropriate behavior to display in the problematic situation. Review the Target Behavior, Competing Behavior, and Antecedent Worksheet to identify those problematic situations. For example, having a child who physically fights after being called a name is a problem situation with an undesirable behavior (the competing behavior). The desired response is to stay away from the situation. At this point, the situation, the trigger, and competing behavior have all been identified. The next steps are to identify self-statement that the child can say. The interventionist should talk to the child about what the child says to oneself in this situation. If the child states, "I think he is not going to get away with calling me a name" and reports arousal of increased heart rate, perspiration, etc., then the interventionist and the child have to come up with more positive self-instructions. If the child has difficulty identifying these problematic situations, then the interventionist may want the child to use the Problem Situations Awareness Worksheet found on page 320. Have the child record instances in which he or she had difficulty throughout the day. The Problem Situations Awareness Worksheet can be kept in a folder for quick access. If the child is having difficulty but is unaware when situation should be recorded, the interventionist or some other adult should remind the child to record the situation. Once the child records 3 or more instances on the Problem Situations Awareness Worksheet, then the interventionist and the child can review these problem situations so that they can identify the self-instructions that would have been helpful.

   ii) Identify the self-instructions that will aid in the problematic situation. The self-instructions have to be believable to the child, have to be ones able to be implemented by the child, and have to impede the competing behaviors that the child wants to reduce. Write the new self-instructions on an index card so that the child can use the card later to remind himself or herself of the self-instructions.

   iii) Teach the self-instructions using behavioral skills training.

      (1) The interventionist recites verbally the self-instructions in a role playing scenario.

      (2) The child and the interventionist recite verbally the self-instructions in the role playing scenario.

(3) The child recites verbally the self-instructions (index card may be used) without assistance from the interventionist.

(4) The child recites the self-instructions repeatedly until the child can recite the self-instructions sub-vocally with minimal lip or mouth movement.

e) Ensure the child self-praise's when meeting a goal. The child uses positive self-statements for the appropriate behavior and meeting goals. Cue the child by asking how the child feels about meeting the goal. Model self-praise, allow the child to practice, and give feedback. If the child can give self-praise, then the reliance on outside or external reinforcers/rewards potentially becomes less frequent.

7) Implement self-management strategies. Once the interventionist and child have been through steps 1-5, it is time for them to implement the strategies. Use the Self-Management Intervention Worksheet on page 321 to document your plan.

Adjustments/Modification

A few considerations are important when implementing self-management. Due to the developmental level of the child, the child may be able to self-monitor aid in the definitions of the competing behaviors, and chose rewards but have difficulty with understanding the triggers or problem situations. In addition, the child may not know how to display the target (desirable) behaviors and/or implement the self-instructions; thus, the child may need social skills training prior to the implementation of self-management. The child may not be truthful in completing the Self-Monitoring Intervention Worksheet or completely understand when inappropriate behavior was displayed. The interventionist or another person may need to check the ratings and provide feedback.

References

Barry, L. M. & Santarelli, G. E. (2000). Making it work at school and home: A need based collaborative, across settings, behavioral intervention. *The California School Psychologist, 5,* 43–51.Batsche, et al., 2008

Batsche, G. M., Castillo, J. M., Dixon, D. N., & Forde, S. (2008). Best practices in designing, implementing, and evaluating quality interventions. In A. Thomas & J. Grimes (Eds.), *Best practices in school psychology V* (pp. 177-193). Bethesda, MD: National Association of School Psychologists.

Hinshaw, S. P. & Melnick, S. (1992). Self-management therapies and attention deficit/hyperactivity disorder. *Behavior Modification, 16*, 253-273.

Hintze, J. M., Stoner, G., & Bull, M. H. (2000). Analogue assessment: Emotional/behavior problems. In E. S. Shapiro & T. R. Kratochwill (Eds.), *Conducting school-based assessment of child and adolescent behavior* (pp. 55-77). New York: Guilford.

Smith, B. W. & Sugai, G. (2000). Functional assessment-based behavior support planning: A self-management case study of a middle school student with EBD. J*ournal of Positive Behavioral Interventions and Supports, 2(4)*, 208-217.

Watson, D.L. & Tharp, R.G. (1993). Self-directed behavior: Self-modification for personal adjustment. Pacific Grove, CA: Brooks/Cole.

Target Behavior, Competing Behavior, and Antecedent Worksheet

Child Name: ____________________________ Date: ______________________________

Interventionist: _________________________ Location: __________________________

1) What behavior(s) do I want to **improve**?

____

____

Examples of the behavior:

____

____

Non-examples of the behavior:

____

____

2) What cues, triggers, situations, etc. make me more likely to display this behavior?

____

____

____

____

Examples of the behavior:

____

____

Non-examples of the behavior:

____

____

3) What cues, triggers, situations, etc. make me more likely to display this behavior?

____

____

____

____

Examples of the behavior:

____

____

Non-examples of the behavior:

____

____

4) What cues, triggers, situations, etc. make me more likely to display this behavior?

____

____

____

____

Target Behavior, Competing Behavior, and Antecedent Worksheet

Child Name: ____________________________ Date: ______________________________

Interventionist: _________________________ Location: __________________________

1) What behavior(s) do I want to **decrease**?

____

____

Examples of the behavior:

____

____

Non-examples of the behavior:

____

____

2) What cues, triggers, situations, etc. make me more likely to display this behavior?

____

____

____

____

Examples of the behavior:

____

____

Non-examples of the behavior:

____

____

3) What cues, triggers, situations, etc. make me more likely to display this behavior?

____

____

____

____

Examples of the behavior:

____

____

Non-examples of the behavior:

____

____

4) What cues, triggers, situations, etc. make me more likely to display this behavior?

____

____

____

____

Reinforcer List

Child's Name: ______________________ Date: ______________________

Interventionist: ______________________

Directions: The interventionist and the child should develop a list of potential rewards for displaying the appropriate behaviors. The interventionist and child the child should negotiate this list as well as the amount of the reward (e.g., how many chips, how much time on the computer, etc.)

Reward	How much?
1. ______________________	1. ______________________
2. ______________________	2. ______________________
3. ______________________	3. ______________________
4. ______________________	4. ______________________
5. ______________________	5. ______________________
6. ______________________	6. ______________________
7. ______________________	7. ______________________
8. ______________________	8. ______________________
9. ______________________	9. ______________________
10. ______________________	10. ______________________

Problem Situations Awareness Worksheet

Child's Name: ____________________________ Date: ________________________________

Directions: If you had a problem situation, write the date, the time the problem situation occurred, where you were, what happened, what you said to yourself, what you felt, and what you did.

Date	Time	Location	What happened?	What did you say to yourself?	How did you feel?	What did you do?

Self-Management Intervention Worksheet

Child's Name: ____________________ Date of Implementation: ____________________

Interventionist: ____________________ Date Completed: ____________________

1) What behaviors do I want to increase?

2) What behaviors do I want to decrease?

3) Please attach the Self-Monitoring Intervention Worksheet.

4) What rewards will the child receive? ____________________

5) What are the short- and long-term goals?
   Short-Term Goal: ____________________
   Long-Term Goal: ____________________

6) What antecedent manipulation strategies is the interventionist going to use?

7) When is the interventionist going to use the antecedent manipulation strategies?

8) What are the child's self-instructions?

9) What are example self-praise statements that the child will use?

10) How often will the interventionist review the self-management intervention?

Interventionist Signature: ____________________

Child Signature: ____________________

Self-Management: Procedural Integrity Checklist

Age/Grade:	2nd Grade – High School
Setting:	School, Home, In-patient
Individual or Group:	Individual
Tier:	2 & 3
Desired/ Appropriate Behavior:	Homework completion, academic performance, on-task behaviors, anger management, exercising, work productivity
Skill Level:	Fluency to generalization

Self-management is a behavioral intervention that teaches children how to recognize their own behavior, to decide which behaviors they want to increase and decrease, to set goals, and to select strategies to meet their goals. The procedural integrity checklist is completed by an observer (e.g., principal, assistant principal, school psychologist, treatment specialist, behavior specialist, counselor, lead teacher) who is familiar with the Self-Management procedure. The observer will observe the individual interventionist implementing the Self-Management procedure and provide feedback. The Self-Management: Procedural Integrity Checklist – Session One Training is completed at the time when the interventionist and the child are completing steps 1-3 of the Self-Management procedure. The Self-Management: Procedural Integrity Checklist – Session Two Training is completed at the time when the interventionist and the child are completing steps 4-5 of the Self-Management procedure. The Self-Management: Procedural Integrity Checklist – Implementation is completed at the time when the interventionist and the child are implementing the Self-Management procedure.

Procedure for Integrity Checklist Observer

Session One Training

1) Arrange to be at the meeting when the interventionist and child discuss the self-management intervention, defining target behaviors and competing behaviors, and making decisions about self-monitoring.
2) Complete the Self-Management: Procedural Integrity Checklist – Session One Training (see page 325) information about the interventionist, child, location, date, time, observer name, and observer signature.
3) Observe for the presence of behaviors 1-6 on the Checklist and mark Yes if present or No if not present. If there is not an opportunity to observe a behavior, then mark N/O for not observed.
4) Count the number of behaviors marked Yes and write the number on the line for "Number of behaviors marked Yes."
5) Write the total number of behaviors observed (i.e., the total behaviors marked Yes or No).
6) Calculate the percent marked Yes. A chart is provided for determining the percent marked Yes.
7) Write any constructive feedback comments in addition to any notations made beside any individual behavior in the "Feedback" section.

8) Provide the interventionist, at an appropriate time, with oral feedback regarding the session one training, starting with positive behaviors observed, and a copy of the Self-Management: Procedural Integrity Checklist – Session One Training. *The feedback should be provided the same day of the observation.*

Session Two Training

1) Arrange to be at the meeting when the interventionist and child set goals and develop the self-management plan.
2) Complete the Self-Management: Procedural Integrity Checklist – Session Two Training (see page 326) information about the interventionist, child, location, date, time, observer name, and observer signature.
3) Observe for the presence of behaviors 1-6 on the Checklist and mark Yes if present or No if not present. If there is not an opportunity to observe a behavior, then mark N/O for not observed.
4) Count the number of behaviors marked Yes and write the number on the line for "Number of behaviors marked Yes."
5) Write the total number of behaviors observed (i.e., the total behaviors marked Yes or No).
6) Calculate the percent marked Yes. A chart is provided for determining the percent marked Yes.
7) Write any constructive feedback comments in addition to any notations made beside any individual behavior in the "Feedback" section.
8) Provide the interventionist, at an appropriate time, with oral feedback regarding the session two training, starting with positive behaviors observed, and a copy of the Self-Management: Procedural Integrity Checklist – Session Two Training. *The feedback should be provided the same day of the observation.*

Implementation

1) Determine a time to observe the interventionist and child at a time when the self-management intervention is being implemented. The interventionist and child should not be notified of the observation. Review a copy of the Self-Management Intervention Worksheet prior to conducting the observation. Have a copy of the Self-Management Intervention Worksheet available for reference during the observation.
2) Complete the Self-Management: Procedural Integrity Checklist – Implementation (see page 327) information about the interventionist, child, location, date, time, observer name, and observer signature.
3) Observe for the presence of behaviors 1-4 on the Checklist and mark Yes if present or No if not present. If there is not an opportunity to observe a behavior, then mark N/O for not observed.
4) Count the number of behaviors marked Yes and write the number on the line for "Number of behaviors marked Yes."
5) Write the total number of behaviors observed (i.e., the total behaviors marked Yes or No).
6) Calculate the percent marked Yes. A chart is provided for determining the percent marked Yes. If less than 80% of behaviors are marked Yes, then provide feedback immediately to the interventionist and conduct another observation the next day or as soon as possible.

7) Write any constructive feedback comments in addition to any notations made beside any individual behavior in the "Feedback" section.

8) Provide the interventionist, at an appropriate time, with oral feedback regarding the implementation of the intervention, starting with positive behaviors observed, and a copy of the Self-Management: Procedural Integrity Checklist – Implementation. *The feedback should be provided the same day of the observation.*

9) Observe the interventionist and child implementing the Self-Management procedure approximately every other week or twice a month after the initial observation.

Self-Management: Procedural Integrity Checklist
Session One Training

Interventionist: ______________________ Date: __________ Time: __________

Child: ______________________ Observer: ______________________

Location: ______________________ Signature: ______________________

N/O = Not Observed

Behaviors to Observe	Yes	No	N/O	Comments
1) The interventionist and child decide to use the self-management intervention.				
2) The interventionist and/or child define target behaviors to increase and competing behaviors to decrease.				
3) The interventionist and/or child identify the antecedents (cues, triggers, signals) for the target and competing behaviors.				
4) The interventionist and/or child select an appropriate self-monitoring form.				
5) The interventionist trains the child on self-monitoring form using role play.				
6) The interventionist implements Problem Situations Awareness Worksheet (if appropriate) by giving examples and role playing.				

Number of behaviors marked Yes = _____ out of _____ = ______ %

Feedback:

Percent
1 out of 6 = 17%
2 out of 6 = 33%
3 out of 6 = 50%
4 out of 6 = 67%
5 out of 6 = 83%
6 out of 6 = 100%

Self-Management Procedural Integrity Checklist
Session Two Training

Interventionist: ______________________ Date: __________ Time: __________

Child: ______________________ Observer: ______________________

Location: ______________________ Signature: ______________________

N/O = Not Observed

Behaviors to Observe	Yes	No	Comments
1) The interventionist reviews the data from the self-monitoring sheet. Based on the child's performance, the interventionist and child decide to either continue with self-monitoring or implement self-management.			
2) The interventionist and child set long-term and short-term goals.			
3) The child and the interventionist negotiate rewards.			
4) The child and the interventionist review the Problem Situations Awareness Worksheet to determine the antecedent manipulations.			
5) The interventionist and the child select the self-management strategies they will use.			
6) The interventionist reviews the Problem Situations Awareness Worksheet to identify self-instructions. The interventionist trains the child on self-instructions using the cue card and role playing.			

Number of behaviors marked Yes = _____ out of _____ = ______ %

Feedback:

Percent
1 out of 6 = 17%
2 out of 6 = 33%
3 out of 6 = 50%
4 out of 6 = 67%
5 out of 6 = 83%
6 out of 6 = 100%

Self-Management Procedural Integrity Checklist
Implementation

Interventionist: ______________________ Date: __________ Time: __________

Child: ______________________ Observer: ______________________

Location: ______________________ Signature: ______________________

N/O = Not Observed

Behaviors to Observe	Yes	No	N/O	Comments
1) The selected self-management strategies are being used.				
2) The child is self-monitoring the behaviors.				
3) The interventionist is giving appropriate feedback periodically to the child on the behavior.				
4) The child is being rewarded for meeting the goals set (evidence may be through an interview or permanent record).				

Number of behaviors marked Yes = _____ out of _____ = ______ %

Percent
1 out of 4 = 25%
2 out of 4 = 50%
3 out of 4 = 75%
4 out of 4 = 100%

Feedback:

Pleasant Events Diary

Age/Grade:	6th grade – High School
Setting:	School, Clinic, In-patient
Individual or Group:	Individual
Tier:	2 & 3
Desired/ Appropriate Behavior:	Positive mood, healthy behaviors, social behaviors, relax/calm (reduction in nervous behaviors)
Skill Level:	Fluency to maintenance; not used for acquisition of skills

Rationale & Research Support

Pleasant Events Diary is an intervention that is used as a treatment for adolescents who experience negative moods/behaviors that are characterized as sadness, irritability, or nervousness that is atypical of their peer group. Behaviors that children may exhibit include but are not limited to inappropriate emotional response or no emotional response to a situation, social withdrawal, excessive sleeping, reduction in sleeping, excessive communication about a topic (i.e., perseveration), excessive motoric behaviors (e.g., fidgety, pacing, repetitive motions), changes in diet or weight, changes in activity level, physical or verbal aggression, and social rejection. The intervention may be implemented as a stand-alone or supplementary treatment.

The Pleasant Events Diary is a Behavior Activation Treatment specifically targeting contextual factors that affect behavior. The premise is that children who exhibit the aforementioned behaviors do so because (a) reward (reinforcement) availability is low or nonexistent for healthy behaviors (e.g., exercising; eating healthy; being active in the home, school, community; having good bi-directional relationships; and communicating with others) and/or (b) the negative behaviors being displayed are rewarded at a much higher rate, frequency, duration, or magnitude (Lejuez, Hopko, & Hopko, 2001). For example, a child may not be obtaining peer attention for attempts at social communication but obtains adult attention for verbally complaining. Another example is children who experience repetitive thoughts, such as worrying, which allow them to avoid experiencing and or participating in activities or situations and the associated emotional consequence. Worry might function to avoid (negative reinforcement) greater stimulation and distress (Hayes, Strosahl, & Wilson, 1999).

The theory behind Behavior Activation Treatment, and thus the Pleasant Events Diary, acknowledges there may be feelings and cognitions that exist apart from the exhibited behaviors. However, the primary goal is to change the behaviors of the individual to ones that are healthier for the individual so that the individual can obtain the desired goals. Each child or individual sets values on different aspects of life. For example, one child may put more focus on academic goals, while another child may focus more on social relationships (Callaghan, 2006). The Pleasant Events Diary allows and fosters the process for individual goals. The Pleasant Events Diary has been successful in treating depression and anxiety in adolescents (Hopko, Robertson, & Lejuez, 2006).

Materials

1) Daily Mood Chart
2) Daily Activity Log
3) Life Areas Assignment
4) Pleasant Events Schedule
5) Activity Identification Ranking Sheet
6) Activity Hierarchy
7) Self-Identification of Possible Rewards
8) Master Log
9) Pleasant Events Diary

Procedure for Interventionist

The Pleasant Events Diary intervention will take 10-12 sessions. The first few sessions will take approximately one hour; however, as the child becomes more fluent with monitoring behavior and events, the sessions can be reduced to 15-30 minutes. The interventionist can be a psychologist or a counselor, although some research suggests that people who are involved with the daily life of the child (i.e., activities, events, progress monitoring, etc.) are a better choice as an interventionist because they can ensure integrity of the intervention. Another potential way to implement the intervention is to have a counselor or psychologist to conduct the first few sessions (i.e., rationale, progress monitoring of mood and activity, and contextual factors) and then have the primary caregiver (e.g., parent, teacher, behavior specialist, etc.) to implement the remaining sessions. See the Progression of the Pleasant Events Diary Intervention on page 334 for the schedule of sessions and goals of the sessions. The interventionist should read and become familiar with all the materials, procedures, and progression of sessions prior to implementation.

1) Discuss with the child the reason for the child being involved in the session. Discuss the specific behaviors that are of concern and that are unique to the child; do not have a general discussion of children who are sad or nervous.
    a) Give examples of when the child displays the behaviors.
    b) Ask the child to give other examples of when the behaviors are displayed by prompting the child with questions.
    c) Explain to the child that other children and adults can experience the same behaviors, thoughts, and feelings as the child and provide examples of some of the other behaviors, thoughts, and feelings that children can have besides those that the child endorsed.
    d) Explain the overall progression of the sessions (obtaining data for baseline, assessing for pleasant activities, the Pleasant Events Diary, the length treatment sessions, which will be discussed later).

2) Explain the Daily Mood Chart to the child.
   a) Read the directions on the Daily Mood Chart on page 335 to the child.
   b) Model for the child how to rate mood on a separate Daily Mood Chart.
   c) Determine with the child when and where the child should rate (e.g., at school during 1st period in the back of the room) to rate the child's mood. Choose a time of day when the child is most likely to exhibit the behaviors.
   d) Determine with the child where the Daily Mood Chart should be located (e.g., in a folder that the child carries to school and home every day, the child's belongings such as a backpack or purse).
   e) Ask if the child feels he or she will need prompting to remember to rate in the future.
3) Explain the Daily Activity Log on page 336 to the child.
   a) Read the directions on the Daily Activity Log to the child.
   b) Model for the child how to log activities on a separate Daily Activity Log.
   c) Determine with the child how often and where the child should log the activities (e.g., every 60 minutes at his desk). Choose a time of day when the child is most likely to exhibit the behaviors.
   d) Determine with the child where the Daily Activity Log should be located (e.g., in a folder that the child carries to school and home every day).
   e) Ask if the child needs prompting to remember to log the activities.
4) Discuss with the child the importance of the collecting the Daily Mood Chart and Daily Activity Log data for a week. These data are important for several reasons:
   - to understand the child's activity level,
   - to understand the mood level of the child for the week,
   - to be able to create an individual plan unique to the child, and
   - to determine if the intervention, Pleasant Events Diary, is effective over time.
5) Check with the child one to two times between sessions to ensure the child is collecting information. This check should be a brief check of the Daily Mood Chart and Daily Activity Log, a time to offer praise for logging mood and activity, and an opportunity to answer any questions.
6) Review the Daily Activity Log and Mood Chart for approximately 10 minutes at the beginning of the second session. The discussion between the interventionist and child should address two ideas:
   a) if there are any relationships between activity level and mood charting and
   b) if there are patterns between certain contextual factors and mood. For example, if a child earned a "C" on a paper and the child rated a sad mood, then the interventionist may ask if the child reacts this way to similar grades. The same type of questions are asked if the child the child reports being happy about a contextual factor.
7) Focus the remainder of the second session on the Life Areas Assignment on page 337 or the Pleasant Events Schedule on page 339. You can decide to conduct one or the other or both. Sometimes a

child needs more written prompts (i.e., Pleasant Events Schedule) rather than open-ended questions (Life Areas Assignment). Make this decision based on the child's unique needs.

a) Read the directions to the child of either the Life Areas Assignment or the Pleasant Events Schedule. Next, assist the child in completing the first item or two to ensure the child understands the directions.

b) Allow the child ample opportunity to answer the items to ensure that if the child does not understand an item, then the child can receive assistance.

c) If the child fills out the Life Areas Assignment, make sure the child identifies and writes behaviors that are observable and measurable. A non-example is "I want a better relationship with my mom." A good example is "I want to spend time playing a game with my mom."

d) Completing the Life Areas Assignment or Pleasant Events Schedule may take the rest of the session. If there is not sufficient time in the session for the child to complete the selected forms, then reschedule the next session for the next day or two. Remind the child to continue to complete the Daily Activities Log and Daily Mood Chart.

8) Have the child complete the Activity Identification Ranking Sheet on page 349, Activity Hierarchy on page 350, and the Self-Identification of Possible Rewards on page 351 in the third session.

a) Review with the child the responses on the Life Areas Assignment and/or Pleasant Events Schedule to refresh the child's memory.

b) Read the directions for the Activity Identification Ranking Sheet to the child. Assure the child that the activities do not have to put in any order at first. The child just needs to understand that only 15 activities identified as most enjoyable or pleasant should be placed on the Activity Identification Sheet. Once all 15 activities have been identified, the child then rank orders the 15 items. Review with the child the Activity Hierarchy on page 350 by reading the directions.

i) Define the word "easiest" in the directions. Easiest can be defined as those activities that the child has quick access to, activities that take little response effort from the child, etc. For example, a child may find reading a book and making a new friend as pleasant activities. However, it may be easier to read a book (quicker access and little response effort) versus making a new friend (has quick access to peers but may require more response effort). Level 1 activities should be activities that the child engages in currently.

ii) Fully participate in completing this form, as a child may need help in discerning levels of easy tasks.

c) Finally, explain the purpose of the Self-Identification of Possible Rewards List on page 351: Once the Pleasant Events Diary is implemented, the child will be recognized for positive, healthy behavior change. Have the child identify possible rewards to earn when the child has met the goals on the Master Log. Read the Self-Identification of Possible Rewards directions to the child and have the child complete the form.

9) Review with the child the Master Log (see page 352) directions and how to complete the form.

a) Complete with the child the first few activities to chart for the first week. Select activities from the Activity Hierarchy, starting with Level 1 activities in column 1. Over time, activities from the next higher level on the Activity Hierarchy should be selected. Assist the child in completing (a) the number of times the child would like to complete the activity and (b) the duration of the activity in the columns under Ideal Goal, which is a long-term goal. A child is not expected to reach the Ideal Goal the first week. In the next group of columns, the child writes the short-term goal for a week.

b) Make a copy of the Master Log each week as it is updated during each session. Keep one copy and have the child keep the other copy to review during the next session.

c) The Master Log will be completed each week by adding activities and/or increasing the frequency and duration of the activities. When activities are added to the Master Log, the additional activities should be taken from the next highest level on the Activity Hierarchy until all levels and activities are incorporated.

10) Review with the child the Pleasant Event Diary directions and model how to complete the form and track progress. The child will track the progress on the activities listed on the Master Log on the Pleasant Event Diary on page 354 throughout the week until the next session.

11) Review with the child weekly the progress on the Daily Mood Chart, Daily Activity Log, and Pleasant Event Diary. Trouble shoot with the child any issues with not meeting goals, not tracking progress, etc. However, if the child meets a goal on the Master Log, the child should be able to pick a reinforcer (reward) off the Possible Rewards List each week that a goal is met.

References

Callaghan, G. M. (2006). The Functional Idiographic Assessment Template (FIAT) system. *The Behavior Analyst Today, 7,* 357-398.

Hayes, S. C., Strosahl, K. D., & Wilson, K. G. (1999). *Acceptance and commitment therapy: An experiential approach to behavior change*. New York: Guilford.

Hopko, D. R., Robertson, S. M., & Lejuez, C. W. (2006). Behavioral Activation for Anxiety Disorders. *The Behavior Analyst Today, 7,* 212-233.

Lejuez, C. W., Hopko, D. R., & Hopko, S. D. (2001). A brief Behavioral Activation Treatment for Depression: Treatment manual. *Behavior Modification, 25,* 255-286.

McPhillamy, C. & Lewinsohn, P. M. (1971). *The Pleasant Events Schedule. Eugene: University of Oregon.*

Progression of the Pleasant Events Diary Intervention

Session	Steps in Intervention	Goals for Session
1	1-4	Rationale & Initiation of Baseline (Daily Mood Chart & Daily Activity Log)
Step 5 is to check in with the child in between sessions 1 & 2		
2	6-7	Review Baseline Data, Conduct Life Areas Assignment or Pleasant Events Schedule
3	8-10	Complete Activity Identification Ranking Sheet, Activity Hierarchy, and Self-Identification of Possible Rewards
4-to end	11	Review Progress on the Master Log, Pleasant Events Diary, Mood Log, and Activity Log

Note: Sessions 1-3 can be completed within the first two weeks of intervention initiation. The interventionist is highly encouraged to check in with the child between sessions to make sure that the child is collecting data as well as implementing/completing the Pleasant Events Diary. This schedule is based on a 50-60 minute session.

Daily Mood Chart

Name: ______________________________ Month: ______________________________

Directions:

1) At the end of the rating period (e.g., day, morning, afternoon), rate your mood the "highest" or "lowest" that you felt during that time period by placing a dot in the box that best describes your mood.

2) If you have had high and low moods on the same day, place two dots.

3) Rate any anxiety or irritability that you may have on a scale from 0-3 (0=None to 3=High).

High Mood	+3																														
	+2																														
	+1																														
Average																															
Low Mood	-1																														
	-2																														
	-3																														
Anxiety																															
Irritability																															
Rating	Period (day)	1	2	3	4	5	6	7	8	9	10	11	12	13	14	15	16	17	18	19	20	21	22	23	24	25	26	27	28	29	30

What made you have a good day?

What made you have a bad day?

TIER

Daily Activity Log

Name: ______________________________ Week of: ______________________

Directions: Log your activities hour by hour as accurately as you can for one week. Please record all activities regardless of how trivial they may seem, such as sleeping, eating, watching television, studying, getting ready for bed, getting ready for school/work, etc. Write in your activity in each hour. If you did two activities in an hour, write both in the time slot (e.g., you might write sleeping/getting ready in the 6-7am slot).

	Sunday	Monday	Tuesday	Wednesday	Thursday	Friday	Saturday
6 - 7am							
7 - 8am							
8 - 9am							
9 - 10am							
10 - 11am							
11 - 12pm							
12 - 1pm							
1 - 2pm							
2 - 3pm							
3 - 4pm							
4 - 5pm							
5 - 6pm							
6 - 7pm							
7 - 8pm							
8 - 9pm							
9 - 10pm							
10 - 11pm							
11 - 12am							
12 - 1am							
1 - 2am							
2 - 3am							
3 - 4am							
4 - 5am							
5 - 6am							

Life Areas Assignment

Adapted and modified from Hayes, Strosahl, and Wilson, 1999

Directions: You need to determine the activities you would like to accomplish or do more often. In identifying these activities, you need to consider activities in the following areas:

1) Family Relationships - What type of brother/sister, son/daughter, cousin, or family member do you want to be? What qualities are important in your relationship with family members?

2) Social Relationships - What would be an ideal friendship be like for you? How would a friend act or feel towards you? How would you act or feel towards your friend? What would you and your friend do? What areas could you improve in your relationships with your friends? How could your friends improve their relationship with you?

3) Education/School - What would you like to improve in your classes? What would you like to improve in a subject /class? What would you like to improve in your overall education? Would you like to participate in something at school that you are currently not participating in as regularly as you would like? How are your overall study habits? How are your organizational skills? How is your time management?

4) Hobbies/Recreation - Are there any special interests that you have? Is there any interest that you would like to pursue? Is there a new hobby or recreation that you would like to experience?

5) Volunteer Work/Charity - What contributions would you like to make to your community? What contributions would you like to make to your school, church, or neighborhood?

6) Physical/Health Issues - Do you wish to improve your diet, sleep, exercise, etc.?

7) Spirituality - What, if anything, does spirituality mean to you? Are you satisfied with this area of your life?

8) Psychological/Emotional Issues - What do you want out of the sessions? Are there any areas that you would like to explore?

Life Areas Assignment

Name: ______________________________ Date: ______________________________

Directions: Describe activities that you would like to accomplish in these areas. You may feel that one of the listed areas is not one in which you want to accomplish activities; in that case, just answer N/A or not applicable.

1) Family Relationships

____

____

____

2) Social Relationships

____

____

____

3) Education/School

____

____

____

4) Hobbies/ Recreation

____

____

____

5) Volunteer Work/ Charity

____

____

____

6) Physical/Health Issues

____

____

____

7) Spirituality

____

____

____

8) Psychological/emotional Issues

____

____

____

Pleasant Events Schedule

Modified and adapted from McPhillamy, C. & Lewinsohn, P. M. (1971).

Name: ______________________________ Date: ____________________

Directions: This schedule is designed to find out about the things you have enjoyed during the past month. The schedule contains a list of events or activities which people sometimes enjoy. You will be asked to go over the list twice; the first time you will rate each event or note how many times it has happened in the past month, and the second time you will rate each event on how pleasant it has been for you. There are no right or wrong answers.

On the following pages you will find a list of activities, events, and experiences. HOW OFTEN HAVE THESE EVENTS HAPPENED IN YOUR LIFE IN THE PAST MONTH? Please answer this question by rating each item on the following scale:

0 = This has not happened in the past 30 days.

1 = This has happened a few times (1 to 6) in the past 30 days.

2 = This has happened often (7 or more) in the past 30 days.

Important: Some items will list more than one event; for these items, mark how often you have done any of the listed events. For example, item number 10 is "Doing art work (painting, sculpture, drawing, movie-making, etc.)." You should rate item 10 on how often you have done any of these forms of art work in the past month.

Since this list contains events that might happen to a wide variety of people, you may find that many of the events have not happened to you in the past 30 days. It is not expected that anyone will have done all of these things in one month.

Go through the list a second time indicating how pleasant each event has been for you. Please rate each item using the following scale:

0 = This event is not pleasant for me.

1 = This event may be pleasant for me.

2 = This event is very pleasant for me.

How Often	How Pleasant		
______	______	1.	Wearing expensive or formal clothes
______	______	2.	Talking about sports
______	______	3.	Meeting someone new of the same sex
______	______	4.	Taking tests when well prepared
______	______	5.	Going to a rock concert
______	______	6.	Playing baseball or softball
______	______	7.	Planning trips or vacations

How Often	How Pleasant	
		8. Buying things for myself
		9. Being at the beach
		10. Doing art work (painting, sculpture, drawing, movie-making, etc.)
		11. Rock climbing or mountaineering
		12. Reading the Scriptures or other sacred works
		13. Playing golf
		14. Rearranging or redecorating my room
		15. Going to a sports event
		16. Reading a "How to Do It" book or article
		17. Reading stories, novels, poems, or plays
		18. Breathing clean air
		19. Thinking up or arranging songs or music
		20. Saying something clearly
		21. Boating (canoeing, kayaking, motorboating, sailing, etc.)
		22. Pleasing my parents
		23. Doing arts and crafts
		24. Watching TV
		25. Talking to myself
		26. Camping
		27. Working in student government
		28. Working on machines (cars, bikes, motorcycles, tractors, etc.)
		29. Thinking about something good in the future
		30. Playing cards
		31. Completing a difficult task
		32. Laughing
		33. Solving a problem, puzzle, crossword, etc.
		34. Criticizing someone
		35. Having lunch with friends
		36. Playing tennis
		37. Taking a shower
		38. Woodworking, carpentry
		39. Writing stories, novels, plays or poetry

How Often	How Pleasant	
______	______	40. Being with animals
______	______	41. Riding in an airplane
______	______	42. Exploring (hiking away from known routes, spelunking, etc.)
______	______	43. Having a frank and open conversation
______	______	44. Singing in a group
______	______	45. Thinking about myself or my problems.
______	______	46. Working on my job
______	______	47. Going to a party
______	______	48. Going to church functions (socials, classes, bazaars, etc.)
______	______	49. Speaking a foreign language
______	______	50. Going to service, civic, or social club meetings
______	______	51. Being in a sporty or expensive car
______	______	52. Playing a musical instrument
______	______	53. Making snacks
______	______	54. Snow skiing
______	______	55. Being helped
______	______	56. Wearing informal clothes
______	______	57. Combing or brushing my hair
______	______	58. Acting
______	______	59. Taking a nap
______	______	60. Being with friends
______	______	61. Solving a personal problem
______	______	62. Being in the city
______	______	63. Taking a bath
______	______	64. Singing to myself
______	______	65. Making food or crafts to sell or give away
______	______	66. Playing pool or billiards
______	______	67. Being with my grandparent
______	______	68. Playing chess or checkers
______	______	69. Doing craft work (pottery, jewelry, leather, beads, weaving, etc.)
______	______	70. Weighing myself
______	______	71. Putting on make-up, fixing my hair, etc.

How Often	How Pleasant	
		72. Designing or drafting
		73. Visiting people who are sick, shut in, or in trouble
		74. Cheering, rooting
		75. Bowling
		76. Being popular at a gathering
		77. Watching wild animals
		78. Having an original idea
		79. Gardening, landscaping, or doing yard work
		80. Reading essays or technical, or academic literature
		81. Wearing new clothes
		82. Dancing
		83. Sitting in the sun
		84. Just sitting and thinking
		85. Seeing good things happen to my family or friends
		86. Going to a fair, carnival, circus, zoo, or amusement park
		87. Talking about philosophy or religion
		88. Planning or organizing something
		89. Listening to the sounds of nature
		90. Dating
		91. Having a lively talk
		92. Listening to the radio
		93. Having friends come over to visit
		94. Playing in a sporting competition
		95. Introducing people who I think would like each other
		96. Giving gifts
		97. Going to school or government meetings, court sessions, etc.
		98. Getting massages
		99. Getting letters, cards, or notes
		100. Watching the sky, clouds, or a storm
		101. Going on outings (to the park, a picnic, or a barbecue, etc.)
		102. Playing basketball
		103. Buying something for my family

How Often	How Pleasant	
______	______	104. Photography
______	______	105. Giving a speech or lecture
______	______	106. Reading maps
______	______	107. Gathering natural objects (wild food, rocks, driftwood, etc.)
______	______	108. Wearing clean clothes
______	______	109. Helping someone
______	______	110. Being in the mountains
______	______	111. Hearing jokes
______	______	112. Going to a revival or crusade
______	______	113. Talking about my health
______	______	114. Seeing beautiful scenery
______	______	115. Eating good meals
______	______	116. Improving my health (getting new glasses, changing my diet, etc.)
______	______	117. Being downtown
______	______	118. Wrestling or boxing
______	______	119. Hunting or shooting
______	______	120. Playing in a musical group
______	______	121. Hiking
______	______	122. Going to a museum or exhibit
______	______	123. Writing papers, essays, articles, reports, memos, etc.
______	______	124. Doing a job well
______	______	125. Having spare time
______	______	126. Fishing
______	______	127. Loaning something
______	______	128. Pleasing teachers
______	______	129. Counseling someone
______	______	130. Going to a health club, sauna, bath, etc.
______	______	131. Having someone criticize me
______	______	132. Learning to do something new
______	______	133. Going to a "drive-thru" (Dairy Queen, McDonald's, etc.)
______	______	134. Complimenting or praising someone
______	______	135. Thinking about people I like

How Often	How Pleasant	
______	______	136. Taking revenge on someone
______	______	137. Being with my parents
______	______	138. Horseback riding
______	______	139. Talking on the telephone
______	______	140. Having daydreams
______	______	141. Kicking leaves, sand, pebbles, etc.
______	______	142. Playing lawn sports (e.g., badminton, croquet, shuffleboard, horseshoes, etc.)
______	______	143. Going to the movies
______	______	144. Being alone
______	______	145. Budgeting my time
______	______	146. Cooking meals
______	______	147. Being praised by people I admire
______	______	148. Outwitting a "superior"
______	______	149. Feeling the presence of the Lord in my life
______	______	150. Doing a project in my own way
______	______	151. Doing "odd jobs" around the house
______	______	152. Crying
______	______	153. Being told I'm needed
______	______	154. Being at a family reunion or get-together
______	______	155. Giving a party or get-together
______	______	156. Washing my hair
______	______	157. Coaching someone
______	______	158. Going to a restaurant
______	______	159. Seeing or smelling a flower or plant
______	______	160. Being invited out
______	______	161. Receiving honors (civic, academic, etc.)
______	______	162. Using cologne, perfume, or aftershave
______	______	163. Having someone agree with me
______	______	164. Reminiscing, talking about old times
______	______	165. Getting up early in the morning
______	______	166. Having peace and quiet

How Often	How Pleasant	
______	______	167. Doing experiments or other scientific work
______	______	168. Visiting friends
______	______	169. Writing in a diary
______	______	170. Playing football
______	______	171. Being counseled
______	______	172. Saying prayers
______	______	173. Giving massages
______	______	174. Hitchhiking
______	______	175. Meditating or doing yoga
______	______	176. Seeing a fight
______	______	177. Doing favors for people
______	______	178. Talking with people in class
______	______	179. Being relaxed
______	______	180. Being asked for my help or advice
______	______	181. Thinking about other people's problems
______	______	182. Playing board games (Monopoly, Scrabble, etc.)
______	______	183. Sleeping soundly at night
______	______	184. Doing heavy outdoor work (cutting wood, clearing land, farm work, etc.)
______	______	185. Reading the newspaper
______	______	186. Snowmobiling or dune-buggy riding
______	______	187. Being in a body-awareness, sensitivity, encounter, therapy, or "rap" group
______	______	188. Dreaming at night
______	______	189. Playing ping pong
______	______	190. Brushing my teeth
______	______	191. Swimming
______	______	192. Being in a fight
______	______	193. Running, jogging, or doing gymnastic, fitness, or field exercises
______	______	194. Walking barefoot
______	______	195. Playing Frisbee or catch
______	______	196. Doing housework or laundry; cleaning things
______	______	197. Listening to music

How Often	How Pleasant	
		198. Arguing
		199. Knitting, crocheting, embroidery, or fancy needlework
		200. Amusing people
		201. Going to a barber or beautician
		202. Having house guests
		203. Being with someone I love
		204. Reading magazines
		205. Sleeping late
		206. Starting a new project
		207. Being stubborn
		208. Going to the library
		209. Playing soccer, rugby, hockey, lacrosse, etc.
		210. Preparing a new or special food
		211. Bird watching
		212. Shopping
		213. Watching people
		214. Building or watching a fire
		215. Winning an argument
		216. Selling or trading something
		217. Finishing a project or task
		218. Confessing or apologizing
		219. Repairing things
		220. Working with others as a team
		221. Bicycling
		222. Telling people what to do
		223. Being with happy people
		224. Writing letters, cards, or notes
		225. Talking about politics or public affairs
		226. Asking for help or advice
		227. Going to banquets, luncheons, potlucks, etc.
		228. Talking about my hobby or special interests
		229. Smiling at people

How Often	How Pleasant	
______	______	230. Playing in sand, a stream, the grass
______	______	231. Talking about other people
______	______	232. Having people show interest in what I have said
______	______	233. Going on field trips, nature walks, etc.
______	______	234. Expressing my love to someone
______	______	235. Caring for houseplants
______	______	236. Having coffee, tea, a coke, etc., with friends
______	______	237. Taking a walk
______	______	238. Collecting things
______	______	239. Playing handball, paddleball, squash, etc.
______	______	240. Sewing
______	______	241. Suffering for a good cause
______	______	242. Remembering a departed friend or loved one, visiting the cemetery
______	______	243. Doing things with children
______	______	244. Beachcombing
______	______	245. Being complimented or told I have done well
______	______	246. Being told that I'm loved
______	______	247. Eating snacks
______	______	248. Staying up late
______	______	249. Having family members or friends do something that makes me proud of them
______	______	250. Going to auctions, garage sales, etc.
______	______	251. Thinking about an interesting question
______	______	252. Doing volunteer work; working on community service projects
______	______	253. Water skiing, surfing, scuba diving
______	______	254. Receiving money
______	______	255. Defending or protecting someone
______	______	256. Hearing a good sermon
______	______	257. Winning a competition
______	______	258. Making a new friend
______	______	259. Talking about my job or school
______	______	260. Reading cartoons, comic strips, or comic books

How Often	How Pleasant	
		261. Borrowing something
		262. Traveling with a group
		263. Seeing old friends
		264. Teaching someone
		265. Using my strength
		266. Traveling
		267. Attending a concert, opera, or ballet
		268. Playing with pets
		269. Going to a play
		270. Looking at the stars or moon
		271. Being coached

Activity Identification Ranking Sheet

Adapted and modified from Hayes, Strosahl, and Wilson, 1999

Name: ______________________________ Date: ______________________

Directions: Write your most desired 15 activities from the Pleasant Events Schedule in the first column in any order. Then, rate each activity from least difficult to achieve to the most difficult to achieve with 1 being the easiest and 15 being the most difficult.

Activity	Ranking
1)	
2)	
3)	
4)	
5)	
6)	
7)	
8)	
9)	
10)	
11)	
12)	
13)	
14)	
15)	

Activity Hierarchy

Adapted and modified from Hayes, Strosahl, and Wilson, 1999

Name: ______________________________ Date: ______________________

Directions: After you have completed the Activity Identification Ranking Sheet, rank the activities by assigning them to a level by writing your top 3 easiest activities under Level 1, the 4th through 6th activities in Level 2, 7th through 9th activities in Level 3, 10th through 12th activities in Level 4, and 13th through the 15th activities in Level 5.

Level 1 (1st through 3rd)

1) ______________________________

2) ______________________________

3) ______________________________

Level 2 (4th through 6th)

1) ______________________________

2) ______________________________

3) ______________________________

Level 3 (7th through 9th)

1) ______________________________

2) ______________________________

3) ______________________________

Level 4 (10th through 12th)

1) ______________________________

2) ______________________________

3) ______________________________

Level 5 (13th through 15th)

1) ______________________________

2) ______________________________

3) ______________________________

Self-Identification of Possible Rewards

Directions: Write your favorite things, activities, and special events or items that may serve as potential rewards.

Name: ______________________________ Date: ______________________________________

My favorite things, activities, and special things to do or get!

1) ____

2) ____

3) ____

4) ____

5) ____

6) ____

7) ____

8) ____

9) ____

10) ____

11) ____

12) ____

Master Log

Directions: Now that you have identified your 15 activities from your Activity Hierarchy, you have to plan on how you will complete these activities in your daily life. The Master Log is a useful way to help plan and track your progress. You should log three to five activities during the first week. The number of activities will differ or change each week. Your participation will be important in achieving your goal. It is important that you challenge yourself but just as important is that the goals are ones you can achieve!

1) Select and write the first few activities from the Activity Hierarchy to log for the coming week in the Activity column.
2) The first group of columns addresses an activity and your Ideal Goal, which is a long term goal. You are not necessarily expected to reach the Ideal Goal the first week. However, you should put what you would eventually like to be able to accomplish in a week. In the two columns immediately following the Activity column, you will list two things about your Ideal Goal:
    a. the number of times (#) you would like to complete the activity in a week and
    b. the duration of the activity (you may write *UF*, representing that the activity will continue **Until Finished** regardless of the duration). The duration should be the number of minutes or hours the activity will last.
3) In the next group of columns, write what your short term goal is for the coming week. For each activity selected for a given week, write down the frequency (#) and duration goals in the appropriate columns.
    a. Both you and the interventionist should have a copy of the Master Log, and it should be completed on a weekly basis.
4) Each week you and your interventionist will review the Pleasant Event Diary to record on the Master Log the number of times that you met both the frequency and duration goals in the "Did" column. If you met or exceeded the goal one week, you should write a more challenging goal for the next week and continue to do this until you have reached your Ideal Goal. Each time you achieve one of your Ideal Goals, you will add a new activity from your Activity Hierarchy.

Master Log

Adapted and modified from Lejuez, C. W., Hopko, D. R., & Hopko, S. D. (2001)

Name: ____

			Week:				Week:			
	Ideal Goal		**Goal**		**Did**		**Goal**		**Did**	
Activity	**#**	**Duration**	**#**	**Duration**	**#**	**Duration**	**#**	**Duration**	**#**	**Duration**
1)										
2)										
3)										
4)										
5)										
6)										
7)										
8)										
9)										
10)										
11)										
12)										
13)										
14)										
15)										

Pleasant Events Diary

Directions: Record your daily progress towards your Master Log goals using the Pleasant Event Diary. As you did on the Master Log, you will write down the goal frequency and duration of each activity you have selected that week in the appropriate columns. Select a time of day or several times a day that you will record your activity. For example, you could select after lunch and at bedtime as your times to record your progress. Chose times that you are most likely to remember to log your progress.

Circle a "Y" if you have engaged in the activity and "N" if you have not engaged in the activity. If you meet the frequency and duration goal for the week, you may circle "G" for meeting the goal as well as circling "Y." Once you have met the goal, your last entry will be circling a "Y" and circling "G." You can always continue to engage in the activity after the goal has been met.

Pleasant Events Diary

Adapted and modified from Lejuez, C. W., Hopko, D. R., & Hopko, S. D. (2001)

Name: ______________________ Week: ______________________

Time(s) you will record your progress: ______________________

	Goal								
Activity	**#**	**Duration**	**Sunday**	**Monday**	**Tuesday**	**Wednesday**	**Thursday**	**Friday**	**Saturday**
			Y N G	Y N G	Y N G	Y N G	Y N G	Y N G	Y N G
			Y N G	Y N G	Y N G	Y N G	Y N G	Y N G	Y N G
			Y N G	Y N G	Y N G	Y N G	Y N G	Y N G	Y N G
			Y N G	Y N G	Y N G	Y N G	Y N G	Y N G	Y N G
			Y N G	Y N G	Y N G	Y N G	Y N G	Y N G	Y N G
			Y N G	Y N G	Y N G	Y N G	Y N G	Y N G	Y N G
			Y N G	Y N G	Y N G	Y N G	Y N G	Y N G	Y N G
			Y N G	Y N G	Y N G	Y N G	Y N G	Y N G	Y N G
			Y N G	Y N G	Y N G	Y N G	Y N G	Y N G	Y N G
			Y N G	Y N G	Y N G	Y N G	Y N G	Y N G	Y N G
			Y N G	Y N G	Y N G	Y N G	Y N G	Y N G	Y N G
			Y N G	Y N G	Y N G	Y N G	Y N G	Y N G	Y N G
			Y N G	Y N G	Y N G	Y N G	Y N G	Y N G	Y N G
			Y N G	Y N G	Y N G	Y N G	Y N G	Y N G	Y N G
			Y N G	Y N G	Y N G	Y N G	Y N G	Y N G	Y N G

Comments:

____

____

TIER

Pleasant Events Diary: Procedural Integrity Checklist

Age/Grade:	6th grade – High School
Setting:	School, Clinic, In-patient
Individual or Group:	Individual
Tier:	2 & 3
Desired/ Appropriate Behavior:	Increasing positive mood, increasing healthy behaviors, increasing social behaviors, increasing relax/calm (reduction in nervous behaviors)
Skill Level:	Fluency to maintenance; not used for acquisition of skills

The checklist is divided into two parts. Part one of the checklist is used to conduct observations in the session while the intervention is being conducted. Part two of the checklist addresses evidence that the child is collecting data (i.e., Daily Mood Chart, Daily Activity Log, and Pleasant Events Diary) with the appropriate frequency and is using feedback from the intervention. The evidence for part two is gathered by looking at the documentation or other evidence sources.

Procedure for Integrity Checklist Observer

1) Complete the Procedural Integrity Checklist (see page 358) information about the interventionist, child, location, date, time, observer name, and observer signature.
2) Assess the interventionist's implementation of the Pleasant Events Diary. An initial observation should occur during the first 3 sessions.
3) Observe the interventionist for the presence of behaviors under Part 1: Sessions on the Checklist and mark Yes if present or No if not present.
4) Evaluate the presence of products under Part 2: Data Collection on the Checklist and mark Yes if present or No if not present. Data Collection of Part 2 is based on child's documentation, child folders, or interviews. Part 2 of the checklist may be completed during or after the Part 1 observation.
5) Count the number of behaviors marked Yes on Part 1 and Part 2 and write the number on the line for "Number of behaviors marked Yes."
6) Calculate the percent marked Yes. A chart is provided for determining the percent marked Yes. If fewer than four behaviors are marked Yes, then provide feedback immediately to the interventionist and conduct another observation the next day or as soon as possible.
7) Write any constructive feedback comments in addition to any notations made beside any individual behavior in the "Feedback" section.
8) Provide the interventionist, at an appropriate time, with oral feedback regarding the implementation of the intervention, starting with positive behaviors observed, and a copy of the Pleasant Events Diary: Procedural Integrity Checklist. *The feedback should be provided the same day of the observation.*

9) Observe the interventionist implementing the Pleasant Events Diary procedure approximately every other week or twice a month after the initial observations.

Pleasant Events Diary: Procedural Integrity Checklist

Interventionist: ______________ Date: ________ Time: ________

Child: ______________ Observer: ______________

Location: ______________ Signature: ______________

Part 1: In Session – Behaviors to Observe	Yes	No	Comments
Session 1			
1) The interventionist explains the rationale for the intervention.			
2) The interventionist explains the progression of the intervention (data collection, Pleasant Events Diary, the intervention sessions, etc.).			
3) The interventionist explains the Daily Mood Chart.			
4) The interventionist explains the Daily Activity Log.			
5) The interventionist explains the importance of data collection.			
Session 2-3			
6) The interventionist and child review the baseline data.			
7) The interventionist ensures the child completes the Life Areas Assignment or Pleasant Events Schedule.			
8) The interventionist ensures the child completes the Activity Identification Ranking Sheet.			
9) The interventionist ensures the child completes the Activity Hierarchy.			
10) The interventionist ensures the child completes the Self-Identification of Possible Rewards.			
11) The interventionist explains the Master Log.			
12) The interventionist assists the child in completing the Master Log.			
13) The interventionist explains the Pleasant Event Diary.			
Sessions 4-12			
14) The interventionist reviews progress on the data collection forms (Pleasant Events Diary, Daily Mood Chart, Daily Activity Log).			
15) The interventionist ensures that the child is rewarded when goals on the Master Log are met.			
16) The child selects new activities from the Activity Hierarchy to place on the Master Log.			

Feedback:

Part 2: Data Collection – Products to Observe	Yes	No	Comments
17) There is evidence the child is charting mood on a daily basis.			
18) There is evidence the child is logging daily activities.			
19) There is evidence the child is logging activities in the Pleasant Event Diary.			

Feedback:

Sessions & Data Collection (Part 1 and Part 2)

Number of behaviors marked Yes = _____ out of 19 = ______ %

Percent
1 out of 19 =5%
2 out of 19 = 11%
3 out of 19 = 16%
4 out of 19 = 21%
5 out of 19 = 26%
6 out of 19 = 32%
7 out of 19 = 37%
8 out of 19 = 42%
9 out of 19 = 47%
10 out of 19 = 53%
11 out of 19 = 58%
12 out of 19 = 63%
13 out of 19 = 68%
14 out of 19 = 74%
15 out of 19 = 79%
16 out of 19 = 84%
17 out of 19 = 90%
18 out of 19 = 95%
19 out of 19 = 100%

Habit Reversal

Age/Grade:	Preschool – High School
Setting:	School, Home, Clinic, In-patient
Individual or Group:	Individual
Tier:	2 & 3
Desired/ Appropriate Behavior:	Reduction in repetitive (habit) behaviors, thumb sucking, hair twirling, hair pulling, stuttering, tics, etc.
Skill Level:	Acquisition to Generalization

NOTE: This intervention is best implemented by someone with behavioral training (e.g., school psychologist, behavior therapist, behavior interventionist). Individuals without prior behavioral training should seek the assistance of someone with the appropriate training to implement this intervention.

Rationale & Research Support

Habit disorders can be defined as repetitive behaviors that serve no recognizable social function but may negatively affect the individual (Hansen, Tishelman, Hawkins, & Doepke, 1990). Due to the repetitive nature of the behavior, habit disorders in children may cause social distress as well as physical injury. Four main "classes" of habit disorders are recognized by professionals and observed in children: vocal and/or motor tics, "nervous" habits, stuttering, and Tourette's Disorder. Although some debate exists as to the actual terminology, most experts would agree with the areas of research that fit into these classes.

Tics are habitual, potentially involuntary movements of small groups of muscles that are caused by spasms, chorea, or tremors (Billings, 1978). Some examples of motor tics include shoulder shrugging, arm or neck jerking, facial grimacing, or excessive eye blinking. Examples of vocal tics include persistent coughing or throat clearing not caused by illness, barking, or coprolalia (i.e., repetitive use of obscene language). These vocal tics may be maintained by muscle tension reduction following a tic occurrence, which negatively reinforces the tic behavior (Evers & Van De Wetering, 1994). That is, once the tic occurs, the muscle tension reduces. Thus, the likelihood of the tic reoccurring to remove the muscle tension in the future is increased. Two reasons may explain why controlling tics can be problematic. One, the person may not be aware that he or she is displaying the tic and therefore may encounter difficultly trying to control it. Second, the negative reinforcing properties of "ticing" to reduce muscle tension are difficult to control without intervention.

"Nervous" habits can be defined as constant, repetitive behaviors that serve no social function but may serve a self-stimulatory function (Hansen, Tishelman, Hawkins, & Doepke, 1990) and/or an environmental restriction (e.g., when presented with an environment with motor restrictions like sitting in a dress, the "nervous" habit is more reinforcing than in other environments). The term *nervous* has implications that the behaviors are to reduce anxiety. Little empirical evidence directly links all of the behaviors to anxiety. These behaviors/habits often involve manipulation of some part of the body, such as the hands or mouth. Examples of "nervous" habits include nail biting, hair pulling/twirling, thumb sucking, chewing on lips or cheeks, constant scratching, skin picking, or bruxism (i.e., chronic and/or acute teeth grinding). Another type of habit is stuttering. Stuttering involves whole and part-word repetitions, blocking, hesitations, and prolongations during speech.

The fourth type of habit disorder is Tourette's Disorder. This disorder involves both motor and vocal tics that seem to occur in clusters, with the tics being active for a period of time and then dissipating (Dedmon, 1990). The factors underlying the development and maintenance of Tourette's are unclear, a number of potential explanations have been offered. One explanation is that the person experiences a tension reduction after the occurrence of the tics associated with Tourette's Disorder.

Habit Reversal has been shown to reduce habit disorders with children (e.g., Shumaker, 2009; Woods & Luiselli, 2007; Woods & Miltenberger, 1996). The original work and procedures are provided below. Habit Reversal is a package intervention, meaning that it has several components. Several studies have used variations of the procedures. In the adaptation/modification section, these variations are discussed further.

Materials

1) Competing Response Practice
2) Social Support Worksheet

Procedure for Interventionist

Azrin and Nunn (1973) proposed the Habit Reversal procedure as a treatment for nervous habits and muscle tics. The original procedure consisted of four phases, with a number of techniques specific to each phase. In the original treatment, a total of nine techniques are introduced to the child in one 2-hour treatment session. However, some of the techniques are explained to the child and/or the caregiver but not actually implemented until after the initial session for homework. In follow up sessions, the interventionist checks to see if the intervention is working. The interventionist may have to reteach certain steps, provide feedback, and/or give praise. Several modifications have either simplified some steps or added others. In some studies, Habit Reversal has taken longer (over more sessions) due to the age of the child, development level, awareness of the habit, etc.

1) The **Awareness Phase** is introduced first because the rest of the treatment is contingent upon the child being aware of each occurrence of the target behavior. Four techniques are considered to help bring about awareness. One or any combination of the four techniques may be used in this phase; however, equally important is the consideration that each technique may or may not be warranted. Each child is unique in presentation of a habit.

   a) The first technique is **Response Description**.

      i. Ask the child to fully describe and identify the dominant vocal and motor tic/behaviors.

      ii. Direct the child to demonstrate the dominant vocal and motor tic/behaviors.

         (a) This technique is often used in front of a mirror while the child is describing the habit.

   b) The second technique is **Response Detection**.

      i. Instruct the child to acknowledge either with a verbal response or physical gesture each occurrence of the behavior in the session.

      ii. Verbally state to the child when the child does not state or gesture that the behavior occurred.

   c) The third technique is **Early Warning**.

Teach the child to recognize the earliest signs of the behavior.

For example, a child with a hair pulling habit is taught to be aware as soon as the hand starts towards the hair. For tics and Tourette's Disorder, a child often has a premonitory urge or sensation, which precedes the tic or repetitive behavior, which in turn serves the function of reducing the aversive urge or stimulus. If a child experiences the premonitory urges or sensations, the identification of the urges or sensations that precede the unwanted tic or repetitive behavior is considered paramount for this particular technique. If a child does not experience these urges, this technique may not be useful. However, if the child demonstrates a clear sequence of behaviors prior to the actual habit behavior, this technique can be considered.

d) The final awareness technique is **Situation Awareness Training**.

i. Ask the child to describe all of the situations in which the behavior occurs.

ii. Ask the child to describe how the behavior is acted out in these situations. This technique may or may not be warranted as the behavior may not cause the child social problems; the child may not be aware that the behavior causes social problems; or the technique may not be age appropriate.

2) The second phase of the Habit Reversal procedure is the **Competing Response Phase**. The goal of this phase is to engage in a behavior that produces tensing of muscles opposite to those used in the target behavior. To be considered a competing response, the behavior should "(1) be opposite to the movement, (2) be capable of being maintained for several minutes, (3) be producing heightened awareness by an isometric tensing of the muscles involved in the movement, (4) be socially inconspicuous, and (5) strengthen the muscles antagonistic to the tic movement for the muscle tics" (Azrin & Nunn, 1973, p. 623).

a) Teach the child the Competing Response.

b) Have the child perform the competing behavior which is to isometrically tense the antagonistic muscle for up to 3 minutes up to 3 minutes contingent upon awareness of the urge to engage in or the actual occurrence of the target behavior.

c) Teach a family member or caregiver and/or the child how to use the Competing Response Practice sheet on page 366. The family member should have the child practice in as many locations, times, etc. as possible, particularly in the times and locations that the habit is most frequently displayed. For example, if the child sucks the thumb in the car then the practice should take place in the car.

3) The third phase is the **Motivation phase**. The goal of this phase is to motivate the child to implement the procedures in the Awareness and Competing Response phases. This phase employs three techniques.

a) The first technique is **Social Situations.**

Ask the child to describe situations in which the target behavior (i.e., habit) is embarrassing, physically injuring, and/or seemingly awkward.

b) The second technique is **Social Support**. This technique is demonstrated to the caregiver and child but actual implementation is done outside the session.

i. Teach the family or friends to provide verbal and physical praise to the child for not engaging in the target behavior.

ii. Teach the family how to use the Social Support Worksheet on pages 367-368.

iii. Teach and remind the child to practice the competing response technique if the caregiver, interventionist, other adult notice an occurrence of the target behavior that goes unnoticed by the child. An example social support is having the family practice the competing response together to show support during a time in which the habit is likely to occur (See Competing Response Practice and Social Support Journals).

c) The final motivational technique is **Public Display.** This technique is demonstrated to the caregiver and child but actual implementation is done outside the session.

Have the caregiver plan a time or times in which the child can demonstrate the competing response to show control of the habit in front of a group of family members or friends.

4) The final phase is **Generalization**. The goal of this phase is to enhance generalization of the results of the treatment to all areas of the child's life.

a) The technique is **Symbolic Rehearsal**.

i. Ask the child to imagine one of the situations discussed during Situation Awareness Training in the Awareness Phase.

ii. Ask the child to state the situation and instead of engaging in the habit have the child state the competing behavior.

iii. Role play with the child the situation while the child appropriately engages in the competing behavior.

iv. Praise the child for each step that was completed correctly.

Adjustments/Modification

Miltenberger, Fugua, and McKinley (1985) evaluated the original Habit Reversal procedure and a simplified intervention consisting of 1) awareness training (response description and detection), 2) self-monitoring (see Self-Monitoring Intervention), and 3) competing response training for the treatment of motor tics. They found that the full version and the simplified version of Habit Reversal were both effective. From this study, the authors concluded that the only necessary components of the Habit Reversal treatment were awareness training and competing response training. Miltenberger and Fuqua (1985) also demonstrated that the competing response must be applied contingent upon the target behavior. In a follow-up study, Sharenow, Fuqua, and Miltenberger (1989) demonstrated that the competing response does not need to be similar to the target behavior to be effective.

Relaxation Training is often described as an additive technique in the Habit Reversal intervention. This training is often added because some children who experience anxiety or verbally express that they have anxiety often engage in the habitual behavior(s) to reduce the aversive stimuli (anxiety).

References

Azrin, N. H. & Nunn, R. G. (1973). Habit reversal: A method of eliminating nervous habits and tics. *Behaviour Research and Therapy, 11*, 619-628.

Billings, A. (1978). Self-monitoring in the treatment of tics: A single subject analysis. *Journal of Behavior Therapy and Experimental Psychiatry, 9,* 339-342.

Dedmon, R. (1990). Tourette syndrome in children: Knowledge and services. *Health and Social Work, 15,* 107-115.

Evers, R.A.F., & Van De Wetering, B.J.M. (1994). A treatment model for motor tics based on a specific tension-reduction technique. *Journal of Behavior Therapy and Experimental Psychiatry, 25,* 255-260.

Hansen, D.J., Tishelman, A.C., Hawkins, R.P., & Doepke, K.J. (1990). Habits with potential as disorders: Prevalence, severity, and other characteristics among college students. *Behavior Modification, 14,* 66-80.

Miltenberger, R.G. & Fuqua, R.W. (1985). A comparison of contingent versus non-contingent competing response practice in the treatment of nervous habits. *Journal of Behavior Therapy and Experimental Psychiatry, 16,* 195-200.

Miltenberger, R. G., Fuqua, R. W., & McKinley, T. (1985). Habit reversal with muscle tics: Replication and component analysis. *Behavior Therapy, 16,* 39-50.

Sharenow, E, L., Fuqua, R. W., & Miltenberger, R. G. (1989). The treatment of muscle tics with dissimilar competing response practice. *Journal of Applied Behavior Analysis, 22,* 3542.

Shumaker, D. M. (2009). Habit Reversal Treatment of Repetitive Hand Writing in a 7-Year-Old Child with a Learning Disability. *Clinical Case Studies*, *8*(3), 163-173.

Woods, J. E. & Luiselli, J. K. (2007). Habit reversal treatment of a vocal and motor tics in a child with Tourette's syndrome. *Clinical Case Studies, 6*, 181-189.

Woods, D. M. & Miltenberger, R. G. (1996) A review of habit reversal with childhood habit disorders. *Education & Treatment of Children (ETC), 19(2)*, 197.

Competing Response Practice

Directions: Every time the child practices the competing response, log the dates, times, place(s) practiced, etc. Use the journal provided below. An example is provided.

Child's Name :_________________________________ Week of: ______________________

What is the competing response: ____

Date	Time	How many minutes did ________ (child's name) practice?	Where was I when I was practicing?

Social Support Worksheet

Directions: Friends and family give positive verbal, physical, and gestures to the child for **<u>not engaging</u>** in the habit or behavior. Friends and family are to give this praise throughout the day to your child. The caregivers and the interventionist will determine how often the praise should be given. However, the more often the caregiver can give the social support, the better. Put a tally mark in each hour that the caregiver gave positive feedback. If the caregiver gave positive feedback 3 times in one hour, the caregiver will have 3 tally marks in the hour block. Block out times in which the caregiver are not with the child (for example, at school). The caregiver can ask the child's teacher to give positive feedback to the child during the school hours. This form can go to school. If the caregiver is the teacher, then send a copy home to the parent once the procedure is explained to the parent.

Example

	Sunday	**Monday**
5am	Asleep	Asleep
6am	Asleep	Asleep
7am	Asleep	I,I,I,I,I,I,I,I,I,I,I,I,I
8am	Asleep	school
9am	I,I,I,I,	school
10am	I,I,I,I,I,I,I,I,I	school
11am	I,I,I,I,I,I,I	school
12pm	I,I,I,I,I,I	school
1pm	I,I,I,I,I,I,I,I	school
2pm	I,I,I,I,I,I	school
3pm	I,I,I,I,I,I,I,I	school
4pm	I,I,I,I,I,I	I,I,I,I,I,I,I,I
5pm	I,I,I,I,I,I	I,I,I,I,I,I
6pm	I,I,I,I,I,I,I,I,I,I	I,I,I,I,I,I
7pm	I,I,I,I,I,I,I,I,I	I,I,I,I,I,I,I,I,I,I
8pm	Asleep	I,I,I,I,I,I,I
9pm	Asleep	Asleep

Social Support Worksheet

Child's Name: ______________________________ Week of: ______________________

Person(s) Giving Positive Feedback: ____

	Sunday	Monday	Tuesday	Wednesday	Thursday	Friday	Saturday
5am							
6am							
7am							
8am							
9am							
10am							
11am							
12pm							
1pm							
2pm							
3pm							
4pm							
5pm							
6pm							
7pm							
8pm							
9pm							
10pm							
11pm							
12am							

TIER

Habit Reversal: Procedural Integrity Checklist

Age/Grade:	Preschool – High School
Setting:	School, Home, Clinic, In-patient
Individual or Group:	Individual
Tier:	2 & 3
Desired/ Appropriate Behavior:	Reduction in repetitive (habit) behaviors, thumb sucking, hair twirling, hair pulling, stuttering, tics, etc.
Skill Level:	Acquisition to Generalization

Habit Reversal has been shown to reduce habit disorders with children (e.g., Shumaker, 2009; Woods & Luiselli, 2007; Woods & Miltenberger, 1996). The original work and procedures are provided below. Habit Reversal is a package intervention, meaning that it has several components. Several studies have used variations of the procedures. In the adaptation/modification section, these variations are discussed further.

Procedure for Integrity Checklist Observer

1) A designated adult who is familiar with the procedures (e.g., principal, assistant principal, school psychologist, treatment specialist, behavior specialist, counselor, lead teacher) completes the Procedural Integrity Checklist (see page 371) information about the adult, group (class, period, etc.), location, date, time, and observer's name.
2) A designated adult who is familiar with the procedures (e.g., principal, assistant principal, school psychologist, treatment specialist, behavior specialist, counselor, lead teacher) observes the person implementing the Habit Reversal intervention. An initial observation should occur during first and possibly the second session and then follow up monthly.
3) The observer watches the interventionist for the presence of behaviors on the Checklist and marks Yes if present or No if not present. If there was not an opportunity to observe some of the behaviors, then mark N/O for not observed. For example, if the interventionist is only implementing the first phase of the intervention, the sections for the following phases will be considered "not observed." In addition, if the interventionist is only choosing one type of strategy such as "Response Description" but not "Early Warning," then the observer would put N/A for not applicable
4) At the completion of the observation, count the number of behaviors marked Yes and write the number on the line for "Number of behaviors marked Yes."
5) Write the total number of behaviors observed (i.e., the total behaviors marked Yes or No) and the percent marked Yes.
6) Write any constructive feedback comments in addition to any notations made beside any individual behavior in the "Feedback" section.
7) At an appropriate time following each observation, the observer provides the interventionist with oral feedback regarding their implementation of the intervention, starting with positive behaviors observed, and a copy of the Habit Reversal Procedural Integrity Checklist. The feedback should be provided the same day of the observation.

8) After the initial observation, the observer should observe the interventionist implementing the Habit Reversal intervention 2-8 times depending on the length of the implementation (i.e., approximately twice a month).

The Checklist provided below has all the phases of the intervention in one document. However, if the interventionist does not complete all phases in one session, either note the dates the techniques were taught or copy the checklist and complete the portion of the checklist you, the observer, completed in one session and then repeat this for the next session.

Habit Reversal: Procedural Integrity Checklist

Interventionist: ______________________ Date: __________ Time: __________

Child: ______________________ Observer: ______________________

Location: ______________________ Signature: ______________________

N/O = Not Observed or N/A Not applicable

Behaviors to Observe	Yes	No	N/O Or N/A	Comments
Awareness Phase				
1) Response Description. a) The child describes and identifies the dominant vocal and motor tic/behaviors.				
b) The child demonstrates the dominant vocal and motor tic/behaviors.				
2) Response Detection. a) The child acknowledges either with a verbal response or physical gesture each occurrence of the habit behavior in the session.				
b) The interventionist states to the child when the child does not acknowledge that the habit behavior occurred.				
3)Early Warning. a) The child was taught to be aware of the earliest signs (antecedents) of the behavior.				
4) Situation Awareness Training. a) The child describes all of the situations in which the behavior occurs.				
b) The child describes how the behavior is acted out in these situations.				

Awareness Phase Integrity = _____/7 x 100 = _____% or number of accurately completed items/total number of items ______/_______ x 100 = ______% The interventionist may have not needed to conduct each phase of the awareness training. There are 7 total sub steps that the interventionist can implement in items 1-3.

Competing Response Phase				
5) A competing response has been taught to the child by considering the five areas: a) opposite to the movement or habit, b) capable of being maintained for several minutes, c) produces heightened awareness by an isometric tensing of the muscles involved in the movement, d) socially inconspicuous, and e) strengthens the muscles antagonistic to the tic or habit.				
6) Have the child perform the competing behavior which is to isometrically tense the antagonistic muscle for up to 3 minutes up to 3 minutes contingent upon awareness of the urge to engage in or the actual occurrence of the target behavior.				
7) The interventionist taught a family member or caregiver and/or the child how to use the Competing Response Practice sheet				
Competing Response Phase Integrity = _____/7 x 100 = _____%. There are 7 total sub steps that the interventionist implements in items 1-3.				
Motivation Phase				
8) Social Situations The child discussed situations in which the target behavior (i.e., habit) is embarrassing, physically injuring, and/or seemingly awkward.				
9) Social Support a) The family or friends are taught to provide verbal and physical praise to the child for not engaging in the target behavior b) The family is taught how to use the Social Support Worksheet c) Teach and remind the child to practice the competing response technique if the caregiver, interventionist, other adult notice an occurrence of the target behavior that goes unnoticed by the child.				

10) Public Display The interventionist and caregiver develop a plan in which the child can demonstrate the competing response to show control of the habit in front of a group of family members or friends.				
Motivational Phase Integrity = _____/5 x 100 = _____%. There are 5 total sub steps that the interventionist implements in items 1-3.				
Generalization Phase				
11) The technique is **Symbolic Rehearsal**.				
a) The interventionist asks the child to imagine one of the situations discussed during Situation Awareness Training.				
b) The child states the situation and instead of engaging in the habit the child states the competing behavior.				
c) The interventionist and child role plays the situation with the child appropriately engages in the competing behavior.				
d) The child is praised for each step that was completed correctly.				
Generalization Phase Integrity = _____/4 x 100 = _____%				

Awareness & Competing Response Phases	Motivational Phase	Generalization Phase
1 out of 7 = 14%	1 out of 5 = 20%	1 out of 4 = 25%
2 out of 7 = 29%	2 out of 5 = 40%	2 out of 4 = 50%
3 out of 7 = 43%	3 out of 5 = 60%	3 out of 4 = 75%
4 out of 7 = 57%	4 out of 5 = 80%	4 out of 4 = 100%
5 out of 7 = 71%	5 out of 5 = 100%	
6 out of 7 = 86%		
7 out of 7 = 100%		

All Phases of Habit Reversal	
1 out of 23 = 4%	13 out of 23 = 57%
2 out of 23 = 9%	14 out of 23 = 61%
3 out of 23 = 13%	15 out of 23 = 65%
4 out of 23 = 17%	16 out of 23 = 70%
5 out of 23 = 22%	17 out of 23 = 74%
6 out of 23 = 26%	18 out of 23 = 78%
7 out of 23 = 30%	19 out of 23 = 83%
8 out of 23 = 35%	20 out of 23 = 87%
9 out of 23 = 39%	21 out of 23 = 91%
10 out of 23 = 44%	22 out of 23 = 96%
11 out of 23 = 48%	23 out of 23 = 100%
12 out of 23 = 52%	

All Phases: Number of behaviors marked Yes = _____ out of _____ = ______ %

Feedback:

Conducting Direct Observations

Conducting Direct Observations

Direct behavior observations are conducted by an observer (e.g., behavior specialist, school psychologist, guidance counselor, social worker, teacher, etc.) for the purpose of systematic recording of behavior (Haynes & O'Brien, 2000). The observer is typically not the primary person interacting with the children. Specifically, the observer should be someone who can sit and observe the children in their environment while not interacting with any adult or child who is present and not having any primary responsibility to instruct or care for the children. Collecting data using behavioral observations is beneficial to determine specific components of the environment (e.g., triggers, cues, signals, antecedents that set the occasion for the behavior and/or consequences that maintain the behaviors) that may be contributing to the behaviors as well as to determine current rates at which behaviors occur in order to measure effectiveness of interventions.

When data are collected prior to the implementation of an intervention, they are referred to as baseline data. The same behavioral observations are conducted throughout an intervention and compared to baseline data in order to determine if rates of behavior are increasing or decreasing as desired. For example, if an observer used a rating scale to judge a child's behavior during baseline and then the observer used a different method in intervention, the person trying to make a determination of successfulness would be comparing two different measurements. Collecting data through direct observation allows one to determine effectiveness of interventions and determine if changes in interventions are needed as soon as the data indicate. Direct behavior observation data also reduce bias and opinion-based decisions on the effectiveness of the intervention.

Direct observations are used widely by school psychologists and other professionals as an assessment procedure. Both natural and systematic direct observations are used to observe and assess student behavior (Hintze, Volpe, & Shapiro, 2002). Natural, or nonsystematic, observations refer to a situation when an observer enters a specific situation and observes what is going on without any predetermined behavior in mind. Natural observation is helpful when an observer does not have specific behaviors in mind or does not know the specific behaviors of concern. It also allows the observer to observe a variety of interactions, situations, and specific variables in the environment in order to gain precision in targeting behaviors for a systematic observation. For example, if referral concerns are vague and indicate that the child exhibits disruptive behaviors without specific behaviors reported, the observer should begin with a natural or nonsystematic observation in order to determine operational definitions of the reported disruptive behaviors. However, systematic direct observations have a specific behavioral goal based upon behaviors that have been operationally defined prior to the observation and are conducted at a specified time and summarized in a standardized manner (Hintze, et al., 2002). For example, if the child has been engaged in behavioral interventions with little success and target behaviors are defined as talking without permission and out of seat, the observer should begin with a systematic observation of the defined target behaviors. Systematic direct observation is conducted when specific, defined behaviors are already determined and the purpose of the observation is to determine specific rates of the occurrence of the behavior. This type of observation is typically used when completing a Functional Behavioral Assessment.

Several different types of observational methods can be used for both natural/nonsystematic as well as for systematic observations. Watson and Steege (2003) indicate that the appropriate observation type to be used in a given situation should be driven by several different considerations. The first consideration is the dimension of the behavior, which includes topography, frequency, and duration. The topography is the observable behavior or the "what" that is occurring. For example, if a referral indicates disruptive behavior, the topography of that behavior is the specific actions from the child that are disruptive (e.g., talking, walking around the room, etc.). The frequency and duration are the number of times a behavior occurs during a set time frame and the length of time a behavior occurs, respectively. The second consideration is the goal of the intervention. If the goal of the intervention is to reduce the frequency of talking behavior during whole group instruction, then an appropriate observation to choose would be a frequency observation. The third consideration includes the basic pragmatic considerations such as time, resources, and experience of the observer.

Various types of observation procedures are used both prior to the implementation of an intervention and during the implementation of an intervention in order to determine the effectiveness. In the following sections, a description of the different types of observation is given. Once all the observations are described, then examples of each type of observation are presented.

Nonsystematic Observations

Nonsystematic observations are those that do not include specific information (such as operational definitions, setting, antecedents, and consequences) about target behaviors.

1) One type of nonsystematic observation is a Narrative Recording Observation. This type of observation requires the observer to record events and behaviors like a script by simply writing down, descriptively, what is observed. This type of observation is useful for identifying potential behaviors for systematic observations and can provide clues to possible intervention components.

2) Another type of nonsystematic observation is a Sequence or Contingency Analysis, also called an ABC (Antecedent-Behavior-Consequence) observation. This type of observation breaks down the narrative recording into descriptions of antecedents, the behaviors that follow, and the consequences that result. This observation can help to form a hypothesis about functional relationships and behavioral chains. An ABC observation is helpful in identifying potential behaviors for systematic observations and can also provide clues to possible interventions.

Systematic Observations

Systematic observations are those that have specific goals and target behaviors. Prior to conducting a systematic observation, the observer should have specific operational definitions of the target behaviors to be observed. An operational definition is one that is objective, clear, measurable, and observable. It refers only to the characteristics of the behavior and the environment (Batsche, Castillo, Dixon, & Forde, 2008; Hintze, et al., 2000). This definition should pass the Stranger test, which indicates that it should be detailed enough that if a stranger observed the behavior, he or she would be able to accurately identify and record the occurrence of the behavior based upon the operational definition. An example of an operational definition for vocalizing is "any academically irrelevant vocalization or verbal noise made by the child. Vocalizing includes such things as humming, making unusual vocal noises, speaking, whispering, or making noises with one's teeth. A non-example of a definition of vocalizing is 'talking out.'"

1) Frequency (also called Event Recording) Observation is an observation that counts the frequency of the occurrence of the target behavior during certain observation periods (e.g., seconds, minutes, etc.). This type of observation is best for behaviors that have a clear beginning or end. An example behavior is throwing paper across the room or raising hand to get permission to speak. This

behavior is quick and has a specific beginning and ending time, allowing for a tally mark to be used to indicate the occurrence of the behavior. Examples of behaviors that would not be appropriate for frequency recording are pencil tapping or talking. These behaviors can occur continuously and present a difficulty when the observer must determine a clear beginning and ending in order to determine frequency of occurrence (Haynes & O'Brien, 2000; Hintze, et al. 2002; Watson & Steege, 2003). Another consideration for frequency recording is the length of time it takes for the behavior to start and end. Specifically, each occurrence should take approximately the same amount of time (e.g., throwing paper). An example of a behavior that is not appropriate for frequency recording is noncompliance. Occurrences of noncompliance can be a simple refusal to pick up a pencil or a tantrum that lasts 10 - 20 minutes. With frequency recording, these two occurrences would be given the same amount of "weight" or importance and recorded as one occurrence of noncompliance each; however, the tantrum is clearly different than refusing to pick up a pencil (Hintze, et al., 2002; Watson & Steege, 2003).

2) Duration Recording is a type of systematic observation that involves recording the total amount of time a behavior occurs (Watson & Steege, 2003). This type of observation is best for those that are continuous in nature (e.g., on-task behavior, tantrums, etc.). One type of duration observation is a scatterplot that is a visual representation of the duration of the behavior through the shading in of the times that the behavior occurs. The results are typically reported in one of two ways. First, results can be reported as an average duration of each occurrence. For example, if a student engages in tantrums 4 times in one day with the following durations, 10 minutes, 15 minutes, 8 minutes, and 22 minutes, the total minutes of tantrumming is 55 minutes (i.e., 10+15+8+22 = 55 total minutes tantrumming). The average is then calculated by dividing 55 minutes/4 tantrums, approximately 14 minutes. The average time of all of the tantrums is reported. Second, results can be reported as a total time that the behavior occurred (e.g., the student engaged in tantrums for 55 minutes during the entire school day).

3) Latency Recording is a type of systematic observation that requires the observer to measure the elapsed time between the occurrence of a stimulus and the initiation of a specific behavior. For example, one of the most commonly used behaviors for latency recording is noncompliance, or specifically, the amount of time between a directive being given and the compliance of the individual receiving the directive. This type of observation should be used when the presenting concern is the amount of time that occurs between an opportunity to engage in a behavior and the actual engagement in a behavior (Hintze, et al., 2002).

4) Interval Recording is a systematic observation that is used for continuous behaviors, or more specifically, behaviors for which a beginning and end is difficult to judge. These behaviors may often occur at a higher rate, and the observer needs to know about the occurrence and non-occurrence of the behavior during a specific period of time. For example, off-task during whole group instruction is a behavior that is often used for interval recording. The observation period is broken down into intervals of time—generally smaller intervals are more accurate—during which the behaviors are coded to have occurred or not occurred during each interval. For example, a 30-minute block of instructional time can be broken down into 10-second intervals. Some device (stopwatch or signal device such as a beep tape, mp3 audio recording, MotivAider®, etc.) can be used to indicate the beginning of each interval as the observer watches the behaviors.

a) Partial Interval Recording is a type of interval observation in which the observer records the occurrence of the target behavior any time during the observation. For example, during a 10-second partial interval observation, if the student is briefly off-task one time during the 10-second interval, three times during the interval, or off-task the entire interval, the interval is coded that the student was off-task during that interval. If the student was off-task and talking to a peer during the last 5 seconds of one interval and the first 5 seconds the next interval, both intervals are recorded as off-task.

b) Whole Interval Recording is a type of interval observation in which the occurrence of the target behavior is coded if it occurs throughout the entire interval. Using the previous example with off-task behavior, the off-task behaviors must have occurred during the entire 10-second interval for the interval to be coded as off-task.

c) Momentary Time Sampling is an interval recording observation that is often referred to as "spot checking." During this observation, the observer looks at a student only at predetermined points in time and records if the behavior occurs during that specific time. For example, during a 30-second momentary time sampling observation, the observer looks up at the end of the 30-second interval and records the occurrence or nonoccurrence of the target behavior.

When conducting observations, the first thing to do is to collect baseline data. Baseline data observations are those that are conducted prior to implementing any specific behavior intervention. The purpose is to have specific data to indicate the current performance of the child. These data are used to make comparisons to the data that are collected following the implementation of the intervention. These comparisons will allow the interventionist to determine if the intervention has resulted in improvements in the child's behavior (i.e., the unwanted target behavior has decreased or the appropriate target behaviors have increased).

Continued observations throughout the implementation of the intervention are called progress monitoring. Progress monitoring should be on-going as any intervention is implemented to determine effectiveness. The same observations that were conducted during baseline data collection should be conducted during progress monitoring so that the data are comparable. The interventionist, as well as others involved in the intervention (e.g., school psychologist, counselor, social worker, teachers, etc.), should be involved in periodic reviews to make decisions about the effectiveness of the intervention.

References

Batsche, G. M., Castillo, J. M., Dixon, D. N., & Forde, S. (2008). Best practices in designing, implementing, and evaluating quality interventions. In A. Thomas & J. Grimes (Eds.), *Best practices in school psychology V* (pp. 177-193). Bethesda, MD: National Association of School Psychologists.

Haynes, S. N. & O'Brien, W. H. (2000). *Principles and practice of behavioral assessment.* New York, NY: Plenim Publishers.

Hintze, J. M., Volpe, R. J., & Shapiro, E. S. (2002). Best practices in the systematic direct observation of student behavior. In A. Thomas & J. Grimes (Eds.), *Best practices in school psychology IV*. Washington, DC: National Association of School Psychologists.

Watson, T. S. & Steege, M. W. (2003). *Conducting school-based functional behavioral assessments: A practitioner's guide.* New York, NY: The Guilford Press.

Example Observations

Each type of observation described above has a sample observation below in order to provide an example of how the observation form could be completed. In the sample observations, the example information is either provided in italics for those observations that require written information, or it is provided in red for the observations that require slash marks. Additionally, the calculations are complete at the end of each observation to provide an example of the summary of the data.

The observations that are coded for time have an interval indicator for the minutes and seconds of the observation (e.g., 1.1, 1.2). For example, 1.1 indicates the 1 minute 10 second mark of the interval, and an interval of 0.15 indicates the 15 second mark of the interval. Each of these interval marks indicates the end of the interval.

Specifically, if using a stopwatch for the momentary time sampling observation, the observer starts the stopwatch and looks up at 15 seconds. The slash is placed in the box if the behavior occurred. If using a stopwatch for a partial interval observation, the behavior is observed for the duration of the interval, and at the end of the interval (indicated by 1.1), the observer puts a slash in the box in which the behavior occurred or leaves the box blank if the behavior did not occur and then moves to the next interval.

If using a MotivAider®, the time can simply be set at the interval being used (e.g., 15 seconds or 10 seconds), and the behavior can be recorded when the timer reaches zero and vibrates. It is important to note that if using a MotivAider® for observations, the observer will need to indicate somewhere that the interval is over. The purpose of this indication is important because a MotivAider® does not denote what specific interval is being observed; therefore, a mark indicating the end of the interval (e.g., interval 1.1 is over) should be used in order to keep the observer's place (e.g., a slash can be placed in the heading of each interval to indicate it is complete).

Example Narrative Observation

Student Name: *First Last*

Teacher: *T. Name*

Observer Name: *First Last*

Date/Time: *10/5/13, 10:30 – 11:00*

Activity: *whole group math instruction followed by independent seat work*

- *Children entered the classroom from recess.*
- *Target student entered last and was dragging behind the other children.*
- *Teacher had a few math problems on the board for children to work on during the transition back from recess.*
- *As the children worked, the teacher instructed them to get their books and open to page 35.*
- *Target student walked slowly to his desk after circling the room a few times prior to sitting down.*
- *Other children were done with 2 board problems before target student sat down. While he was circling the room, the teacher instructed him to sit at his desk and begin working. He looked at the teacher and continued to circle the room. The teacher continued talking to other children and ignored the target student.*
- *The student eventually sat in his seat (approximately 3.5 minutes after walking in the room). Once seated, he was reminded that he was to get his math book and open to page 35. He immediately picked up his book; however, he turned the pages slowly by turning only 1 at a time until he got to page 35. This was ignored by the teacher.*
- *While the teacher is instructing and the children are expected to keep their eyes on her and follow along in their books as well as verbally answer questions, target student puts his head on his desk. When instructed to pick up his head, he takes a while to pick up his head and then puts his head back down.*
- *Once the children are given individual worksheets to complete, he begins to work on his sheet and finishes quickly at which time he puts his head back on his desk.*

Summary

Based on this observation, it is determined that noncompliance and off-task will be the target behaviors. Those behaviors will be observed using specific direct observations to determine specific rates of off-task behavior as well as percentage of compliance to commands and the latency of compliance to commands that are given by the teacher.

Narrative Observation

Student Name: Teacher:

Observer Name: Date/Time:

Activity:

Summary

Example ABC Observation

Date/Time	Setting	Antecedent	Behavior	Consequence
When did the behavior occur?	**Where did the behavior occur?**	**What happened immediately prior (i.e., triggered) to the behavior?**	**Describe the problem behavior**	**What happened after the behavior occurred?**
10/10/2013 *8:45*	*Circle time (whole group on the carpet)*	*Teacher told student to sit down on his animal.*	*Student walked to the back of the room beside his bookbag and took a toy out of his bookbag.*	*Teacher assistant followed the student and took the toy from him then escorted with physical prompt on the elbow to his spot on the carpet.*

ABC Observation

Date/Time	Setting	Antecedent	Behavior	Consequence
When did the behavior occur?	**Where did the behavior occur?**	**What happened immediately prior (i.e., triggered) to the behavior?**	**Describe the problem behavior**	**What happened after the behavior occurred?**

TIER

Example Frequency / Event Recording

Student Name: *First Last* Teacher: *T. Name* Date: MM/DD/YYYY

Observer: *First Last* Start Time: *8:15* Stop Time: *8:45*

Behavior Observed: *Talking out without permission (any verbal comment that the child does not have teacher permission to engage in) In the case that the child is talking when all children have been given permission to talk, this is not considered talking without permission.*

Day	Frequency Count
Monday	~~1~~ ~~2~~ ~~3~~ ~~4~~ ~~5~~ ~~6~~ ~~7~~ ~~8~~ 9 10 11 12 13 14 15 16 17 18 19 20 21 22 23 24 25 26 27 28 29 30 31 32 33 34 35 36 37 38 39 40 41 42 43 44 45 46 47 48 49 50
Tuesday	1 2 3 4 5 6 7 8 9 10 11 12 13 14 15 16 17 18 19 20 21 22 23 24 25 26 27 28 29 30 31 32 33 34 35 36 37 38 39 40 41 42 43 44 45 46 47 48 49 50
Wednesday	1 2 3 4 5 6 7 8 9 10 11 12 13 14 15 16 17 18 19 20 21 22 23 24 25 26 27 28 29 30 31 32 33 34 35 36 37 38 39 40 41 42 43 44 45 46 47 48 49 50
Thursday	1 2 3 4 5 6 7 8 9 10 11 12 13 14 15 16 17 18 19 20 21 22 23 24 25 26 27 28 29 30 31 32 33 34 35 36 37 38 39 40 41 42 43 44 45 46 47 48 49 50
Friday	1 2 3 4 5 6 7 8 9 10 11 12 13 14 15 16 17 18 19 20 21 22 23 24 25 26 27 28 29 30 31 32 33 34 35 36 37 38 39 40 41 42 43 44 45 46 47 48 49 50

Frequency / Event Recording

Child Name: ____________________ Teacher: ____________________ Date: ____________________

Observer: ____________________ Start Time: ____________ Stop Time: ____________________

Behavior Observed: ____

____

Day	Frequency Count
Monday	1 2 3 4 5 6 7 8 9 10 11 12 13 14 15 16 17 18 19 20 21 22 23 24 25 26 27 28 29 30 31 32 33 34 35 36 37 38 39 40 41 42 43 44 45 46 47 48 49 50
Tuesday	1 2 3 4 5 6 7 8 9 10 11 12 13 14 15 16 17 18 19 20 21 22 23 24 25 26 27 28 29 30 31 32 33 34 35 36 37 38 39 40 41 42 43 44 45 46 47 48 49 50
Wednesday	1 2 3 4 5 6 7 8 9 10 11 12 13 14 15 16 17 18 19 20 21 22 23 24 25 26 27 28 29 30 31 32 33 34 35 36 37 38 39 40 41 42 43 44 45 46 47 48 49 50
Thursday	1 2 3 4 5 6 7 8 9 10 11 12 13 14 15 16 17 18 19 20 21 22 23 24 25 26 27 28 29 30 31 32 33 34 35 36 37 38 39 40 41 42 43 44 45 46 47 48 49 50
Friday	1 2 3 4 5 6 7 8 9 10 11 12 13 14 15 16 17 18 19 20 21 22 23 24 25 26 27 28 29 30 31 32 33 34 35 36 37 38 39 40 41 42 43 44 45 46 47 48 49 50

Example Duration Recording Observation

Student Name: *First Last* Teacher: *T. Name* Observer: *First Last*

Target Behavior Observed: *Tantrum (crying, whining, or screaming that may or may not include any form of physical aggression such as pushing, hitting or knocking things off of tables, desks, or walls)*

Date of Observation	Start and Stop Times of Observation	Time when Target behavior started	Time when Target behavior stopped	Length of time that the behavior lasted
10/15/2013	*9:30 – 10:30*	*9:55*	*10:15*	*20 minutes*

Duration Recording Observation

Student Name: ____________________ Teacher: ________________________ Observer: _______________________

Target Behavior Observed: ____

____

Date of Observation	Start and Stop Times of Observation	Time when Target behavior started	Time when Target behavior stopped	Length of time that the behavior lasted

Example Duration Observation (Scatterplot)

Date: *10/14/13*

<table>
<tr><th></th><th>1</th><th>2</th></tr>
<tr><td>8:00-8:30</td><td></td><td></td></tr>
<tr><td>8:30-9:00</td><td style="background:gray"></td><td></td></tr>
<tr><td>9:00-9:30</td><td style="background:gray"></td><td></td></tr>
<tr><td>9:30-10:00</td><td></td><td></td></tr>
<tr><td>10:00-10:30</td><td></td><td style="background:gray"></td></tr>
<tr><td>10:30-11:00</td><td></td><td></td></tr>
<tr><td>11:00-11:30</td><td></td><td></td></tr>
<tr><td>11:30-12:00</td><td></td><td></td></tr>
<tr><td>12:00-12:30</td><td></td><td></td></tr>
<tr><td>12:30-1:00</td><td></td><td></td></tr>
<tr><td>1:00-1:30</td><td></td><td></td></tr>
<tr><td>1:30-2:00</td><td></td><td></td></tr>
<tr><td>2:00-2:30</td><td style="background:gray"></td><td></td></tr>
<tr><td>2:30-3:00</td><td></td><td></td></tr>
<tr><td>3:00-3:30</td><td></td><td></td></tr>
</table>

Behavior 1: Sleeping in class

Date: *10/15/13*

<table>
<tr><th></th><th>1</th><th>2</th></tr>
<tr><td>8:00-8:30</td><td></td><td></td></tr>
<tr><td>8:30-9:00</td><td></td><td></td></tr>
<tr><td>9:00-9:30</td><td></td><td style="background:gray"></td></tr>
<tr><td>9:30-10:00</td><td></td><td style="background:gray"></td></tr>
<tr><td>10:00-10:30</td><td></td><td></td></tr>
<tr><td>10:30-11:00</td><td></td><td></td></tr>
<tr><td>11:00-11:30</td><td></td><td style="background:gray"></td></tr>
<tr><td>11:30-12:00</td><td></td><td></td></tr>
<tr><td>12:00-12:30</td><td></td><td></td></tr>
<tr><td>12:30-1:00</td><td></td><td></td></tr>
<tr><td>1:00-1:30</td><td></td><td></td></tr>
<tr><td>1:30-2:00</td><td></td><td></td></tr>
<tr><td>2:00-2:30</td><td></td><td></td></tr>
<tr><td>2:30-3:00</td><td style="background:gray"></td><td></td></tr>
<tr><td>3:00-3:30</td><td></td><td></td></tr>
</table>

Behavior 2: Tantrums

Summary Chart

Date	**Behavior 1**		**Behavior 2**	
	# occurrences	Average Duration	# occurrences	Average Duration
10/14/13	*2*	*45 minutes*	*1*	*30 minutes*
10/15/13	*1*	*30 minutes*	*2*	*45 minutes*

Duration Observation (Scatterplot)

Date: ___________________ Date: ___________________

	1	2
8:00-8:30		
8:30-9:00		
9:00-9:30		
9:30-10:00		
10:00-10:30		
10:30-11:00		
11:00-11:30		
11:30-12:00		
12:00-12:30		
12:30-1:00		
1:00-1:30		
1:30-2:00		
2:00-2:30		
2:30-3:00		
3:00-3:30		

Behavior 1:

	1	2
8:00-8:30		
8:30-9:00		
9:00-9:30		
9:30-10:00		
10:00-10:30		
10:30-11:00		
11:00-11:30		
11:30-12:00		
12:00-12:30		
12:30-1:00		
1:00-1:30		
1:30-2:00		
2:00-2:30		
2:30-3:00		
3:00-3:30		

Behavior 2:

Summary Chart

Date	**Behavior 1**		**Behavior 2**	
	# occurrences	Average Duration	# occurrences	Average Duration

Example Latency Recording Observation

Student Name: *First Last* Date: *10/18/2013*

Observer: *First Last* Teacher: *T. Name*

Target Behavior Observed: *Initiation Compliance (amount of time from the time the adult gives the child a direction to the time the child begins to comply with the direction)*

Date of Observation	Start and Stop Times of Observation	Prompt given and time of prompt	Time when behavior was initiated	Latency between prompt and behavior
10/18/2013	*8:45 – 9:30*	*9:02 - Teacher told student to put paper in her folder*	*9:07*	*5 minutes*

Latency Recording Observation

Student Name: ______________________ Date: ________________________________

Observer: _________________________ Teacher: _____________________________

Target Behavior Observed:____

____

Date of Observation	Start and Stop Times of Observation	Prompt given and time of prompt	Time when behavior was initiated	Latency between prompt and behavior

Example Compliance Training Observation (Systematic Observation)

Student Name: Sample Student Start Time: ________ End Time: ________ Date: ______________

Adult Behavior						Child Behavior		Adult Beh
Instruction	**(2)** **Proximity (P)**	**(3)** **Eye Contact (EC)**	**(4)** **Descriptive (Desc)**	**(5)** **Directive (D)**	**(6)** **5 sec wait**	**(7)** *IC*	**(8)** *CC*	**(9)** **CP**
1 sit down	/	/	/		/	/		/
2 put paper in box			/	/	/	/	/	/
3 put hands in lap	/		/	/	/		/	/
4								
5								
6								
7								
8								
9								
10								
	# of P/ # of opportunities (opps)	**# of EC/ # of opps**	**# of Des/ # of opps**	**# of D/ # of opps**	**# of 5 sec/ # of opps**	**# of IC/ # of opps**	**# of CC/ # of opps**	**# of CP/ # of opps**
Total	2/3	1/3	3/3	2/3	3/3	2/3	2/3	3/3
%	67%	33%	100%	67%	100%	67%	67%	100%

Tally Time In	IIIIII	**Duration of Observation (time)**	15:00	**# of tally marks/ time**	6/15	**Rate per minute:** .4 per minute

Tally Negative Attention	IIIIIIIIIIIIIIIIII	**Duration of Observation (time)**	15:00	**# of tally marks/ time**	18/15	**Rate per minute:** 1.2 per minute

Compliance Training Observation

Student Name: ________________ Start Time: ________ End Time: ________ Date: ____________

	Adult Behavior					Child Behavior		Adult Beh
Instruction	(2) Proximity (P)	(3) Eye Contact (EC)	(4) Descriptive (Desc)	(5) Directive (D)	(6) 5 sec wait	(7) *IC*	(8) *CC*	(9) CP
1								
2								
3								
4								
5								
6								
7								
8								
9								
10								
	# of P/ # of opportunities (opps)	# of EC/ # of opps	# of Des/ # of opps	# of D/ # of opps	# of 5 sec/ # of opps	# of IC/ # of opps	# of CC/ # of opps	# of CP/ # of opps
Total								
%								

Tally Time In		Duration of Observation (time)		# of tally marks/ time		Rate per minute:
Tally Negative Attention		Duration of Observation (time)		# of tally marks/ time		Rate per minute:

TIER

Example Partial Interval Observation (10-second)

	1.1	1.2	1.3	1.4	1.5	1.6	2.1	2.2	2.3	2.4	2.5	2.6	3.1	3.2	3.3	3.4	3.5	3.6
Off-Task			/			/	/	/	/	/								
Vocalizing						/	/							/				

	4.1	4.2	4.3	4.4	4.5	4.6	5.1	5.2	5.3	5.4	5.5	5.6	6.1	6.2	6.3	6.4	6.5	6.6
Off-Task											/	/						
Vocalizing						/												

	7.1	7.2	7.3	7.4	7.5	7.6	8.1	8.2	8.3	8.4	8.5	8.6	9.1	9.2	9.3	9.4	9.5	9.6
Off-Task																		
Vocalizing		/									/							

	10.1	10.2	10.3	10.4	10.5	10.6	11.1	11.2	11.3	11.4	11.5	11.6	12.1	12.2	12.3	12.4	12.5	12.6
Off-Task																		
Vocalizing						/												

	13.1	13.2	13.3	13.4	13.5	13.6	14.1	14.2	14.3	14.4	14.5	14.6	15.1	15.2	15.3	15.4	15.5	15.6
Off-Task	/	/	/	/				/										
Vocalizing																		

	16.1	16.2	16.3	16.4	16.5	16.6	17.1	17.2	17.3	17.4	17.5	17.6	18.1	18.2	18.3	18.4	18.5	18.6
Off-Task			/	/	/											/		
Vocalizing																		

	19.1	19.2	19.3	19.4	19.5	19.6	20.1	20.2	20.3	20.4	20.5	20.6
Off-Task			/			/						
Vocalizing							/					

Target Behavior One:

19 /120 total intervals = 16 %

Target Behavior Two:

8 /120 total intervals= 7 %

Name: ____________________

Date: ____________________

Time: ____________________

DIRECTIONS:

1) Define one or two target behaviors to be observed and place them in the first column of the observation form.
2) Use a stopwatch or a beep tape and observe for 10-second intervals.
3) If the behavior(s) occur(s) any time during that 10 second interval place a slash (/) in that interval.
4) Calculate total percentages of the occurrence of each behavior.

Partial Interval Observation (10-second)

	1.1	1.2	1.3	1.4	1.5	1.6	2.1	2.2	2.3	2.4	2.5	2.6	3.1	3.2	3.3	3.4	3.5	3.6
Off-Task																		
Vocalizing																		

	4.1	4.2	4.3	4.4	4.5	4.6	5.1	5.2	5.3	5.4	5.5	5.6	6.1	6.2	6.3	6.4	6.5	6.6
Off-Task																		
Vocalizing																		

	7.1	7.2	7.3	7.4	7.5	7.6	8.1	8.2	8.3	8.4	8.5	8.6	9.1	9.2	9.3	9.4	9.5	9.6
Off-Task																		
Vocalizing																		

	10.1	10.2	10.3	10.4	10.5	10.6	11.1	11.2	11.3	11.4	11.5	11.6	12.1	12.2	12.3	12.4	12.5	12.6
Off-Task																		
Vocalizing																		

	13.1	13.2	13.3	13.4	13.5	13.6	14.1	14.2	14.3	14.4	14.5	14.6	15.1	15.2	15.3	15.4	15.5	15.6
Off-Task																		
Vocalizing																		

	16.1	16.2	16.3	16.4	16.5	16.6	17.1	17.2	17.3	17.4	17.5	17.6	18.1	18.2	18.3	18.4	18.5	18.6
Off-Task																		
Vocalizing																		

	19.1	19.2	19.3	19.4	19.5	19.6	20.1	20.2	20.3	20.4	20.5	20.6
Off-Task												
Vocalizing												

Target Behavior One:

____/120 = _______%

Target Behavior Two:

Name: ____

Date: ____

Time: ____

DIRECTIONS:

1) Define one or two target behaviors to be observed and place them in the first column of the observation form.
2) Use a stopwatch or a beep tape and observe for 10-second intervals.
3) If the behavior(s) occur(s) any time during that 10 second interval place a slash (/) in that interval.
4) Calculate total percentages of the occurrence of each behavior.

Example Whole Interval Observation (10-second)

	1.1	1.2	1.3	1.4	1.5	1.6	2.1	2.2	2.3	2.4	2.5	2.6	3.1	3.2	3.3	3.4	3.5	3.6
Off-Task			/			/				/			/		/	/		
Out of seat	/													/				

	4.1	4.2	4.3	4.4	4.5	4.6	5.1	5.2	5.3	5.4	5.5	5.6	6.1	6.2	6.3	6.4	6.5	6.6
Off-Task											/	/						
Out of seat						/												

	7.1	7.2	7.3	7.4	7.5	7.6	8.1	8.2	8.3	8.4	8.5	8.6	9.1	9.2	9.3	9.4	9.5	9.6
Off-Task																		
Out of seat		/									/							/

	10.1	10.2	10.3	10.4	10.5	10.6	11.1	11.2	11.3	11.4	11.5	11.6	12.1	12.2	12.3	12.4	12.5	12.6
Off-Task			/					/										
Out of seat						/												

	13.1	13.2	13.3	13.4	13.5	13.6	14.1	14.2	14.3	14.4	14.5	14.6	15.1	15.2	15.3	15.4	15.5	15.6
Off-Task	/							/					/	/				/
Out of seat																		

	16.1	16.2	16.3	16.4	16.5	16.6	17.1	17.2	17.3	17.4	17.5	17.6	18.1	18.2	18.3	18.4	18.5	18.6
Off-Task	/				/						/					/		
Out of seat																		

	19.1	19.2	19.3	19.4	19.5	19.6	20.1	20.2	20.3	20.4	20.5	20.6
Off-Task			/			/				/		
Out of seat							/					

Name: ______________________________

Date: ______________________________

Time: ______________________________

Target Behavior One:

22 /120 = 18 %

Target Behavior Two:

DIRECTIONS:

1) Define one or two target behaviors to be observed and place them in the first column of the observation form.
2) Use a stopwatch or a beep tape and observe for 10-second intervals.
3) If the behavior(s) occur(s) during the entire 10 seconds of the interval, place a slash (/) in that interval.
4) Calculate total percentages of the occurrence of each behavior.

Whole Interval Observation (10-second)

	1.1	1.2	1.3	1.4	1.5	1.6	2.1	2.2	2.3	2.4	2.5	2.6	3.1	3.2	3.3	3.4	3.5	3.6
Off-Task																		
Out of seat																		
	4.1	4.2	4.3	4.4	4.5	4.6	5.1	5.2	5.3	5.4	5.5	5.6	6.1	6.2	6.3	6.4	6.5	6.6
Off-Task																		
Out of seat																		
	7.1	7.2	7.3	7.4	7.5	7.6	8.1	8.2	8.3	8.4	8.5	8.6	9.1	9.2	9.3	9.4	9.5	9.6
Off-Task																		
Out of seat																		
	10.1	10.2	10.3	10.4	10.5	10.6	11.1	11.2	11.3	11.4	11.5	11.6	12.1	12.2	12.3	12.4	12.5	12.6
Off-Task																		
Out of seat																		
	13.1	13.2	13.3	13.4	13.5	13.6	14.1	14.2	14.3	14.4	14.5	14.6	15.1	15.2	15.3	15.4	15.5	15.6
Off-Task																		
Out of seat																		
	16.1	16.2	16.3	16.4	16.5	16.6	17.1	17.2	17.3	17.4	17.5	17.6	18.1	18.2	18.3	18.4	18.5	18.6
Off-Task																		
Out of seat																		

	19.1	19.2	19.3	19.4	19.5	19.6	20.1	20.2	20.3	20.4	20.5	20.6
Off-Task												
Out of seat												

Name: ______________________________

Date: ______________________________

Time: ______________________________

Target Behavior One:

____/120 = _______%

Target Behavior Two:

DIRECTIONS:

1) Define one or two target behaviors to be observed and place them in the first column of the observation form.
2) Use a stopwatch or a beep tape and observe for 10-second intervals.
3) If the behavior(s) occur(s) during the entire 10 seconds of the interval, place a slash (/) in that interval.
4) Calculate total percentages of the occurrence of each behavior.

Example Momentary Time Sampling Observation Form

Child	C1	C2	C3	C4	C5	C1	C2	C3	C4	C5	C1	C2	C3	C4	C5	C1
Time	0.15	0.30	0.45	1.00	1.15	1.30	1.45	2.00	2.15	2.30	2.45	3.00	3.15	3.30	3.45	4.00
Behavior 1	/			/				/								
Behavior 2											/					
Behavior 3													/	/	/	

Child	C2	C3	C4	C5	C1	C2	C3	C4	C5	C1	C2	C3	C4	C5	C1	C2
Time	4.15	4.30	4.45	5.00	5.15	5.30	5.45	6.00	6.15	6.30	6.45	7.00	7.15	7.30	7.45	8.00
Behavior 1			/				/									
Behavior 2																
Behavior 3																

Child	C3	C4	C5	C1	C2	C3	C4	C5	C1	C2	C3	C4	C5	C1	C2	C3
Time	8.15	8.30	8.45	9.00	9.15	9.30	9.45	10.00	10.15	10.30	10.45	11.00	11.15	11.30	11.45	12.00
Behavior 1					/											
Behavior 2																
Behavior 3																

Child	C4	C5	C1	C2	C3	C4	C5	C1	C2	C3	C4	C5	C1	C2	C3	C4
Time	12.15	12.30	12.45	13.00	13.15	13.30	13.45	14.00	14.15	14.30	14.45	15.00	15.15	15.30	15.45	16.00
Behavior 1	/				/	/	/	/						/		
Behavior 2		/														/
Behavior 3																

Child	C5	C1	C2	C3	C4	C5	C1	C2	C3	C4	C5	C1	C2	C3	C4	C5
Time	16.15	16.30	16.45	17.00	17.15	17.30	17.45	18.00	18.15	18.30	18.45	19.00	19.15	19.30	19.45	20.00
Behavior 1					/											
Behavior 2		/														
Behavior 3																

Child 1 (C1): gray shirt	**Total and Percent for Each Behavior**	
Child 2 (C2): red striped shirt	Behavior 1 Total:	13 /80 = 16.25 %
Child 3 (C3): black jacket	Behavior 2 Total:	4 /80 = 5 %
Child 4 (C4): green shorts/white shirt	Behavior 3 Total:	3 /80 = 5 %
Child 5 (C5): glasses		
	Date: 10/3/2013	
Observer's Name: First Last - Position	Start Time: 8:45	
	Activity: Math independent work	

Behavior 1: Off-Task Behavior 2: Vocalizing Behavior 3: Playing with Objects

Momentary Time Sampling Observation Form

Child	C1	C2	C3	C4	C5	C1	C2	C3	C4	C5	C1	C2	C3	C4	C5	C1
Time	0.15	0.30	0.45	1.00	1.15	1.30	1.45	2.00	2.15	2.30	2.45	3.00	3.15	3.30	3.45	4.00
Behavior 1																
Behavior 2																
Behavior 3																
Child	C2	C3	C4	C5	C1	C2	C3	C4	C5	C1	C2	C3	C4	C5	C1	C2
Time	4.15	4.30	4.45	5.00	5.15	5.30	5.45	6.00	6.15	6.30	6.45	7.00	7.15	7.30	7.45	8.00
Behavior 1																
Behavior 2																
Behavior 3																
Child	C3	C4	C5	C1	C2	C3	C4	C5	C1	C2	C3	C4	C5	C1	C2	C3
Time	8.15	8.30	8.45	9.00	9.15	9.30	9.45	10.00	10.15	10.30	10.45	11.00	11.15	11.30	11.45	12.00
Behavior 1																
Behavior 2																
Behavior 3																
Child	C4	C5	C1	C2	C3	C4	C5	C1	C2	C3	C4	C5	C1	C2	C3	C4
Time	12.15	12.30	12.45	13.00	13.15	13.30	13.45	14.00	14.15	14.30	14.45	15.00	15.15	15.30	15.45	16.00
Behavior 1																
Behavior 2																
Behavior 3																
Child	C5	C1	C2	C3	C4	C5	C1	C2	C3	C4	C5	C1	C2	C3	C4	C5
Time	16.15	16.30	16.45	17.00	17.15	17.30	17.45	18.00	18.15	18.30	18.45	19.00	19.15	19.30	19.45	20.00
Behavior 1																
Behavior 2																
Behavior 3																

Child 1 (C1):	**Total and Percent for Each Behavior**	
Child 2 (C2):	Behavior 1 Total:	/80 = %
Child 3 (C3):	Behavior 2 Total:	/80 = %
Child 4 (C4):	Behavior 3 Total:	/80 = %
Child 5 (C5):		
	Date:	
Observer's Name:	Start Time:	
	Activity:	

Behavior 1: Behavior 2: Behavior 3:

Intervention Observation Forms

Some of the interventions described in this book have an observation form that is to be used with the intervention. Each observation form has directions for the collection of baseline data as well as directions for the collection of progress monitoring data.

The observation forms are in the following order:

1) Good Behavior Game
2) PreCorrection
3) Mystery Motivator
4) Time-In
5) Compliance Training
6) Positive Peer Reporting
7) Variable Ratio – Variable Interval
8) Structured Breaks

Good Behavior Game Observations

Baseline Data Collection

1) Using the target behaviors as selected in the procedures of the GBG, the observer should conduct observations prior to beginning the intervention during the specified time that GBG will be implemented. The observer can be the interventionist or an external observer such as the school psychologist, behavior specialist, counselor, etc. Each of the target behaviors should be written into the form and labeled as Behavior 1, Behavior 2, and/or Behavior 3.

2) The observer should conduct at least three different observations using a Momentary Time Sampling procedure. Momentary Time Sampling means that the observer observes if the behavior(s) are present only at the beginning of each interval. The observation is 15-second intervals. For example, at 30 seconds into the observation, the observer will look up to see what behaviors are present. The observer will put a slash through the corresponding box(es) to indicate that the behavior was present. Then, the observer moves to the next interval and waits for that 15-second interval to begin (in this scenario, 45 seconds) and repeats the steps.

3) For Tier 1, the observer randomly selects five children for observation. The observation should last for 20 minutes with 15-second intervals. At the beginning of each interval, the observer looks at the selected child for 3 seconds and records the observed behaviors. Each of the 5 children should be defined by some description, typically using clothes or location in the room. For example, the first child can be described as "child with white shirt" or "child sitting in front desk." For Tier 2, the observer observes only the target child or children during the specified times. Each interval will be observing just the one child, rather than rotating from one child to a different child.

4) The observer should count the number of marks for each behavior and write the total number of times each behavior occurred in the summary of the observation. Divide this total by the total number of intervals observed to equal the total percentage of occurrence of each behavior during the observation. Use these totals for baseline and conduct additional observations weekly for the use of progress monitoring.

Progress Monitoring

1) Continue to use Momentary Time Sampling observations at least once per week as the intervention is being conducted.

2) The interventionist should review all data collected following the implementation of the intervention and compare to the percentages of behavior collected during baseline. This comparison is to determine if GBG is increasing/decreasing the targeted behaviors.

Good Behavior Game – Momentary Time Sampling Observation Form

Child	C1	C2	C3	C4	C5	C1	C2	C3	C4	C5	C1	C2	C3	C4	C5	C1
Time	0.15	0.30	0.45	1.00	1.15	1.30	1.45	2.00	2.15	2.30	2.45	3.00	3.15	3.30	3.45	4.00
Behavior 1																
Behavior 2																
Behavior 3																
Child	C2	C3	C4	C5	C1	C2	C3	C4	C5	C1	C2	C3	C4	C5	C1	C2
Time	4.15	4.30	4.45	5.00	5.15	5.30	5.45	6.00	6.15	6.30	6.45	7.00	7.15	7.30	7.45	8.00
Behavior 1																
Behavior 2																
Behavior 3																
Child	C3	C4	C5	C1	C2	C3	C4	C5	C1	C2	C3	C4	C5	C1	C2	C3
Time	8.15	8.30	8.45	9.00	9.15	9.30	9.45	10.00	10.15	10.30	10.45	11.00	11.15	11.30	11.45	12.00
Behavior 1																
Behavior 2																
Behavior 3																
Child	C4	C5	C1	C2	C3	C4	C5	C1	C2	C3	C4	C5	C1	C2	C3	C4
Time	12.15	12.30	12.45	13.00	13.15	13.30	13.45	14.00	14.15	14.30	14.45	15.00	15.15	15.30	15.45	16.00
Behavior 1																
Behavior 2																
Behavior 3																
Child	C5	C1	C2	C3	C4	C5	C1	C2	C3	C4	C5	C1	C2	C3	C4	C5
Time	16.15	16.30	16.45	17.00	17.15	17.30	17.45	18.00	18.15	18.30	18.45	19.00	19.15	19.30	19.45	20.00
Behavior 1																
Behavior 2																
Behavior 3																

Child 1 (C1):	**Total and Percent for Each Behavior**	
Child 2 (C2):	Behavior 1 Total:	/80 = %
Child 3 (C3):	Behavior 2 Total:	/80 = %
Child 4 (C4):	Behavior 3 Total:	/80 = %
Child 5 (C5):		
	Date:	
Observer's Name:	Time:	
Group:	Activity:	

PreCorrection Observation

Baseline Data Collection

1) The observer should conduct observations of the target behaviors during the specified time (e.g., recess, going to the cafeteria) selected in step 2 of the PreCorrection procedure.

2) The observer should conduct at least three different observations using a Momentary Time Sampling procedure. Momentary Time Sampling means the observer observes if the behavior or behaviors are present only at the beginning of each interval. The observation is in 15-second intervals. For example, at 30 seconds into the observation, the observer looks up to see what behaviors are present. The observer makes a slash mark through the corresponding box(es) to indicate that the behavior was present. Then, the observer moves to the next interval box and waits until the next 15-second interval begins at 45 seconds and repeats the steps. On the Momentary Time Sampling Observation Form, the behaviors are generically listed as Behavior 1, Behavior 2, and Behavior 3. Determine what Behavior 1 represents (e.g., talking without permission) and then determine what Behaviors 2 and 3 represent.

3) The observer should observe for 20 minutes with 15-second intervals. For Tier 1, the observer should select five children at random for observation. Write the names of the first randomly selected student at the bottom of the Momentary Time Sampling Observation Form on the line Student1 (S1) and so on for each student. At the beginning of each interval, the observer looks at the target child (i.e., S1 = the first randomly selected student, S2 = the second randomly selected student, etc.) for 3 seconds and records the observed behaviors. For Tier 2, only the target children are observed during the specified times.

4) The observer should calculate the percent of frequency of each behavior during the observation. Use these percentages for determining baseline described in step 3 of the PreCorrection procedures.

Progress Monitoring

1) Conduct additional observations and calculate the percentage weekly for progress monitoring when the intervention is being conducted.

2) Compare the percentage of each behavior each week to the baseline and any previously monitored weeks to determine if PreCorrection is increasing/decreasing the targeted behaviors.

PreCorrection: Momentary Time Sampling Observation Form

Child	C1	C2	C3	C4	C5	C1	C2	C3	C4	C5	C1	C2	C3	C4	C5	C1
Time	0.15	0.30	0.45	1.00	1.15	1.30	1.45	2.00	2.15	2.30	2.45	3.00	3.15	3.30	3.45	4.00
Behavior 1																
Behavior 2																
Behavior 3																
Child	C2	C3	C4	C5	C1	C2	C3	C4	C5	C1	C2	C3	C4	C5	C1	C2
Time	4.15	4.30	4.45	5.00	5.15	5.30	5.45	6.00	6.15	6.30	6.45	7.00	7.15	7.30	7.45	8.00
Behavior 1																
Behavior 2																
Behavior 3																
Child	C3	C4	C5	C1	C2	C3	C4	C5	C1	C2	C3	C4	C5	C1	C2	C3
Time	8.15	8.30	8.45	9.00	9.15	9.30	9.45	10.00	10.15	10.30	10.45	11.00	11.15	11.30	11.45	12.00
Behavior 1																
Behavior 2																
Behavior 3																
Child	C4	C5	C1	C2	C3	C4	C5	C1	C2	C3	C4	C5	C1	C2	C3	C4
Time	12.15	12.30	12.45	13.00	13.15	13.30	13.45	14.00	14.15	14.30	14.45	15.00	15.15	15.30	15.45	16.00
Behavior 1																
Behavior 2																
Behavior 3																
Child	C5	C1	C2	C3	C4	C5	C1	C2	C3	C4	C5	C1	C2	C3	C4	C5
Time	16.15	16.30	16.45	17.00	17.15	17.30	17.45	18.00	18.15	18.30	18.45	19.00	19.15	19.30	19.45	20.00
Behavior 1																
Behavior 2																
Behavior 3																

Child 1 (C1):	**Total and Percent for Each Behavior**	
Child 2 (C2):	Behavior 1 Total & Percent:	/ 80 = %
Child 3 (C3):	Behavior 2 Total & Percent:	/ 80 = %
Child 4 (C4):	Behavior 3 Total & Percent:	/ 80 = %
Child 5 (C5):		
Observer's Name:	Time:	Date:
Group:	Activity:	

TIER

Mystery Motivator Observation

Baseline Data Collection

1) Using the target behaviors as selected in the procedures of the Mystery Motivator, an observer should conduct observations prior to beginning the intervention during the specified time that MM will be implemented.
2) The observer should conduct at least 3 different observations using a momentary time sampling procedure. Momentary time sampling means that the observer observes if the behavior(s) are present only at the beginning of each interval. The observation is 15-second intervals. For example, at 30 seconds into the observation, the observer will look up to see what behaviors are present. The observer will put a slash through the corresponding box(es) to indicate that the behavior was present. Then, the observer moves to the next interval and waits until 45 seconds and repeats the steps.
3) For Tier 1, the observer should select five random children for observation. The observation should last for 20 minutes with 10-second intervals. At the beginning of each interval, the observer looks at the target child for 3 seconds and records the observed behaviors. For Tier 2, only the target child is observed during the specified times.
4) The observer should total the percentage of occurrence of each behavior to determine average exhibition of the target behavior during the observation. Use these totals for baseline and conduct additional observations weekly for the use of progress monitoring.

Progress Monitoring

1) Continue to use Momentary Time Sampling observations at least once per week as the intervention is being conducted.
2) Percentage of each behavior should be compared to determine if MM is increasing/decreasing the targeted behaviors.

Mystery Motivator: Momentary Time Sampling Observation Form

Child	C1	C2	C3	C4	C5	C1	C2	C3	C4	C5	C1	C2	C3	C4	C5	C1
Time	0.15	0.30	0.45	1.00	1.15	1.30	1.45	2.00	2.15	2.30	2.45	3.00	3.15	3.30	3.45	4.00
Behavior 1																
Behavior 2																
Behavior 3																

Child	C2	C3	C4	C5	C1	C2	C3	C4	C5	C1	C2	C3	C4	C5	C1	C2
Time	4.15	4.30	4.45	5.00	5.15	5.30	5.45	6.00	6.15	6.30	6.45	7.00	7.15	7.30	7.45	8.00
Behavior 1																
Behavior 2																
Behavior 3																

Child	C3	C4	C5	C1	C2	C3	C4	C5	C1	C2	C3	C4	C5	C1	C2	C3
Time	8.15	8.30	8.45	9.00	9.15	9.30	9.45	10.00	10.15	10.30	10.45	11.00	11.15	11.30	11.45	12.00
Behavior 1																
Behavior 2																
Behavior 3																

Child	C4	C5	C1	C2	C3	C4	C5	C1	C2	C3	C4	C5	C1	C2	C3	C4
Time	12.15	12.30	12.45	13.00	13.15	13.30	13.45	14.00	14.15	14.30	14.45	15.00	15.15	15.30	15.45	16.00
Behavior 1																
Behavior 2																
Behavior 3																

Child	C5	C1	C2	C3	C4	C5	C1	C2	C3	C4	C5	C1	C2	C3	C4	C5
Time	16.15	16.30	16.45	17.00	17.15	17.30	17.45	18.00	18.15	18.30	18.45	19.00	19.15	19.30	19.45	20.00
Behavior 1																
Behavior 2																
Behavior 3																

Child 1 (C1):	**Total and Percent for Each Behavior**	
Child 2 (C2):	Behavior 1 Total & Percent:	/ 80 = %
Child 3 (C3):	Behavior 2 Total & Percent:	/ 80 = %
Child 4 (C4):	Behavior 3 Total & Percent:	/ 80 = %
Child 5 (C5):		
Observer's Name:	Time:	Date:
Group:	Activity:	

TIER

Time-In Observation

Baseline Data Collection

1) The observer should conduct observations of the target behaviors during the specified time (e.g., reading period, going to the cafeteria) selected in step 1 of the Time-In procedure.
2) The observer should conduct at least three different observations using a Momentary Time Sampling procedure. Momentary Time Sampling means the observer observes if the behavior or behaviors are present only at the beginning of each interval. The observation is in 10-second intervals. For example, at 30 seconds into the observation, the observer looks up to see what behaviors are present. The observer makes a slash mark through the corresponding box(es) to indicate that the behavior was present. Then, the observer moves to the next interval box and waits until the next 10-second interval begins at 40 seconds and repeats the steps. Observe for 20 minutes with 10-second intervals.
3) The observer should calculate the percent of frequency of each behavior during the observation. Use these percentages for determining the baseline described in number one under Adjustments/Modifications of the Time-In procedures.

Progress Monitoring

1) The observer should conduct additional observations and calculate the percentage weekly for progress monitoring when the intervention is being conducted.
2) The interventionist should compare the progress monitoring data to baseline data and any previously monitored weeks to determine if Time-In is increasing/decreasing the targeted behaviors.

Time-In: Momentary Time Sampling Observation Form

Behavior	1.0	1.1	1.2	1.3	1.4	1.5	2.0	2.1	2.2	2.3	2.4	2.5	3.0	3.1	3.2	3.3	3.4	3.5
TB1																		
TB2																		

Behavior	4.0	4.1	4.2	4.3	4.4	4.5	5.0	5.1	5.2	5.3	5.4	5.5	6.0	6.1	6.2	6.3	6.4	6.5
TB1																		
TB2																		

Behavior	7.0	7.1	7.2	7.3	7.4	7.5	8.0	8.1	8.2	8.3	8.4	8.5	9.0	9.1	9.2	9.3	9.4	9.5
TB1																		
TB2																		

Behavior	10.0	10.1	10.2	10.3	10.4	10.5	11.0	11.1	11.2	11.3	11.4	11.5	12.0	12.1	12.2	12.3	12.4	12.5
TB1																		
TB2																		

Behavior	13.0	13.1	13.2	13.3	13.4	13.5	14.0	14.1	14.2	14.3	14.4	14.5	15.0	15.1	15.2	15.3	15.4	15.5
TB1																		
TB2																		

Behavior	16.0	16.1	16.2	16.3	16.4	16.5	17.0	17.1	17.2	17.3	17.4	17.5	18.0	18.1	18.2	18.3	18.4	18.5
TB1																		
TB2																		

Behavior	19.0	19.1	19.2	19.3	19.4	19.5	20.0	20.1	20.2	20.3	20.4	20.5
TB1												
TB2												

Name: ____

Date: ____

Time: ____

Target Behavior One (TB1): ____________________________

Target Behavior Two (TB2): ____________________________

Target Behavior One:

___ / 120 = _______%

Target Behavior Two:

___ / 120 = _______%

Compliance Training Observation

Baseline Data Collection

1) The observer should conduct at least 3 different observations of the target behavior (i.e., compliance) prior to beginning the intervention.

2) The compliance training observation is a systematic observation that allows the interventionist to determine the specific percentage of compliance as well as the specific rate of both positive and negative attention provided to the child.

3) For Tier 1, the observer should select five random children for observation. For Tier 2 or Tier 3, only the target child is observed during the specified times.

4) The observer should put a tally mark for the interventionist behaviors related to each instruction in columns 1-6 and 9. Put a tally mark for each behavior exhibited by the child in columns 7 and 8. Definitions of each behavior are included in the intervention procedures.

5) In the total row, the observer should count the number of tally marks in each column and then count the number of opportunities. For example, the interventionist may have given only 8 instructions; thus, there are only 8 opportunities instead of 10. In this scenario, the interventionist may have been in proximity only 5 times out of the 8 instructions; therefore, the fraction would be 5 proximities/8 opportunities.

6) In the percentage row, the observer should calculate the total fraction as a percentage. In the above example, 5 proximities/8 opportunities would be .625 multiplied by 100, which equals 62.5% proximity.

7) The observer should put a tally mark in the specified box for each negative attention given for inappropriate behavior (for each time the interventionist gives an inappropriate facial or gestural prompt toward the child and/or verbal reprimand or redirection). Put a tally mark in the specified box for each positive attention or Time-In for appropriate behavior.

8) The observer should total the number of tally marks for negative attention and divide it by the number of minutes observed. For example, if the interventionist gave 30 negative attentions in a 7minute period, the ratio would be 30/7 = 4.29 negative attentions per minute. Total the number tally marks for positive attention in the same manner. The rationale is that the positive attention should outweigh the negative attention. If the interventionist gave 1 positive comment per minute and 4.29 negative comments per minute for inappropriate behavior, then the interventionist should increase the amount of positive attention and decrease the amount of negative attention.

Progress Monitoring

1) Continue to use Compliance Training observations at least once per week as the intervention is being conducted.

2) Compare the percentage of each adult and child behavior to baseline data to determine if the intervention is increasing/decreasing the targeted behaviors.

Compliance Training Observation

Student Name: ______________________ Start Time: ________ End Time: ________ Date: ______________

Adult Behavior						Child Behavior		Adult Beh
Instruction	(2) Proximity (P)	(3) Eye Contact (EC)	(4) Descriptive (Desc)	(5) Directive (D)	(6) 5 sec wait	(7) *IC*	(8) *CC*	(9) CP
1								
2								
3								
4								
5								
6								
7								
8								
9								
10								
	# of P/ # of opportunities (opps)	# of EC/ # of opps	# of Des/ # of opps	# of D/ # of opps	# of 5 sec/ # of opps	# of IC/ # of opps	# of CC/ # of opps	# of CP/ # of opps
Total								
%								

Tally Time In		**Duration of Observation (time)**		**# of tally marks/ time**		**Rate per minute:**

Tally Negative Attention		**Duration of Observation (time)**		**# of tally marks/ time**		**Rate per minute:**

TIER

Positive Peer Reporting Observation

Baseline Data Collection

1) For the Positive Peer Reporting (PPR) observation, the target behaviors are as follows: Positive Behaviors, Negative Behaviors, No Behaviors, or No Opportunity. For positive or negative behaviors, the observer should indicate additional criteria that include whether the target child initiated the interaction or a peer initiated the interaction. Definitions of each behavior follow:
    a) Positive behaviors (PB) include any of the following behaviors: cooperation (e.g., sharing materials common to a learning activity), assisting peers with a task or activity (e.g., providing materials, explaining a task), and/or appropriate verbal behaviors (e.g., any socially and developmentally appropriate conversation devoid of insults, yelling, teasing, etc.).
    b) Negative behaviors (NB) include any of the following behaviors: aggression (e.g., hitting, kicking, pinching, biting, taking something away from a peer), and or inappropriate verbalizations (e.g., yelling, teasing).
    c) Target-child initiation (T) is any positive and/or negative behavior initiated by the target child to a peer (e.g., target child offers a toy truck to a peer).
    d) Peer initiation (P) is any positive or negative behavior initiated by a peer to the target child (e.g., peer offers truck to the target child).
    e) No behavior (No) indicates that a child is either in proximity (P) to a peer (i.e., less than 2 feet from peer) and exhibits no verbal or social behavior or is not in proximity (N) to a peer (i.e., 2 or more feet from peer and having no verbal or social behavior) and exhibits no verbal or social behavior.
    f) No opportunity (O) indicates that the target child is engaged in 1:1 interaction with teacher or in the bathroom.
2) An observer should conduct observations prior to beginning the intervention during the specified time that PPR will be implemented.
3) The observer should conduct at least three different observations using a partial interval observation procedure. A partial interval observation means that the observer indicates the presence of the behaviors at any time during each interval. If the behaviors are present, note in the corresponding box(es) by using a slash mark to indicate that the behavior occurred during that interval. The observation uses 10-second intervals.
4) The observer should total the percentage of occurrence of each behavior to determine average exhibition of the target behavior during the observation. Use these totals for baseline, and additional observations should be conducted weekly for the use of progress monitoring.

Progress Monitoring

1) The observer should continue PPR observations at least once per week as the intervention is being conducted.
2) The observer should compare the percentage of each behavior to baseline data to determine if PPR is increasing/decreasing the targeted behaviors.

PPR Behavioral Observation – 10 second Partial Interval

	1.1	1.2	1.3	1.4	1.5	1.6	2.1	2.2	2.3	2.4	2.5	2.6	3.1	3.2	3.3	3.4	3.5	3.6	4.1	4.2	4.3	4.4	4.5	4.6	5.1	5.2	5.3	5.4	5.5	5.6
PB T/P																														
NB T/P																														
No P/N/O																														

	6.1	6.2	6.3	6.4	6.5	6.6	7.1	7.2	7.3	7.4	7.5	7.6	8.1	8.2	8.3	8.4	8.5	8.6	9.1	9.2	9.3	9.4	9.5	9.6	10.1	10.2	10.3	10.4	10.5	10.6
PB T/P																														
NBT/P																														
No P/N/O																														

	11.1	11.2	11.3	11.4	11.5	11.6	12.1	12.2	12.3	12.4	12.5	12.6	13.1	13.2	13.3	13.4	13.5	13.6	14.1	14.2	14.3	14.4	14.5	14.6	15.1	15.2	15.3	15.4	15.5	15.6
PB T/P																														
NBT/P																														
No P/N/O																														

	16.1	16.2	16.3	16.4	16.5	16.6	17.1	17.2	17.3	17.4	17.5	17.6	18.1	18.2	18.3	18.4	18.5	18.6	19.1	19.2	19.3	19.4	19.5	19.6	20.1	20.2	20.3	20.4	20.5	20.6
PB T/P																														
NB**T/P**																														
No P/N/O																														

Name: ____________________ Observer: ____________

Date/Time: ________________ Phase/Session: _________

Positive Behaviors:
Target Initiated: _____ _____%
Peer Initiated: _____ _____%
Negative Behavior:
Target Initiated: _____ _____%
Peer Initiated: _____ _____%
No Behaviors:
Proximity: _____ _____%
No Proximity: _____ _____%
No opportunity: _____ _____%
IOA A/A+D x 100% _______%

PPR Operational Definitions

Positive behaviors (PB): any of the following behaviors: cooperation (e.g., sharing materials common to a learning activity), assisting peers with a task or activity (e.g., providing materials, explaining a task), and/or appropriate verbal behaviors (e.g., any socially and developmentally appropriate conversation devoid of insults, yelling, teasing, etc.).

Negative behaviors (NB): any of the following behaviors: aggression (e.g., hitting, kicking, pinching, biting, taking something away from a peer), and or inappropriate verbalizations (e.g., yelling, teasing).

Target/peer initiations.

Target-child initiation (T): any positive and/or negative behavior initiated by the target child to a peer (e.g., target child offers a toy truck to a peer).

Peer initiation (P): any positive or negative behavior initiated by a peer to the target child (e.g., peer offers truck to the target child).

No behavior (No): **(P)** a child being in proximity to a peer (i.e., less than 2 feet from peer) and exhibiting no verbal or social behavior) and **(N)** a child not being in proximity (i.e., 2 or more feet from peer and having no verbal or social behavior).

No opportunity (O): 1:1 interaction with teacher, in the bathroom,

Other: ________________________________

TIER

Variable Ratio – Variable Interval Observation

Baseline Data Collection

1) Using the target behaviors as selected in the Variable Ratio – Variable Interval (VR-VI) procedures, an observer should conduct observations prior to beginning the intervention.
2) The observer should conduct at least three different observations prior to beginning the intervention using a frequency/event recording procedure. Frequency/event recording means that the observer counts the frequency of the occurrence of the target behavior during the observation period.
3) The observer should total the frequency of occurrence of each behavior to determine the number of times the target behavior occurs during the observation. Use these totals for baseline and additional observations should be conducted weekly for the use of progress monitoring.

Progress Monitoring

1) The observer should continue the Frequency/event recording observations at least once per week as the intervention is being conducted.
2) The observer should compare percentage of each behavior to baseline data to determine if VR-VI is increasing/decreasing the targeted behaviors.

Variable Ratio – Variable Interval Frequency / Event Recording

Student Name: ____________ Teacher: ____________ Date: ____________

Observer: ____________ Start Time: ________ Stop Time: ____________

Behavior Observed: ____

Day	Frequency Count
Monday	1 2 3 4 5 6 7 8 9 10 11 12 13 14 15 16 17 18 19 20 21 22 23 24 25 26 27 28 29 30 31 32 33 34 35 36 37 38 39 40 41 42 43 44 45 46 47 48 49 50
Tuesday	1 2 3 4 5 6 7 8 9 10 11 12 13 14 15 16 17 18 19 20 21 22 23 24 25 26 27 28 29 30 31 32 33 34 35 36 37 38 39 40 41 42 43 44 45 46 47 48 49 50
Wednesday	1 2 3 4 5 6 7 8 9 10 11 12 13 14 15 16 17 18 19 20 21 22 23 24 25 26 27 28 29 30 31 32 33 34 35 36 37 38 39 40 41 42 43 44 45 46 47 48 49 50
Thursday	1 2 3 4 5 6 7 8 9 10 11 12 13 14 15 16 17 18 19 20 21 22 23 24 25 26 27 28 29 30 31 32 33 34 35 36 37 38 39 40 41 42 43 44 45 46 47 48 49 50
Friday	1 2 3 4 5 6 7 8 9 10 11 12 13 14 15 16 17 18 19 20 21 22 23 24 25 26 27 28 29 30 31 32 33 34 35 36 37 38 39 40 41 42 43 44 45 46 47 48 49 50

TIER

Structured Breaks Scatterplot Observation

Baseline Data Collection

1) The observer should use the defined target behaviors defined by the interventionist for the intervention.
2) When a target behavior is exhibited, the observer should either place a tally mark in the corresponding box for the time that the behavior occurred for a behavior that does not last more than 1 minute or shade the time from beginning to end for behaviors that last longer than a brief occurrence (i.e., more than 1 minute). The number of shaded areas in a day will indicate the frequency as well as the duration of the behavior that occurred.
3) The observer should summarize the data each day to indicate the number of occurrences of each behavior and the average duration of each behavior.

Progress Monitoring

1) The observer should continue Scatterplot observations at least once per week as the intervention is being conducted.
2) The observer should total frequency and duration of each target behavior to compare to baseline data and determine if intervention is increasing/decreasing the targeted behaviors.
3) During the intervention, the interventionist should also indicate the number of break cards used and the time of day each card is used.

Structured Breaks Scatterplot Observation

Date: ___________________

	1	2
8:00-8:30		
8:30-9:00		
9:00-9:30		
9:30-10:00		
10:00-10:30		
10:30-11:00		
11:00-11:30		
11:30-12:00		
12:00-12:30		
12:30-1:00		
1:00-1:30		
1:30-2:00		
2:00-2:30		
2:30-3:00		
3:00-3:30		

Behavior 1:

Date: ___________________

	1	2
8:00-8:30		
8:30-9:00		
9:00-9:30		
9:30-10:00		
10:00-10:30		
10:30-11:00		
11:00-11:30		
11:30-12:00		
12:00-12:30		
12:30-1:00		
1:00-1:30		
1:30-2:00		
2:00-2:30		
2:30-3:00		
3:00-3:30		

Behavior 2:

Summary Chart

Date	**Behavior 1**		**Behavior 2**		**Break Cards**
	# Occurrences	Average Duration	# Occurrences	Average Duration	# Break Cards Used and time of day

Glossary

Acquisition –Beginning learning in any situation is the acquisition level of learning. It requires the complex process of combining information from multiple sources.

Active Engagement – 80% of the children are engaged in exercises or activities that include but are not limited to writing, answering questions, discussions. It is NOT passive listening or silent reading.

Antecedent – A stimulus that sets the occasion for a behavior is an antecedent.

Baseline – Data and/or observations collected prior to the implementation of an intervention.

Behavior Intervention Plan - a plan developed for children exhibiting behavioral difficulties. This plan includes targeted behaviors, intervention strategies, reinforcers, consequences, collecting and monitoring data, as well as positive behavioral strategies

Consequence – A stimulus that occurs after the behavior and maintains the behavior is a consequence.

Contingent Praise – Positive praise (verbal or physical contact) that is contingent on the child complying with the commands given.

Effective Instruction Delivery – A way to give commands that makes it more likely that children comply. The main components associated with EID are eye contact, directive statements, descriptive wording, close proximity, and a 5-second wait for initiated compliance.

Fluency – A phase of the instructional hierarchy with which the focus is to increase the speed of the child's responding. The child has the skills to complete a task but completes the task slowly.

Functional Behavior Assessment – An assessment utilized to evaluate a child's behavior and determine the purpose or function of that behavior.

Generalization – For a skill to be considered to be generalized, it must occur across various settings, people and stimuli as well as over time. This is a crucial component of skill acquisition and if it is not occurring then a skill should not be considered mastered.

Instructional Level – The level that is optimal for instruction and learning new information. The student should experience approximately 90% success with this material. This reading text should be challenging, but not frustrational. With normal classroom instruction and appropriate support (such as vocabulary lists and reading guides), a student should be able to identify 90-95% of the words and comprehend 75-90% of the material.

Interventionist – Anyone designated as implementing an intervention or the person primarily responsible for implementing an intervention is an interventionist. Depending on the setting and circumstances an interventionist may be a general teacher, special education teacher, teacher assistant, school psychologist, behavior specialist, clinician, parent, or another appropriate adult.

Maintenance – When a child has learned a skill and continues to demonstrate the skill after teaching has been discontinued.

Momentary Time Sampling – An interval recording observation that is often referred to as "spot checking." During this observation, the observer only looks at a student at predetermined points in time and records if the behavior occurred during that specific time. For example, during a 30-second momentary time sampling observation, the observer looks up at the end of the 30-second interval and records the occurrence or nonoccurrence of the target behavior.

Negative Punishment – If an inappropriate or undesirable behavior is displayed/performed, then a reward is lost to decrease the likelihood of the behavior reoccurring.

Negative Reinforcement – If an appropriate or desirable behavior is displayed/performed, then an aversive task, event, etc. is removed or prevented to increase the likelihood of the behavior reoccurring.

Observer – Anyone designated as the person conducting an integrity check is an observer. Depending on the setting and circumstances an observer may be a principal, assistant principal, school psychologist, treatment specialist, behavior specialist, counselor, lead teacher, or other appropriate adult other than the interventionist.

Operational Definition – A definition of a behavior or task that is clear, observable, and measureable.

Positive Punishment – If an inappropriate or undesirable behavior is displayed/performed, then a punisher is provided to decrease the likelihood of the behavior reoccurring.

Positive Reinforcement – If an appropriate or desirable behavior is displayed/performed, then a reward is provided to increase the likelihood of the behavior reoccurring.

Progress Monitoring – Ongoing data collection throughout the implementation of an intervention.

Prosocial – A positive, social behavior that benefits others and is intended to be positive towards others.

Replacement Behavior – A behavior that is an acceptable appropriate replacement behavior for the unwanted target behavior.

Target Behavior – One or more behavior that his unwanted and being targeted for change.

Time In – Any verbal praise, physical gesture, or appropriate physical contact when the child behaves appropriately, or differential reinforcement for appropriate behavior.